DK EYEWITNESS TRAVEL

NMC IRR

We hope you enjoy this book. Please return or
renew it by the due date. You can renew it at
www.norfolk.gov.uk/libraries or by using our free
library app. Otherwise you can phone
0344 800 8020 - please have your library card and
PIN ready. You can sign up for email reminders too.

BOLIVIA

ARGENTINA

Tierra del
Fuego

Santiago Area by Area

**Plaza de Armas and
Santiago Centro**
Pages 58–77

**West of Santiago
Centro**
Pages 78–85

**Northeast of
Santiago Centro**
Pages 86–95

0 km   300

0 miles   300

**Northern
Patagonia**
Pages 226–239

**Southern
Patagonia and
Tierra del Fuego**
Pages 240–257

DK EYEWITNESS TRAVEL

Chile
& Easter Island

Penguin
Random
House

Managing Editor Aruna Ghose
Senior Editorial Manager Savitha Kumar
Senior Design Manager Priyanka Thakur
Project Editor Sandhya Iyer
Project Designer Stuti Tiwari Bhatia
Editor Divya Chowfin
Designer Neha Dhingra
Senior Cartographic Manager Uma
Bhattacharya
Cartographer Mohammad Hassan
DTP Designer Azeem Siddiqui
Senior Picture Research Coordinator
Taiyaba Khatoon
Picture Researcher Shweta Andrews

Contributors Wayne Bernhardson, Declan
McGarvey, Kristina Schreck

Photographers Demetrio Carrasco, Nigel
Hicks

Illustrators Chinglemba Chingtham, Surat
Kumar Mantoo,
Arun Pottirayil, T. Gautam Trivedi

Printed and bound in Malaysia

First published in the UK in 2011 by
Dorling Kindersley Limited
80 Strand, London WC2R 0RL

17 18 19 20 10 9 8 7 6 5 4 3 2 1

**Reprinted with revisions 2013,
2016, 2018**

Copyright © 2011, 2018 Dorling Kindersley
Limited, London
A Penguin Random House Company

All rights reserved. No part of this
publication may be reproduced, stored in
a retrieval system, or transmitted in any
form or by any means, electronic,
mechanical, photocopying, recording or
otherwise, without the prior written
permission of the copyright owner.

Published in the UK by Dorling Kindersley
Limited.

A CIP catalog record is available from the
British Library.

ISBN 978-0-2413-0600-0

Floors are referred to throughout in
accordance with American usage; ie the
"first floor" is at ground level.

MIX
Paper from
responsible sources
FSC   FSC™ C018179
www.fsc.org

Introducing Chile and Easter Island

A historic and modern building standing
side-by-side in downtown Santiago

Santiago Area by Area

Guanaco grazing in the Parque Nacional
Torres del Paine

**The information in this
DK Eyewitness Travel Guide is checked regularly.**
Every effort has been made to ensure that this book is as up-to-date as possible
at the time of going to press. Some details, however, such as telephone numbers,
opening hours, prices, gallery hanging arrangements and travel information are
liable to change. The publishers cannot accept responsibility for any consequences
arising from the use of this book, nor for any material on third party websites, and
cannot guarantee that any website address in this book will be a suitable source of
travel information. We value the views and suggestions of our readers very highly.
Please write to: Publisher, DK Eyewitness Travel Guides, Dorling Kindersley,
80 Strand, London, WC2R 0RL, UK, or email: travelguides@dk.com.

◄ **Title page** Vineyards in Chile's Colchagua Valley   **Front cover image** Lake Pehoé and the peaks of Cuernos del Paine, Parque
Nacional Torres del Paine   **Back cover image** The 15 *moai* at Ahu Tongariki, Easter Island

Contents

Street art depicting a Chilean city scene, Valparaíso

Casa Museo Isla Negra

HOW TO USE THIS GUIDE

This guide helps you get the most from your visit to Chile and Easter Island. It provides detailed practical information and expert recommendations. *Introducing Chile and Easter Island* maps the country and its regions, sets it in historical and cultural context, and describes events and festivals through the year. *Chile and Easter Island*

Region by Region is the main sightseeing section. It covers all the important sights, with maps, photographs, and illustrations. Information on hotels, restaurants, shops, entertainment, and sports is found in *Travelers' Needs*. The *Survival Guide* has advice on everything from travel to medical services, banks, and communications.

Santiago Area by Area

Chile's capital, dealt with in a separate section, is divided into three sightseeing areas. Each area has its own chapter, which opens with an introduction and a list of the sights described. All sights are plotted on an *Area Map*. The key to the map symbols is on the back flap.

Sights at a Glance lists the chapter's sights by category: Historic Streets and Buildings, Museums and Galleries, Parks and Gardens, and so on.

A locator map shows where the area is in relation to other parts of the city.

1 Area Map
Sights are numbered on a map. Within a chapter, information on each sight follows the numerical order on the map. Sights in each area are also located on the Santiago Street Finder maps on pages 106–13.

All pages relating to Santiago have red thumb tabs.

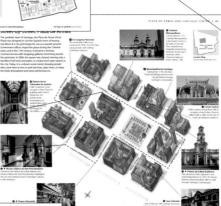

2 Street-by-Street Map
This gives a bird's-eye view of the key area in a chapter.

A suggested route for a walk is shown in red.

Story boxes explore specific subjects further.

3 Detailed information
All sights in Santiago are described individually. Addresses, telephone numbers, opening hours, and other practical information are provided for each entry. The key to all symbols used in the information block is shown on the black flap.

1 Introduction
The landscape, history, and character of each region is outlined here, revealing how the area has developed over the centuries and what it offers visitors today.

Chile and Easter Island Region by Region

Apart from Santiago, Chile is divided into six regions, each with a separate chapter. The best places to visit are numbered on a *Regional Map* at the beginning of each chapter.

Each region can be identified quickly by its color coding. A complete list of color codes is shown on the inside front cover.

2 Regional Map
This map shows the road network and gives an illustrated overview of the region. All the sights are numbered and there are also useful tips on getting around.

The visitors' checklist provides all the practical information needed to plan your visit.

3 Detailed information
Important places to visit are described individually. Major towns have maps with sights picked out and described.

4 Chile and Easter Island's Top Sights
Historic buildings are dissected to reveal their interiors; museums and galleries have color-coded floorplans; and national parks have maps showing facilities and trails. Driving tours explore areas of exceptional interest.

Stars indicate the features or sights that no visitor should miss.

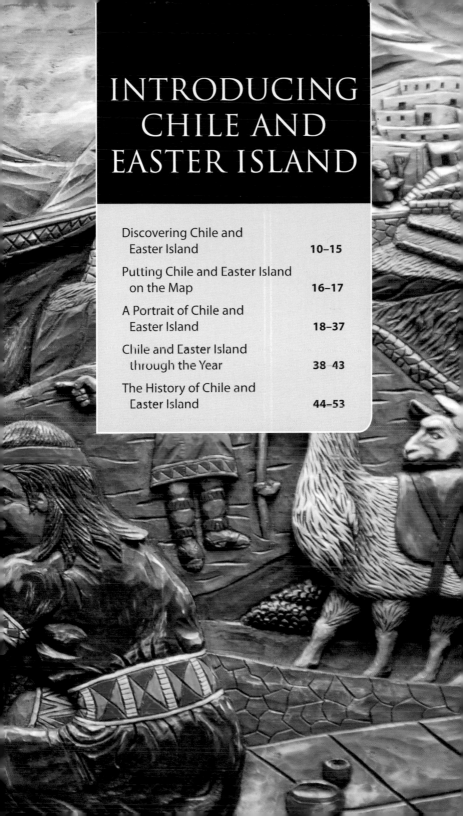

INTRODUCING CHILE AND EASTER ISLAND

DISCOVERING CHILE AND EASTER ISLAND

The following tours cover all of Chile's highlights. To start, there are two two-day city tours – one of the capital, Santiago, and one of the historic port of Valparaíso. (Visiting the city of Punta Arenas can also take up two days, but this is part of the longer Patagonian itinerary.) Both city tours can be appended to any of the three week-long tours detailed here, which cover the Atacama, Patagonia, and the

South Pacific. Since most visitors to Chile will arrive in Santiago, it makes sense to spend a few days exploring the capital before setting off on a wider tour. From here, it is possible to travel north, toward the Atacama Desert, or south, toward Patagonia. Visitors should note that, due to the country's distinct geography, getting from one destination to another can be time-consuming.

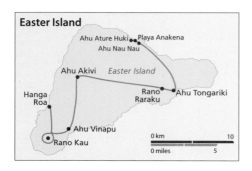

Easter Island

Key

— A Week in the South Pacific:
   The Chilean Islands

— A Week in the Atacama

— A Week in the South:
   Puerto Varas & Paine

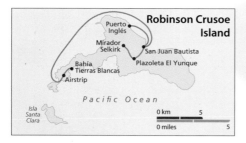

See inset map
above left

Easter
Island

A Week in the South Pacific: The Chilean Islands

- Head to the archaeological museum in **Hanga Roa**.

- Explore the **Rano Kau crater** and the **Orongo ceremonial village**.

- Stare in awe at the great *moai* of **Easter Island**.

- Relax at a **South Pacific beach**.

- Enjoy the antics of a large colony of **southern fur seals**.

- Visit the sites that inspired the tale of **Robinson Crusoe**.

Parque Nacional Torres del Paine, Patagonia
This national park offers a variety of landscapes, including glacial lakes and dramatic, jagged ice peaks.

◄ Carved depiction of traditional mountain life in Chile

Atacama

Pisagua
Humberstone and Santa Laura
Iquique
Cerro Pintados

Pacific Ocean

BOLIVIA

CHILE

El Tatio
Calama
San Pedro de Atacama
Valle de la Luna
Salar de Atacama
Lakes of the Altiplano

0 km 100
0 miles 100

ARGENTINA

A Week in the Atacama

- Visit the archaeological museum in **San Pedro de Atacama**.
- Spend some time flamingo-watching at the shallow salt lakes of **Salar de Atacama**.
- Enjoy a sunset in the **Valle de la Luna**, or a sunrise amid the geysers at **El Tatio**.
- Go guanaco- and bird-watching in the **Lakes of the Altiplano**.
- Explore the historic district of **Iquique** (with a side trip to the beach).
- Visit the nitrate-era ghost towns **Humberstone** and **Santa Laura**.
- Admire the geoglyphs on the hillsides of **Cerro Pintados**.

Arica
Iquique
Calama
Antofagasta

See inset map above

Copiapó

O c e a n   La Serena

Robinson
Crusoe
Island

See inset map left

Valparaíso
Santiago

Concepción

Temuco

Puerto Varas   Parque Nacional Vicente Pérez Rosales
Puerto Montt

Coyhaique

See inset map right

Puerto Natales

Punta Arenas

Patagonia

Torres del Paine
Cuernos del Paine

ARGENTINA

Puerto Natales

CHILE

Isla Magdalena
Seno Otway
Punta Arenas

0 km 100
0 miles 100

A Week in the South: Puerto Varas & Paine

- Explore the historic district of **Puerto Varas**.
- Hike around the active volcano **Volcán Osorno**.
- Take a raft or kayak down the **Petrohué**.
- Tour the city of **Punta Arenas**.

- Enjoy amazing views in the **Parque Nacional Torres del Paine**.
- Go day-trekking to the **Horns**.
- Visit a colony of **Magellanic penguins**.

Two Days in Santiago

Sprawling Santiago has a compact historic center.

- **Arriving** Santiago's airport (SCL) is 10 miles (17 km) northwest of downtown. Buses, shuttles, and taxis connect it with the city center.
- **Moving on** Frequent intercity buses connect Santiago with the scenic port of Valparaíso in less than two hours.

Day 1
Morning Stroll through the patios of the **Palacio de La Moneda** *(see p68)*, the Colonial-era presidential palace; then, take in an exhibition at the **Centro Cultural Palacio La Moneda** *(see p68)* – a cultural center beneath the Plaza de la Ciudadanía's reflecting pools.

From the Moneda, tour the **Museo Chileno de Arte Precolombino** *(see pp64–5)*, in the old Royal Customs House, which has ancient art and artifacts from throughout the Americas. Have lunch at the museum café or in the colorful **Mercado Central**'s fish and seafood market *(see pp76–7)*.

Afternoon Pay a visit to **La Chascona** *(see p91)*, one of poet Pablo Neruda's three eccentric houses. Afterward, explore the parkland of **Cerro Santa Lucía** *(see p74)* and enjoy the views, or go to the **Museo Nacional de Bellas Artes** *(see p75)* to see its Roberto Matta paintings.

Day 2
Morning Visit the **Museo de la Memoria y los Derechos Humanos** *(see p80)* to learn the grim tale of the Pinochet dictatorship and its aftermath, which gives valuable insight into Chile's past and present. For an idea of how Santiago's 19th-century elite lived, tour the **Palacio Cousiño** *(see p84)*, built by the mine and wine fortunes of a Portuguese immigrant family.

Afternoon After lunch, cross town to **Viña Cousiño-Macul**

The Neo-Classical facade of Santiago's Museo Nacional de Bellas Artes

(see p144), one of several wineries still within city limits.

Two Days in Valparaíso

Its historic port and scenic hilly neighborhoods have earned Valparaíso UNESCO World Heritage Site status. Explore the city on foot.

- **Arriving** Santiago is two hours away by frequent intercity buses.

Day 1
Morning Only small parts of the Barrio Puerto waterfront are open to the public, but there are still architectural monuments like the Primera Zona Naval, the **Monumento a los Heroes de Iquique** war memorial *(see p125)*, and the **Edificio de la Aduana** (Customs Building; *see p124)*.

To the east, the El Almendral neighborhood includes the Arco Británico, erected by the British community, and the massive **Congreso Nacional** *(see p129)*, moved here from Santiago by the Pinochet dictatorship.

Afternoon Explore Cerro Alegre and Cerro Concepcíon by taking any of the city's **funiculars** *(ascensores)* *(see pp130–31)*, and wandering the winding streets. In the process, don't miss the fine arts museum in the renovated **Palacio Baburizza** *(see p126)*, an elegant nitrate-era mansion.

Day 2
Morning Pay a visit to Cerro Bellavista's **La Sebastiana** *(see p128)*, another of poet Pablo Neruda's houses that's open to the public. Since 2014, visitors have been able to explore all of Neruda's homes independently, with an audio guide (available in English, French, German, Portuguese, and Spanish) providing all the information needed to enjoy them.

Afternoon At the risk of a poetry overdose, take an afternoon excursion to **Casa Museo Isla Negra** *(see pp136–7)*, Neruda's beachfront house south of Valparaíso, about an hour away by road. Despite the name, Isla Negra is not an island. Visitors can remain for hours in the grounds (which also include a restaurant). The poet is buried here and visitors can view his tomb.

The plaza in front of Palacio de La Moneda, Chile's presidential headquarters

Puerto Varas, with the Iglesia Sagrado Corazón de Jesús in the background

A Week in the South: Puerto Varas & Paine

- **Duration** Seven days, with a possible extension of two to three days.

- **Airports** Puerto Montt for Puerto Varas, and Punta Arenas for Torres del Paine.

- **Transport** This route is best traveled by bus or rental car.

Day 1: Puerto Varas
Take a walking tour of **Puerto Varas**'s *(see p211)* historic neighborhoods, with their 19th-century architecture, then tour the shoreline of **Lago Llanquihue** *(see p210)*. Consider a detour to **Frutillar** *(see pp210–11)*, the most self-consciously Germanic town here, for its Museo Colonial Alemán and the Teatro del Lago, a stunning performing arts center built on pilings that extend into the lake.

Day 2: Parque Nacional Vicente Pérez Rosales
At the east end of the lake is the **Volcán Osorno**'s perfect cone *(see p214)*. Darwin witnessed the eruption of this volcano while anchored near Puerto Montt. Shuttles from Puerto Varas reach the ski area where, in summer, lifts carry hikers into the high country. However, the summit requires a technical climb, and is suitable for experienced climbers only.

Day 3: Petrohué
Petrohué *(see p215)* is the starting point for the bus-boat shuttle to Bariloche, Argentina, but it also has an elite hotel and the Museo Pioneros de la Patagonia, a private museum on the area's history. For the more adventurous, there's hiking around the volcano's base or, alternatively, a white-water rafting or kayaking excursion down the **Río Petrohué** *(see p214)*.

Day 4: Punta Arenas
With clear weather and a window seat, the flight from Puerto Montt to Punta Arenas includes glimpses of **Parque Nacional Torres del Paine** *(see pp246–7)* from the air. Once in **Punta Arenas** *(see pp250–51)*, take in the sights around the lushly landscaped Plaza Muñoz Gamero, including wool-rush mansions such as the Casa Braun-Menéndez, now home to the **Museo Regional Braun Menéndez** *(see p250)*. Wool fortunes also paid for elaborate crypts at the **Cementerio Municipal** *(see p251)*.

Day 5: Torres del Paine
Take a bus via Puerto Natales or hire a car to the famous **Parque Nacional Torres del Paine** *(see pp246–7)*, a UNESCO World Biosphere Reserve and trekker's paradise. Take a day hike on the Sendero Salto Grande to see the thunderous falls from Lago Sarmiento and enjoy the views.

Day 6: Los Cuernos
The park's best hike goes to the base of the granite needles known as **Los Cuernos** *(see p247)* ("The Horns"). It's a full day's hike, but it also marks the starting point for **The W**, a three-day trekking route *(see p248)*, which involves camping or staying at various *refugios* (shelters) along the way. The *refugios* offer bunks, hot showers, meals, and even wine, but reservations are essential.

Day 7: Punta Arenas
Traveling from the park back to the city takes up most of the day, but if you have time, take a detour to the Magellanic penguin colony at **Seno Otway** *(see p251)*. With an extra day, consider a trip to the penguin-saturated **Isla Magdalena** *(see p251)*, an island in the Strait of Magellan that also features a historic lighthouse. A daily ferry and rigid inflatables make day trips from Punta Arenas.

The iconic silhouette of Volcán Osorno, in the Parque Nacional Vicente Pérez Rosales

A Week in the Atacama

- **Duration** Seven days, with possible extensions.
- **Airport** Arrival at Calama, departure from Iquique.
- **Transport** Buses travel from Calama to San Pedro, and from San Pedro to Iquique via Calama. Alternatively, hire a car from Calama to Iquique.

Houses, palm trees and lush mountains in San Juan Bautista, Robinson Crusoe Island

Day 1: San Pedro de Atacama

Travel from **Calama** (see p174) to **San Pedro de Atacama** (see p178), and walk through the village center, stopping for a visit at the Museo Arqueológico, the legacy of Jesuit scholar Gustavo Le Paige, who explored the desert for artifacts. Toward evening, take a trip to the **Pukará de Quitor** (see p178), a 12th-century fortification, or visit the Incan administrative site of **Catarpe** (see p178).

Day 2: Salar de Atacama

Any exploration of the enormous salt flats of **Salar de Atacama** (see p179), south of San Pedro, should include the limestone lagoon of Laguna Céjar and the flamingo-filled site of Laguna Chaxa. As sunset approaches, take an excursion to the **Valle de la Luna** to observe the changing hues of the Andean peaks (see p180).

Day 3: El Tatio

Leave before dawn for the sprawling site of **Geisers de Tatio** (see p175), as it is a two-hour drive through altitudes upward of 14,000 ft (4,300 m). The aim is to arrive at daybreak, when the fumaroles are at their most active. Temperatures are below freezing, but bring your bathing suit to take a dip in one of the semi-natural heated pools.

Return to San Pedro for the night. The town's lack of artificial light means that stargazing (see p181) is a popular activity here. Several agencies in town offer guided tours to the best spots.

Day 4: Lakes of the Altiplano

Where the Andes rise to the east, there's a cluster of high-altitude lakes, including the saline **Salar de Tara** (see p179) and the freshwater **Laguna Miscanti** (see p179) and **Laguna Miñeques** (see p179), which are home to nesting colonies of Andean and Chilean flamingoes, and many other birds. Vicuñas, vizcachas, foxes, and other mammals are also frequently sighted here.

Day 5: Iquique

It's a six-hour bus ride from Calama to the port of **Iquique** (see pp170–71), whose historic district features an abundance of Georgian and Victorian constructions dating from the nitrate boom of the 19th and early 20th centuries. In the 1930s, miners scraped and processed nitrates that made a handful of Chileans (and a few foreigners) very rich – until petroleum-based fertilizers overtook them. Iquique is a beach town, though the Pacific can be cool here, and a center for recreational paragliding.

Tandem paragliding off the **Cerro Dragón** dune is a special experience.

Day 6: Humberstone and Santa Laura

On the high, barren pampa just above Iquique are the ghost towns of **Humberstone** and **Santa Laura** (see p172). The desert air has kept these former company towns, now a UNESCO World Heritage Site, in a photogenic state of preservation.

Day 7: Cerro Pintados

The pre-Colombian peoples of the Andes left a record of their passing in the abstract and figurative geoglyphs that cover the hillsides throughout much of the northern Atacama. At **Cerro Pintados** (see p173), part of the Reserva Nacional Pampa del Tamarugal, there's a nearly uninterrupted string of these designs that can be accessed via a 3-mile (5-km) hillside path. It's best visited in the early morning, when the representations of birds, fish, and llamas are not backlit.

To extend your trip…
Pisagua, accessible by car from Iquique, was once Chile's most northerly nitrate port. Its historical sights now include an elaborate theater, a clock tower, and a train station. It suffered an unsavory period as a prison camp for victims of the Pinochet regime, but the primary activity here now is kelp-gathering.

The adobe church in the village of San Pedro de Atacama

Colorful motorboats moored at the port of Hanga Roa, Easter Island

Day 1: Hanga Roa
Arrive in **Hanga Roa** *(see pp262–3)*, home of the **Museo Antropológico P. Sebastián Englert** *(see p263)*. Named for a resident Franciscan scholar, the museum provides an introduction to South Pacific geography, archaeology, and ethnology. Visit archaeological landmarks such as the Ahu Tautira, **Ahu Tahai** *(see p262)*, and Ahu Vai Uri, with their standing *moai* statues, and appreciate the religious artwork at the Iglesia Hanga Roa, the Catholic church. Have a sunset dinner at any of the local restaurants.

Day 2: Rano Kau
Start the morning with a hike on the Ruta Patrimonial Te Ara o Rapa Nui, a footpath that passes several *ahus* (stone platforms) en route to the scenic **Rano Kau** crater *(see p264)*. Follow the rim to the ceremonial village of **Orongo** *(see p264)*, site of the so-called **Birdman** cult *(see p264)* that flourished in the 18th and 19th centuries. A visitor center on site offers information in two languages (Spanish and English).

Back in town, have a quick lunch at any of the restaurants on Te Pito Te Henua, opposite the soccer field. Afterward, grab a cab to **Ahu Vinapu** *(see p264)*, east of the airport. Though most of the *moai* lie broken on the ground, the platforms that once held them are some of the island's most elaborate. Another short road leads to **Ahu Akivi** *(see pp264–5)*, where seven restored *moai* overlook a ceremonial area.

Day 3: Meeting the Moai
Rent a car or a motorcycle, or even a bicycle, to loop around the island's archaeological sites. The most important is **Rano Raraku** *(see pp266–7)*, where unfinished *moai* stand or lie in place on the inner and outer slopes of a water-filled crater second only to Rano Kau in its scenic appeal. It's easy to spend hours here, so bring lunch.

A short drive to the east, **Ahu Tongariki** *(see p265)* is the island's largest platform, with 15 *moai*. They were toppled by a tsunami in 1960, but have since been restored. It's also one of the island's top rock art sites, with petroglyphs of marine life and cultural artifacts, including ancient inscribed stone tablets. Continue along the island's north shore to the site of **El Gigante** *(see p267)*, the largest *moai* ever, before returning to Hanga Roa. Dine at Tataku Vave, a popular seafood restaurant.

Day 4: Playa Anakena
Before leaving the island, visit **Playa Anakena** *(see p265)*, the island's best sandy beach, which is also home to standing *moai* at **Ahu Ature Huki** and **Ahu Nau Nau**.

Day 5: San Juan Bautista
After arriving at Robinson Crusoe's airstrip, catch the launch boat (included in the airfare) to **San Juan Bautista** *(see p268)*, the island's only town. Alternatively, hike from the airstrip to San Juan (the launch will deliver baggage to your accommodation), with a detour to the fur-seal colony at **Bahía Tierras Blancas** *(see p269)*.

Day 6: Selkirk's Sights
To see what castaway Alexander Selkirk saw for so many years, climb the trail to the **Mirador Selkirk** *(see p269)*, a saddle where two plaques commemorate his years of exile. Other hikes include **Plazoleta El Yunque** *(see p269)* and **Sendero Salsipuedes** *(see p268)* for views of the backcountry and the village. Alternatively, hire a launch to visit Puerto Inglés, where Selkirk may have camped. For dinner, enjoy some Juan Fernández lobster (actually a crayfish).

Day 7: Crusoe from the Sea
Hire a launch for excursions to otherwise inaccessible parts of the island, including the little-visited western shore. The launch can then drop you at the airstrip for your return flight.

Impressive *moai* statues at Ahu Tahai, in Hanga Roa, Easter Island

Putting Chile and Easter Island on the Map

Chile runs along the western edge of South America and is wedged between the Andes in the east and the Pacific Ocean in the west. It is bordered by the countries of Peru and Bolivia in the north and Argentina in the east. The most striking aspect of Chile is its thin, long shape – spanning some 2,600 miles (4,190 km) from 17° to 56° latitude south, there is no area of Chile that measures more than 186 miles (300 km) in width. The nation is divided into 15 *regiones* (regions) and is occupied by more than 18.2 million inhabitants, of whom some 6 million live in Santiago. Chile also claims Easter Island, Robinson Crusoe Island, and a slice of Antarctica as part of its territory. Hanga Roa, the main city on Easter Island, lies about 2,350 miles (3,780 km) west of Santiago.

Key

━━ Highway
━━ Major road
── Railway
━━ International border

PERU

Arica ✈

Iquique ○ ✈

Calama ○

Antofagasta ✈

CHILE

Copiapó ○

La Rioja ○

La Serena ○
Ovalle ○

San Ju

Valparaíso ✈ ○ Santiago
Robinson Crusoe Island
San Antonio ○ *Río Maipo*
Rancagua ○

Talca ○ *Río Maule*

Chillán ○
Concepción ○
Los Ángeles ○
Río Bío Bío

Temuco ○ ✈
✈ Neuquén

Valdivia ○

Osorno ○

Puerto Montt ○ ✈

Castro ○

Quellón ○
Golfo Corcovado

Comodoro Rivadavia ○

Coyhaique ○

Golfo de Penas

El Calafate ○
Bah Gran

Puerto Natales ○

✈ ○ Punta Arenas

Ushuaia ○

Pacific Ocean

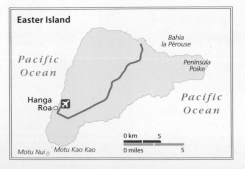

Easter Island

Pacific Ocean

Bahía la Pérouse

Península Poike

Hanga Roa ✈

Pacific Ocean

Motu Nui ○   Motu Kao Kao

0 km   5
0 miles   5

For keys to symbols *see back flap*

Aerial view of the Andes, with Chile to the right and Argentina to the left

A PORTRAIT OF CHILE AND EASTER ISLAND

A narrow sliver of land on the western edge of South America, Chile is an area of diverse natural beauty, a model of economic prosperity, a politically stable nation, and an emerging paradise for wine connoisseurs. While the mainland is varied both in geography and culture, isolated by the Pacific, Easter Island enthralls with its iconic *moai* and Polynesian heritage.

Extending over 39 degrees of latitude, Chile embraces a stunning variety of terrain, from the world's driest desert to the ice fields of Patagonia and Antarctica. However, most of this area is unsettled, with the majority of Chile's 16.3 million inhabitants living in the sprawling capital of Santiago and in a handful of other urban centers. A part of Chilean territory, Easter Island is the most remote place on the globe to be populated; its few thousand inhabitants live in the small capital town of Hanga Roa.

Evidence of human presence in Chile dates from as far back as 13,000 BC, and until the 15th century numerous indigenous groups flourished here. The following centuries saw the Spanish conquest of Chile and an influx of immigrants from Europe. The Mapuche, who number about 1.5 million, are the largest indigenous group; there are also far smaller and more isolated groups of Aymara, Rapa Nui, and other peoples. These different groups are harmonious, creating an inclusive atmosphere where visitors can easily feel at home.

Modern-day Chile has emerged as Latin America's safest country and has excellent tourist facilities. It is a land of both relaxation and adventure, offering an incredible range of activities, from skiing down volcano slopes and hiking through rain forest to surfing and wildlife-watching. Chile's many vibrant festivals offer an insight into the nation's rich cultural heritage. This multidimensional land has something for everyone.

Moai atop the Ahu Tautira platform near Hanga Roa's pier, Easter Island

◀ Lago Pehoé with the Los Cuernos peaks in the background, Parque Nacional Torres del Paine

Llamas in the vicinity of Volcán Pomerape and Volcán Parinacota, at Parque Nacional Lauca

Land and Nature

Chile's natural spaces are extensive given the lack of dense human population. The northern third of the country is the arid Atacama desert, known for its otherworldly landscapes. It is bordered on the south by the Mediterranean Central Valley, Chile's agricultural belt, and the rain forests, lakes, and snowcapped volcanoes of the Lake District. Farther south, the land breaks to form the many fjords, granite peaks, and awe-inspiring glaciers of Patagonia.

The natural wealth of this land supports the bulk of Chile's economy, with the result that industries such as mining, agriculture, and fishing have, till recently, taken precedence over conservation. On Easter Island, centuries of human intervention have destroyed the island's native forests and palm stands. Growing concern about threats to the ecology has spawned initiatives across Chile. Patagonia Sin Represas, for instance, opposes plans for hydroelectric plants in southern Chile. The Conservation Land Trust, founded by environmentalist Douglas Tompkins, promotes ecotourism and sustainable farming.

Economy

Chile's economy stands out among its South American neighbors for its stability, minimal corruption, and overall health. Its foundations, interestingly, were laid during the Pinochet regime which replaced socialist economic policies with plans based on privatization, free market, and stable inflation. By the 1990s, Chile had experienced an economic boom with a seven percent average annual growth. The country faced the 2008 economic slowdown with over US$20 billion in a sovereign wealth fund, averting a major crisis.

A major exporter of minerals, Chile has emerged as the world's top copper producer, and the state-run Codelco is the largest copper mining agency on the globe. Thriving tourism, along with fishing and subsistence farming, is the backbone of Easter Island's economy.

Fishing boats docked at Hanga Roa, Easter Island

Economic prosperity has brought about rapid development, reducing poverty. Chile's vast pay inequality, however, is still a problem, along with *pituto*, or nepotism, common even in the most modern corporations.

Politics and Government

After years of military dictatorship, Chile has emerged as a strong democratic republic which operates under a constitution. The government comprises the executive, judiciary, and legislative branches, and is led by the president, who is both the head of state and head of government. The country itself consists of 15 administrative regions and the capital.

Annexed by the Chilean navy in 1888, Easter Island is a province of the Valparaíso region (Región V). Its residents were granted Chilean citizenship only in 1966, and in 2007, the island was recognized as a special territory of Chile.

Sports and Arts

As in all Latin American countries, *fútbol* (soccer) is a national craze in Chile. Since the last few decades, the country has also made news in the field of tennis with international medal winners such as Nicolás Massú and Fernando González. Golf, skiing, and surfing are popular sports among Chileans. The rodeo remains a much-loved sport in the countryside.

Chile has produced a number of composers and musicians of international renown. While pianist Claudio Arrau remains unparalleled in the arena of classical music, acts such as Congreso and Los Jaivas have brought Chilean folklore into the limelight. Santiago's Teatro Municipal *(see p73)* is the country's foremost cultural institution and hosts world-class opera, symphony, and ballet performances. Chile boasts a rich and long-standing tradition of theater, which

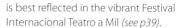

The late Chilean pianist Claudio Arrau (1903–91)

is best reflected in the vibrant Festival Internacional Teatro a Mil *(see p39)*.

Chile's key contribution, however, is in the field of literature. Chilean writers and poets have enjoyed worldwide acclaim, most notably the Nobel laureates Pablo Neruda and Gabriela Mistral.

People and Society

There is a staggering contrast between urban and rural lifestyles in Chile. Santiago is known for its cosmopolitan finesse and great cultural and culinary scene. While the new-age residents of this metropolis are fashionable and tech-savvy, many people in the countryside still cook over wood-burning stoves and plough their fields with oxen. Spanish is the official language, but some indigenous people speak their own languages. Christianity is the predominant religion, though folk religion remains important for many ethnic and rural groups. On Easter Island, religious practices reflect the syncretization of Christian and Polynesian beliefs. Overall, Chilean society is both tolerant and friendly.

Flags flutter over Plaza de la Constitución, Santiago

Landscape and Wildlife

Hemmed in by the towering Andes mountain range in the east, the Pacific Ocean in the west, a vast desert in the north, and thousands of islands and glaciers in the south, Chile incorporates a range of landscapes, from farmlands and forests to lakes and ice fields. A total of 25 percent of Chile's land mass is made up of 49 national reserves, 16 national monuments, and 36 national parks. An additional 11 million acres was set aside for new national parks in 2017. A part of the geothermally active Pacific Ring of Fire, Chile is also home to a total of 90 live volcanoes and plenty of thermal hot springs. Stretching over 2,670 miles (4,300 km), the environs, flora and fauna of the country can change dramatically in the space of a single day of traveling.

Sparkling waters off the white sands of Playa Anakena, on Easter Island

Plateau and Coastal Desert

Chile's desert is the driest in the world. It is composed largely of sand, salt basins, mineral-rich peaks, and volcanoes, interspersed with oases that are fed by aquifers. Near the coast, a Pacific fog known as *camanchaca* provides enough moisture for cacti, shrubs, and lichen.

Chilean flamingoes can be seen on the saline altiplano lakes searching for tiny crustaceans, whose carotenoids give the birds their pink color.

Vicuñas, the smallest of the camelids, graze in groups at high altitudes.

The vizcacha is a long-tailed, yellow and brown rodent, part of the chinchilla family. It feeds on vegetation and can frequently be seen at twilight, when it is most active.

Central Valley

The flat, green valleys of central Chile are divided by the Andes and coastal mountains, and watered by rivers that descend from the Andes. The Mediterranean-like climate here is conducive to agriculture – mostly fruits and vegetables – and to wine production.

The quisco dominates the lower Andes and is one of the few cacti that can withstand cold and snow.

The Chilean palm has a smooth, gray trunk that is rotund in the middle or upper reaches.

The Andean condor, Chile's national bird, is one of the world's largest fowls, with a wingspan of over 9 ft (3 m).

Tectonic Activity

The towering Andes mountain range and the hundreds of volcanoes that make up the spine of Chile are the result of plate tectonics: the movement of interlocking plates of the earth's crust that ride on molten material (magma) in the mantle. Along the Chilean coast, the Nazca plate and the South American plate collide and create a subduction zone, whereby the Nazca plate is forced under the South American plate, creating the Peru-Chile Trench. As one of the fastest-moving plates, the Nazca is capable of triggering spectacular earthquakes, such as the 8.8-magnitude quake that struck central Chile in February 2010, and the 9.5-magnitude earthquake in Valdivia in 1960, the strongest recorded in the world.

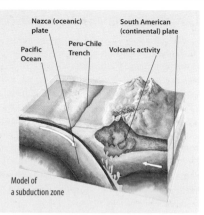

Nazca (oceanic) plate
South American (continental) plate
Pacific Ocean
Peru-Chile Trench
Volcanic activity

Model of a subduction zone

Lake District and Chiloé
The lush Lake District is characterized by snowcapped volcanoes, crystalline lakes and rivers, emerald farmland, and dense Valdivian rain forest. It is home to the alerce, the second-oldest tree on the planet, and the nalca, whose leaves can reach 7 ft (2 m) in diameter.

Patagonia and Tierra del Fuego
The windswept pampa grassland of Patagonia forms part of a region packed with granite peaks, glacier fields, fjords, and sheep ranches known as estancias. Adventure-seekers come here for trekking, fly-fishing, and mountain climbing in dramatic, untamed wilderness.

Copihue, or the Chilean bellflower, is a waxy red flower which grows in twisted vines around trees and plants. It is Chile's national flower.

The guanaco, a camelid, exists in robust populations in the wild and can be spotted throughout Patagonia.

The pudú is the world's smallest deer, reaching just 33 inches (85 cm) in length. It lives in the dense underbrush of temperate rain forests.

Pumas are agile animals with an exceptional leaping ability. These elusive cats can usually only be seen when feeding on a fresh kill.

Monkey-puzzle, or araucaria, is an evergreen conifer whose branches and razor-sharp leaves take on an umbrella shape.

The huemul, or South Andean deer, is an endangered species that is shy, solitary, and stocky, with large ears and short legs.

The Biodiversity of Chile

A paradise for nature lovers, Chile has a varied landscape which supports a wealth of flora and fauna. It is considered a "continental island" because it is isolated from neighboring countries by the Andes mountains, the Pacific Ocean, and the arid Atacama desert. As a result, more than half of its flora is endemic. This is especially true of southern Chile's Valdivian forest, South America's only temperate rain forest, which extends into parts of Argentina. Chile has 10 Biosphere Reserves that are part of UNESCO's program. Each reserve promotes the conservation of biodiversity for future generations. In regrettable contrast, most of Easter Island's native forests and fauna have disappeared as a result of many centuries of human activity.

Key
- Fertile lowland
- Scrubland
- Evergreen forest
- Grassland, with some scrub
- Barren warm or cold desert

Robinson Crusoe Island *(see pp268–9)*, through geological isolation, has produced a hothouse of endemic flora that represents two-thirds of the island's vegetation and the highest density of endemic plants in the world. The island has been a UNESCO-designated World Biosphere Reserve since 1997. However, botanists fear that the introduction of alien plant species now threatens the island's ecosystem.

| 0 km | 300 |
| 0 miles | 300 |

Unsurpassed Delights

Chile's microclimates, geographical isolation, and varying topography offer visitors a chance to experience contrasting landscapes and myriad flora within short distances. Rare phenomena, such as the coastal *camanchaca*, a fog that feeds vegetation in the otherwise barren Atacama Desert, are examples of the country's unique biodiversity. In addition, Chile's growing interest in nature conservation has boosted animal populations throughout the country, and several private foundations have established reserves to encourage the expansion of Chile's protected areas and preserve its unique flora and fauna.

The arid Atacama explodes with wildflowers after a (rare) period of rain. This phenomenon is known as the Desierto Florido *(see p185)*.

The firecrown hummingbird, an endemic and dimorphic species of Robinson Crusoe Island, is one of the rarest birds in the world.

Parque Nacional Lauca *(see pp168–9)* is northern Chile's hot spot for viewing fauna. It has large representations of the country's four camelid species – alpaca, guanaco, llama, and vicuña – over 140 species of birds, and unusual fauna such as the vizcacha, a relative of the chinchilla.

Parque Nacional La Campana *(see p139)* is home to the magnificent *Nothofagus obliqua*. This tree is the northernmost representation of the 10 *Nothofagus*, or southern beech, species of Chile.

Parque Nacional Alerce Andino *(see p217)* harbors large stands of the coniferous alerce, which date to over 3,500 years. This area is part of the Valdivian rain forest belt, where one-third of the plant species are remnants of the Gondwana supercontinent,

Whale Conservation

The waters off Chile's shores are home to over half the world's whale species. Indeed, Herman Melville's masterpiece *Moby Dick* was based on a giant albino sperm whale, Mocha Dick, that harassed ships near Chile's Isla Mocha in the 19th century. Fresh sightings of the humpback, blue, and southern right whales in recent times signal the comeback of a mammal once nearly hunted into extinction. Several non-profit associations have formed to study whale behavior, and in 2008, the Chilean government designated all national waters a whale sanctuary. Although the whale sightings are fairly unpredictable, Punta Arenas is a good place to embark on a boat trip from.

Isla Magdalena *(see p251)* hosts nesting colonies of Magellanic penguins from November to March each year. The largest temperate-climate penguin, members of this species share parental responsibilities equally and can be seen marching comically in single file from their nesting burrows to the sea in the morning and afternoon.

A breaching humpback whale

Arica

Iquique

Calama

Reserva Nacional
Los Flamencos

*Atacama
Desert*

Copiapó

La Serena

ña del Mar

Rancagua

Chillán

*aldivian
Forest*

Parque
Nacional
Conguillío

Puerto
Montt

*Parque
Nacional
Chiloé*

*Parque
Nacional
Torres del
Paine*

Punta
Arenas

Peoples of Chile and Easter Island

According to studies at the archaeological site of Monte Verde in southern Chile, the first inhabitants of this country arrived around 13,000 years ago. Over the following centuries, these nomadic tribes populated the length of Chile, either as land hunters or fisherfolk, and they eventually became settled farmers and herders. From the 16th century onward, Chile experienced sporadic immigration at intervals – first the Spaniards and later German, Swiss, English, Croatian, and Italian arrivals. Today, the majority of the 16.3 million Chileans are mestizo – people of mixed ethnic and European ancestry. Indigenous people are a minority, with a total population of roughly 1.75 million.

Aymara dancers in bright fiesta clothing in Arica

Mapuche silver jewelry includes a pectoral pendant known as a *trapelacucha*.

A **makuň** is a colorful, finely woven poncho worn by Mapuche men and boys.

Many Mapuche live in the Lake District, often on *reducciones*, or reservations, where they are engaged in a battle to repatriate land taken by settlers or the government over the last centuries.

Indigenous Chileans

Chile was the last country to be conquered by the Spanish, yet what remains of Chile's indigenous groups today represents about 11 percent of the population. The principal indigenous group is the Mapudungun-speaking Mapuche, with about 1.5 million members, or 84 percent of the total indigenous population. Just nine of Chile's original 14 indigenous groups remain, and several have only very few members.

The Aymara is Chile's second-largest ethnic group, with around 100,000 members. They live in Chile's northern desert and depend on the llama and alpaca for meat, wool, and cargo transportation. Their native language is also known as Aymara.

The Rapa Nui are descendants of the Polynesians who arrived on Easter Island around AD 1200. Their population declined greatly during the 19th century due to war, famine, and sickness, and they number about 6,000 today.

Fuegians encompass the indigenous groups that existed in Tierra del Fuego and Patagonia. A few, such as the Selk'nam, are now nearly extinct, while others, such as the Yaghan, have been reduced to a handful.

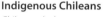

Immigrants

While Chile did not witness mass immigration, European settlers did play a major role in shaping the culture, architecture, and cuisine of regions such as the Lake District and Patagonia. Valparaíso, during its heyday in the 1800s, was a cosmopolitan center, with settlers from England, Italy, Ireland, and Germany each stamping their unique identity in the distinct neighborhoods they created.

Croatians came to Chile for economic opportunity in the latter part of the 19th century and settled in Patagonia, specifically in modern-day Porvenir and Punta Arenas. Today, one in four residents in the region is of Croatian descent.

German and Swiss immigrants arrived in the mid-19th century as part of the Law of Selective Immigration. The law, introduced in 1845, sought to populate the Lake District with people whom the Chilean government considered to be of a high social and cultural status. A sculpture in Puerto Montt commemorates the immigration.

Mestizos and Non-Indigenous Chileans

Although the majority of Chileans are mestizo, each region in Chile displays well-defined cultural styles. These distinct traditions have been heavily influenced by the various immigrant communities that settled throughout the country.

A **boina** is a knitted beret that often features a pompón tassle.

Comfortable baggy pants are well-suited for rough outdoor chores

Baqueanos are Patagonian ranch hands who are entrusted to herd sheep and cattle. They are identified by their distinct attire.

Tough working boots are sometimes topped with homemade leather gaiters.

The Roma community in Chile lives in the Central Valley. This semi-nomadic group, originally from Europe, is recognized by their long, colorful skirts and their tent settlements on the outskirts of towns.

Chilotes, people of the Chiloé archipelago, consider themselves distinct from their mainland compatriots, and speak with a clear regional accent. Most Chilotes have a mix of Spanish, Chono and Huilliche ancestry.

Huasos

Residing mainly in the Central Valley, huasos are Chilean cowboys who roam the countryside on their horses. The earliest huasos lived and worked on large Colonial ranches. Today, members of this community are identifiable by their straw hats and ponchos, and many are adept horsemen. Over the years, huasos have become central to Chilean folkloric culture and they play an integral role in most parades and celebrations, particularly Fiestas Patrias, where they perform the cueca *(see p28). They also sing the* tonada *(see p29), a folk song that is accompanied by a guitar.*

A *huaso* on horseback rounding up sheep

Music and Dance

Chile's lively music and dance scene mirrors the diversity of its cultural traditions. International contemporary music appeals to the majority of the urban population, while rural citizens favor folkloric music derived from the Nueva Canción Chilena (New Chilean Song) era, as well as Latin music from Argentina and Mexico. In northern Chile, folk styles such as the *sajuriana* and *cachimbo* are popular. Chile's national dance is the *cueca*, which appeared in the early 1800s. It originated in Spain and is thought to be the evolution of a creole fusion of Spanish, Arab, and African influences.

Fiesta de San Pedro features performances by dancers donned in traditional bright costumes and colorful headgear.

Dance

Chilean dance is conventionally associated with the folkloric cueca, which mimics the courtship of the rooster and hen. The dance is generally performed during the Fiestas Patrias celebrations (see pp36–7), when participants turn out in ceremonial dress.

Traditionally attired men appear in striped ponchos, flat-brimmed sombreros, and boots with spurs.

Women in ceremonial dress wear long, brightly colored skirts with sashes and jackets.

Waving a handkerchief, female dancers respond coyly to their suitors.

The traditional *cueca*, danced primarily at Fiestas Patrias, is much loved in rural areas. The *cueca chora* or *bravo* is the urban equivalent, with lyrics that are more associated with city life. The *cueca* in Chiloé *(see pp218–25)* is distinct in that the vocalist has a more important role than the musicians.

Traditional Music

Chilean music owes much to its indigenous traditions and folklore. Among this diversity, Andean music is characterized by lyrics that allude to spirits of the earth, nature, and mountains. Also founded on harmony with nature, Mapuche music follows melodic patterns and ancestral rhythms that are transmitted orally. The Rapa Nui people of Easter Island base their music on Polynesian rhythms that have been influenced by Latin sounds and cadences. Chile is also rich in folkloric music, which is derived from indigenous forms that have been heavily influenced by European music.

Rapa Nui music comprises chanting and singing to instruments such as the *kauaha* (made from the jaw bone of a horse), drums, and accordions. Often, families form a choir and compete in annual contests.

The *trutruka* is a trumpet used in Mapuche music.

The *kultrun* is designed with symbols representing the cosmic structure.

The Mapuche define rhythms as *kantun* (instrumental) or *öl* (ceremonial). Their instruments include the *kultrun*, a drum made of wood and leather, and the *trutruka*, a trumpet made of bamboo and a cow horn. Rich and melodious, the sound reflects close contact with nature.

Contemporary Sounds

In the 1980s, urban music was associated with politics: Los Prisioneros was Chile's most popular band, along with Fiskales Ad Hok and Electrodomésticos. Today, rock, pop, classical, jazz, and hip hop can be heard in all major urban centers.

Classical and jazz music both have ample audience in Chile, which has produced important composers and conductors. Claudia Acuña is Chile's best-known jazz performer, while Claudio Arrau was one of the 20th century's foremost pianists.

Chilean rock band La Ley have achieved international stardom, as have the rock group Los Tres. Other modern pop and rock bands include Los Bunkers, Lucybell, Chancho en Piedra, and Javiera y Los Imposibles.

Nueva Canción Chilena

The nation's most influential contribution to Latin American music is the Nueva Canción Chilena. The genre arose in the early 1960s and is based on Andean rhythms. Its original artists wrote lyrics that focused on social justice for native cultures and those persecuted under the Pinochet dictatorship. Musicians Victor Jara and Violeta Parra were pioneers who disseminated the genre throughout Latin America, and influenced popular Chilean bands such as Inti-Illimani and Los Jaivas.

Musician Victor Jara (1932–73)

Cumbia, a music genre that originated in Colombia, has been very popular among the working classes across Latin America. The lyrics often tackle issues such as life, love, and troubles, and its tinny rhythm is popular for dancing at weddings and parties. The best-known local band is La Sonora Palacios.

Andean music originated in the high plateau areas of the Andes and is instantly recognizable by the sound of *quena* flutes, pan pipes, and *charango* lutes.

Bombo legüero, an Andean skin drum

Zampoña, a pan pipe made of bamboo

A 10-string *charango* lute

The melodic *tonada* is similar to the *cueca* except that it is not danced. It arose in Spain and shows Arab and Andalucian influences. Popular Chilean groups include the Huasos Quincheros.

Folklore instruments such as the pan flute and *quena* (a traditional six-hole bamboo flute) are the essentials of Andean music, and are often combined with the *charango* lute and violin.

Literature, Theater, and Cinema

Chile is called a nation of poets, and has been the home of literary giants throughout its history. Among the early writers are such names as Alonso de Ercilla y Zúñiga (1533–94) and Francisco Núñez de Pineda y Bascuñan (1607–82). In the last few centuries, Chile has produced two Nobel laureates and many novelists and playwrights of international renown. Since the end of Pinochet's dictatorship era, artists in literature, theater, and cinema have delved into subjects that address modern themes and come to terms with the turmoil of Chile's past.

Antonio Skármeta, a Chilean writer exiled during the dictatorship years

Spanish cover of Isabel Allende's *The House of the Spirits*

Literature

Chile's earliest literary works, dating from the 16th century, mostly relate tales of conquest and colonialism. Prominent in this genre are the Spanish nobleman Alonso de Ercilla y Zúñiga's poem *La Araucana*, describing the Spanish conquest of Chile, and Francisco Núñez de Pineda's *Cautiverio Feliz*, a chronicle of his capture by Mapuches. Such early works tended to romanticize the events they described.

Literature in the 19th and 20th centuries witnessed a turn toward more realistic works. Santiago-born Alberto Blest Gana (1830–1920) is considered the father of the Chilean novel for his authentic portrayal of Chilean history and life in his *Martín Rivas* (1862). In the 20th century, Chile became a major player in the Latin American literary boom, producing influential poets such as Vicente Huidobro (1893–1948), a leading figure in the emergence of avant-garde poetry in the Hispanic world. Huidobro created an experimental verse called Creationism, which sought to bring to life experiences and themes through word play. His 1931 poem "Altazor" was written while he was in Europe, and it became a part of that continent's avant-garde movement. Other prominent 20th-century poets include Nobel laureates Gabriela Mistral and Pablo Neruda (*see p91*), whose works centered on themes of love and politics respectively. During the second half of the 20th century, the forerunners of Chile's burgeoning literature scene included Nicanor Parra (b.1914), a self-described "anti-poet", who shunned traditional poetic styles and was a major influence on the 1950s' American Beat writers.

The Pinochet dictatorship spawned several major works by exiled writers such as Luís Sepúlveda (b.1949), Antonio Skármeta (b.1940), José Donoso (1924–96), and Isabel Allende (b.1943), many of them writing on themes of exile and loss. A prominent writer of novels such as *The House of the Spirits*, Allende was an exponent of Latin America's Magical Realism movement that blended seemingly normal situations with an element of fantasy.

Magic Realism lost favor in the 1990s with the rise of the Nueva Narrativa Chilena (New Chilean Narrative). The term, coined by writer Jaime Collyer (b.1955), defined the post-dictatorship era and Chile's introduction to consumerism

Gabriela Mistral

Latin America's first Nobel Prize winner, Gabriela Mistral (1889–1957) was a teacher and feminist turned poet, with a unique and lyrical voice that spoke of love and betrayal, life and death, and the

Gabriela Mistral receiving the Nobel Prize in 1945

Latin American experience in poetical works such as *Ternura* and *Desolation*. Mistral, born Lucila Godoy y Alcayaga, spent much of her adult life outside Chile, as a consul in Spain, France, Italy, and the US, and as a professor in Mexico, and in Vassar College and Barnard University in New York. Mistral was of mixed Amerindian and Basque origin, and celebrated the mestizo race in *Tala*, her second collection of poems that contemplated the blend of Latin American and European culture.

and globalization. This movement produced writers including Gonzalo Contreras and Alberto Fuguet, whose stories such as "Mas Estrellas Que en el Cielo" dispel the notions of Magic Realism. The literary rebel Roberto Bolaño (1953–2003) was the posthumous winner of 2009's National Book Critics Circle Award for his epic novel *2666*.

Theater

Theater appeared in the late 19th century as mostly amateur productions of European plays, and comedies and dramas based on daily Chilean life. However, the founding of the Teatro Experimental in the late 1930s by the Universidad de Chile established theater as a powerful and socially relevant art form. The subsequent sprouting of theater houses across Chile spawned a boom in productions ranging from folkloric themes to the popular European-origin drama form, the Theater of the Absurd.

By the 1960s and 1970s, political radicalization propelled dramatists to bring theater to the masses. A complete censorship of media during the 1970s and 1980s led to the emergence of the dramatic arts as society's way of discussing grievances. The Ictus Theater Group, one of the longest-running companies in Chile, played a prominent role in pushing theater's boundaries with plays such as *Andrés of La Victoria* (1985), the plot of which centered around a priest killed by military police. In the late 1980s, the Gran Circo Teatro produced *La Negra Ester*, by Andrés Pérez, that became the most artistically and commercially successful play in Chilean history. The masked performance was based on a popular love tragedy, and signaled a departure from most contemporary drama based on social criticism.

Today, Santiago has dozens of independent and state-sponsored theater houses, including the venerable Teatro Municipal *(see p73)*, the Teatro Nacional, San Ginés, and Universidad Católica, all of which host performances from classical to cutting-edge. Theater takes center stage with the annual Festival Internacional Teatro a Mil *(see p39)*, which features myriad theatrical performances in cultural centers, theaters, and city streets.

Poster of *La Negra Ester* playing at Teatro Oriente, Santiago, in 2009

Cinema

The Chilean film industry dates from the early 20th century; its first black and white movie, *The Development of a People*, dates from 1920. Cinema flourished in the 1940s with the founding of the studio Chile Films, but declined until a short revival in the 1960s. During this decade filmmakers combined shades of experimental European cinema and Chilean culture to create art house and national classics. Films of this genre included Patricio Kaulen's *Long Journey* (1967) and Miguel Littín's *The Jackal of Nahueltoro* (1969). Littín later became the subject of Gabriel García Márquez's book *Clandestine in Chile* (1986). In 1968, the unconventional director Raúl Ruiz (1941–2011) produced the cult classic *Tres Tristes Tigres*, based on Chilean society.

The dictatorship stifled creative filmmaking and exiled cinematic artists, as a result of which just seven films were made in over a decade. The return to democracy led to cinema's comeback with a new wave of Chilean filmmaking.

Today, Chile produces a dozen films a year and receives nominations at international film festivals. In 2005, *Mi Mejor Enemigo* (My Best Enemy) by Alex Bowen entered the competition at the Cannes Film Festival after winning the best Spanish-language film at Spain's Goya awards. Other films to have garnered international publicity include *Tony Manero* (2008) by Pablo Larraín, a bleak portrayal of marginality during the 1970s; *The Maid* (2008) by Sebastián Silva, which won the Sundance Festival's World Cinema Jury Prize; *No* (2012), starring Gael García Bernal, which deals with the transition to democracy in 1989; and *Neruda* (2016), a critically-acclaimed film about the life of Chile's Nobel laureate.

Still from the classic art house film *The Jackal of Nahueltoro* (1969)

Chilean Art and Architecture

Pre-Colonial art in Chile chiefly comprised rock art, of which northern Chile has fine examples. In the Colonial era, both art and architecture were initially influenced by Spanish cultural and ecclesiastical elements. With the influx of immigrants from other European countries in the 19th century, techniques and designs diversified and each region showed trademark styles of the groups that settled there. Today, Chile is among the world's most architecturally prolific countries and has a thriving art scene.

The massive Gigante de Atacama geoglyph in northern Chile

Mapuche textiles woven in traditional geometric patterns

Art

While pre-Hispanic art in Chile reached a level of sophistication, Colonial-era art was limited to portraits and landscapes of criollo life. Today, however, with the integration of immigrant groups into society and the freedom of post-dictatorship Chile, the art world is giving rise to international stars, and Santiago alone is home to dozens of cultural centers and galleries.

Indigenous and Colonial Art

Chile's northern desert and altiplano region has some of the world's largest collections of petroglyphs and geoglyphs, including the 400-ft (121-m) high Gigante de Atacama. Colonial art in Chile did not exhibit complexity, other than the Rococo-style sculptures, paintings, and silverwork produced in the Jesuit workshops of Calera de Tango in the early 1700s. Mapuche silverwork is also remarkable in its intricacy.

Ornate silver croziers and monstrances were among the popular ecclesiastical artifacts crafted by skilled Jesuits in the 16th century.

Vessel shaped to resemble a bird

Ceramic pottery in animistic and geometric designs, metalwork, and textile weaving were among the traditional crafts of the Diaguita culture (300 BC–AD 1500) in northern Chile.

Contemporary Art

The nation's artistic scene blossomed with the inauguration of Santiago's Museo Nacional de Bellas Artes *(see p75)* in 1880. Renowned artists of that time were Fernando Alvarez de Sotomayor and Arturo Gordon, whose works depicted Chilean life. Among contemporary Chilean artists are Surrealist painter Roberto Matta and Hyperrealist Claudio Bravo.

Absent Feet by Eugenio Dittborn (b.1943) is part of his "Airmail Paintings" series, which could be folded up and sent via post to the location of the exhibition.

Paisaje Lo Contador is a well-known canvas by Arturo Gordon, a member of the Generación del Trece group of artists who depicted the lives of the common man, a rare subject in the early 1900s.

Architecture

Chilean architecture is a potpourri of a number of influences. In the early decades of colonization, Chilean towns were modeled after Spanish towns, with a central square surrounded by a cathedral and government buildings with large patios, bare walls, and wrought-iron gates. In the 20th century, Santiago's nouveau riche built their houses to resemble European Neo-Classical mansions. Modern Chileans have adapted North American bungalows, skyscrapers, and malls that reflect the country's economic boom over the past 20 years.

Colonnaded passageway bordering the yard at Convento de San Francisco *(see p72)*, Santiago

Colonial

Much of the country's Colonial architecture has succumbed to earthquakes, with the exception of a few 17th-century churches in the desert north and a handful of haciendas in the Central Valley.

The Iglesia San Francisco de Chiu-Chiu *(see p174)* is Chile's oldest church. Its twin bell towers, chañar-wood ceilings, and white-washed walls are characteristic of 17th-century adobe churches in the Atacama.

The Casa Colorada *(see p63)*, named for its rose-tinted walls, is built of brick and stone around a central patio.

Neo-Classical

Triangular pediments, hefty columns, and domed roofs are quintessential elements of government buildings in Santiago, and are evidence of the city's preference for Neo-Classical architecture during the 19th century.

Palacio de La Moneda *(see p68)* is the best example of 19th-century Neo-Classical structures found in the capital. Opened as the mint in 1805, the building became the presidential palace in 1845.

Vernacular

Over the centuries, Chileans have constructed their buildings with local resources and according to climatic needs. In some cases, the influence of European immigrants is also visible – Valparaíso, for example, is noted for its Victorian-style buildings.

Estancias in Patagonia are low-slung ranches encircled with cypresses or pines, which provide protection against the region's howling winds.

Wooden shingles dominate the German-styled homes in the Lake District and prevent the rain from seeping in.

Chiloé's *palafitos* *(see p221)*, built during a wave of strong commercial expansion in the 19th century, enabled fishermen to live closer to the sea.

Sports in Chile

Conventional sports such as soccer, tennis, and rodeo are Chile's favorite pastimes. However, extreme sports are quickly gaining popularity given the country's wealth of destinations suited to such activities. Chile's numerous rivers are formidable challenges for white-water rafting and kayaking, while well-designed trails and challenging peaks draw trekkers to national parks, and the desert regions attract a growing number of mountain-bikers. Hang gliding and helicopter skiing are other adrenaline-fueled activities on offer.

Getting up close to glaciers using crampons and ropes

Colo-Colo is the only Chilean soccer team to have won the prestigious South American competition Copa Libertadores de América (in 1991). The team is named for a fierce Mapuche chief who fought against Spanish conquistadores.

Soccer

The nation's most popular sport, soccer is played by Chileans of all ages and social classes. The sport was introduced in Valparaíso by British immigrants who established the Federación de Fútbol de Chile in 1895.

The FIFA World Cup returned to South America after a 12-year interval, when it was held in Chile in 1962. The Chilean team, in official red, blue, and white, finished in third place.

Alexis Sánchez was one of the key players in Chile's squad as the country hosted, and won, the 2015 Copa América. He scored the winning penalty in the final against Argentina.

Tennis

Generally an upper-class sport, tennis is most common at private clubs. Nicolás Massú and Fernando González, both now retired, won the gold medal at the 2004 Olympics in the doubles competition; however, no Chilean player ranks in the world's top 100 at present.

Fernando González's impressive career includes the semifinals at the 2009 French Open, where he was pitted against the Swedish player Robin Söderling.

Marcelo Ríos was the first Latin American tennis player to rank number 1 in the world, in 1998.

Rodeo

Chile's national sport, the rodeo arose in the 16th century when cattle from haciendas were gathered together and branded as a means of identification. The stars of the rodeo are the huasos (cowboys), who skillfully steer their horses around a medialuna, or half-moon arena, and attempt to corral and pin a cow against the wall. The occasion calls for formal garb, which includes a poncho, wide-brimmed hat, leather leg protectors and pinwheel-sized spurs. Huasos compete in a number of annual rodeo events, the largest being the Campeonato Nacional de Rodeo, or National Championship of Chilean Rodeo, held in Rancagua (see p146).

Huasos use a number of deft maneuvers in their efforts to win the rodeo. This includes such moves as the sliding stop, which involves galloping sideways.

A **collera**, or two-man team, work to nudge a calf against a padded arena wall. The *collera* gains top points for pinning the rear of the calf.

Surfing

Despite the cold waters of the Humboldt current that runs along Chile's southern and central coast, surfing is popular with both residents and visitors thanks to consistent waves and a myriad of empty beaches. Pichilemu (see p150), Iquique (see pp170–71), and Arica (see pp164–5) are three of the hot surf spots.

US champion Tyler Fox was one of many big names to attend the 2008 Chile World Tow-In at Punta de Lobos surf break in Pichilemu. This week-long surf festival was one of the most extreme events ever held in the country

Skiing and Snowboarding

From mid-June to early October, skiers and snowboarders head to the Andes for world-class terrain, a relaxed ambience, and relatively short lift lines. The principal resorts are found in Chile's Central Valley (see pp118–59).

Nevados de Chillán *(see p156)*, Valle Nevado, and Ski Portillo, Chile's top ski resorts, host many North American and European ski teams who come to train in summer.

The slopes of Volcán Villarrica *(see p202)*, an active, smoking volcano, are popular with numerous professional snowboarders, notably Markku Koski from Finland.

Fiestas Patrias

The most important holidays of the year, Fiestas Patrias (Patriotic Festivals) celebrate Chile's Independence Day, informally called the Dieciocho, on September 18, and Armed Forces Day on September 19. Chile's true independence came on February 12, 1818, but the formally recognized date honors the nation's first attempt at secession from Spain, on September 18, 1810. In the weeks leading up to the festival, the country comes together to celebrate all things Chilean, including regional culture, traditional food, and dance. Armed Forces Day is marked by a grand military parade in Santiago. Chileans decorate their town streets and fasten flags on vehicles in a show of nationalist pride, and it is common to see children dressed in traditional dresses and *huaso* suits.

Chilean troops participating in a military parade

The *fonda* or *ramada* is a temporary structure, erected as a party hall, which is made of either wooden poles and a thatched roof, or a circus-like tent. Nearly every town in Chile has its own *fonda*, featuring a stage for live bands, a dance area with just a dirt or sawdust floor, and beverage and food stands surrounded by tables and chairs.

Military Parade

The Armed Forces Day, also known as the Día de las Glorias del Ejército (Day of the Glories of the Military) was designated a holiday in 1915 to celebrate freedoms gained and victories won by Chile's military since the country's inception.

Traditional Food and Drink

The barbecue reigns during the patriotic holidays, often carrying on for days and shared among friends and family. Other emblematic foods define the holidays, most having arisen from the countryside.

Empanada is a kind of turnover made with pastry dough and stuffed with *pino*, a mixture of beef, onions, half a boiled egg, raisins, and olives. The dish is then baked in a clay oven.

Chicha is an alcoholic drink made from fermented fruit, most commonly apples or grapes, and produced toward the end of the summer. However, *chicha* is not commonly drunk outside of the Fiestas Patrias. Mapuches make a regional *chicha* using corn, called *muday*.

The *cueca* (see p28), Chile's national dance, is a common sight during Fiestas Patrias. Women dress in flouncy, floral cotton dresses and men in black pants, spurs and boots, a wide-brimmed *huaso* hat, and a white jacket or poncho.

Over half a million spectators attend the parade, which is often accompanied by displays of the military's latest acquisitions in planes, war vehicles, and technological gadgetry.

Rodeo contests take place throughout rural villages up and down the country during Fiestas Patrias. Chile's national sport, the rodeo attracts hordes of enthusiastic spectators to the *medialuna*, where such events are held.

The parade, held in Parque Bernardo O'Higgins (see p85) in Santiago, includes the army, navy, air force, and the police marching Prussian-style along a gigantic cement esplanade in the middle of the park. More than 7,000 troops participate.

Kite-flying is a hugely popular activity, especially as spring breezes rise over the festive weeks.

Anticucho, a dish of marinated and skewered meat

Asados, or barbecues, are synonymous with Fiestas Patrias. Popular items include the *anticucho*, a type of shish kabob, which dates back to the Incan empire. The barbecue usually starts off with a *choripán*, a sausage sandwiched in a piece of crusty bread and topped with *pebre*, a tomato and cilantro salsa.

Piscola, along with the *pisco sour*, is the popular cocktail of the day. A simple concoction of *pisco*, cola, and ice, it is a major party starter during Fiestas Patrias.

CHILE AND EASTER ISLAND THROUGH THE YEAR

Festivals are colorful, joyous events in Chile, often carrying on for days if they fall close to a weekend. The northern desert region is home to the country's most vibrant festivals, featuring bright costumes and lively parades. Although most festivals commemorate religious events or venerate saints, there is also a strong influence of pre-Christian and pre-Colonial tradition. While New Year's Eve is celebrated with fireworks and family reunions, Christmas is a relatively brief event with little fanfare. February is the country's official summer break, when most Chileans go on holiday. Across Chile, a variety of *costumbrista* festivals showcase the country's diverse local arts and crafts, foods, and industry.

Children dancing during the Fiestas Patrias celebrations

Spring

Central Chile has temperate weather conditions during the spring months. In the desert north, temperatures are moderate – the days are not too hot, nor are the evenings cold. Farther south, the Lake District experiences intermittent rainfall. In Patagonia, however, the weather can be blustery and changeable. With off-season rates, mostly pleasant weather, and the lack of summertime crowds, spring is generally considered a good time to visit Chile.

September

Fiestas Patrias *(Sep 18 and 19)*, throughout Chile. The country's Independence Day and Armed Forces Day are celebrated with much revelry *(see pp36–7)*. People spill onto the streets and music reverberates through the air.

Festival de Cine Internacional *(Sep)*, Viña del Mar. This film festival showcases contemporary Latin American films. It is also attended by filmmakers hoping to win the PAOA, the prize for excellence.

October

Festival de los Mil Tambores *(1st weekend of Oct)*, Valparaíso. The arrival of spring is celebrated with the Thousand Drums Festival. The streets come alive with the sound of rhythmic drumbeats, outdoor theater, and dance performances.

Día de la Raza *(Oct 12)*, throughout Chile. This festival was originally held to commemorate the discovery of the Americas by Columbus. Today, it celebrates Chile's diverse indigenous peoples. In Santiago, Mapuche Indians parade through the streets, dressed in typical costumes and playing music on traditional instruments.

Día de las Iglesias Evangélicas y Protestantes *(Oct 31)*, throughout Chile. This relatively new national holiday (started in 2008) marks the date that German theologian Martin Luther challenged the Catholic Church.

El Ensayo *(late Oct/early Nov)*, Santiago. Club Hípico *(see p85)* plays host to Chile's main horse-racing derby and the oldest stakes race in South America.

November

Feria del Libro *(early Nov)*, Santiago. This annual book festival, displaying the works of Latin American authors, is held at the Centro Cultural Estación Mapocho *(see p77)*.

Festival de Colonias Extranjeras *(Nov)*, Antofagasta. Immigrants and their descendants from around the world celebrate their varied heritage with food, music, and dance.

A performer in a vibrant mask at the Festival de Colonias Extranjeras

Traditional dances at the Fiesta Grande de la Virgen de Rosario

Summer

A number of Chile's major festivals, especially music events, take place during the summer months. December through February is the best time to visit the beaches, the Lake District, and Northern Patagonia. During January and February, sizable vacationing crowds are drawn to the beaches and resort-towns. In southern Chile, strong gales are common, but cool ocean currents moderate temperatures in the northern deserts.

December
Inmaculada Concepción *(Dec 8)*, throughout Chile. This religious festival is celebrated in a variety of venues across the country, with the most extraordinary event held at the Santuario de la Virgen de Lo Vasquez, on the road to Valparaíso. Up to 100,000 devotees make an arduous pilgrimage to this sanctuary, often barefoot or on their knees.
Fiesta Grande de la Virgen de Rosario *(late Dec)*, Andacollo. This festival draws up to 150,000 pilgrims, who come to worship the patron saint of mining at the village of Andacollo in northern Chile. It features costumed and masked performers, feasting, and sports such as horse racing and cockfighting.

Noche Buena *(Dec 24)*, throughout Chile. On Christmas Eve, most Chileans meet their extended families, enjoy a late dinner, and attend midnight mass. Children receive gifts from the Viejo Pasquero (Old Man Christmas), while adults enjoy *cola de mono*, or monkey's tail, a traditional Chilean drink made of coffee and *aguardiente*.

Santa distributing gifts at Christmas

Navidad *(Dec 25)*, throughout Chile. Nearly all businesses are closed and the streets are quiet as Chileans rest in their homes.
Carnaval Cultural de Valparaíso *(Dec 25–31)*, Valparaíso. The city's yearly cultural carnival runs through the week leading up to New Year's Eve. It features street performances of theater and dance, music shows, art exhibitions, cinematic events, food stalls, and much more.
Fin de Año *(Dec 31)*, throughout Chile. One of Chile's liveliest festivals is best celebrated in Santiago or on the coast, especially in Valparaíso, where revelers pour into the city for street parties and firework displays. The celebration in Valparaíso is regarded as the largest fireworks event in the world.

January
Año Nuevo *(Jan 1)*, throughout Chile. Quiet streets and closed businesses are the norm on this day, as Chileans recover from the previous evening's *carrete* (party).
Festival Internacional Teatro a Mil *(Jan–early Feb)*, Santiago. The city's top cultural event. Dozens of theater and dance productions by national as well as international artistes are presented. Large-scale street shows draw thousands of onlookers. Alongside performances of established actors, emerging talent is also showcased.
Semana Musical de Frutillar *(late Jan–early Feb)*, Frutillar. Set against a spectacular volcanic backdrop, Frutillar's concert hall plays host to a music festival each year. A series of virtuoso performances of different genres that range from jazz and ballet to chamber music and symphony keep the audiences enthralled.

A giant puppet parading during Santiago's Festival Internacional Teatro a Mil

February

Tapati Rapa Nui *(early Feb)*, Easter Island. Residents of the island celebrate their Polynesian heritage during this 2-week festival *(see p263)*. One of the best and most popular events in Chile, it boasts sophisticated productions of local dance, chant, and song. A variety of competitions, such as horse racing, woodcarving, fishing, body decoration, and making *kai kai* (string figures), are also held.

Derby de Viña del Mar *(1st Sun of Feb)*, Viña del Mar. A major equestrian event, this annual derby draws thousands of racing enthusiasts to the Sporting Club track.

Encuentro Folclórico *(early Feb)*, Ancud. This festival promotes folkloric music, traditional dance, distinct cuisine, and the arts and crafts of the verdant archipelago of Chiloé.

Festival Costumbrista Chilote *(mid-Feb)*, Chiloé. Spread over a weekend, this fascinating cultural festival celebrates the unique culture, folklore, and gastronomy of Chiloé. Visitors can sample over 50 kinds of local dishes and beverages, learn about traditional tools and their use, and buy arts and crafts.

Noche Valdiviana *(3rd Sat of Feb)*, Valdivia. A popular night-long celebration, when lighted boats fill the Río Valdivia and the skies are filled with dazzling fireworks.

Residents of Easter Island performing at the Tapati Rapa Nui celebrations

Festival Internacional de la Canción de Viña del Mar *(last week of Feb)*, Viña del Mar. A 5-day music festival that features competitions between rock, pop, and folkloric music by Chilean as well as popular international bands. The winners are decided by the roaring approval of the crowd.

Carnaval de Putre *(end Feb)*, Putre. The pocket-sized village of Putre in the Andean highlands hosts a big party for its carnival. Aymara Indians from the region are drawn to the celebration. The music, costumed events, as well as the food represent the village's Andean heritage.

Autumn

By March, the summer vacations are over, but many Chileans continue to head to the beach and other outdoor destinations in search of sunny skies during the last of the warm days. Semana Santa, or Easter week, is a popular time for a quick escape to resort towns or neighboring countries. In the Central Valley, the autumn harvest of ripened grapes brings on the yearly wine festivals.

March

Festival de la Vendimia *(Mar)*, Chilean wine valleys. The annual grape harvest is celebrated with events that feature food stands, exhibitions, wine tastings, grape-crushing, and more. Festivals generally begin in early March in northern wine valleys such as Limaní, and continue through late March in the southern Bío Bío.

April

Viernes Santo *(Fri before Easter)*, throughout Chile. Some commemorate Good Friday with re-enactments of Christ's death on the cross, while others flock to fishmongers in order to abide by the religious edict of avoiding meat on this day.

Fiesta de Cuasimodo *(1st Sun after Easter)*, throughout Chile. Priests visit the sick and disabled who were unable to attend church on Easter. They are accompanied by *huasos* (cowboys) in a grand parade. Historically, *huasos* protected the priests from bandits. This is followed by a feast.

Huasos watched by crowds at the Fiesta de Cuasimodo

May

Glorias Navales *(May 21)*, throughout Chile. This event commemorates the 1879 Battle of Iquique during the War of the Pacific *(see p49)*. Military ceremonies are held in Santiago, Valparaíso, and Iquique. Traditionally, the president also presents his or her State of the Union address.

Winter

Winter months bring chilly temperatures to Patagonia and wet conditions to the Lake District. The northern desert region hosts some of the country's largest festivals during this time. The ski season starts in the south, with many events and competitions at ski resorts.

June

Fiesta de San Pedro *(Jun 29)*, throughout Chile. People on the coast honor St. Peter, the patron saint of fishermen, by carrying his statue out to a harbor and wishing for fortune, good weather, and large catches. Inland, especially at San Pedro de Atacama in northern Chile, residents celebrate St. Peter as the patron saint of the Catholic church with mass and costumed processions.

Spirited dancing by costumed young men at the Festival de La Tirana

July

Festival de La Tirana *(Jul 12–16)*, La Tirana. A 5-day event *(see p173)* that fuses pre-Colombian traditions with Catholic ceremony, during which as many as 200,000 people visit the village of La Tirana to honor the Virgen de la Carmen with dances. Performers wear costumes and dragon masks.

Fiesta de la Virgen del Carmen *(Jul 16)*, Santiago. This celebration honors Chile's armed forces, the fight for independence, and the Virgen de la Carmen, patron saint of the nation.

Carnaval de Invierno *(3rd weekend of Jul)*, Punta Arenas. An event that seeks to cheer up the dark days of winter with night-time parades, folkloric dances, and fireworks.

Public Holidays

Año Nuevo (Jan 1)
Viernes Santo (Mar/Apr)
Día del Trabajo (Labor Day, May 1)
Glorias Navales (May 21)
St. Peter and St. Paul Day (Jun 29)
Asuncion de la Virgen (Assumption of Mary, Aug 15)
Fiestas Patrias (Sep 18 & 19)
Día de la Raza (Oct 12)
Día de las Iglesias Evangélicas y Protestantes (Oct 31)
Día de Todos los Santos (All Saints' Day, Nov 1)
Fiesta Inmaculada Concepción (Dec 8)
Navidad (Dec 25)

Masked Chileans parading down a narrow street in San Pedro de Atacama during the Fiesta de San Pedro

Climate of Chile

Covering a distance of some 2,600 miles (4,190 km) from north to south, Chile experiences a wide range of weather conditions. The northern section is an extreme desert that rarely sees rain, though it can have dramatic storms with flash floods. The Central Valley enjoys a Mediterranean climate of dry summers and mild, but wet, winters. Torrential downpours can last weeks during winter in the Lake District and fjord lands, especially in Chiloé, while Patagonia's legendary weather can change in a matter of hours from sunshine to gale-force winds or rain. Isolated from the mainland, Easter Island is influenced largely by the Pacific Ocean, but despite the exposure to cooling oceanic winds, it faces occasional droughts and forest fires, as well as rainstorms.

Norte Grande and Norte Chico are arid, with little or no rainfall. The high desert days are warm, but cold at night.

A road passes through a snowy landscape in southern Chile

The Central Valley climate is also called Mediterranean due to warm, dry summers, and mild winters with moderate rainfall.

ROBINSON CRUSOE ISLAND

°C/F			
20/68			22/72
13/55	15/59	16/61	15/59
	10/50	10/50	
11 hrs	10 hrs	13 hrs	14 hrs
100 mm	160 mm	60 mm	20 mm
Month Apr	Jul	Oct	Jan

VALDIVIA

°C/F			
	17/63	17/63	23/73
	11/52		11/52
8/46		7/45	
	5/41		
11 hrs	9 hrs	10 hrs	10 hrs
234 mm	394 mm	127 mm	66 mm
Month Apr	Jul	Oct	Jan

Easter Island

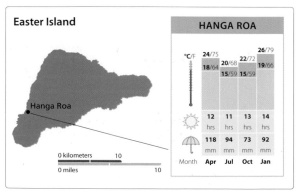

Hanga Roa

| 0 kilometers | 10 |
| 0 miles | 10 |

HANGA ROA

°C/F			
24/75		22/72	26/79
18/64	20/68		19/66
	15/59	15/59	
12 hrs	11 hrs	13 hrs	14 hrs
118 mm	94 mm	73 mm	92 mm
Month Apr	Jul	Oct	Jan

Northern Patagonia experiences winter precipitation in the form of rain and light snow. Strong winds affect open areas in summer.

Southern Patagonia has highly changeable weather during summer. The winters are cold with mild snowfall.

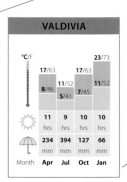

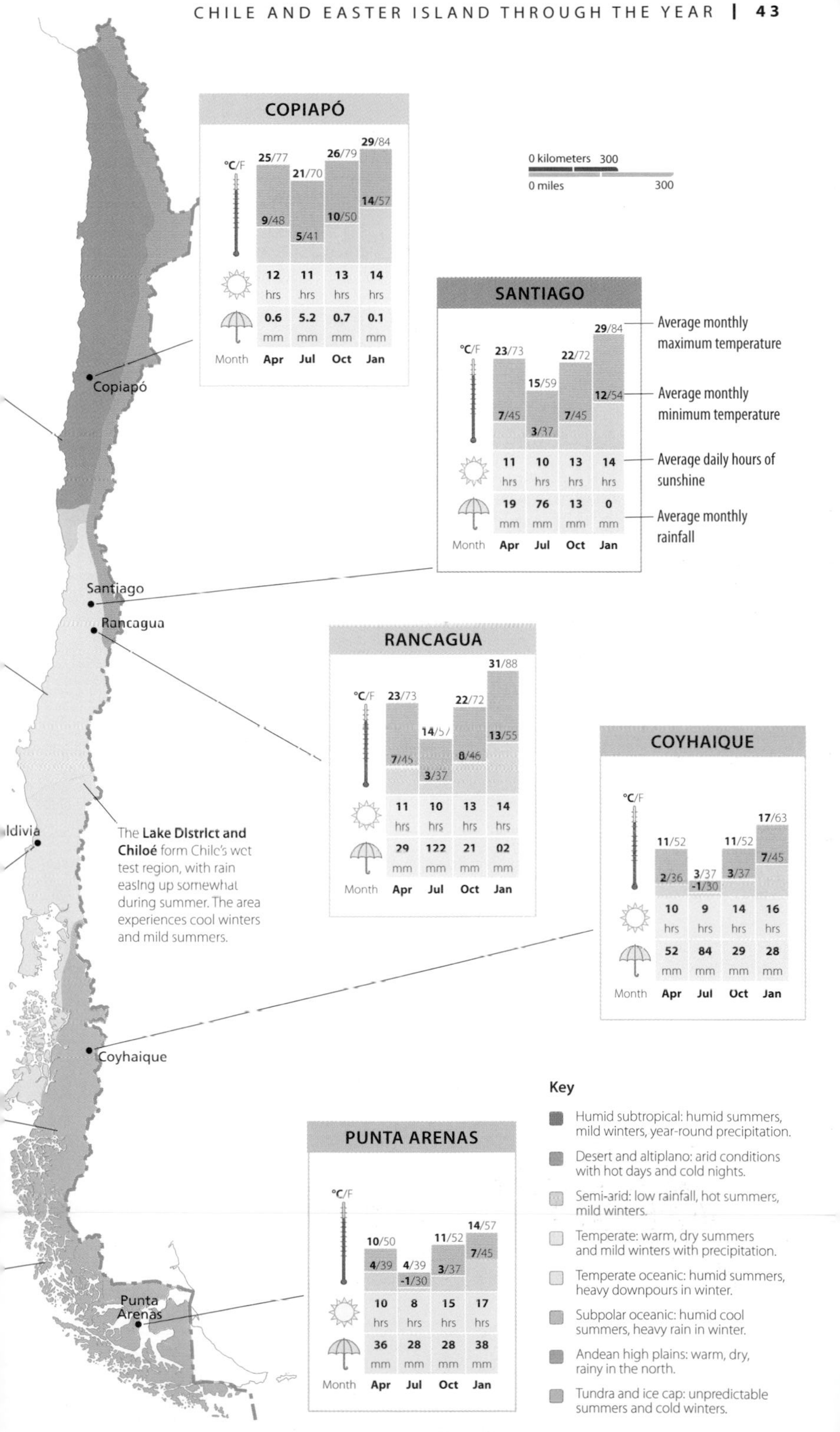

COPIAPÓ

°C/F			
25/77	21/70	26/79	29/84
9/48	5/41	10/50	14/57

12 hrs	11 hrs	13 hrs	14 hrs
0.6 mm	5.2 mm	0.7 mm	0.1 mm
Month	Apr	Jul	Oct	Jan

0 kilometers 300
0 miles 300

SANTIAGO

°C/F			
23/73	15/59	22/72	29/84
7/45	3/37	7/45	12/54

11 hrs	10 hrs	13 hrs	14 hrs
19 mm	76 mm	13 mm	0 mm
Month	Apr	Jul	Oct	Jan

Average monthly maximum temperature

Average monthly minimum temperature

Average daily hours of sunshine

Average monthly rainfall

Copiapó

Santiago

Rancagua

RANCAGUA

°C/F			
23/73	14/57	22/72	31/88
7/45	3/37	8/46	13/55

11 hrs	10 hrs	13 hrs	14 hrs
29 mm	122 mm	21 mm	02 mm
Month	Apr	Jul	Oct	Jan

COYHAIQUE

°C/F			
11/52	3/37	11/52	17/63
2/36	-1/30	3/37	7/45

10 hrs	9 hrs	14 hrs	16 hrs
52 mm	84 mm	29 mm	28 mm
Month	Apr	Jul	Oct	Jan

Idivia

The **Lake District and Chiloé** form Chile's wettest region, with rain easing up somewhat during summer. The area experiences cool winters and mild summers.

Coyhaique

PUNTA ARENAS

°C/F			
10/50	4/39	11/52	14/57
4/39	-1/30	3/37	7/45

10 hrs	8 hrs	15 hrs	17 hrs
36 mm	28 mm	28 mm	38 mm
Month	Apr	Jul	Oct	Jan

Punta Arenas

Key

- Humid subtropical: humid summers, mild winters, year-round precipitation.
- Desert and altiplano: arid conditions with hot days and cold nights.
- Semi-arid: low rainfall, hot summers, mild winters.
- Temperate: warm, dry summers and mild winters with precipitation.
- Temperate oceanic: humid summers, heavy downpours in winter.
- Subpolar oceanic: humid cool summers, heavy rain in winter.
- Andean high plains: warm, dry, rainy in the north.
- Tundra and ice cap: unpredictable summers and cold winters.

THE HISTORY OF CHILE AND EASTER ISLAND

Despite Chile's isolation, its history is an epic one involving ancient settlements and empires. The country also played a role in the European age of exploration and colonization and created its own rich independence period. Equally complex is the history of Easter Island, which, owing largely to its seclusion in the remote South Pacific, is subject of much debate in modern times.

The first humans to reach the Americas were hunter-gatherers who crossed the Bering Strait via a land bridge. Although pinpointing the date of arrival is difficult, the immigration of these groups took place in waves over many thousands of years, the last one occuring some 10,000 years ago.

Evidence from excavations at Monte Verde, just north of Puerto Montt in the Lake District, show that the earliest human settlement in Chile may date from more than 13,000 years ago.

By 6000 BC, crops such as potatoes, squash, and beans had become the livelihood of the settled communities of Atacameño, Aymara, and Diaguita in the Atacama and foothills of the Andes. The Aymara also herded llamas and alpacas for meat and wool, bartering their goods with groups such as the Chango fisherfolk for products from the valleys and the coast. Farther south, the land was peopled by the Mapuche and the closely related Pewenche, Huilliche, and Puelche, all semi-sedentary agriculturalists who subsisted autonomously. In what is now Patagonia, the Chonos, Kawéskar, and Yámana –

collectively known as Canoe Indians – lived off fish and shellfish from the fjords and channels along the Pacific coast and the Strait of Magellan. The Tehuelche hunted game on the Patagonian steppe, while the Selk'nam (Ona) were land-based hunters on the big island of the Tierra del Fuego archipelago.

Isolated from mainland Chile, Easter Island followed a separate trajectory of events, and its history is today a controversial subject. The first settlers arrived about 1,000 years ago from eastern Polynesia to what was then a densely forested island. Their descendants forged a complex society, best remembered by the iconic statues known as *moai* found at various locations around the island. However, the construction of the *moai*, coupled with a fast-growing population that reached unsustainable levels, deforested the island and led to clan warfare and the eventual collapse of this society. The arrival of the Europeans and, later, the island's annexation by Chile suppressed (but failed to dislodge) a culture that is now beginning to reclaim its status.

13,000 BC Establishment of Monte Verde, Chile's first-known settlement

Depiction of the settlement at Monte Verde

1000 Polynesian settlers arrive on Easter Island

| 14,000 BC | AD1 | 400 | 800 | AD 1200 |

6000 BC Cultivation of crops such as potatoes, beans, and squash in the central Andes

Moai on Ahu Akivi, Easter Island, dating from c.1000–1600

◀ José de San Martín and Bernardo O'Higgins at the end of Chile's struggle for independence, April 5, 1818

La Fundación de Santiago, Pedro Lira's painting of Valdivia founding the city

The Incan Empire

During the 15th century, the Incas, the best known of the central Andean empires, extended their power southward up to the latitude of present-day Santiago, reaching a maximum extent around AD 1438. However, their control over peripheral areas, including modern-day Chile, was precarious, depending upon cooperation and tribute from various peoples. Intrigues within the empire, following the death of the emperor Huayna Capac (c.1527), led to a civil war that paved the way for the invading Spaniards.

Exploration and Colonization

The voyages of Christopher Columbus (1451–1506) began an epoch of exploration and acquisition that brought most of what is now Latin America under Spanish control by the 1494 Treaty of Tordesillas. In 1520, Ferdinand Magellan (1480–1521) became the first European to reach Tierra del Fuego and navigate the passage

Spanish explorer Francisco Pizarro (c.1471–1541)

now known as the Strait of Magellan. In the 1530s, the Spaniard Francisco Pizarro and his brothers divided and conquered the Inca empire. Pizarro's partner and rival Diego de Almagro was the first to explore and try to take what is now Chile, in an overland expedition in 1535, but poor planning and logistics stopped him from advancing beyond the Aconcagua valley in central Chile, and many of his men and animals died crossing the high Andes. Pedro de Valdivia's 1541 expedition was more successful, establishing the capital of Santiago, as well as the coastal cities of La Serena, Valparaíso, and Concepción, the interior town of Villarrica, and the riverside city of Valdivia. He also sent forces south to explore the Strait of Magellan from the western side, helping establish Chile's claim to the continent's southernmost areas.

Initial good relations between the Mapuche and the Spanish soon deteriorated, leading to the Araucanian wars which lasted over three centuries. Valdivia himself died in the 1553 Battle of Tucapel against the Mapuche, but his exploits and organizational skills laid the foundation for the country that would become Chile.

The main goal of the conquistadores was to get rich and, when the gold they hoped for proved an illusion, they and their successors had to find alternatives. The Spanish Crown, with a vested interest in the new colonies, offered them wealth in the form of *encomiendas*, where power over large areas of land and its indigenous inhabitants were "entrusted" (*encomendado*)

1438 Consolidation of the Inca Empire

1520 Magellan discovers Tierra del Fuego and the Strait of Magellan

1492 Columbus's first voyage

Pedro de Valdivia

1598 Mapuche uprising expels Spaniards from area south of Río Bío Bío

1400 **1450** **1500** **1550** **1600**

Incan ruler Huayna Capac

1494 Treaty of Tordesillas divides the New World between Spain and Portugal

1535 Diego de Almagro begins expedition to Chile from Peru

1528 Francisco Pizarro first lands in Peru

1541 Pedro de Valdivia founds the city of Santiago

1565 First Audiencia de Chile, held in the city of Concepción

to Spanish settlers. At the same time, the Catholic Church saw in this system an opportunity for evangelizing millions of possible converts. Both these factors became the basis of economic and social reorganization in the absence of Incan authority.

The *encomienda* lost its value as the indigenous population declined under the impact of smallpox (brought by the Spanish) and other diseases. In some cases, population numbers fell by more than 90 percent, and there were no more Indians to pay tribute. Mortality rates were highest in the coastal lowlands, where the climate favored the propagation of disease.

Chilean leader Bernardo O'Higgins (1778–1842)

With no one to pay tribute, the Spaniards adapted by creating large rural estates, commonly known as haciendas, although their profitability was limited as there was no labor to work them. This changed as lower-class Spaniards cohabited with indigenous women, creating the mestizo population. However, this brought new social problems: the *latifundistas* (landowners) monopolized the best agricultural lands, while the mestizos became resident laborers, and neighboring *minifundistas* (peasants) struggled to put enough on the table.

Collapse of Colonialism

The issue of access to land divided Chileans well into the 20th century, but in the short term, it was less significant than their increasing alienation from Spain. Although there was a governor in Santiago, Chile was an administrative subdivision of the Lima-based Viceroyalty of Peru, which in turn depended on Spain for authority. Local *criollos* (South American-born Spaniards) grew restive with Madrid's rule, as their interests began to diverge from those of the Europeans. Events came to a head when Napoleon's invasion of Spain undercut the empire's control over its distant colonies. Figures on the empire's periphery, such as Chile's Bernardo O'Higgins, son of the Viceroy of Lima, and Argentina's José de San Martín, represented the aspirations of the *criollo* population, and led the campaign for independence.

A 19th-century lithograph depicting life on a Chilean hacienda

1722 Dutchman Jacob Roggeveen is the first European to land on Easter Island, at a time of peace among the island's inhabitants

Captain James Cook

1774 Captain James Cook visits Easter Island to find local society in disarray

| 1650 | 1700 | 1750 | 1800 |

1740 Bahía Corral, marking the river entrance to Valdivia, is secured with 17 forts

1778 Birth of Bernardo O'Higgins

1808 Napoleon invades Spain

The declaration of independence in 1818, painted by Chilean artist Pedro Subercaseaux in 1945

Independence and Republic

As the tensions between Spain and the *criollos* exacerbated, and Spain's European relations grew problematic, Chilean patriots plotted to overthrow the Spaniards. Led by O'Higgins, they declared a governing junta in 1810. The declaration unleashed a Royalist reaction that culminated in the 1814 Battle of Rancagua, with many high-profile rebels imprisoned on the Juan Fernández archipelago as a result. O'Higgins fled across the Andes to Mendoza, where he joined forces with Argentine liberator José de San Martín. Three years later, San Martín's Ejército de los Andes (Army of the Andes) defeated the Spaniards at Chacabuco and entered Santiago with an invitation for him to become Chile's Supreme Director. San Martín declined in favor of O'Higgins and proceeded north to liberate Peru.

After overseeing Chile's declaration of independence in 1818, O'Higgins spent five tumultuous years as head of state, consolidating the country but angering conservatives who objected to his secularism and social activism.

Over the following years, the influence of pro-business politicians and landowners grew until, after a brief civil war that ended in 1830, Santiago-born entrepreneur Diego Portales emerged as the power behind a new conservative regime. Portales was responsible for the Constitution of 1833, which created a centralized government and installed Roman Catholicism as the official religion. Portales's constitution lasted until 1925.

On the economic front, the country enjoyed a boom during this period, thanks to a silver strike at Chañarcillo, in the Atacama region, that enriched the national treasury. Additionally, the mid-19th century California Gold Rush made

1810 Creation of Primera Junta de Gobierno (First Governing Body)

1833 Constitution of 1833

1837 Diego Portales executed in a brief uprising

Diego Portales (1793–1837)

1818 Chile declares independence

1810

1825

1840

1814 Battle of Rancagua

1823 Bernardo O'Higgins exiled to Lima

1830 Discovery of silver deposits at Chañarcillo by muleteer Juan Godoy

1849 California Gold Rush

1817 Battle of Chacabuco

Statue of Juan Godoy at Copiapó

Valparaíso a major stopover for ships rounding Cape Horn, and San Francisco became a huge market for Chilean wheat. The key beneficiaries of this boom were the landowners; resident laborers and the peasantry formed a permanent underclass of have-nots that would become one of Chile's great social dilemmas in the 20th century.

Nitrate extraction plant in the Atacama desert

Territorial Expansion

At the time of independence, Chile's territory stretched only from Copiapó in the Atacama to Concepción in the Central Valley, plus a few precarious outliers such as Valdivia and Chiloé.

Beyond Copiapó, Bolivia and Peru held the Atacama's nitrate-rich lands. In Bolivia, these were controlled by Chilean investors, who balked at paying export taxes at the port-city of Antofagasta. In a move to negate this, Chilean military occupied the city in 1879. When Bolivia invoked Peruvian assistance, it unleashed the 4-year War of the Pacific, which ended in an overwhelming Chilean victory. Not only did Chile gain Antofagasta, it also occupied Peru's southern provinces of Tacna, Arica, and Tarapacá, and even the capital, Lima. It eventually returned Lima and Tacna to Peru, but kept Arica and Tarapacá to form its present northern border.

The 1879 Battle of Tarapacá, War of the Pacific

While consolidating its northern frontier, Chile also looked south, where just beyond Río Bío Bío, the Mapuche-controlled lands of Arauco were a dangerous frontier for settlers. Only the Patagonian territories, in and around Punta Arenas and in the vicinity of present-day Aisén, were under definitive Chilean control.

In 1881, the government concluded a series of treaties with the Mapuche that finally ended the Araucanian wars. In the process, it opened the area south of the Bío Bío to European immigration, mainly German, that left a visible impact on the landscape, with its shingled houses and dairy farms. At the same time, the country's growing navy solidified its presence from the desert north to Patagonia and beyond. A wool boom that started in the mid-1870s made the Magallanes region especially prosperous. In 1888, Chile also annexed Easter Island.

Around this time President José Manuel Balmaceda faced a brief civil war for attempting to distribute the nation's new-found riches more evenly through the population. This ended with his suicide in 1891, and the consolidation of conservative power.

Naval combat between Chile and Peru, War of the Pacific

José Manuel Balmaceda (1840–91)

1881 Treaty with the Mapuche ends Araucanian wars

1883 War of the Pacific ends with victory for Chile

1855

1870

1870 Patagonian wool boom

1879 War of the Pacific begins as Chileans occupy the port-city of Antofagasta

1885

1888 Annexation of Easter Island

1891 Civil war and suicide of President Balmaceda

Escuela Santa María de Iquique, site of the 1907 massacre

Economic Decline

With revenues booming from the profits of the mining and shipping industries, Chile had reason for optimism at the start of the 20th century. Yet there were clouds on the horizon. In 1907, one of the most notorious incidents in Chilean labor history occurred when the police and military slaughtered hundreds of striking workers and their family members, who had occupied a school in the mining town of Iquique to protest against low salaries and poor working conditions. At the same time, synthetic nitrates began to replace the low-yield ores of the Atacama mines. As a result,

many mining *oficinas* (company towns) and ports withered from lack of traffic. Meanwhile, the opening of the Panama Canal in 1914 reduced commerce around Cape Horn, so the thriving port of Valparaíso went into sudden decline. Almost simultaneously, World War I nearly eliminated trade with traditional partners such as the UK and Germany. Chile was, in effect, on its own.

As the nitrate mines closed, many miners moved to Santiago and other cities, where they became part of an increasingly militant working class. The rural population found limited opportunities in the countryside, especially as large rural estates still monopolized the best land; smallholders, whose marginal properties often lacked basic amenities such as irrigation water, were unable to support growing families.

The New Constitutionalism

Despite the depressing social and economic conditions, the 1920s began auspiciously in Chile with the election of reformer Arturo Alessandri as president. Alessandri realized

Ships at Valparaíso harbor, depicted by Edward Willmann in 1840

1907 Massacre of striking miners at Escuela Santa María de Iquique

1914 Inauguration of Panama Canal

1920 Arturo Alessandri elected president

1925 Constitution of 1925; Alessandri resigns under pressure from Carlos Ibáñez del Campo

Arturo Aless (1868–1950

1931 Ibáñez del Campo resigns and goes into exile

1910　　　　**1920**　　　　**1930**　　　　**1940**

1910 Chile Exploration Company begins mining copper at Chuquicamata

1923 Chuquicamata sold to Anaconda Copper Company

Copper at Chuquicamata

1929 Great Depression begins in the US

1927 Ibáñez del Campo becomes president and de facto dictator

the seriousness of the situation, but could not overcome a conservative congress. This soon provoked a military coup, which resulted in Alessandri's resignation and exile, as well as the new Constitution of 1925, which created a more powerful executive and separated church and state. However, the Great Depression of the 1930s combined with the authoritarian tendencies of the new president, army general Carlos Ibáñez del Campo, paved the way for Alessandri's return. The following decades brought political fragmentation with an electorate evenly divided among a radical left, a bourgeois center, and an authoritarian right.

During this period, copper became Chile's prime revenue earner, and the US-owned Anaconda Copper Company exerted an enormous influence in the country, even as urban and rural discontent festered. Elected in 1964, President Eduardo Frei Montalva tried to deal with these issues through land reform and by promoting the participation of Chilean investors in the mining sector. However, Frei's well-intentioned measures could not satisfy either side. The far left would accept nothing less than confiscation of the large estates and nationalization of the copper industry, while the landowners and mining magnates resisted any change to the status quo. In 1970, the election of the socialist Salvador Allende Gossens changed everything.

The Allende Presidency

Allende, who first ran for president in 1952, was a true radical who envisioned a total transformation of Chilean society. In 1970, in a close election, he finished first, though his

Carlos Ibáñez del Campo (1877–1960)

leftist Unidad Popular coalition candidacy won 36.6 percent of the vote, while his opponents Jorge Alessandri Rodríguez and Radomiro Tomic took 34.9 percent and 27.8 percent respectively. In the absence of a clear majority, the election passed to the Congress who, by custom, chose the leading candidate as president. Once in office, Allende nationalized the copper industry, but also confiscated some 7,700 sq miles (20,000 sq km) of agricultural land for redistribution, encouraging informal occupation of private landholdings that resulted in rural violence. At the same time, Allende tried to satisfy the urban working class with large wage increases and spending deficits that contributed to runaway inflation.

However, these measures failed to satisfy groups such as the rightist Patria y Libertad and leftist Movimiento de Izquierda Revolucionaria, who helped make the country ungovernable, with the result that political assassinations became commonplace. In the midst of this chaos, Allende appointed General Augusto Pinochet Ugarte as commander-in-chief of the army.

Salvador Allende, elected president on October 24, 1970

Eduardo Frei Montalva (1911–82)

1973 Allende appoints Augusto Pinochet Ugarte as commander-in-chief of the armed forces

1970 Salvador Allende elected as president

| 1950 | 1960 | 1970 |

1952 Salvador Allende runs for presidency for the first time; Ibáñez del Campo elected

1964 Eduardo Frei Montalva elected to presidency

1971 Chilean Congress nationalizes copper mines

Augusto Pinochet Ugarte

General Augusto Pinochet on a visit to Los Andes, July 1987

The Pinochet Regime

A little-known careerist, Augusto Pinochet surprised almost everyone when, barely three weeks after his appointment as commander-in-chief, he led a sudden brutal coup that overthrew Salvador Allende, who committed suicide as the air force attacked Santiago's presidential palace on September 11, 1973. The following months were even more brutal, as the armed forces locked down the country with a curfew, banned political parties, imprisoned political dissidents, and executed many in campaigns such as General Sergio Arellano Stark's so-called Caravan of Death. At least 3,000 died or "disappeared," and many more were tortured. Pinochet also sent agents beyond Chile's borders to kill exiled Carlos Prats, his predecessor as commander-in-chief, and Allende's former foreign minister, Orlando Letelier.

Pinochet had no compunction about increasing his personal power, or accumulating personal wealth despite cultivating an image of incorruptibility. However, he also tried to remake Chilean society. Implementing his beliefs in free-market capitalism, he oversaw a wholesale transformation of the economy, eliminating government regulations, privatizing health and pension plans, encouraging foreign investment, and selling off most state enterprises. An economic recovery gave him sufficient confidence to hold a plebiscite in 1980, to extend his "presidency" until 1989 and ratify a new constitution. Despite some dubious rules, he won the plebiscite by a wide margin and, even more confidently, permitted political parties to operate openly in 1987. The Constitution of 1980, written by conservative lawyer Jaime Guzmán, stipulated another plebiscite, in 1988, that could extend his mandate until 1997. This time, however, a coalition of centrist and center-left parties rallied against him and, galvanized by a bold televised appearance from socialist politician Ricardo Lagos, the vote was emphatically against Pinochet.

Restoring Democracy

In 1989, the center-left aligned Concertación coalition's candidate Patricio Aylwin won the presidency, but Guzmán's constitution limited political change to a snail's pace. Among other provisions, it created the lifetime position of Institutional Senator that allowed former presidents, such as Pinochet himself, to assume a congressional role that also stipulated legislative immunity. Four years later, the Concertación's Eduardo Frei Ruiz-Tagle won the presidency and, as the economy grew steadily, with only minor

1974 Assassination of General Carlos Prats in Buenos Aires, Argentina

Celebrations following the plebiscite against Pinochet

1988 Pinochet loses plebiscite

1989 Patricio Aylwin elected as president

1975　　　　**1980**　　　　**1985**　　　　**1990**　　　　**1995**

1976 Assassination of Orlando Letelier in Washington DC

1980 Plebiscite approves Constitution of 1980 and eight more years of Pinochet's rule

1987 Political parties once again operate openly

1991 Lawyer Jaime Guzmán assassinated in Santiago

1973 Military coup deposes Salvador Allende

1994 Eduardo Frei Ruiz-Tagle elected president

Eduardo Frei Ruiz-Tagle, president 1994–2000

tinkering, there was neither demand nor support for investigating the Pinochet dictatorship's human rights abuses. Convinced of his immunity, Pinochet traveled freely both at home and abroad, until, on a medical visit to London in October 1998, he found himself under house arrest on the order of Spanish judge Báltazar Garzón, who requested his extradition in an investigation into deaths and disappearances of Spanish citizens in the 1973 coup.

Garzón never achieved Pinochet's extradition to Spain, but the London detention broke the spell. Soon thereafter, Chilean judge Juan Guzmán successfully challenged Pinochet's immunity and opened investigations into the Caravan of Death and other cases, as well as questionable overseas bank accounts that destroyed whatever credibility remained. While never convicted before his death in late 2006, Pinochet was effectively exorcised from public life.

Post-Pinochet Chile

The election of Ricardo Lagos in 2000 marked the consolidation of Chilean democracy. Before his 6-year term ended, the third consecutive Concertación president managed to amend some of the constitution's most anti-democratic provisions, eliminating non-elected senators and restoring the president's authority to remove the commander-in-chief of the armed forces. It also reduced the presidential term to four years, but allowed ex-presidents to run for non-consecutive re-election. Chile's Concertación governments have largely continued the economic course set by their predecessors. While these policies have led to Latin America's most stable economy, the gap between rich and poor has grown rather than diminished and unemployment remains higher than desirable.

In 2006, Chileans made history by choosing the Concertación's Michelle Bachelet, a former defense minister, as the country's first female president. After initial ups and downs, Bachelet drew praise for her handling of the Chilean economy during the global crisis of 2009. In March 2010, her term expired and Sebastián Piñera, the opposition Alianza party's candidate, became president. Bachelet then succeeded Piñera in 2014, to become president for a second term.

Michelle Bachelet and former president Ricardo Lagos

1998 Pinochet placed under house arrest in London

2005 Riggs Bank case uncovers secret Pinochet bank accounts

2010 Sebastián Piñera elected president; central Chile struck by a major earthquake followed by several aftershocks

2014 A billion people watch the rescue of 33 trapped Chilean miners

2017 Chile suffers the worst forest fires since records began

2000	2005	2010	2015	2020

2000 Ricardo Lagos elected president; Pinochet freed to return to Chile

2006 Michelle Bachelet elected president; Pinochet dies in December

2015 Volcán Villarrica and Volcán Calbuco erupt; floods in Atacama Desert

2014 Michelle Bachelet elected president again

Pinochet's coffin on a gun carriage

SANTIAGO AREA BY AREA

Santiago at a Glance

The capital, Santiago, is the largest city in Chile, home to more than one-third of the country's population. Urban Santiago covers an area of 248 sq miles (641 sq km) across a basin between the Andes to the immediate east and the coastal cordillera to the west. The Río Mapocho bisects the city, and Santiago's main points of interest lie along the river. These include the neighborhoods of Las Condes, Vitacura, Providencia, Bellavista, and Santiago Centro (also known as downtown Santiago). Residential areas fan out into the foothills of the Andes, and toward the west, away from Parque Metropolitano de Santiago.

Locator Map

Catedral Metropolitana *(see p62)* is an iconic landmark on the Plaza de Armas. It is the city's largest Catholic church and the seat of the Archdiocese of Santiago de Chile. The cathedral is built in a Neo-Classical style that can be seen in most of downtown's major buildings.

PLAZA DE ARMAS AND SANTIAGO CENTRO *(See pp58–77)*

WEST OF SANTIAGO CENTRO *(See pp78–85)*

Club Hípico's architectural grandeur *(see p85)*, set amid the faded elegance of the República neighborhood, is a testament to Santiago's economic boom during the late 19th century.

0 km   1
0 miles   1

◄ The Providencia and Las Condes districts of Santiago, with the Andes in the background

Barrio El Golf *(see p94)* is part of the larger neighborhood of Las Condes, which is nicknamed Sanhattan for its modern, glitzy skyscrapers. Dozens of excellent restaurants line Avenida Isidora Goyenechea and Avenida El Bosque in Barrio El Golf.

NORTHEAST OF SANTIAGO CENTRO
(See pp86–95)

Galería Isabel Aninat is one of a dozen modern art galleries in the Barrio Vitacura *(see pp94–5)* that display exhibits by both established artists and new Chilean talent.

Parque Metropolitano de Santiago *(see pp88–9)* is a forested recreational park and the lungs of Santiago. The park features walking trails, a botanical garden, swimming pools, the city zoo, and a cable car for aerial views.

PLAZA DE ARMAS AND SANTIAGO CENTRO

Established in 1541 by Pedro de Valdivia, the Plaza de Armas began as the civic and commercial nucleus of Santiago. The area around it became site of the court of law, the cathedral, the governor's palace, and the residential homes of Chile's principal conquistadores. Over the years, many of these buildings fell victim to earthquake or fire, and what remains today dates largely from the 18th century. The plaza and Santiago Centro are now the major social hub of downtown Santiago, where locals and visitors alike relax and are entertained by street performers.

Sights at a Glance

Historic Buildings, Streets, and Neighborhoods

2 Correo Central
3 Palacio de la Real Audiencia
4 Municipalidad de Santiago
5 Casa Colorada
7 Paseos Ahumada and Huérfanos
8 Palacio de los Tribunales de Justicia
9 Ex Congreso Nacional
10 Palacio Alhambra
11 Cancillería
12 Palacio de La Moneda
13 Centro Cultural Palacio La Moneda
14 Plaza Bulnes
15 Bolsa de Comercio
16 Club de la Unión
17 Barrio París-Londres
19 Biblioteca Nacional
20 Teatro Municipal
24 Barrio Lastarria
28 Posada del Corregidor
30 Mercado Central
31 Centro Cultural Estación Mapocho

Churches and Cathedrals

1 Catedral Metropolitana
18 Iglesia y Convento de San Francisco
21 Iglesia San Agustín
22 Basílica y Museo de la Merced
29 Iglesia de Santo Domingo

Museums and Galleries

6 *Museo Chileno de Arte Precolombino (pp64–5)*
25 Museo de Artes Visuales
26 Museo Nacional de Bellas Artes
27 Museo de Arte Contemporáneo

Sites of Interest

23 Cerro Santa Lucía

See also Street Finder maps 2 & 3

◄ The magnificent central nave of Catedral Metropolitana

For keys to symbols *see back flap*

Street-by-Street: Plaza de Armas

The symbolic heart of Santiago, the Plaza de Armas (Arms Plaza) was designed to suit the Spanish norm of leaving one block of a city grid empty for use as a parade ground. Government offices ringed the plaza during the Colonial years, and in the 17th century, it became a thriving commercial area with shopping galleries stretching around the perimeter. In 2000, the square was cleared, leaving only a handful of tall trees and palms, to create more open spaces in the city. Today, it is a vibrant social center drawing people who come here to rest on park benches, play chess, or enjoy the lively atmosphere and street performances.

❾ Ex Congreso Nacional
This venerable edifice was constructed 1858–76 in the Neo-Classical style, with striking Corinthian columns.

❽ Palacio de los Tribunales de Justicia
Chile's Supreme Court occupies a Neo-Classical building with French influences. An architectural masterpiece, its vaulted glass-and-metal ceiling runs the length of the edifice.

❻ ★ Museo Chileno de Arte Precolombino
Housed in the Palacio de la Real Aduana, the Museo Chileno de Arte Precolombino highlights the arts and symbols of pre-Columbian cultures in the Americas.

❼ ★ Paseos Ahumada and Huérfanos
These two bustling pedestrian walkways are lined with shopping centers, cafés, and restaurants.

Key
— Suggested route

For hotels and restaurants in this area see p276 and p290

1 Catedral Metropolitana
Consecrated in 1775, Catedral Metropolitana is the fourth church to be built on this site. This cathedral was originally designed by Bavarian Jesuits, but it received a Neo-Classical makeover from 1780 to 1789.

PLAZA DE ARMAS AND SANTIAGO CENTRO

Locator Map
See also Street Finder maps 2 & 3

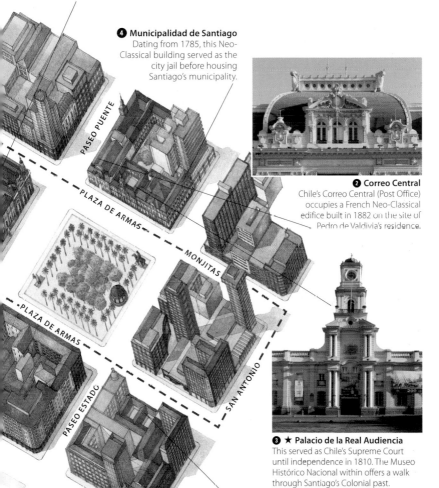

4 Municipalidad de Santiago
Dating from 1785, this Neo-Classical building served as the city jail before housing Santiago's municipality.

PASEO PUENTE

PLAZA DE ARMAS

MONJITAS

PLAZA DE ARMAS

PLAZA DE ARMAS

PASEO ESTADO

SAN ANTONIO

2 Correo Central
Chile's Correo Central (Post Office) occupies a French Neo-Classical edifice built in 1882 on the site of Pedro de Valdivia's residence.

3 ★ Palacio de la Real Audiencia
This served as Chile's Supreme Court until independence in 1810. The Museo Histórico Nacional within offers a walk through Santiago's Colonial past.

5 Casa Colorada
One of the last 18th-century structures left in Santiago, Casa Colorada features a second story, uncommon in its day.

0 meters   50
0 yards   50

❶ Catedral Metropolitana

Plaza de Armas. **City Map** 2 E2.
Tel (02) 2696-2777. 🚇 Plaza de
Armas. **Open** 12:30–7pm Mon–Sat,
10am–7pm Sun. 🔱

Set on the western side of the
Plaza de Armas, the Catedral
Metropolitana was inaugurated
in 1775 and is the fourth church
to be built on this site, after previous structures were destroyed
in earthquakes. The cathedral is
considered the most important
in Chile and is the seat of the
Archdiocese of Santiago de Chile.
The original design was conceived
by Bavarian Jesuits, whose influence can be seen in the cathedral's
imposing, handcarved cedar
doors and wooden pews, despite
the church having undergone an
endless series of renovations
and architectural alterations.
 The grand interior is 295 ft
(90 m) long and divided into
three naves. The right nave
holds an urn that guards the
hearts of war heroes who
fought the Concepción battle
during the War of the Pacific
(1879–83). It also holds the
vestige and altar of Santa Teresa
de los Andes, Chile's first saint.
Highlights in the central nave
include the organ, imported
from London in 1850; the
cathedral's original 18th-century
pulpit; and the central altar,
constructed in Munich in 1912.
Behind the altar is the crypt
where Chile's past cardinals and
archbishops are buried. The left
nave is the Iglesia de Sagrario
(Tabernacle Church), a national

The Baroque facade of the Catedral Metropolitana

monument and site of the first
parish that was founded in the
country. The cathedral's Capilla
del Centesimo Sacramento (the
Hundredth Sacrament Chapel)
is covered in beautiful silver-
work crafted by Jesuits.
 The cathedral houses Jesuit
artwork and other religious
imagery in the **Museo de Arte
Sagrado**, a small yet atmospheric museum reached
through the church.

❷ Correo Central

Plaza de Armas 983. **City Map** 2 E2.
Tel (02) 2956-0303. 🚇 Plaza de
Armas. **Open** 9am–6:30pm Mon–Fri,
10am–2pm Sat. 📷 🌐 **correos.cl**

Historically known as the site
of the first house built in early
Santiago, the Correo Central
was initially the residence of
the city's founding father, Pedro
de Valdivia. Later it served as
the Governing Council, and
following independence, as the

presidential residence until 1846.
In 1881, a fire destroyed part of
the edifice. Soon after, the government planned a grand post office
at the Plaza de Armas, enlisting
the help of architect and musician
Ricardo Brown, who adapted his
design using the actual base
and partial walls of the existing
building. He expanded the walls
to a thickness of 4 ft (1 m) and
topped the roof with metal. In
1908, in a bid to beautify the
building, architect J. Eduardo
Ferham renovated the facade
in Renaissance style, adding a
third floor and a glass cupola.
 Today, the Correo Central
has a small postal museum
and stamp collection on the
first floor to memorialize
the history of Correos de
Chile (Post Office of Chile).

❸ Palacio de la Real Audiencia

Plaza de Armas 951. **City Map** 2 E2.
Tel (02) 2411-7010. 🚇 Plaza de
Armas. **Open** 10am–6pm Tue–Sun.
📷 🚫 cameras without flash allowed.
🌐 **museohistoriconacional.cl**

Built between 1804 and 1808,
the Neo-Classical Palacio de
la Real Audiencia has been
witness to some of the most
important events in Chile. In
1811, the palace was the site
of Chile's first National Congress,
and later it housed the govern-
mental offices of Chile's first
president and liberator, Bernardo
O'Higgins. During the 20th
century, the edifice housed
the City Hall and the post office.

Old post-office artifacts at the Correo Central

Located in this old palace, the **Museo Histórico Nacional** charts Chile's history through a chronological display of exhibits from the Colonial period to the military coup of 1973. Exhibit rooms are spread around a central courtyard and feature rare 18th-century paintings and furniture such as a sacristy wardrobe. Built in Baroque polychrome modeled in a Spanish-Renaissance style, the wardrobe guarded sacred ornaments for Catholic ceremonies. Reproductions of home interiors depict daily life in Colonial Chile, as do traditional clothing and agricultural instruments. There are also sections dedicated to transportation and education. The temporary exhibit hall, called Sala Plaza de Armas (Heritage Square), features displays about Chilean culture and customs.

Sacristy wardrobe, c.1760, at the Museo Histórico Nacional

❹ Municipalidad de Santiago

Plaza de Armas s/n. **City Map** 2 E2. **Tel** (02) 2713-6000. Plaza de Armas. **Closed** to the public.
municipalidaddesantiago.cl

Although Santiago's municipal building is closed to the public, its exterior architecture is easily appreciated from the Plaza de Armas. Originally founded in 1548 as the *cabildo*, or Colonial town hall, this was also the site of the city's first jail. Three buildings on the site were subsequently destroyed by earthquakes or fire. In 1785,

Modern-day facade of the Municipalidad de Santiago

Italian architect Joaquin Toesca, who had already put his signature Neo-Classical stamp on many of Santiago's buildings, rebuilt the town hall. In 1883, following the transfer of the jail to new premises, the town hall offices expanded, but within a decade the edifice succumbed to a major fire. Renovations began apace and by 1895 the Santiago Municipality was installed in the restored building. This still maintained the previous structure's Neo-Classical style, but now displayed touches of Italian Renaissance, in the form of arched doorways and three enormous frontal windows framed by columns. Today, the front facade bears a coat of arms given by Spain.

❺ Casa Colorada

Merced 860. **City Map** 2 E2. **Tel** (02) 2386-7400. Plaza de Armas. **Closed** to the public.
santiagocultura.cl

One of the few remaining Colonial structures in the capital, the Casa Colorada (Red House) is highly regarded as a pristine

example of Colonial architecture designed for the bourgeoisie of Chile. Built in 1770, it was the home of Don Mateo de Toro y Zambrano (1727–1811), a wealthy entrepreneur and the first Count of the Conquest, a title he bought from the Spanish Crown. Toro y Zambrano went on to serve as a senior military leader and Royal Governor during Spanish rule. On September 18, 1810, he was elected the first president of the newly formed government junta during Chile's fledgling struggle for independence. In 1817, after the Battle of Chacabuco *(see p18)*, revolutionaries José San Martín and Bernardo O'Higgins stayed at the Casa Colorada, followed by Lord Cochrane *(see p207)*.

The Casa Colorada is unique in that it has two floors, which was unusual at the time. The family originally lived on the second floor and rooms on the first floor were used as Don Mateo's offices. The building was built with a brick facade painted red (hence the name) and reinforced with decorative stone along the base, arched windows with forged iron balconies, and a central patio.

Red exterior of the Casa Colorada

❻ Museo Chileno de Arte Precolombino

Inaugurated in 1981, the highly regarded Museo Chileno de Arte Precolombino is dedicated exclusively to the study of the artistic and symbolic legend of cultures throughout Latin America. The museum is housed in the impressive Neo-Classical Palacio de la Real Aduana, which was built between 1805 and 1807 as the Royal Customs House, and which later served as the National Library and Court of Law. The permanent exhibits are divided into six cultural regions. Of special interest is the valuable collection of pre-Columbian textiles and excellent ceramics. There are also interesting temporary exhibitions.

Neo-Classical facade of the palatial building housing the museum

Ceramic Art
The Bahía, Tolita, and Jama-Coaque cultures of coastal Ecuador produced elaborate human and animal figurines, and representations of temples, in addition to ornate everyday items such as tripod vases and yucca graters.

★ Chinchorro Mummy
Now extinct, the Chinchorro (see p165) lived in northern Chile and southern Peru, where they practiced mummification for over 3,500 years. They used sticks, vegetation, and mud to preserve bodies 2,000 years before the Egyptians began mummifying their dead.

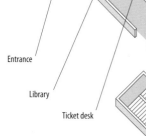

Entrance

Library

Ticket desk

Basement

Gallery Guide

The first floor has three temporary exhibition halls where in-depth displays focus on a particular culture. Galleries on the museum's second floor feature permanent exhibitions on indigenous groups from across the Americas. There is a café and a space for outdoor events at the museum's entrance patio.

For hotels and restaurants in this area see p276 and p290

★ Incan *Quipu*
The expansive Incan empire kept complex judicial data and business transactions on record using the *quipu*, a knotted counting instrument that could only be deciphered by the record keeper.

Second floor

Sergio Larraín Garcia-Moreno

Hailed as a charismatic bon vivant and visionary advocate of Latin American and European art, Sergio Larraín Garcia-Moreno (1905–99) was the founder of the Museo Chileno de Arte Precolombino. An architect with a passionate interest in archaeology and ancient American cultures, Larraín began to trade and sell modern art to buy pre-Columbian relics.

eHe convinced the Santiago Municipality and the city mayor to let him convert the old, fire damaged Royal Customs House into a museum, and employed experts to procure artifacts from private collections located across Europe and the Americas. The museum opened with 1,500 exhibits in 1981; today, the collection is double in size.

Chilean collector Sergio Larraín Garcia-Moreno

The Central Andes displays of textiles, ceramics, and metal-work form the museum's largest collection

First floor

★ Andean Textiles
The early domestication of alpacas and llamas allowed Central Andean cultures such as the Paracas and Nazca (100 BC–AD 300) to create aesthetic textiles. Culturally and politically symbolic designs conveyed a user's ethnic identity.

Key
🟦 Mesoamerican
🟦 Caribbean
⬜ Intermediate
🟦 Amazonian
⬜ Central Andes
⬜ Southern Andes
⬜ Temporary exhibition space
⬜ Non-exhibition space
⬜ Chile before Chile

Moche Masks
The sophisticated Moche people (AD 100–800) of Peru were pioneers in metalworking, creating intricate jewelry and funerary masks inlaid with precious stones.

❼ Paseos Ahumada and Huérfanos

City Map 2 E2. 😊 Plaza de Armas.
🖉 🖥 📷

Pedestrianized in 1977 by closing 12 blocks to motor vehicles, Paseo Ahumada and Paseo Huérfanos are two walkways flanked by numerous shopping galleries, restaurants, electronics stores, and commercial businesses. Catering to a bustling downtown population, the *paseos* take on a lively ambience, with thousands of people walking to and fro all day. Street performers add to the excitement of a stroll here.

Paseo Ahumada stretches from Avenida del Libertador Bernardo O'Higgins, popularly called Avenida Alameda, to the Mercado Central *(see pp76–7)*. It is cut across by a number of streets, most notably by Agustinas, whose junction with Ahumada is the site of the former Hotel Crillón. The first story of this edifice is occupied by **Galería Crillón**, one of many downtown *galerías* – labyrinthine shopping centers brimming with stores selling everything from handicrafts to designer wear.

Paseo Huérfanos runs parallel to Agustinas and crosses Paseo Ahumada near the historic **Banco de Chile**. Built in 1921–25 by Viennese architect Alberto Siegel, the bank boasts ornate interiors and old-fashioned teller windows that are worth a look.

Pedestrians taking a break on the busy Paseo Ahumada

❽ Palacio de los Tribunales de Justicia

Compañía de Jesús, esq. Morandé.
City Map 2 E2. **Tel** (02) 2412-5700.
😊 Plaza de Armas. **Open** 9am–2pm Mon–Fri. Note: IDs to be left at the front desk.

Constructed between 1905 and 1930, the Palacio de los Tribunales de Justicia exhibits both Neo-Classical and Greco-Roman features. The colossal building stretches from *calles* Morandé to Bandera, covering an area of around 43,000 sq ft (4,000 sq m). Since its early days, it has often been the scene of public protests. In 1818, Chile's First National Government Assembly was convened here. Designed by the French architect Emilio Doyere, the building is entered through a marble stairway that is flanked by two fine caryatids. Although the edifice has a somber, institutional facade, its interior offers a stunning example of 20th-century architecture. An open three-story central hall is encircled with wraparound interior balconies and topped with a vaulted glass-and-metal ceiling. Located above the entrance is a bas-relief of a condor clutching a book inscribed with the letters LEX, the Latin term for Law.

Today, the palace houses Chile's Supreme Court, the Court of Appeals, the Military and Police Courts, as well as the Supreme Court Library.

❾ Ex Congreso Nacional

Catedral 1158. **City Map** 2 E2. **Tel** (02) 2674-7800. 😊 Plaza de Armas. **Open** 9am–2pm last Sun of May.

An imposing Neo-Classical structure with massive columns similar to those of the Pantheon in Rome, the Ex Congreso Nacional was designated a National Monument in 1976. Beginning in 1858, the building's construction experienced a series of delays and was only completed in 1876, under the direction of architect Manuel Aldunate. In 1895, the building nearly burned to the ground and was rebuilt by architect Emilio Doyere in 1901.

Congressional sessions were held in this building until the dissolution of the Congress by former dictator Augusto Pinochet in 1973. Today, it houses the Santiago offices of the Senate as well as the Chamber of Deputies.

The edifice is surrounded by lush, exotic gardens that are open to the public. The statue of the Virgin that dominates the grounds was placed in memory of the 2,000 people who were killed in a fire at the Iglesia Compañía de Jesús in 1863, which was located nearby.

Formal gardens fronting the entrance to Ex Congreso Nacional

⓪ Palacio Alhambra

Compañia de Jesús 1340. **City Map** 2 D2. **Tel** (02) 2698-0875. 🚇 La Moneda. **Closed** for restoration. Ⓦ **snba.cl**

An extraordinary architectural gem, the Palacio Alhambra stands out in a neighborhood dominated chiefly by Neo-Classical structures and modern storefronts. Built between 1860 and 1862, Alhambra was modeled after the eponymous Moorish palace in Granada, Spain. The architect Manuel Aldunate designed the *palacio* for Francisco Ossa Mercado, a wealthy silver-mine owner, politician, and military lieutenant. Aldunate traveled to Spain to study the original Alhambra Palace. Upon his return, he created a smaller version of it with elaborate plaster ceilings and carved pillars, and replicated the lion fountain from its Court of Lions. Following Ossa's death, the *palacio* was bought by Don Julio Garrido Falcón, a millionaire and renowned Chilean philanthropist, who donated the building to the National Society of Fine Arts in 1940.

Today, the palace houses the Society's offices and operates as a cultural center offering art classes and hosting a variety of exhibitions. Due to restoration work, it is closed to the public until further notice.

Moorish motifs and arches at Santiago's Palacio Alhambra

⓫ Cancillería

Teatinos 180. **City Map** 2 E2. **Tel** (02) 2827-4200. 🚇 La Moneda.

Chile's Ministry of Foreign Relations, or Cancillería, is located in an impressive 17-story building that was formerly the Hotel Carrera. Open from 1940 to 2003, this was the grandest hotel of its time. It was designed by architect Josué Smith Solar (with help from his son José), who was already well known for his design of the Club Hípico *(see p85)*. The hotel's guests included Fidel Castro, Henry Kissinger, Charles de Gaulle, Nelson Rockefeller, Indira Gandhi, and Neil Armstrong, among others.

Hotel Carrera was most famous for its proximity to the Palacio de La Moneda *(see p68)* during the infamous coup d'état in 1973 *(see p52)*, when it acted as a temporary home for nearly every international journalist reporting in the country. Most of the images of the presidential building being bombarded were taken from the hotel's windows and rooftop. The hotel itself was slightly damaged by the shelling.

In 2004, the hotel sold for US$24 million and was renovated to accommodate some 1,200 employees of the Ministry of Foreign Relations. Today, most of the building's interiors, other than the lobby, are unrecognizable from its hotel era. The lobby features beautiful marble columns that rise up to a towering 49 ft (15 m), and a striking mural made of opal glass. Painted by the Spanish artist Luis Egidio Meléndez, this mural is a depiction of the discovery of the Americas.

Opal-glass mural behind the gleaming marble columns in Cancillería's lobby

The palace guard outside the stately Neo-Classical Palacio de La Moneda

⑫ Palacio de La Moneda

Avenida Alameda, between Calles Morandé & Teatinos. **City Map** 2 E3. **Tel** (02) 2690-4000. 🚇 La Moneda. **Open** 9am–5pm Mon–Fri. 🎥 Note: book 1 wk in advance by email (visitas@presidencia.cl); passport needed to gain entry.

The immaculately preserved Palacio de La Moneda is Chile's presidential headquarters. Built between 1784 and 1799 by the Spanish, it was inaugurated in 1805 as the Casa de Moneda, the nation's mint. From 1845, it housed the republican government offices, and also served as the presidential residence till 1958. Designed by Italian master architect Joaquin Toesca (1745–99), the palace was the largest building erected in any of Spain's colonies during the 18th century, and is considered one of the finest examples of Neo-Classical architecture in Chile.

At the northeastern side of the Palacio de La Moneda is the **Plaza de la Constitucíon**, an expansive grassy space crisscrossed by walkways and fronted by a triangular cement esplanade. Visitors can present their passports here to enjoy a stroll through the palace's patios. This easy access might seem odd to visiting foreigners used to more stringent security at other presidential head-quarters. The plaza was

designed in the 1930s to create Barrio Cívico, the country's political and administrative center; other civic buildings around the plaza include the Ministry of Foreign Relations, Ministry of Labor, the Intendente, and the Central Bank of Chile. At the plaza's southern corner is a statue of Chile's former president Salvador Allende, who perished here during the coup d'état of 1973 (see p52) that ushered in the Pinochet regime. It is possible to watch the ceremonial changing of the guard that takes place at the plaza at 10am every other day. From the plaza, visitors can enter the palace's interior courtyards that comprise the Patio de los Cañones – named for the two 1778 Peruvian-made cannons that are on display here – and the Patio de los Naranjos, named for the orange trees that adorn it.

⑬ Centro Cultural Palacio La Moneda

Plaza de La Ciudadanía Nº 26. **City Map** 2 E3. **Tel** (02) 2355-6500. 🚇 La Moneda. **Open** 9am–8:30pm daily. 🎥 🎞 💺 🖉 🖪 🏠 w ccplm.cl Note: access is via elevators at ground level on the plaza or from sloping walk-ways at Calles Morandé and Teatinos.

A pet project of former president Ricardo Lagos, the cutting-edge Centro Cultural Palacio La Moneda was inaugurated in 2006 as part of the 2010 Bicentennial Project that introduced new museums and improved road infra-structure in the capital. The cultural center is located just southwest of the Palacio de La Moneda, in what once served as the palace's basement.

Designed by noted Chilean architect Cristián Undurraga, the cultural center features three subterranean floors that surround a spacious central hall made of cement and glass. Three large salons host international traveling exposi-tions as well as shows by well-known Chilean artists. This facility also houses the Arts Documentation Center library; the National Film Archive, with a digital library and a movie theater that can accommodate over 200 people; a number of restaurants and cafés; and a superb artesanía store that showcases arts and crafts from the length of Chile. The sprawling Plaza de la Ciudadanía, landscaped with gorgeous walkways and reflecting pools, acts as the roof for the underground cultural center.

Contemporary interior of the Centro Cultural Palacio La Moneda

Fountain adorning the tree-lined walkway leading to Plaza Bulnes

⓮ Plaza Bulnes

Northern end of Paseo Bulnes. **City Map** 2 E3. La Moneda.

Named for the six-block pedestrian esplanade at the end of which it stands, Plaza Bulnes has been the site of military and patriotic celebrations during the years of the Pinochet dictatorship as well as a center for dissident protests that continued long after the return to democracy (see p53).

In 1975, General Pinochet established the controversial Eternal Flame of Liberty at the plaza. This flame was regarded by many as a visible monument to the dictatorship, and dissidents regularly attempted to extinguish it as a form of protest.

In 1979, the remains of revolutionary hero and Chile's first president Bernardo O'Higgins (see p157) were moved from the Cementerio General (see p90) to the plaza by the Pinochet regime. This was done in an attempt to create a patriotic altar that represented a supposed symbolic return to traditional historical values.

Plaza Bulnes was renovated in 2005 and now features an underground crypt holding the remains of Bernardo O'Higgins that can be viewed through a glass window. The Eternal Flame of Liberty was finally put out during the course of the renovations.

⓯ Bolsa de Comercio

La Bolsa 64. **City Map** 2 E3. **Tel** (02) 2399-3000. Universidad de Chile. **Open** 9:30am–5pm Mon–Fri. **W** bolsadesantiago.cl Note: passport or ID needed to gain entrance.

Launched in 1884 with only 160 incorporated companies, Chile's stock market expanded rapidly to include twice the number of companies within a decade. The early years of the 20th century continued to be a time of tremendous good fortune for the Chilean economy, mostly due to the boom in metal and nitrate mining in the northern deserts.

The financial nerve center of the capital, today this area is a micro-district comprising charming cobblestone streets and historic buildings. At the heart of this economic hub is the Bolsa de Comercio, Santiago's lively stock exchange. It is housed in a French Renaissance-style triangular structure, with Roman pillars and a slate roof with a cupola. This elegant old building was built in 1917 by Emilio Jecquier, who was already famous for his design of the Museo Nacional de Bellas Artes (see p75). Visitors need to show their passports or IDs to enter the interiors of the building and witness the hustle and bustle of the stock market business. Although considerable modern technology has been installed during the past few decades, the interiors of the Bolsa de Comercio retain their original splendor.

Historic structures lining a cobblestone street in La Bolsa

⓰ Club de la Unión

Avenida Alameda 1091. **City Map** 2 E3. **Tel** (02) 2428-4600. Universidad de Chile. **W** clubdelaunion.cl Note: entry via invitation only.

The exclusive Club de la Unión is an architectural gem constructed between 1917 and 1925 by noted Chilean architect Alberto Cruz Montt (1879–1955) in French Neo-Classical style. The club boasts spacious dining rooms, halls, a private art gallery, and the longest carved oak bar in the country. The ornate interior of the club features gleaming marble walls, antique furnishings, crystal chandeliers, and other finery. The club operated as a men's-only association until 2006, when it invited its first female member.

The on-site restaurant is open to non-members.

Bolsa de Comercio's interior, reflecting a mix of the old and new

Neptune's fountain, in Cerro Santa Lucía ▶

⓱ Barrio París-Londres

Londres and París. **City Map** 2 F3.
Tel (02) 2800-1898. ⓜ Universidad de
Chile. Londres 38: **Tel** (02) 2800-1898.
Open 10am–1pm & 3–6pm Tue–Fri,
10am–2pm Sat.◪ on request, in
Spanish only. ⓦ **londres38.cl**

With small, artful mansions, the
tiny neighborhood known as
Barrio París-Londres (because
it consists of the two parallel
streets) is an architectural oasis in
an area cluttered with parking
garages and utilitarian buildings
that hark back to the 1960s and
1970s. Laid out in 1922, the *barrio*
was constructed over the gardens
of the Convento de San Francisco.
It was conceived by the architect
Ernesto Holzmann, who believed
that downtown Santiago lacked
attractive neighborhoods that
were within walking distance
of services and shops. After
purchasing the gardens of the
Convento de San Francisco, he
enlisted architects to create what
he envisioned as a "model block
residence," one he hoped to reproduce in other parts of the city.

The neighborhood is well
preserved today, and is delightful
for its elegant ambience, cafés,
and courtyards. Within a four-
block radius of winding, cobblestone streets are styles such as
French Neo-Classical (Londres 70),
Italian Neo-Renaissance (Londres 65),
and Neo-Colonial (Londres 65).

The building at Londres
38 was infamous during the

An old mansion on a quiet, cobbled street
of Barrio París-Londres

Awe-inspiring magnificence of the Medina Library at Biblioteca Nacional

dictatorship years (1973–90)
as a torture center. Visitors can
explore the exhibits pertaining
to the repressions of the Pinochet
years here.

⓲ Iglesia y Convento de San Francisco

Londres 4. **City Map** 2 F3. **Tel** (02)
2639-8737. ⓜ Universidad de Chile.
Open 9:30am–1:30pm & 3–6pm
Mon–Fri, 10am–2pm Sat & Sun.◪
♿ ♦ ⓦ **museosanfrancisco.com**

The oldest surviving building
in Santiago, the Iglesia y
Convento de San Francisco
is a national monument with
distinct architectural details
from various eras. Pedro de
Valdivia first erected a chapel
here in the 16th century in
honor of the Virgen del
Socorro, whose image he had
brought with him and who,
he believed, had protected
the conquistadores against
Indian attacks. In 1618, the
Franciscan Order established
a church of stone walls and
coffered ceilings, expanding
the complex to include cloisters,
gardens, and an infirmary. With
the exception of the church's
bell towers, the structure
survived two major earthquakes.
The current tower was designed
by Fermín Vivaceta in 1857 in
Neo-Classical style.

The giant stones used to build
the walls of the original church
are still visible, as are the nave's
intricately carved woodwork
and the grand doors carved
from cedar. The convent's lush
and tranquil patio and tiled roofs

are early examples of the
traditional architecture of Chile
(see pp32–3). Set in the church is
the **Museo San Francisco**, with
an extremely valuable series
of 17th-century paintings that
narrate the life of St. Francis de
Assisi. Also on display are antique
locks, paintings representing
the life of the Virgen del
Socorro, a graph indicating
the lineage of the Franciscans,
and the Salon Gabriela Mistral,
which houses the poet's
Nobel Prize medal *(see p30)*.

⓳ Biblioteca Nacional

Avenida Alameda 651. **City Map** 2 F3.
Tel (02) 2360-5272. ⓜ Santa Lucía.
Open 9am–6pm Mon–Thu, 9am–5pm
Fri. ◪ ♿ ⓦ **bibliotecanacional.cl**

An imposing building that
occupies a whole city block,
the Biblioteca Nacional was built
1914–27 by architect Gustavo
García Postigo in the style of
the French Academy. Its interiors
have marble staircases, bronze
balustrades, painted murals, and
carved wood detail in a highly
ornamental style, unusual in a
20th-century building. The
library boasts one of Latin
America's most valuable
collections of Colonial-era l
iterary works – it is estimated
that 60 percent of everything
printed during this period
can be found in the handsome
Medina Library on the second
floor. Works include *Mística
Teología* from Mexico (1547), *La
Doctrina Cristina* from Peru (1584),
and chronicles of explorers such
as Sir Francis Drake.

⑳ Teatro Municipal

Agustinas 794. **City Map** 2 F2.
Tel (02) 2463-1000. 🚇 Universidad
de Chile. 🚻 🎫 noon & 4:30pm
Mon, Wed & Fri (email visitas@
municipal.cl). 📧 🌐 **municipal.cl**

Built between 1853 and 1857,
the Teatro Municipal is Chile's
most important venue for
classical music, opera, and
theater. The theater was
originally designed by architect
Claude François Brunet des
Baines in an elegant, French
Neo-Classical style with a well-
proportioned and symmetrical
facade. Its first ever performance
was an Italian production of
Verdi's *Ernani*. Soon the theater
became the cultural and social
center of Santiago's elite, who
contributed heavily to the
production of important opera
performances. In 1870, a raging
fire nearly razed the theater.
However, architect Lucien
Henault successfully restored
the building to its earlier
splendor, and it was reopened
in 1873.

The theater foyer, La Capilla,
features two sculptures by
Nicanor Plaza – *Prólogo* and
Epílogo. The main concert hall
has a capacity of 1,500, not
including the private Sala Arrau
salon on the second floor, with
space for 250. The interior hall
was designed after the Paris
Opera house with lateral
viewing boxes and a large
ceiling cupola, whose grand
crystal chandelier dates from
1930. The theater's massive
curtain weighs 2,645 lb (1,200 kg)
and was made in Germany in
1995 using burgundy mohair
velvet. Throughout the theater
there are costume workshops,
rehearsal studios, dressing
rooms, and set design studios.
The Philharmonic Orchestra,
Santiago Ballet, and Municipal
Theater Chorus are all permanent residents. Many great
artistes have graced this stage,
including Plácido Domingo, Igor
Stravinsky, Anna Pavlova, and
Chilean pianist Claudio Arrau.

㉑ Iglesia San Agustín

Agustinas 828. **City Map** 2 E2.
Tel (02) 2638-0978. 🚇 Universidad de
Chile. **Open** 7:30am–8:30pm Mon–
Sat, noon–6pm Sun. ⛪

The construction of the Iglesia
San Agustín, formerly known as
Templo de Nuestra Señora de
Gracia, marked the founding
of the Catholic Augustinian
mission in Chile. Augustinians
reached Chile from Peru in
1595 and erected their first
church here in 1625. In 1647,
an earthquake destroyed the
church, along with most of the
city. Rebuilt in 1707, the church
was toppled again, by an earthquake in 1730. It was restored
by architect Fermín Vivaceta,
who added columns to the
facade and bell towers. A
curious aspect of San Agustín
is the *Cristo de Mayo* statue.
After the 1647 earthquake,
priests salvaged the intact
statue to find that Christ's
crown of thorns had fallen
around his neck, which
appeared miraculous given
that the diameter of the crown
was smaller than that of the
head. Priests paraded through
the rubbled streets of Santiago
to celebrate this event, and
in the ensuing decades the
commemoration of May 13
grew into the city's most venerable religious festival. Today,
followers still celebrate May 13,
but on a much smaller scale.

Colonnaded nave of the ornate Baroque
Basilica de la Merced

㉒ Basilica y Museo de la Merced

Mac Iver 341. **City Map** 2 F2. **Tel** (02)
2664-9189. 🚇 Plaza de Armas.
Open 10am–6pm Mon–Fri. 🚻 ⛪
🌐 **museolamerced.cl**

Established by the Order of the
Blessed Mary of Mercy – who
arrived with the first expedition
to Chile – the Basilica de la
Merced was built in 1566.
During the city's early years, it
was patronized by the elite,
some of whom are buried within
its walls. These include Governor
Rodrigo de Quiroga and his wife
Inés de Suarez, the first Spanish
woman in Chile. The present-day
basilica was built in 1760 and
later adorned with Neo-Classical
touches by architect Joaquín
Toesca. The Baroque interiors
feature a hand-carved pulpit
and a Virgen la Mercedes from
1548. The church also boasts the
largest organ in Chile. On the
second floor of the basilica is
the Museo de la Merced, an
interesting collection of Easter
Island artifacts, Colonial art,
and 18th-century figurines.

Simple, classical lines of the whitewashed Teatro Municipal

The lush and beautifully landscaped Cerro Santa Lucía

㉓ Cerro Santa Lucía

Avenida Alameda 499. **City Map** 2 F2.
Santa Lucía. **Open** Mar–Sep:
9am–6pm daily; Oct–Feb: 9am–8pm
daily.

Rising above the bustle of
Santiago, the Santa Lucía hill
is a lush park that was once the
strategic defense point for conquistador Pedro de Valdivia, who
founded Santiago at this very
spot in 1541. Following the
conquest, local Mapuches named
the hill Huelén, meaning Sadness
or Pain. In 1871, Mayor Benjamin
Vicuña Mackenna transformed
the 226-ft (69-m) high denuded
outcrop into a veritable Eden,
with dense foliage, Gothic-style
iron balustrades, stone walkways,
statuary, fountains, and lookout
points. Vicuña was buried here
in the tiny chapel, **Capilla la
Ermita**. Other historical
curiosities include a 6-ft (2-m)
high stone carved with a
passage taken from a letter
sent to Charles V, Holy Roman
Emperor, by Pedro de Valdivia,
chronicling the land features
of Chile. There is also a statue
representing the Dissidents
Cemetery that was once part
of Cerro Santa Lucía; dissidents

referring to non-Catholics or
to those who had committed
suicide. At the summit sits
Castillo Hidalgo, built by
Royalists in 1816 during the
Chilean War of Independence.

The principal access point
to the hill, from Avenida
Alameda, is at the **Plaza
Neptuno** monumental staircase, or up a cobblestone road
across from Calle Agustinas.
Visitors can also take the glass
elevator from Calle Huérfanos,
but that only operates
occasionally. A tradition
since the 18th century,
there is a cannon boom
at noon every day.

㉔ Barrio Lastarría

José Victorino Lastarría. **City Map** 3 B4.
Universidad Católica.
barrio lastarria.com Plaza Mulato
Gil de Castro: Merced, esq. Lastarría.
Open 11am–midnight Mon–Fri.
Centro Gabriela Mistral: Av O'Higgins
227. **Tel** (02) 2556-5500. **Open** 10am–
9pm Tue–Sat, 11am–9pm Sun.
gam.cl

Also known as Barrio Parque
Forestal, the charming Barrio
Lastarría is a fashionable neighborhood for artists, actors, and other
young and creative members of
society. On Calle Lastarría, and
along the narrow streets that
branch from it, there are cafés,
restaurants, high-end *artesanía*
shops, art galleries, bookstores,
and a couple of boutique clothing
stores, which together provide
a wonderful atmosphere for
shopping and strolling. Located
in the middle of Calle Lastarría is
the serene and sober **Iglesia de
Vera Cruz**, dating from 1858.
The church was designed by
architects Claudio Brunet des
Baines and Fermín Vivaceta in
Neo-Classical style using rich
red and sunflower tones.

Barrio Lastarría's prime
attraction is the tiny **Plaza
Mulato Gil de Castro**. Named
for the famed 19th-century
portrait painter José Gil de
Castro who lived in the *barrio*,
the plaza was once the patio of
a former house. A small, outdoor
book and antiques fair is held
here from Thursdays to Saturdays.

An art center, named after
the first Latin American Nobel
Prize winner for Literature,
the **Centro Gabriela Mistral**,
regularly hosts concerts, theatre

Weekly antiques fair at Plaza Mulato Gil de Castro, Barrio Lastarría

For hotels and restaurants in this area see p276 and p290

Art Nouveau ceiling and balconies at the Museo Nacional de Bellas Artes

and dance performances. It is set in a remarkable building and is a maze of little plazas and cafés. The center also has airy exhibition spaces on the ground floor where up-and-coming Chilean artists display their works. Free tours in Spanish can be requested at the information desk.

㉕ Museo de Artes Visuales

José Victorino Lastarria 307. **City Map** 3 B4. **Tel** (02) 2664-9337 Universidad Católica. **Open** 11am–7pm Tue–Sun. Sun free. mavi.cl

Opened in 1994, the Museo de Artes Visuales is the ideal place to view contemporary Chilean sculpture, painting, photography, and conceptual art. The museum's permanent collection comprises over 1,500 works by artists such as Samy Benmayor, a Neo-Expressionist painter; Gonzalo Cienfuegos, who uses a variety of media, including oil and acrylic; and Rodrigo Cabezas, best known for his three-dimensional assemblies. Located on the second floor, the **Museo Arqueológico de Santiago** is a compact salon with over 3,300 artifacts from pre-Columbian Chile, including a Chinchorro mummy, hallucinogenic tablets from Atacama, everyday utensils and tools, and decorative finery from the Aymara, Mapuche, Fuegino, and Rapa Nui cultures (see pp26–7).

㉖ Museo Nacional de Bellas Artes

Palacio de Bellas Artes, Parque Forestal. **City Map** 2 F2. **Tel** (02) 2499-1600. Bellas Artes. **Open** 10am–6:45pm Tue–Sun. mnba.cl

First established in 1880 as the Museo de Pintura Nacional, and housed in the Parque Quinta Normal (see pp80–81), the Museo Nacional de Bellas Artes is the oldest and one of the most important art museums in South America. The lovely palace in which it is housed today was built to celebrate Chile's centennial in 1910. It was designed by French-Chilean architect Emilio Jecquier, who created a French Neo-Classical edifice with Art Nouveau details, including a grand vaulted glass ceiling manufactured in Belgium and a facade modeled after the Petite Palais in Paris. In front of the museum is a large bronze sculpture by Chilean artist Rebeca Matte, Unidos en la Gloria y la Muerte (United in Death and Glory), from 1922.

The museum's permanent collection numbers 2,700 works and is divided according to aesthetic, historic, and thematic criteria. Early works include Colonial art – which principally centered on religious themes and the fusion of Spanish and indigenous cultures – 19th-century paintings of landscapes, and portraits of major figures in Chilean history, the most famous of which are by José Gil de Castro. The most valuable paintings here are by Roberto Matta, the 20th-century Surrealist. Since

1990, the museum has drawn major traveling expositions from artists including Damien Hirst and David Hockney.

㉗ Museo de Arte Contemporaneo

Palacio de Bellas Artes, Parque Forestal. **City Map** 2 F1. **Tel** (02) 2977-1751. Bellas Artes. **Open** 11am–7pm Tue–Sat, 11am–6pm Sun. mac.uchile.cl

Facing the tree-lined Parque Forestal, the Museo de Arte Contemporaneo (MAC) is housed in the Palacio de Bellas Artes, but is accessed by a separate western entrance. The museum, founded in 1947 by Marco A. Bontá, features over 2,000 works in its permanent collection. These include 600 paintings, 80 sculptures, and 250 photographs from the end of the 19th century to the present. There are also monthly expositions highlighting international and local artists, and shows such as the Architecture Biennial. The museum has an auxiliary branch at Parque Quinta Normal. The collection features Latin American art, including works by members of the Grupo Signo and Generación del Trece groups (see p32). The influence of Europe in the creation of Chilean artwork is vividly apparent, yet the art features indigenous viewpoints. This is seen in the work of Chilean Hugo Marín, who has melded European technique with pre-Columbian influences. The grounds feature a sculpture by Colombia's famous artist Fernando Botero.

Classical colonnaded entrance to the Museo de Arte Contemporaneo

Vast colonnaded nave of the Iglesia de Santo Domingo

intervened to complete the church's interiors and added brick towers in a Bavarian Baroque style. The church was finally inaugurated in 1808. Today, worshipers pray to the Virgin of Pompeii, whose statue occupies the central altar.

㉘ Posada del Corregidor

Esmeralda 749. **City Map** 2 F1.
Tel (02) 2633-5573. Bellas Artes.
Open 10am–5:30pm Mon–Fri.
W santiagocultura.cl

A national landmark dating from 1750, the Posada del Corregidor is one of the few Colonial adobe buildings left in Santiago. Its thick adobe walls, stone foundations, and second-story wraparound balcony are outstanding examples of urban architecture in 18th-century Chile. In the 1920s, the *posada* became a social center for Santiago's bohemian set.

Although the building's name means the Magistrate's Inn, it was never actually the residence of a magistrate. The *posada* was christened as such – with a bogus plaque – in reference to the Colonial-era magistrate Luis Manuel Zañartu, whose descendant Darío Zañartu purchased the building in 1928.

Today, it operates as an art gallery featuring temporary exhibits of emerging artists, but it once served as a dance hall of dubious reputation known as the Filarmónica. Although the *posada* suffered significant damage in the 2010 earthquake, it has since been restored. The wooden doors and corner pillar are distinctive, and the shady plaza alongside it, with its central fountain, makes an ideal spot for a breather while sightseeing.

㉙ Iglesia de Santo Domingo

Santo Domingo 961. **City Map** 2 E2.
Tel (02) 2633-1584. Plaza de Armas.
Open 8am & 11:30am Mon–Fri,
11:30am Sat, 9am & 11:30am Sun.

The present-day Iglesia de Santo Domingo is the fourth church of the Dominican Order to be built on this site, on land that was initially granted by Spain to the church in 1557. The existing building was designed by architect Juan de los Santos Vasconcelos. Its construction began in 1747 – with the aid of Portuguese masons who were brought over to quarry stone – in a Doric Neo-Classical style that is distinct from other structures in downtown Santiago. In 1795–99, the Italian architect Joaquín Toesca

Virgin of Pompeii, Iglesia de Santo Domingo

㉚ Mercado Central

San Pablo 967. **City Map** 2 E1.
Cal y Canto. **Open** 7am–5pm Mon–Sat, 7am–3pm Sun.
W mercadocentral.cl

Built in 1872 for the National Exposition in Chile, Mercado Central (Central Market) stands on the site of the burned ruins of Plaza de Abasto. The old plaza had been set up in the early 1800s as a means of dispersing the flood of merchants who then occupied the Plaza de Armas. Designed by self-taught architect Fermín Vivaceta, the market is considered one of the most beautiful public structures of its era: the government briefly considered using the building for a fine arts museum. A firm in Glasgow, Scotland, was commissioned to build the grand cast-metal roof that now shelters the market space. The lattices and cutouts of the roof were designed to suck air upward and ventilate the market. Part of the metal

Metalwork pilasters sheltering a busy and brightly lit restaurant at the Mercado Central

For hotels and restaurants in this area see p276 and p290

Intricate arches, cupolas, and metalwork fronting the Centro Cultural Estación Mapocho

design features intertwined balustrades, and two reclining women who represent peace and agriculture. Upon the structure's completion, the firm first assembled the building in Glasgow, then took it apart and shipped the pieces in crates to Chile.

After the 1872 exposition, Mercado Central became a premier market. Although Santiago's major wholesale fish and vegetable market has since moved elsewhere, Mercado Central is still an important commercial center. It is frequented by locals and visitors alike who come to see, smell, and buy the bounty of fish and shellfish found along the Chilean coast, or dine on a local dish at one of the many low-key eateries in and around the market.

③ Centro Cultural Estación Mapocho

Plaza de la Cultura s/n, Balmaceda and Independencia. **City Map** 2 E1. **Tel** (02) 2787-0000. 🚇 Cal y Canto. **Open** 10am–7pm Tue–Sun. 🚗 ♿ 🖥 📷 🅆 estacionmapocho.cl

Inaugurated in 1913, Estación Mapocho was built as a grand terminal for trains that connected Santiago to Valparaíso, northern Chile, and Mendoza in Argentina. The station was designed by renowned Chilean architect Emilio Jecquier, who had studied in France and returned greatly influenced by the Beaux-Arts movement and the teachings of Gustave Eiffel, architect of Paris's Eiffel Tower. The Beaux-Arts style can be readily appreciated in the details of the station's stunning facade, its cupolas, and the columns in the access hall. The station's vast steel roof and skeleton were produced in Belgium by the Haine Saint Pierre construction company, and its interior vaults and marquees were designed by the Paris-based company Casa Daydé. All were later shipped to Chile and assembled there.

Estación Mapocho was one of several public works projects to celebrate the country's centennial in 1910, and construction lasted from 1905 to 1912. It was declared a national monument in 1976. The station closed in 1987 when train services were suspended. The building, abandoned, fell into a state of disrepair. Eventually, the government chose to convert it into a cultural center, reopening it in 1994 as the Centro Cultural Estación Mapocho.

During the restoration, architects rescued the station's facade and preserved most of the edifice's ornate details, including its domed ceilings, stained glass, and masonry. Indeed, much of the attraction of visiting the beautiful Estación Mapocho today is to marvel at the splendor of its architecture and decor. The Centro Cultural now hosts all manner of events, including music concerts, theater performances, and cinema. Many of the original salons have been converted into galleries and spaces for temporary art, dance, and photography exhibits of Chilean artists, but the building is worth a visit in its own right.

The signature event at the center is the austral spring's Feria Internacional del Libro de Santiago. Usually held in October or November, this fortnight-long book fair attracts both Chilean and foreign authors from throughout the Spanish-speaking world, as well as a more international mix. Countries are often invited as special guests. Denmark, Sweden, and Mexico have been invited in the past. Up to-date information on forthcoming book fair-related events can be accessed at www.camaradellibro.cl.

A music workshop at the Centro Cultural Estación Mapocho

WEST OF SANTIAGO CENTRO

The sprawling area west of Santiago Centro encompasses the city's oldest neighborhoods, including Barrio Brasil, Barrio Concha y Toro, Barrio Yungay, and Barrio Dieciocho. These districts were home to the city's elite before they took flight northeast toward the Andean foothills. Few early Colonial buildings remain, but there are plenty of handsome and well-preserved examples of early 20th-century Neo-Classical and French architecture. Some of the capital's most interesting museums and galleries can also be found here, especially around the verdant Parque Quinta Normal, the cultural nucleus of this area.

Sights at a Glance

Historic Buildings, Streets, and Neighborhoods
3 Biblioteca de Santiago
6 Barrio Brasil
7 Barrio Concha y Toro
9 Barrio Dieciocho
10 Confitería Torres
11 Palacio Cousiño

Churches and Cathedrals
12 Basilica de los Sacramentinos

Museums and Galleries
2 Museo Pedagógico Gabriela Mistral
4 Matucana 100
8 Museo de la Solidaridad
   Salvador Allende

Parks and Sanctuaries
1 Parque Quinta Normal pp80–81
13 Parque Bernardo O'Higgins

Sites of Interest
5 Planetario USACH
14 Fantasilandia
15 Club Hípico

See also Street Finder maps 1 & 2

0 meters	500
0 yards	500

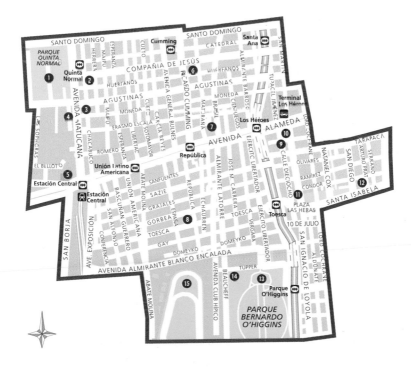

❶ Parque Quinta Normal

Set up in 1842 to propagate foreign plants, Parque Quinta Normal is famous for its wide variety of tree species. Many of these were planted by French naturalist Claudio Gay, whose extensive pioneering studies of Chilean flora and fauna gave birth to the city's Museo Nacional de Historia Natural and to the park itself. In its early years, Quinta Normal was also used for agricultural studies and in 1928 it was incorporated into the University of Chile as the School of Agronomy and Veterinary Sciences. Today, the park is only a fraction of its earlier size, but it remains popular owing to its large lawns and mature trees. The park is also home to a handful of scientific museums, picnic areas, and an artificial lake.

Parque Quinta Normal

① Museo de la Memoria y los Derechos Humanos
② Museo Nacional de Historia Natural
③ MAC Espacio Quinta Normal
④ Museo Artequín
⑤ Museo Ferroviario
⑥ Museo de Ciencia y Tecnología

0 meters 200
0 yards 200

🏛 Museo de la Memoria y los Derechos Humanos

Matucana 501. **Tel** (02) 2597-9600. ⊕ Quinta Normal. **Open** 10am–6pm Tue–Sun. **Closed** public holidays. 🏞 voluntary donations. 💻 📷 🅿 ♿ 🌐 museodelamemoria.cl

The Museum of Memory and Human Rights opened in 2010 as a memorial to the victims of Chile's military dictatorship (1973–90).

Among the items on display are personal letters, official documents, and government propaganda, alongside information on torture methods and some of the implements used, offering vivid and grisly testimony to the horrors of the time, as well as the historical background that led to the rise of the dictatorship.

The building is vast and spacious, utilizing its interior for multimedia exhibits of the notorious regime and its survivors, with the objective of encouraging reflection and debate on human rights.

Although a visit here is a sobering experience, it is also valuable in understanding Chile's past and present.

🏛 Museo Nacional de Historia Natural

Parque Quinta Normal. **Tel** (02) 2680-4603. ⊕ Quinta Normal. **Open** 10am–5:30pm Tue–Sat, 11am–5:30pm Sun & hols (exc Mon). 🏞 🌐 🌐 mnhn.cl

Santiago's museum of natural history is housed in a stately Neo-Classical edifice that was built in 1875 for the city's first International Exposition. The building was handed over to the museum in 1876. The lofty main hall, near the entrance, is dominated by the skeleton of a juvenile fin whale. Displays are divided into 12 categories, including insects, flora, and cultural anthropology. There is also a salon dedicated to the native forests of Chile, with wood slabs showing the age of such giants as alerce, the world's second-oldest tree. The building has been restored after being damaged in the 2010 earthquake (*see p23*).

🏛 MAC Espacio Quinta Normal

Avenue Matucana 464. **Tel** (02) 2681-7813. ⊕ Quinta Normal. **Open** 11am–7pm Tue–Sun (to 6pm Sun). 🏞 📷 ♿ 🌐 mac.uchile.cl

Housed in the Neo-Classical Palacio Versailles, built in the early 1900s and declared a national monument in 2004, this museum is a branch of the Museo de Arte Contemporaneo (*see p75*). In 2005, MAC briefly relocated here while its salons in the Palacio de Bellas Artes were renovated. Since then, this building has been retained by MAC for shows. With 12 spacious salons surrounding a central plaza, the museum hosts large expositions of up-and-coming national

Mature trees in the popular Parque Quinta Normal

The eye-catching glass-and-metal exterior of Museo Artequín

artists and large international expositions such as Germany's Fluxus and the Sao Paulo Biennial.

🏛 **Museo Artequín**

Avenue Portales 3530. **Tel** (02) 2682-5367. 🚇 Quinta Normal. **Open** 9am–5pm Tue–Fri, 11am–6pm Sat & Sun. **Closed** Feb. 🎫 📷 🌐 artequin.cl

An offbeat museum featuring reproductions of the world's greatest painters, the Museo Artequín is located in the gorgeous Pabellón París that was designed to represent Chile at the 1889 Universal Exposition in Paris. The Pabellón's Art Nouveau façade and interiors are the work of French architect Henri Picq. The structure was built using iron, steel, and zinc, in a clear reference to the Industrial Revolution. Also featured were works by contemporary figures such as writer and artist Pedro Lira (1845–1912). The Pabellón was built in Paris, taken apart, and later reassembled at Parque Quinta Normal, where it housed a museum on minerals and metallurgy. In 1992, the Pabellón was renovated and reopened as the present-day Museo Artequín.

The purpose of the museum is to inspire and educate children and adults alike about art through a "real" version of the world's best paintings. On display are prints of some of the world's greatest artists, each represented by a piece for which he is best known. Among the most recognizable international names are Goya, Dalí, Kahlo, and Kandinsky.

🏛 **Museo Ferroviario**

Parque Quinta Normal. **Tel** (02) 2681-4627. 🚇 Quinta Normal. **Open** 10am–5:50pm Tue–Fri, 11am–6:50pm Sat & Sun. 📷 🌐 santiagocapital.cl

Housing one of the most important collections of steam locomotives in Latin America, the Museo Ferroviario is spread across 5 acres (2 ha) in the southwest corner of the Quinta Normal. On display are 16 locomotives and three wagons, the oldest of which is a Rogers locomotive type 22 built in 1893. Locomotive type 20, made by the now defunct Sociedad de Maestranza y Glavanizaciones from Caleta Abarca, is a pristine example of a locally built machine. Also on display is a Kitson-Meyer locomotive built in 1909 in Leeds, UK. This served the Ferrocarril Transandino (Transandine Railway) that, until 1971, connected Los Andes (see p138) in Chile with Mendoza in Argentina – a distance of 154 miles (248 km) across the precarious peaks of the Andes. In all, there were nine locomotives used for the Andean passage, of which only two remain.

Visitors can also view the restored 1923 presidential carriage used by former presidents Arturo Alessandri (1868–1950) and Carlos Ibáñez del Campo (1877–1960).

🏛 **Museo de Ciencia y Tecnología**

Parque Quinta Normal. **Tel** (02) 2681-6022. 🚇 Quinta Normal. **Open** 10am–6:15pm Tue–Fri, 11am–6:15pm Sat & Sun. 📷 🎫 🌐 museodeciencia.cl

Set up in 1985, the Museo de Ciencia y Tecnología was the first interactive

Interactive displays for children at the Museo de Ciencia y Tecnología

museum in the country designed to engage children in science and technology. The museum is housed in a building called the Parthenon, a Greco-Roman-style edifice built in 1884 by Naples-born artist Alejandro Cicarelli and inaugurated by Chilean painter Pedro Lira, who sought to create a permanent exhibition hall for art. Interactive displays are offered on astronomy, geology, mechanics, technology, and many more. Although interesting, it has been overshadowed by the Museo Interactivo Mirador (see p105). In 1887, the Unión de Arte opened the city's first Fine Arts Museum here. It later became the Museo de Arte Contemporaneo (MAC), then in 1974 it was transferred to its current location in Parque Forestal, in central Santiago.

The 1909 Kitson-Meyer engine at Museo Ferroviario

❷ Museo Pedagógico Gabriela Mistral

Chacabuco 365. **City Map** 1 A2. **Tel** (02) 2681-8169. Ⓜ Quinta Normal. **Open** 10am–5pm Mon–Fri, 10am–3:30pm Sat. 🎫 ♿ 🅦 museodelaeducacion.cl

Housed in the Escuela Normal Brígada Walker, the Museo Pedagógico Gabriela Mistral tracks the history and development of education in Chile. The building, originally from 1886, underwent a two-decade renovation and reopened in 2006. The museum is named for Nobel laureate and literary artist Gabriela Mistral *(see p30)*, who was an educator throughout most of her life in spite of having left school at the age of 12. Self-taught and born with a natural verbal dexterity, Mistral became an advocate for education in response to the lack of opportunities for schooling in Chile.

This education museum was launched in 1941 as an exposition by the Museo Nacional de Bellas Artes *(see p75)* to celebrate Santiago's 400th anniversary. Its exhibitions explored the history of education from the Colonial period onward. Following the popular success of the exposition, director Carlos Stuardo combed through grade schools and even industrial and mining schools in search of material and furniture to establish a permanent collection. Today, the collection consists of more than 6,500 historical pieces, including antique maps, school desks, and skills-based teaching apparatus such as sewing machines,

Redbrick facade of the Museo Pedagógico Gabriela Mistral

abacuses, and more. There is also an extensive library of some 40,000 texts covering education, as well as a photo library of 6,000 digitalized images that track the history of education in the country.

❸ Biblioteca de Santiago

Avenida Matucana 151. **City Map** 1 A3. **Tel** 800 220-600. Ⓜ Quinta Normal. **Open** 11am–8:30pm Tue–Fri, 11am–5pm Sat & Sun. ♿ 🖥 🅦 bibliotecasantiago.cl

Opened in 2005, this was Chile's first major public library. It was built near Quinta Normal *(see pp80–81)* in an effort to create a center of cultural and educational development. Housed in a former government supply warehouse built in the 1930s, it has given the people of Santiago access to a vast range of literature, audiovisual and research materials, computer centers, auditoriums, conference rooms, ongoing lectures, and a children's section.

❹ Matucana 100

Avenida Matucana 100, Estación Central. **City Map** 1 A3. **Tel** (02) 2964-9240. Ⓜ Quinta Normal. **Open** 11am–3pm & 4–8pm Mon–Wed, 11am–3pm & 4–9pm Thu & Fri, 5–9pm Sat & Sun. 🖥 🅦 m100.cl

Another gallery founded near Parque Quinta Normal, Matucana 100 is set in a mammoth brick warehouse built in 1911 for the state railway company. The gallery was designed in 2001 to create a space in which a variety of art forms could participate simultaneously – whether cinema, theater, artwork, photography, or music. Over the past decade or so, the center has grown to include a large art gallery and a concert hall. It now focuses solely on contemporary works principally by national artists.

❺ Planetario USACH

Avenida Alameda 3349, Estación Central. **City Map** 1 A4. **Tel** (02) 2718-2909. Ⓜ Estación Central. **Open** Jan & Feb: 11:30am–6pm Tue–Fri, 1:30–7pm Sat, Sun & hols (Mar–Dec: 1:30–6:30pm Sat, Sun & hols only). 🎦 🎫 🅦 planetariochile.cl

The University of Santiago's planetarium is one of Latin America's most prominent astronomy education centers. Its projection dome, the Sala Albert Einstein, has an unusual conical design. Made of copper, it is 72 ft (22 m) in diameter, and has a Carl Zeiss model VI projector that uses 160 lenses, allowing visitors to observe the moon and the solar system, and over 5,000 stars in both hemispheres. Of particular interest are the special expos-itions that highlight discoveries by Chile's top astronomical observatories. The planetarium offers workshops, audiovisual salons, and expositions for both children and adults.

❻ Barrio Brasil

City Map 1 C2. Ⓜ Los Héroes, Santa Ana.

During the early 20th century, Barrio Brasil was a posh

The children's reading room at Biblioteca de Santiago

International Freedom of the Press Fountain at Plazoleta de la Libertad de Prensa, Barrio Concha y Toro

residential neighborhood. By the 1940s, wealthy residents began migrating eastward, toward the Andes. Later, the construction of the Norte-Sur Highway severed the neighborhood from the rest of the city, and Barrio Brasil was by and large forgotten. Thanks to this, the area escaped development and many of its grand early 20th-century Gothic and Neo-Classical mansions have been left intact. As a result, Barrio Brasil is now one of the most picturesque areas in Santiago. It has also experienced a cultural and architectural resurgence, due to the presence of many universities nearby. Artists and musicians have moved in, drawn by Barrio Brasil's eclectic ambience. Today, trendy lofts and funky restaurants sit alongside traditional *picadas* and bars. The streets of nearby **Barrio Yungay** are especially well preserved, the most beautiful being **Pasaje Adriana Cousiño**

between Huérfanos and Maipú, and **Pasaje Lucrecia Valdés** off Compañía between Esperanza and Maipú. Both are cobblestone walkways that exude a strong European feel. Other vestiges of Barrio Yungay's past can be seen at the restaurant Boulevard Lavaud (*see p290*).

❼ Barrio Concha y Toro

City Map 1 C3. 🚇 República.

Dating from the 1920s, Barrio Concha y Toro is one of Santiago's best-preserved neighborhoods, comprising mansions built by the flourishing upper class in the early 20th century. The area was initially owned by engineer-entrepreneur Enrique Concha y Toro and his wife Teresa Cazotte, who reaped a fortune in mining in the late 1800s. They sought to replicate European towns with sinuous cobblestone streets, closely grouped buildings behind a continual facade, and a tiny plaza. The best Chilean architects of the time – Larraín Bravo, Siegel, González Cortés, Machiacao, and Bianchi – were entrusted with the design. They created a cohesive style incorporating influences such as Neo-Gothic, Neo-Classic, Baroque, and even Bauhaus. Highlights include the **Teatro Carrera**, built in 1926 by Gustavo Monckeberg and modeled after the Teatre des Presidents in Paris. The former

home of poet Vicente Huidobro is now the popular Zully restaurant (*see p291*). The picturesque **Plazoleta de la Libertad de Prensa**, often used as a set for television productions, was named in 1994 in honor of the World Press Freedom Day

❽ Museo de la Solidaridad Salvador Allende

República 475. City Map 1 C4. Tel (02) 2689-8761. 🚇 República. Open Apr–Nov: 10am–6pm Tue–Sun; Dec–Feb: 11am–7pm Tue–Sun. 🎟️ Sun free. 🎫 📷 🌐 mssa.cl

Set in the former headquarters of DINA, the secret police during the Pinochet military dictatorship (*see p52*), the Museo de la Solidaridad is the only museum in Latin America consisting entirely of works donated by artists. In an act of solidarity with the government of Salvador Allende (*see p51*), artists in 1971 founded this museum with a collection of more than 400 pieces by such names as Joan Miró, Alexander Calder, Víctor Vasarely, and Roberto Matta. After Salvador Allende's overthrow, the works were hidden in the Museo de Arte Contemporaneo (*see p75*). The museum's administration moved to Paris, where artists continued to donate until the collection reached some 1,500 pieces. The works date from 1950 to 1980, and many of them evoke the social struggle of Latin Americans.

A typical house from the early 1900s in Barrio Brasil

The 19th-century facade of the renowned Confitería Torres

❾ Barrio Dieciocho

City Map 2 D4. Los Héroes.

During the turn of the 20th century Santiago's posh neighborhood was centered around Calle Dieciocho. Wealthy families erected opulent mansions here, as a means of flaunting their newfound fortune from shipping and mining. The constructions reflect the influence of European styles, principally French. Santiago's elite has since moved uptown, yet the architectural gems they built can still be seen, in spite of the fact that the neighborhood looks a little worse for wear. Among its best are the Subercaseaux Mansion at No.190, Residencia Eguiguren at No.102, and the Palacio Astoreca at No.121. The grand buildings are now occupied by university groups, libraries, and other associations.

❿ Confitería Torres

Avenida Alameda 1570. **City Map** 2 D3. **Tel** (02) 2688-0751. Los Héroes. **Open** 10:30am–midnight Mon–Sat. **confiteriatorres.cl**

Opened in 1879, the Confitería Torres is Santiago's oldest café. It served Santiago's politicians, intellectuals, and elite society when the Barrio Dieciocho area was still considered fashionable. Renovations in 2004 salvaged the old red-leather booths, French doors, and long oak bar, and the café's antique ambience is still quite palpable. The Confitería is steeped in history and has produced several emblematic elements of Chile's culinary repertoire. The *barros luco*, a beef sandwich with melted cheese, is named for former president Barros Luco, who ordered one every time he came. The *cola de mono* aperitif of *aguardiente*, milk and coffee, was also invented here.

⓫ Palacio Cousiño

Calle Dieciocho 438. **City Map** 2 D4. **Tel** (02) 2386-7448. Toesca. **Open** 9:30am–4:30pm Mon–Fri. **santiagocultura.cl**

Built between 1870 and 1878, the Palacio Cousiño was the most extravagant mansion of its day. It was designed by French architect Paul Lathoud for the Cousiño family, who had made a fortune in mining and shipping. From Europe, the Cousiños imported walnut and mahogany parquet floors,

brocade tapestries, Italian marble, and French embroidered curtains, along with European artisans to install these fineries. The mansion also housed the country's first elevator. The palace was auctioned off to Santiago's mayor in 1940, who donated it to the city. Subsequently, it was used to house visiting dignitaries such as Golda Meir, Charles de Gaulle, and Belgian king Balduimo. In 1968, the mansion was converted into a museum that preserved the house as it was during the 19th century. Palacio Cousiño is undergoing renovation following the 2010 earthquake, but the garden is open for tours.

Distinctive cupola of Santiago's Basílica de los Sacramentinos

⓬ Basílica de los Sacramentinos

Arturo Prat 471. **City Map** 2 E4. **Tel** (02) 2638-3189. Toesca. **Open** 10am–12:30pm & 4–7pm Tue–Fri.

Designed by architect Ricardo Larraín Bravo, the Basílica de los Sacramentinos was built as an imitation of the Sacré-Coeur of Paris, between 1919 and 1931. The church is notable for its Roman Byzantine architecture and the crypt, a 4,925-ft (1,500-m) long burial chamber that runs underneath. The parquet floors are the first of their kind to be made in Chile. The wooden pulpit, confessionals, and seats were all hand-carved by Salesians, a Roman Catholic order. Also of interest are the French stained glass

Rich furnishings in the central hall of Palacio Cousiño

For hotels and restaurants in this area see p276 and pp290–91

and the organ imported from Germany. The church suffered significant damage in the 2010 earthquake, but it is once again open to the public. The exterior is also lovely, and made more pleasant by Parque Almagro, which lies stretched out before it.

Entrance to Fantasilandia, Chile's largest amusement park

⓭ Parque Bernardo O'Higgins

Between Avenida Beaucheff & Autopista Central. **City Map** 2 D5.
🚇 Parque O'Higgins.
Open 6am–8pm daily. ∅ 🏛
🎌 Fiestas Patrias (Sep 18 & 19).

The capital's second-largest park is a popular recreation area for families and a major staging area for the Fiestas Patrias celebrations *(see pp36–7)*. Named for one of Chile's founding fathers, Bernardo O'Higgins, the park is home to tennis courts, soccer fields, an artificial lake, Santiago's largest indoor music stadium, and a public pool. A curious aspect of the park is the **Campo de Marte**, a gigantic strip of concrete that resembles a landing strip. Military parades take place here every September 19, drawing thousands of spectators.

Among the park's attractions is **El Pueblito**, a mock Colonial village with simple restaurants serving traditional cuisine. Located here are two museums. The **Museo de Huaso** depicts the culture and history of the cowboys of the Central Valley *(see p27)*, while the **Museo de Insectos y Caracoles** houses a collection of butterfly and insect displays. There are also artisan

workshops and fairs at the **Plaza de las Artesanías**. During the Fiestas Patrias, the grounds are bloated to capacity with revelers who come for the *fondas*, or festival centers in tents – a hallmark of this popular park. For days, a veritable patriotic bacchanal takes over the park with nonstop *cueca* music, smoking barbecues, and excessive drinking. The Lollapalooza Chile music festival takes place in late March or early April.

⓮ Fantasilandia

Beaucheff 938. **City Map** 2 D5.
Tel (02) 2476-8600. 🚇 Parque O'Higgins. **Open** noon–8pm daily.
🏛 ∅ 💻 🏛 🆆 fantasilandia.cl

The third-largest amusement park in South America, Fantasilandia is often dubbed the Chilean Disneyland. It opened in 1978 as the brainchild of entrepreneur Gerardo Arteaga, who felt that Santiago had grown insufferably boring for families who were seeking amusement during their spare time. The park offers plenty of knee-trembling rollercoasters and stomach-churning rides such

as Xtreme Fall, Raptor, and Boomerang. There are also more tranquil attractions for younger children including a carousel, the Kids' Zone, and Villa Mágica, with music jamborees and magic acts.

⓯ Club Hípico

Avenida Almirante Blanco Encalada 2540. **City Map** 1 C5. **Tel** (02) 2693-9642. 🚇 Unión Latinoamericana. **Open** for races; schedules vary. 🅿
🆆 clubhipico.cl

Founded in 1870, Club Hípico is Chile's preeminent racetrack and home to South America's oldest stakes race, El Ensayo *(see p38)*, which takes place in late October/early November. It is part of the Triple Corona together with Hipódromo Chile and Valparaíso Derby.

The current racetrack was designed by architect Josué Smith and opened in 1923, the previous track house having succumbed to fire in 1892. The club building is a fine example of early 20th-century architectural grandeur, a result of Chile's economic boom during the late 1800s. Club Hípico features stylish terraces and viewing platforms, restaurants, formal gardens, and a picnic area, set amid the faded elegance of the old República neighborhood.

In total, there are about 1,500 races annually, including the famed Alberto Vial Infante and the Arturo Lyon Peña. The club has also hosted major music concerts, including performances by Iron Maiden, Jonas Brothers, and Linkin Park. Despite the racetrack's roots as an elite social club, it is now frequented by people from all backgrounds.

Spectators following a horse race at Club Hípico

NORTHEAST OF SANTIAGO CENTRO

The neighborhoods northeast of Santiago Centro comprise residential areas built around a commercial center. Until the late 1950s, some of these were nothing more than *parcelas*, or country homes situated on large plots of land, interspersed with slums for Chile's poorer classes. Today, Barrio El Golf has glitzy skyscrapers and posh shops and restaurants; Barrio Bellavista, Santiago's bohemian quarter, sits at the foot of the recreational Parque Metropolitano; and in the north, Barrio Vitacura comprises leafy streets with 20th-century mansions mixed with towering condominiums.

Sights at a Glance

Historic Buildings, Streets, and Neighborhoods
5 Barrio Patronato
7 Plaza Camilo Mori
13 Barrio Suecia
14 Barrio El Golf
15 Barrio Vitacura
18 Pueblo Los Dominicos

Museums and Galleries
3 Museo de Arte Decorativas
6 Casa Museo La Chascona
11 Museo de Tajamares
16 Museo Ralli
17 Museo de la Moda

Parks and Sanctuaries
1 Parque Metropolitano de Santiago *pp88–9*
10 Parque Balmaceda
12 Parque de las Esculturas

Sites of Interest
2 Cementerio General
4 La Vega
8 Patio Bellavista
9 Casa de la Ciudadanía Montecarmelo

See also Street Finder maps 2, 3, 4 & 5

0 meters 800
0 yards 800

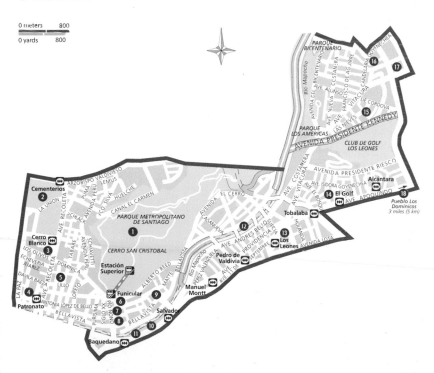

◀ Statue of the Virgin atop Cerro San Cristóbal, in Parque Metropolitano de Santiago

For keys to symbols *see back flap*

❶ Parque Metropolitano de Santiago

Covering some 3 sq miles (7 sq km) of vegetation-clad slopes, the Parque Metropolitano de Santiago was developed between 1903 and 1927 as the lungs of Santiago, encompassing the hills San Cristobal, Pirámide, Bosque, and Chacarillas. Previously bare and dry, the park was reforested with native plants and trees from across Chile and further developed with trails, picnic areas, swimming pools, a cultural center, and a cable car. It is now the city's recreational center and home to the Zoológico Nacional, and offers sweeping views of Santiago and the Andes.

★ Statue of the Virgin
This 45-ft- (14-m-) high statue was donated by France and erected in 1904. It can be seen from most of Santiago Centro.

★ Funicular
This 1925 funicular takes visitors to the top of Cerro San Cristobal and past the park's zoo.

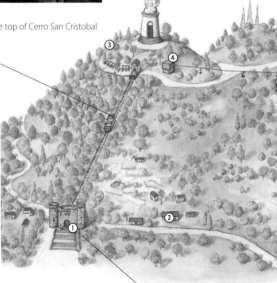

KEY

① **The Pío Nono entrance**, leading directly to the Estación Funicular, forms part of the Plaza Caupolicán garden, with its medieval-style facade and souvenir stands.

② **Zoológico Nacional**

③ **Cerro San Cristobal**

④ **Estación Cumbre**

⑤ **Casa de la Cultura Anahuac**

⑥ **Estación Tupahue**

⑦ **Piscina Tupahue** is one of the most popular pools in the capital.

⑧ **The Jardín Mapulemu** covers over 8 acres (3 ha) of diverse Chilean flora, with interpretative information.

⑨ **Estación Oasis**

⑩ **The alternative entrance** to the park, from Pedro de Valdivia Norte, has two-way traffic open to ascending and descending vehicles. This is also the exit point for all vehicles.

Plaza Caupolicán
The funicular station at Plaza Caupolicán is the main entry point to the park.

Jardín Japonés
Inaugurated in 1997 by Prince Hitachi of Japan, the Japanese Garden features a lotus pond and water wheel. Filled with cherry trees and Japanese maples, this is a tranquil getaway from the bustle and noise of the city.

Enoteca Wine Museum
Housed in the Camino Real restaurant, this museum is a good spot for sampling some of Chile's best vintages.

VISITORS' CHECKLIST

Practical Information
Entrance from Pío Nono & Ave. Pedro de Valdivia Norte. **City Map** 3 B2. **Tel** (02) 2730-1331. free on foot; vehicles pay 3,000 pesos Mon–Fri, 4,000 pesos Sat & Sun. **Open** 10am–6pm daily (summer: to 9pm). Piscina Antilén & Piscina Tupahue: **Closed** Mon. Zoológico Nacional: Entrance from Pío Nono funicular. **Open** 10am–7pm daily (from 1pm Mon; to 5pm in winter). parquemet.cl

Transport
Baquedano.

0 meters 60
0 yards 60

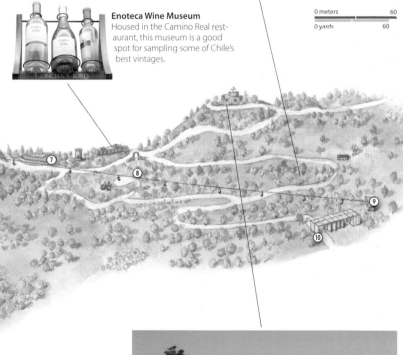

Piscina Antilén
Offering beautiful views of the city, this is Santiago's highest swimming pool and a great respite from the summer heat.

Tombstones at Santiago's famous Cementerio General

❷ Cementerio General

Avenida Alberto Zañartu 951. **City Map** 3 A1. **Tel** (02) 2637-7800. 🚇 Cementerios. **Open** 9am–5:30pm daily. 📷

Santiago's principal cemetery is the final resting place for many of the country's historical figures. Most of the nation's past presidents are buried here, including Salvador Allende, whose remains were moved to this site from Viña del Mar *(see pp132–3)* in 1990. The cemetery opened in 1821 and was inaugurated by Chile's first president, Bernardo O'Higgins, who now rests in a crypt at Plaza Bulnes *(see p69)*. The area was designed as a "city" for the dead, with tree-lined streets and elaborate mausoleums. These run the gamut of styles from Gothic to Egyptian to Greek, and the cemetery's aesthetic appeal is an integral part of its attraction.

Among those buried here are legendary folk singer Violeta Parra; former Senator and leftist Orlando Letelier, who was murdered in Washington, D.C.; noted poet and singer Victor Jara, tortured and shot dead by the Pinochet regime in 1973; and more recently, the Communist Party leader Gladys Marín. There is also a somber monument to the dictatorship era *(see p52)*, a mural by sculptor Francisco Gazitúa called *Rostros* (Faces) that lists thousands of Chileans who were executed.

On the west side of the cemetery is the Dissenters' Patio, a burial sector for the city's Protestants, who had been moved from their earlier burial site at Cerro Santa Lucía in the late 1800s.

❸ Museo de Artes Decorativas

Avenida Recoleta 683. **City Map** 3 A2. **Tel** (02) 2497-1280. 🚇 Cerro Blanco. **Open** 10am–5:30pm Tue–Fri. 📷 **W** artdec.cl

In 1982, the very valuable Coleccion Garcés was donated to the Chilean government and established as the Museo de Artes Decorativas. The museum was moved in 2005 to the old convent of the Centro Patrimonial Recoleta Dominica. The pieces here (more than 2,500) are divided into 20 thematic displays and include beautiful examples of 18th- and 19th-century porcelain, crystal glasses and vases, ornate silver-work, marble and ceramic objects, jewelry, and Greek, Roman, and Oriental art.

The center houses two other collections of interest. The **Museo Histórico Dominico** displays 18th- and 19th-century religious objects such as sacred goblets and priests' clothing. The **Biblioteca Patrimonial Recoleta Dominica** is one of the largest private libraries in Latin America with 115,000 historically important books, maps, and investigative papers covering science and religion.

❹ La Vega

Dávila Baeza 700. **City Map** 2 E1. 🚇 Cal y Canto, Patronato. **Open** 5am–6pm Mon–Sat, 6am–4pm Sun. 🚻 📷 **W** lavega.cl

Located just across Mercado Central, La Vega is Santiago's principal fruit and vegetable market and a must-see for foodies. Amid its chaos of crates and stalls, and the buying and negotiating, La Vega offers an earthy and colorful experience. The market occupies a purpose-built structure covering several city blocks and is surrounded by 100 or more vendors selling everything from sandals to electronics and pet food. At the center of La Vega are the food stalls that sell typical and inexpensive meals such as chicken soup *cazuela*. This is an ideal place to look out for local fruits such as *chirimoya* (a custard apple), *tuna* cactus fruit, and *lucuma*, a butterscotch-flavored fruit used in desserts such as ice cream.

❺ Barrio Patronato

Between Loreto, Bellavista, Dominica and Recoleta streets. **City Map** 3 A3. 🚇 Patronato. **Shops open** 10am–7pm Mon–Fri, 10am–5pm Sat. **W** tiendaspatronato.cl

Occupying over a dozen blocks, Barrio Patronato is a bustling shopping area dominated by clothing stores and small eateries operated in large part by immigrants from Korea, China and the Middle East. During the Colonial period,

Stores and shoppers along a busy lane in Barrio Patronato

For hotels and restaurants in this area see pp276–7 and pp291–2

the *barrio* was a poor residential neighborhood. It was then called La Chimba, which means Other Side of the River. The area continues to be populated by the working class and many of the neighborhood's original adobe houses still stand.

During the late 19th century, Arab immigrants from Syria, Lebanon, and especially Palestine settled in the Patronato neighborhood. They established the city's principal textile commercial center here, selling imported clothing and fabrics, as there was little national production of textiles at the time. Today, Patronato heaves with more than 10,000 shoppers per day, who pack the streets searching for T-shirts, shoes, ball gowns, suits, and trendy clothing at dirt-cheap prices.

Pablo Neruda

Chile's most beloved literary artist, Pablo Neruda has left an indelible mark the world over with his touching poetry about love, politics, history, and the beauty of life and the natural world. Born Neftalí Ricardo Reyes Basoalto on July 12, 1904, Neruda took his pen name from the Czech poet Jan Neruda, in part to hide his earliest works from his father, who did not consider writing a suitable career choice. Neruda was thrust into the limelight with the collection *Twenty Poems of Love and a Song of Despair*.

Pablo Nerudo, Chile's iconic poet and diplomat

Shortly thereafter, he was sent abroad in a series of diplomatic posts that included Argentina, Burma, Mexico, and Spain, where in the mid-1930s he became a vociferous supporter of the Spanish Republic against dictator Francisco Franco. In 1943, he was elected Senator and joined the Communist Party. During this time, Neruda wrote his opus *Canto General* (1950), an encyclopedic work encompassing the entire Latin American continent. In 1971, Neruda won the Nobel Prize for Literature. The poet died from cancer in 1973; his three homes, in Isla Negra, Santiago, and Valparaíso, are now treasured museums.

❻ Casa Museo La Chascona

Fernando Márquez de la Plata 192. **City Map** 3 B3. **Tel** (02) 2777-8741. Ⓜ Baquedano. **Open** 10am–6pm Tue–Sun (Jan & Feb; to 7pm) 🎫 🏛 📷 📷 🎬 **fundacionneruda.org**

Built in 1953 on a steep slope of Cerro San Cristobal in the Bellavista neighborhood, the entrancing Museo La Chascona is one of 20th-century poet Pablo Neruda's three homes. The home was named La Chascona (Woman with Unruly Hair) for Matilde Urrutia, Neruda's secret mistress who lived here alone for a year; Neruda eventually married her in 1966. The house's original blueprints were drafted by Catalan architect Germán Rodríguez. However, Neruda eschewed many of his designs and standard models of home-building. Instead, he used a deeply personal and notably whimsical design of intimate living areas connected by a labyrinth of winding staircases, passageways, and secret doors. His love of the sea is evident in La Chascona's maritime-influenced architectural details such as porthole windows, cozy spaces with creaking floors and arched

ceilings, a dining area that was once fronted by a stream to give the illusion of sailing while dining and a living room that resembles a lighthouse. The interiors exhibit Neruda's vast collection of art and artifacts, bought during his travels around the world.

Neruda was both a friend of former president Salvador Allende and a Communist. After the Pinochet-led coup of 1973, military vandals damaged and flooded the house, and the poet's funeral took place only with great difficulty. The Fundación Pablo Neruda, which operates La Chascona and the poet's two

other residences, later restored La Chascona to its original state. It now contains household items and decorative pieces rescued from the Santiago house, as well as furniture and personal objects from Neruda's office in France, where he was ambassador between 1970 and 1973. Neruda's library holds his Nobel prize medal along with letters, photographs, books, and other publications. It is possible to visit the house with an audio-guided tour on a first-come, first-served basis. While waiting for your turn, the museum café offers a pleasant area in which to relax.

The quaint, almost lyrical grace of the garden at Casa Museo La Chascona

Castillo Lehuedé overlooking
Plaza Camilo Mori

❼ Plaza Camilo Mori

Constitución, esq. Antonia López de
Bello. **City Map** 3 B3. Baquedano.

Located in the heart of the
bohemian neighborhood of
Bellavista, Plaza Camilo Mori
is named for the well-known
Chilean painter whose house
and studio stood here. The
triangular plaza is dominated
by the **Castillo Lehuedé**, a
striking mansion popularly
known as the Casa Rosa (Red
House) that is now a boutique
hotel. This beautiful stone
edifice was built in 1923 by
architect Federico Bieregel
for entrepreneur Pedro
Lehuedé. The plaza is also
home to trendy boutiques
and restaurants, as well as
the **Centro Mori**, which hosts
offbeat theater performances.

❽ Patio Bellavista

Constitución 30. **City Map** 3 B4.
Tel (02) 2249-8700. Baquedano.
Open 10am–2am Sun–Wed, 10am–
4am Thu–Sat.
W patiobellavista.cl

Inaugurated in 2006 as an urban
renewal project, Patio Bellavista
is a large collection of shops
and restaurants that are spread
around an interior square. This
central plaza was originally a

cité, a housing facility for the
working class in the 19th
century. Today, well restored,
Patio Bellavista features over
80 stores selling high-end
artesanía, or crafts, around
two dozen restaurants and
bars, book stores, art galleries,
jewelry shops, as well as the
boutique Hotel del Patio.

There are a number of
outdoor cafés, which are
popular with both locals and
visitors. Patio Bellavista also
hosts a variety of open-air
cultural programs that include
dance performances, live music
shows, as well as exhibitions
of paintings and photography.

❾ Casa de la Ciudadanía Montecarmelo

Bellavista 0594. **City Map** 3 C3.
Tel (02) 2820-2900. Salvador.
Open 9am–7pm Tue–Sat. for
events. **W** providencia.cl

Barrio Bellavista's primary
cultural center, the Casa de la
Ciudadanía Montecarmelo is
located in the building of the
former Montecarmelo Convent,
which in the late 19th century
belonged to the nuns of
Carmelitas de Santa Teresa.
The order was known for its
humility, and its members
were referred to as *descalzos*
(barefoot). Today, operated by
the Corporación Cultural de
Providencia, the beautifully
renovated center conducts
workshops and classes in
photography, art, music, and
dance. It has a year-round

calendar of concerts, cinematic
events, and theater productions
that take place on an outdoor
stage, surrounded by the picturesque brick walls of the old
convent. Montecarmelo also
provides a place for Chilean
authors to showcase new
works of fiction and poetry.

Stark front facade of the Café Literario at
Parque Balmaceda

❿ Parque Balmaceda

Avenida Providencia, between
Baquedano and Del Arzobispo.
City Map 3 C4. Baquedano,
Salvador.

Built in 1927 following the
canalization of Río Mapocho,
Parque Balmaceda is named for
José Manuel Balmaceda, Chile's
erstwhile president and a central
figure in the country's short-lived
Civil War of 1891 *(see p49)*. A statue
commemorating this national
hero stands at the western end
of the park.

The colorful offerings of a gift shop at Patio Bellavista

Sculptures by Chilean artist Federico Assler Browne, Parque de las Esculturas

Parque Balmaceda's central attraction is the relatively new **Fuente Bicentenario**, a fountain which lights up at night in a rainbow of colors. At the foot of the fountain is the **Monumento de Aviación**, an abstract sculpture installed during the Pinochet dictatorship.

The **Café Literario**, located at the center of the park, is well stocked with newspapers and books. An enjoyable place for a stroll, Balmaceda attracts locals from the Providencia and Bellavista neighborhoods, and from downtown Santiago.

⓫ Museo de Tajamares

Avenida Providencia 222.
City Map 3 C4. **Tel** (02) 2223-2700.
⬤ Baquedano. **Open** 10am–5pm Tue–Sat.

Santiago's *tajamares* were a complex series of underground dikes and brick walls that held back Río Mapocho during the 18th century. The mortar used for their construction was a mixture of egg white, limestone, and sand called *cal y canto*. Designed by master architect Joaquín Toesca, these prevented Santiago from flooding for many decades until the modern canal system was developed in the late 19th century.

A part of the city's old *tajamares* was rediscovered during excavations in the Providencia neighborhood in the late 1970s. The Museo de Tajamares, created in 1980, features well-preserved examples of these archaic thick walls and arched dikes. The museum suffered considerable damage during the 2010 earthquake and has reopened after years of renovation.

⓬ Parque de las Esculturas

Avenida Santa María 2205, between Avenue Pedro de Valdivia and Padre Letelier. **City Map** 4 E2. ⬤ Los Leones. **Open** 10am–7pm daily.

Laid out after a massive flooding of Río Mapocho in 1982, Parque de las Esculturas was a creative response to the need to reinforce this area of the river shore. The park was landscaped between 1986 and 1988 by architect Germán Bannen with funds from the Corporación Cultural de Providencia. Serene walking paths meander through the area, which is dotted with some 40 valuable sculptures by contemporary Chilean and international artists, including *Pachamama* by Marta Olvín, *La Pareja* by Juan Egneau, and *Conjunto Escultorico* by Federico Assler. The park also offers views of the snow-capped Andes.

⓭ Barrio Suecia

Avenida Suecia, esq. Avenida Providencia. **City Map** 4 F2.
⬤ Los Leones. ▨ ▣ ▥

A micro-neighborhood, Barrio Suecia is packed with restaurants and bars that exude a North American flavor both in their design and cuisine. The area is dominated by bold and colorful facades.

During its heyday, Barrio Suecia was the city's most popular spot for nightlife. However, focus has now moved elsewhere to areas such as Bellavista. Despite this, young travelers, expatriates, and office workers flock to the neighborhood for happy-hour specials and for the clubs, which remain open until the wee hours of the morning. It can get rather rowdy on the streets however, and pickpockets often take advantage of drunken revelers.

Busy outdoor café in the micro-neighborhood of Barrio Suecia

⑭ Barrio El Golf

Ave. El Bosque & Ave. Isidora Goyenechea. **City Map** 5 B4. El Golf.

Often referred to as Sanhattan for its glitzy skyscrapers and North American feel, Barrio El Golf, a micro-neighborhood, is the city's most modern area and home to many major corporations and embassies. The avenues Isidora Goyenechea and El Bosque comprise the heart of the *barrio*, and are characterized by an abundance of restaurants and several five-star hotels. Little of the neighborhood's residential past can be seen, and most of the former mansions and large homes that remain are now upscale eateries. The Gran Torre Santiago here is the tallest building in Chile – and in South America – at 984 ft (300 m) high. It was designed by Argentine architect César Pelli (of Petronas Towers fame) and can be seen from almost every point in the city. The tower is part of the Costanera Center complex, which includes a mall, cinema, and restaurants. It can be found on Avenida Andres Bello, between Nueva Tajamar and Los Leones, and reached by the Tobalaba metro.

Tiramisu restaurant and café on Avenida Isidora Goyenechea, Barrio El Golf

⑮ Barrio Vitacura

City Map 5 B2. vitacura.cl

Named for the Mapuche chief Butacura (Big Rock) who lived here with his clan at the time of the conquistadores' arrival, Barrio Vitacura was expropriated in the mid-1500s as an *asentamiento* –

Spanish settlements on indigenous land developed into haciendas.

Vitacura lies in the north of the city under the shadow of Cerro Manquehue (Place of the Condors), which is a popular day-hike. Today, Vitacura is the residential neighborhood of the affluent, the politicians, and the aristocracy. It is characterized by towering condominiums, Modernist homes, lush parks, and upscale stores and restaurants. The neighborhood is centered around Avenida Alonso de Córdova and Avenida Nueva Costanera. These two tree-lined streets are populated with luxury goods stores, from Louis Vuitton to Longchamp, and exclusive Chilean and Argentine clothing and interior design stores. More recently, Avenida Nueva Costanera has become the focal point for Santiago's thriving gourmet restaurant scene, with posh eateries such as Tierra Noble, La Mar, and OX *(see p292)*.

The borough's sparkling new municipality building is part of a colossal urban renewal project that also includes **Parque Bicentenario**, a grassy expanse with lagoons and trails that has renovated the banks of

Río Mapocho. This park is the staging center for outdoor festivals, especially wine galas and artisan fairs. An important institution here is the head-quarters of **CEPAL**, the Spanish acronym for the United Nation's Economic Commission for Latin America, which is housed in an architectural landmark designed in the 1960s by Chilean architect Emilio Duhart (1917–2006).

Barrio Vitacura is Santiago's epicenter of high-brow art galleries, boasting more than two dozen venues whose exhibitions highlight Chile's finest artists. Housed in slick, Minimalist-style buildings with bookstores and fashionable cafés, the galleries are in constant motion, hosting exhibitions that provide a space for established and fresh talent. The best-known is **Galería Animal** *(see p99)*, the city's first cutting-edge gallery that launched the idea of presenting art in grand, airy spaces to give the works a more dramatic punch and draw a larger crowd. Galería Animal also offers an extensive range of Chilean art for sale, and frequently rotates its temporary exhibits. In 2008, several heavyweight galleries

Nativity scene on a hill in the Bicentennial Park, Barrio Vitacura

opened to the public, including the transnational AMS Marlborough Chile, Isabel Aninat (known especially for new talent), Arte Espacio, and Patricia Ready. The Patricia Ready gallery hosts temporary art shows featuring top artists such as Carlos Capelan and Bruna Ruffa, and its inaugurations draw Santiago's elite society.

Modern glass exterior of the Patricia Ready art gallery, Barrio Vitacura

⑯ Museo Ralli

Alonso de Sotomayor 4110. **City Map** 5 C1. **Tel** (02) 2206-4220. **Open** 10:30am–5pm Tue–Sun (Jan: Sat & Sun only). **Closed** Feb. **W** museoralli.cl

One of the lesser-known museums in Santiago, the Museo Ralli boasts a small, yet impressive collection of Latin American and European art that includes a handful of works by Salvador Dalí, Marc Chagall, and Joan Miró. This transnational museum – there are other branches in Spain, Uruguay, and Israel – was founded in 1992 by Harry Recanati, an art collector and retired banker who shuns any profit from it. The museum is spread across 32,290 sq ft (3,000 sq m), and is located on a tranquil residential street, where it occasionally hosts temporary exhibits by contemporary European and Latin American artists.

⑰ Museo de la Moda

Avenida Vitacura 4562. **City Map** 5 C1. **Tel** (02) 2219-3623. **Closed** for restoration. **W** museodela moda.cl

Built to honor a family legacy and love of fashion, the Museo de la Moda was established in 2007 by Juan Yarur, who converted his parents' Modernist home into one of the most important fashion museums in the world. Yarur, the grandson of a textile and banking mogul, scoured the globe for a decade in order to compile a nearly encyclopedic collection of more than 10,000 pieces of clothing. These range from the 18th century to

modern day, from classic couture gowns by Chanel and Lanvin to modern frocks by Gaultier and Hollywood memorabilia such as Joan Collins' wardrobe from the 1980s TV series *Dynasty*. Madonna's cone bra, John Lennon's jacket from 1966, and pieces owned by Marilyn Monroe also make an occasional appearance. The utterly stylish and low-lit museum rotates its collections in themes such as "Rock and Roll" and "War and Love", with a special wing devoted to tennis, Yarur's sport of choice. The museum is also a tour through his family home, preserved as it was in the 1960s and 1970s, with a special interpretive area dedicated to his lineage and place in Chilean history. Many items on display are immaculately preserved clothing and accessories once owned by Yarur's mother, Raquel Bascuñán. There is also a restaurant, the Garage, occupying, of course, the family's former garage.

Dresses from the War and Love exhibition, Museo de la Moda

⑱ Pueblo Los Dominicos

Apoquindo 9085. **⊞** Los Dominicos. **Open** 10am–8pm daily. **🅿 💻 📷** **W** culturallascondes.cl

One of Santiago's best and most enticing shopping areas for local arts and crafts, the Pueblo Los Dominicos is a rustic complex housed within the former grounds of the neighboring **Iglesia Los Dominicos**. In 1982, the *pueblo* was expanded and landscaped to resemble a Chilean Colonial village with whitewashed, low-slung adobe buildings that evoke a bygone era. The area was originally a Mapuche settlement headed by chief Apoquindo, whose name was given to the grand avenue that ends here.

Today, the *pueblo* offers 160 small shops to independent artisans for selling wares such as ceramics, leather goods, jewelry, folk art, stained glass, furniture, textiles, clothing, and even animals such as rabbits and birds. Part of the appeal here is that the shops double as workshops, giving visitors a glimpse of the artistic process and an opportunity to interact with the artisans.

The ambience is truly idyllic, enhanced by trickling creeks and the sound of flute music wafting through the village. Saturday and Sunday are the best days to come here, when the Iglesia Los Dominicos holds mass. The church is featured on the Chilean 2,000 peso bill and is a historical monument that provided shelter to revolutionaries during the nation's battle for independence in the 1810s.

GETTING AROUND SANTIAGO

Chile's dynamic capital city is well-connected by an efficient public transport system. Its outstanding metro service is the easiest and cheapest way to access the city's main attractions. Most of the capital's primary sights and services are located in or around central Santiago, which is served by metro lines 1 to 5. However, the metro tends to get crowded during rush hour, when it becomes preferable to use one of the numerous, reasonably inexpensive taxis, radio taxis, and *colectivos* (route taxis). Santiago's buses are smart, environmentally friendly vehicles, although for the most part, short-term visitors will find the bus system less useful than the metro and, late at night, taxis are the better alternative.

A metro shuttle through scenic Santiago

The Metro and Rail Network

The immaculate **Metro de Santiago** is mostly an underground system that covers nearly the entire city and many of its suburbs. Regarded as the most contemporary and extensive metro network in South America, it offers an efficient, fast, and inexpensive way to get around the capital. The network has a total of four lines, but the central Línea 1 and, to a lesser degree, the intersecting Línea 5 are the most useful for visitors. Strangely, there is no Línea 3.

The metro operates from 5:35am to 11:43pm on all weekdays. On Saturdays, it starts operating at 6:30am and stops at 11:45pm; on Sundays and all holidays, it runs from 8am to 11:23pm. Fares vary according to the time of day, with morning and evening rush hours being slightly more expensive. Individual tickets are available, although rechargeable Multivía or Bip! tickets are cheaper and an easy way to avoid standing in long queues. Multi-trip tickets are bought for about US$2.80 and then charged to the required limit; an amount is deducted each time the card is used. These can also be used by multiple passengers, by passing them back and forth across the turnstile. The metro carriages are modern, but have a limited seating capacity. Passengers should stay vigilant about their possessions, as pickpocketing incidents in packed metro cars are not uncommon.

Starting at the Estación Central, a reasonably efficient southbound overland TerraSur commuter rail system reaches Rancagua *(see p146)* and San Fernando *(see p150)*. This rail network is under the aegis of **Empresa de Ferrocarriles del Estado**.

Buses

Transantiago is an ambitious attempt by Chile to eliminate the proliferation of poorly maintained, diesel-guzzling, private buses. The revamped bus system, introduced in 2007, replaced the capital's worst polluters with larger, more comfortable buses. Passengers do not pay in cash, but use Bip! cards, which are also valid on the metro. When metro lines cease operations at night, Transantiago buses ply alongside the main metro routes.

Driving

Driving is mainly useful when leaving the city for excursions. Santiago's narrow streets mean congestion and slow travel times, and parking can be difficult. It is possible to hire vehicles equipped with a compulsory electronic TAG sensor, at car rental companies including **Hertz** and **Budget**.

Chile follows strict driving laws – seat belts are compulsory,

The eco-friendly green-and-white Transantiago buses

A commonly found black-and-yellow Santiago taxi

drink-driving is a serious offence, and drivers must not converse on cell phones.

Taxis, Radio Taxis, and *Colectivos*

The capital has a number of metered yellow-and-black taxis. Fares are reasonable, but passengers are charged more during the night. Taxi drivers are generally courteous and helpful, but some may take indirect routes to hike up the fare. A system of unmarked radio taxis, generally newer vehicles, also operates in Santiago. These do not have meters but charge customers per trip.

Colectivos are shared taxis that accommodate up to four passengers. These black taxis run on fixed prices and routes, and a placard on their roofs displays the destination. **Uber Chile** is also an inexpensive alternative.

Walking

Central Santiago, with several multi-block pedestrian malls, can be easily explored on foot. Parks such as Cerro Santa Lucía and the Parque Metropolitano, across the Río Mapocho, are also great for walkers. Neighborhoods such as Las Condes and Providencia are walkable, but in some parts of the city, the sidewalks need repair and have few wheelchair ramps at corners. Drivers in Santiago generally respect pedestrians, but walkers need to be careful crossing the multi-lane Alameda.

Cycling

Many locals get around on bicycles, but it is better to avoid major avenues such as the Alameda and Avenida Vicuña Mackenna. The streets are sometimes bumpy, but new

bicycle lanes and routes are being introduced. Bike Santiago (www.bikesantiago.cl) offers a bike-sharing scheme that requires a monthly registration fee.

DIRECTORY

The Metro and Rail Network

Empresa de Ferrocarriles del Estado (EFE)
Alameda Bernardo O'l liggins 3170, Estación Central.
Tel (02) 2585-5050. W **efe.cl**

Metro de Santiago
Tel 600 600 9292.
W **metrosantiago.cl**

Buses

Transantiago
Tel 800 730 073.
W **transantiago.cl**

Driving

Budget
Luz 2934, Las Condes. **Tel** (02) 2795-3932. W **budget.cl**

Hertz
Andres Bello 1469, Providencia.
Tel (02) 2360-8666 W **hertz.cl**

Metro de Santiago

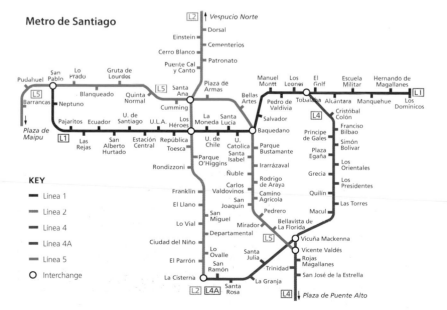

KEY

— Línea 1
— Línea 2
— Línea 4
— Línea 4A
— Línea 5
O Interchange

SHOPPING IN SANTIAGO

Chile's capital city offers a wide range of shopping options, from high-end fashion to wine and local handicrafts. Traditional crafts include clay kitchenware, Mapuche-carved wooden utensils and bowls, and jewelry and art pieces made of *krill* (dyed horse hair). It is also possible to buy ponchos, alpaca and sheep's wool blankets, and thick woolen sweaters. Lapis lazuli, the unique blue stone found solely in Chile and Afghanistan, is used to create exclusive Chilean accessories. In recent years, young fashion designers have eschewed the shopping mall and set up independent, homespun boutique stores in areas such as Bellavista and Bellas Artes. In addition, the rising interest in Chilean gastronomy has spawned several gourmet delicatessens and wine stores in the city.

Textiles and ceramics on display at a shop in the capital

Crafts and Souvenirs

Handicrafts from the Chilean provinces can be purchased in a range of stores across Santiago, although the choice may be restricted. The capital, however, is the best place to purchase the country's unique gemstone, lapis lazuli *(see p303)*, which is used in ornaments, decorative pieces, architectural fittings, and objects of daily use such as salt and pepper shakers. Lapis lazuli is sold in dozens of moderately priced stores lining Avenida Bellavista, between Calle Capellán Abarzúa and Calle Pío Nono. The **Lapis Lazuli House** offers finely crafted items made with this rare blue stone. Those who wish to purchase elegant lapis lazuli jewelry are advised to visit any of the **Morita Gil** stores across the city or **Faba** in Vitacura.

Traditional ceramics, textiles, and decorative objects are available at the **Artesanías de Chile** shops at the Centro Cultural Palacio La Moneda *(see p68)* or Los Domínicos. **Ona** offers some exciting artworks and fashionable clothing made from local products, while **La Verveine** in the Vitacura neighborhood boasts a wide selection of stylish *artesanía* that includes ornamental items for the home.

Simple souvenirs such as T-shirts and keyrings can be found at the stalls lining Patio Bellavista. The most distinctive souvenir shop, though, is probably Santiago's **The Clinic El Bazar**, named for the English clinic in which Chile's former dictator, General Pinochet, was arrested in 1998. The upscale **Pura Artesanos** store in Las Condes carries a range of elegantly designed jewelry, throw rugs, leatherwork, and toys.

Antiques

Shopping for antiques in Santiago is relatively easy as most antique shops are grouped into warehouses. Extensive bargains are on offer at **Antiguedades Balmaceda** where more than 200 independent antique dealers sell household items, furniture, chandeliers, decorative art, jewelry, and wares that date from the early 20th century. **Antiguedades Bucarest** is a shopping gallery that houses dozens of independent stores selling antique items such as gilded mirrors, paintings, wooden furniture, ornaments, and curios from a range of eras.

There are also a number of independent antique shops across Santiago. At the corner of Avenida Italia and Avenida Sucre, over a dozen antique furniture workshops sell mostly refurbished fittings and odd pieces. **Brainworks**, in Providencia's Barrio Italia, specializes in household

Antiques fair at Plaza Mulato Gil de Castro

The high-end Louis Vuitton store at Avenida Alonso de Córdova

acclaimed Surrealist painter Roberto Matta (1911–2002) and the Spanish artist Joan Miró. **Galería Patricia Ready** has vast spaces, a chic café, and a widespread selection of art books. Across the street is **Galería Isabel Aninat**, a long-time gallery that highlights the works of lesser-known Chilean artists. Another site for purchasing Chilean artworks is the **Galería La Sala**. Internationally renowned artists feature prominently at the **Galería A.M.S. Marlborough**. Located in downtown Santiago, **Galería 13** and **Galería Gabriela Mistral** feature mostly young artists who specialize in photography and painting.

items, retro furniture, and reproductions dating from the 1960s and 1970s.

Every Sunday at the Plaza Peru in El Golf, antique vendors display their wares for sale; another popular antique street fair takes place from Thursday to Saturday along the pocket-sized Plaza Mulato Gil de Castro in the Parque Forestal area.

Fashion

Parque Forestal is the hub for fashion created by young Chilean designers. Among the popular designer stores here are **Atelier Carlos Pérez**, a contemporary fashion store, and **Tampu**, which sells modern clothing with indigenous patterns. The most fashionable shops, such as **Cepaz**, **Aji**, and **Makinita de Coser**, can be found at the end of Merced Street and on the corner of Lastarria Street. These stores are a good choice for local fashion and jewelry. **Zapateria Lastarria** is a store that sells handmade shoes for men. **Galería Drugstore** in Providencia features more than 30 locally designed clothing and accessory outlets, including Kebo, which sells frocks by designer Carla Godoy.

Most middle-class Chileans buy the bulk of their clothing at shopping malls that stock national and international brands such as Zara, MNG, and Nine West. Vitacura's Avenida Alonso de Córdova and Avenida Costanera play host to luxury international brands such as Louis Vuitton, Armani, and Burberry.

The epicenter of low-priced fashion is Barrio Patronato (see p90) in Recoleta, where shoppers descend each weekend in search of low-cost clothing at the hundreds of shops here. Shoppers head for **Óptica Bahía** for retro sunglasses, **Orange Blue** for funky clothing and footwear from the 1960s and 1970s, and **Nostalgic** on Calle Bandera for vintage wear and accessories.

Art Galleries

The uptown Barrio Vitacura in eastern Santiago is the heart of Chile's art gallery scene, with no fewer than 15 top galleries spread around Avenida Alonso de Córdova and Avenida Costanera. The most prominent of these is the **Galería Animal**, one of the city's first avant-garde galleries, offering an outstanding collection of contemporary Chilean art, including paintings, sculpture, conceptual pieces, and a handful of artworks by internationally

Sculpture at the Galería Animal

Books and Music

Street kiosks selling local magazines and newspapers are plentiful in Santiago. The stalls located on Paseo Ahumada, between Avenida Alameda and Paseo Huérfanos, sell publications from all around the world at fairly reasonable prices.

English-language magazines are available mainly at the international airport, although some stalls and bookstores in crowded areas occasionally sell *Newsweek* or *Time*. However, a variety of English novels, magazines, guidebooks, and textbooks are available at the **Librería Inglesa** stores found throughout Santiago. **Librería Antartica** shops also have a range of English books.

Santiago's **Feria Chilena del Libro**, with multiple branches around the city, has a decent supply of magazines and books, including a large selection of coffee-table books on Chile and an array of English-language titles. **Librería Eduardo Albers**, known for its travel-oriented selection, is an online-only store.

For music lovers, there are also a number of pocket-sized record stores located throughout the capital.

Browsing through books at Patio Bellavista

Wine and Food

The booming interest in Chile's wine and cuisine, as well as an increased production of gourmet food using local ingredients, has created a brand new culinary scene and shops that cater to it. Although many well-known Chilean wines can be found around the world, wine shops such as **La Vinoteca** and **El Mundo del Vino** offer boutique wines and little-known varietals that are not available elsewhere. Across the interior patio from its namesake restaurant, **Baco** offers the best from the big wineries, in addition to a wide selection from lesser-known *bodegas*.

In Providencia, **Emporio Nacional** is designed to resemble a food shop from the early 1900s, and sells specialty food items from all over the country. On offer are cured meats, different kinds of cheese, and dried nuts and fruits. The various branches of **Emporio La Rosa** serve homemade ice cream, plus take-away food such as empanadas and sandwiches.

Markets

Many of Santiago's markets act as one-stop shopping centers for handicrafts, antiques, art, household items, pets, and plants. The Pueblo Los Dominicos *(see p95)*, an outdoor market designed to resemble a Colonial adobe village, offers a variety of local arts and crafts, as well as a pleasant shopping ambience. At the centrally located, upscale Patio Bellavista *(see p92)*, it is possible to buy clothes, accessories, jewelry, and handicrafts. The **Feria Artesanal Santa Lucía** and **La Aldea** markets have moderately priced local handicrafts from all over Chile. Santiago's most accessible crafts market, **Centro de Exposición de Arte Indígena**, sells Mapuche, Aymara, and Rapa Nui handicrafts. It is open daily, except on Sunday. The sprawling weekend flea market **Persa Bio Bio** sells a range of second-hand goods, but this chaotic market is recommended only for intrepid travelers who have at least a basic knowledge of Spanish.

Shopping Malls

Santiago's shopping malls provide virtually the same stores and quality as most US shopping centers. The three most popular malls are **Parque Arauco**, **Alto Las Condes**, and **Costanera Center**, housing many US, Latin American, and European chains, and depart-mental stores such as Ripley, Falabella, and Almacenes Paris *(see p302)*. Parque Arauco is a vast complex, with a dozen high-end gourmet restaurants, a bowling alley, and an indoor ice-skating rink for children. Both Parque Arauco and Alto Las Condes have megaplex cinemas. The **Mall Apumanque** in Las Condes features mostly small boutiques with locally produced clothing and goods.

Handicrafts on display at one of the adobe shops in Pueblo Los Dominicos

DIRECTORY

Crafts and Souvenirs

Artesanías de Chile
Plaza de la Ciudadanía 26, Subterráneo. **City Map** 2 E3. **Tel** (02) 2697-2784.
🌐 artesaniasdechile.cl

The Clinic El Bazar
Avenida Providencia 2124, Local 9A.
City Map 4 F2.
Tel (02) 2687-4373.

Faba
Avenida Alonso de Córdova 4227.
City Map 5 C2.
Tel (02) 2208-9526.
🌐 lapislazuli.cl

Lapis Lazuli House
Bellavista 08.
City Map 3 B4.
Tel (02) 2732-1419.
🌐 lapislazulihouse.cl

Morita Gil
Los Misioneros 1991.
City Map 4 E1.
Tel (02) 2206-9450.

Ona
Victoria Subercaseaux 295. **City Map** 2 F2.
Tel (02) 2632-1859.
🌐 onachile.com

Pura Artesanos
Avenida Kennedy 5413.
Tel (02) 2211-7875.
🌐 purartesanos.cl

La Verveine
Avenida Las Tranqueras 1535. **Tel** (09) 8729-9351.
🌐 laverveine.cl

Antiques

Antiguedades Balmaceda
Avenida Brasil 1157.
City Map 1 C1.**Tel** (02) 2688-1348.

Antiguedades Bucarest
Avenida Bucarest 34.
City Map 4 F2. **Tel** (02) 2231-0034.

Brainworks
Pasaje Beltrán 330.
City Map 3 C5.
Tel (02) 2791-1539.
🌐 brainworks.cl

Fashion

Aji
C/Lastarria, 316.
City Map 3 A4.
🌐 cepaz.cl/es

Atelier Carlos Pérez
Rosal 388.
City Map 2 F2.
Tel (02) 2664-1463.

Cepaz
C/Lastarria, 316.
City Map 3 A4.
🌐 cepaz.cl/es

Galería Drugstore
Avenida Providencia 2124. **City Map** 4 F2.
Tel (02) 2335-0822.
🌐 drugstore.cl

Makinita de Coser
C/Lastarria, 316.
City Map 3 A4.

Nostalqic
Bandera 569.
City Map 2 E2.
Tel (02) 2672-1937.
🌐 nostalgic.cl

Óptica Bahía
Merced 374
City Map 2 F2.
Tel (02) 2632-7031.
🌐 opticabahia.cl

Orange Blue
Gilberto Fuenzalida 84.
Tel (02) 2761-3808.
🌐 orangeblue.cl

Tampu
Merced 327.
City Map 3 B3.
Tel (02) 2638-7992.

Zapateria Lastarria
Jose Victorino Lastarria 316, Local C.
City Map 3 A4.
🌐 zapaterialastarria.cl

Art Galleries

Galería 13
Girardi 1480.
Tel (02) 2710-3361.
🌐 galeria13.cl

Galería A.M.S. Marlborough
Avenida Nueva Costanera 3723.
City Map 5 B2.
Tel (02) 2799-3180.
🌐 amsgaleria.cl

Galería Animal
Avenida Nueva Costanera 3731.
City Map 5 B2.
Tel (02) 2371-9090.
🌐 galeriaanimal.com

Galería Gabriela Mistral
Avenida Alameda 1381.
City Map 2 E3.
Tel (02) 2406-5618.
🌐 galeriagm.cultural.gob.cl

Galería Isabel Aninat
Espoz 3100.
City Map 5 B1.
Tel (02) 2481-9870.
🌐 galeriaisabelaninat.cl

Galería Patricia Ready
Espoz 3125.
City Map 5 B1.
Tel (02) 2953-6210.
🌐 galeriapready.cl

Galería La Sala
Avenida Alonso de Córdova 2700.
City Map 5 B2.
Tel (02) 2246-7031.
🌐 galerialasala.cl

Books and Music

Feria Chilena del Libro
Huérfanos 670.
City Map 2 F2.
Tel (02) 2345-8380.
🌐 feriachilenadellibro.cl

Librería Antartica
Avenida Kennedy 5413.
Tel (02) 2242-0799.
🌐 antartica.cl

Librería Eduardo Albers
Patria Vieja 358.
Tel (02) 2964-7450.
🌐 albers.cl

Librería Inglesa
Avenida Pedro de Valdivia 47. **City Map** 4 E2
Tel (02) 2231-6270.
🌐 libreriainglesa.cl

Wine and Food

Baco
Nueva de Lyon 105.
City Map 4 F2
Tel (02) 2231-4444.

Emporio Nacional
Avenida Providencia 2124, Local 60.
City Map 4 F2.
Tel (09) 5716-6214.
🌐 emporionacional.cl

Emporio La Rosa
Merced 291. **City Map** 3 B4. **Tel** (02) 2638-9257.
🌐 emporiolarosa.com

El Mundo del Vino
Isidora Goyenechea 3000.
City Map 5 B4.
Tel (02) 2584-1173.
🌐 elmundodelvino.cl

La Vinoteca
Nueva Costanera 3955
City Map 5 B1.
Tel (02) 2953-6290.

Markets

La Aldea
Luis Pasteur 6420, Local 5.
Tel (02) 2219-1009.
🌐 laaldea.net

Centro de Exposición de Arte Indígena
Avenida Alameda 499.
City Map 2 E3.
Tel (02) 2664-1352.

Feria Artesanal Santa Lucía
Avenida Alameda & Carmen.
City Map 2 F3.

Persa Bio Bio
Bío Bío 793.
Tel (02) 2551-0909.
🌐 persa-biobio.com

Shopping Malls

Alto Las Condes
Avenida Kennedy 9001.
Tel (02) 2299-6965.
🌐 altolascondes.cl

Costanera Center
Avenida Andrés Bello 2425. **City Map** 4 F1
Tel (02) 2916-9200.
🌐 costaneracenter.cl

Mall Apumanque
Manquehue Sur 31.
Tel (02) 2246-2614.
🌐 apumanque.cl

Parque Arauco
Avenida Kennedy 5413.
Tel 600 500 0011.
🌐 parquearauco.cl

ENTERTAINMENT IN SANTIAGO

Santiago is the culture capital of Chile, and nearly all of the country's major music, theater, and sports venues are concentrated within its limits. Jazz clubs, intimate bars, and mega stadiums play host to numerous national and international music acts, and the city's Teatro Municipal is home to national dance troupes and orchestras.

Dramatic theater is hugely popular in Santiago. There are dozens of venues around the city and an international theater festival each February. Visitors looking for energy-packed entertainment will love the city's many soccer matches, played between national and visiting teams.

The elegant frontage of the Club Hípico, which hosts concerts by international artists

Information and Tickets

There are limited sources of entertainment information available in Santiago. The most reliable English-language source is the website of *Revolver Magazine*, which is run by a group of expatriates and offers a comprehensive guide to the thriving arts, cultural, and entertainment scene in the city. It features a calendar of events, restaurant guides, art show openings, previews and reviews of concerts and theater shows, and a smattering of fun pieces about travel in Chile as well as cultural-clash topics such as language blunders.

The most popular national newspapers, *La Tercera* and *El Mercurio*, publish entertainment listings in their Friday editions that are slightly more comprehensive and up-to-date than *Revolver Magazine's* website, but are available in Spanish only. Both newspapers also offer full listings, and reviews of music, arts, and theater on their websites: *La Tercera* provides this on its *Entretenimiento* page, and *El Mercurio*, under *Entretención*.

The website **Puro Teatro** focuses on theater reviews and performance schedules.

Tickets for major theater performances, music concerts, and sports events can be bought through **Ticketmaster** and **Punto Ticket** *(see p305)* websites and sales points; Punto Ticket offices can be found in Ripley department stores and Cinemark movie halls. Tickets for performances and more intimate theater or music venues are generally purchased at the venue itself.

Well-stocked newsstand on Paseo Ahumada, Santiago

Bars and Clubs

There are relatively few true bars in Santiago since most double as full-scale restaurants given the city's licensing code, which requires that food be served in all drinking establishments. The best "resto-bar," as they are known, is undoubtedly the Bar Liguria *(see p291)*, which has three addresses in the capital city. The bar pays homage to Chilean kitsch, serving potent drinks in a lively ambience that can get raucous after midnight. **Bar The Clinic** is a politically irreverent drinking spot named for the facility where General Pinochet was arrested in 1998. For expatriates, **Flannery's Geo Pub** serves pints in a convivial atmosphere. Downtown, the sophisticated **Ópera Catedral** draws fashionable businessmen and businesswomen for well-prepared cocktails. The establishment's second-story open-air bar is pleasant during the summer. In Bellavista, there are dozens of bars along Calle Pío Nono, although most cater to college students buying cheap beer in pitchers. Those seeking a low-key ambience will find plenty of bars to choose from at Patio Bellavista *(see p92)*. Bellavista's **Bar Constitución** is an established hot spot with sexy and sleek decor, electro pop DJ music and the occasional live band. After midnight, the dance floor kicks up and the place becomes packed. A number of Chilean DJs got their start at the stylish and low-lit **Club La Feria** lounge and dance club. Those seeking salsa dancing should head to **Havana Salsa** for some racy stepping at this tropical-style club. The 30- to 45-year-old crowd heads to **Las Urracas** to boogie the night away on one of the club's two dance floors, dine on Mexican food in the adjoining restaurant, and rub elbows with the city's TV stars and football players. Santiago's clubs do not get started until after midnight, and in most cases hit their peak well after 2am. Women often get in for free before 2am and may also get drink discounts.

Contemporary Music

Santiago boasts a handful of large venues that pull in well-known international and national acts. The largest of such sites is **Estadio Nacional**, which is also a major sports stadium. Recent shows here have included performances by Iron Maiden, The Rolling Stones, Black Sabbath, Coldplay and Justin Bieber. Equally large is the **Estadio San Carlos Apoquindo** in Las Condes, which has hosted the Black Eyed Peas and Pearl Jam

Tickets for stadium concerts are not sold at the stadiums themselves and must be purchased through ticket vendors.

Santiago's newest large-scale music venue is located in the 19th-century **Club Hípico** *(see p85)*, the city's oldest racetrack, which is occasionally adapted

to showcase headline acts such as Elton John, Depeche Mode, and the Jonas Brothers. It is also the site of the yearly Cumbre de Rock Chileno (Chilean Rock Fest), held in January. Santiago's ultramodern venue **Espacio Riesco** is located on the outskirts of the capital. In addition to hosting bands such as Coldplay, the concert-cum-exhibition hall is known for its yearly electronic and rock music festivals. The downtown district's **Centro Cultural Estación Mapocho** *(see p77)* features Chilean rock, pop, and folk bands, as well as DJ parties; however, the acoustics are not stellar.

The Nuñoa district's **La Batuta** is ever popular for its more intimate music club experience. It highlights local bands or lesser known international acts, hosting mostly rock and hip-hop acts, and some tribute bands. The **Teatro Caupolican** sponsors indie and alternative rock acts, and the edgy **Bar El Clan** hosts nightly acts that are mostly DJ parties and local rock and hip hop bands.

Canadian pop singer, Justin Beiber, at the Estadio Nacional

Santiago's famous **Club de Jazz** is considered one of the best jazz clubs in Latin America and has hosted a who's who of jazz greats during the more than 65 years that it has been open. **La Casa en el Aire**, a tiny bar in the Bellavista area, books folk music acts with nightly live performances. At weekends, **Confitería Torres** is the closest thing to a Buenos Aires tango bar to be found in Santiago. Housed in a Classical building, the venue is worth a visit at any time.

The cavernous space of the Centro Cultural Estación Mapocho, a former train station

Performers at the international theater festival of Santiago a Mil

Classical Music, Dance, and Theater

Performances of classical music, opera, and ballet are held at Santiago's **Teatro Municipal** *(see p73)* from April to December. These are led by the Santiago Philharmonic Orchestra and the Santiago Ballet, along with visiting orchestras and dance troupes. The **Teatro Oriente** often features performances by the Fundación Beethoven and Ballet Folklórico, while the **Teatro Universidad de Chile** puts on modern dance performances and boasts productions by the Chilean National Ballet and the Chilean Symphonic Orchestra.

Theater performances are widespread throughout the city, especially during the **Teatro a Mil** event each January. This grand celebration of theater brings street acts and local and international productions to the stage of more than 15 playhouses. During the rest of the year, cutting-edge productions can be seen at **Teatro Bellavista** and the **Teatro Mori Bellavista**, and comedic and contemporary acts at the **Teatro La Comedia**.

Spectator Sports

Fútbol, or soccer, is Chile's most popular sport, attracting hordes of passionate fans to often thrilling matches. The three best-known teams are Universidad de Chile, Colo-Colo, and Universidad Católica, whose local stadiums are, respectively, Estadio Nacional, **Estadio Monumental**, and Estadio San Carlos de Apoquindo. Soccer matches are best attended with a local who is familiar with stadium procedures. Security guards will often close the gates to rowdy fans, even if they hold a paid ticket, so attendees are well advised to arrive no less than 3 hours early for the bigger or popular matches.

Major horse races take place at the **Club Hípico** *(see p85)* and the **Hipódromo Chile** year-round, drawing large crowds of Chileans. El Ensayo, the major race of the year, and also the oldest stakes race in South America, is held at Club Hípico in late October/early November.

Participation Sports

Most people in Santiago enjoy spending afternoons and weekends in city parks such as the **Parque Metropolitano de Santiago** *(see pp88–9)*, either jogging, walking, or cycling. Gymnasiums are very popular, and can be found throughout the city and in major hotels. On hot summer days, the outdoor public pools at Tupahue and Antilén atop the Parque Metropolitano, or the **Club Providencia**, which offers day passes, are ideal for swimmers. Indoor rock climbing, with classes for beginners, are available at **El Muro** in Las Condes, and **Mall Sport**, a shopping center dedicated exclusively to sports shops, features a climbing wall and skate park.

Entertainment for Children

Santiago, like Chile in general, is very family-friendly, offering plenty of activities and attractions to keep children entertained and active. There are traveling circuses that often set up tents during the summer in the city limits. More permanent thrills include the amusement park **Fantasilandia** *(see p85)* and the **Parque Metropolitano de Santiago** *(see pp88–9)*, where children can ride a funicular and

The outdoor swimming pool at Tupahue, Parque Metropolitano de Santiago

gondola, take a swim, or ride bikes. **Parque Quinta Normal** *(see pp80–81)* has several child-friendly museums such as the **Museo Nacional de Historia Natural**, the **Museo Ferroviaro**, and the **Museo Artequín**. Farther afield, the **Museo Interactivo Mirador** is designed to give children an introduction to science and technology via interactive exhibits and workshops, and there is a 3D cinema with educational and entertaining features. The shopping mall **Parque Arauco** *(see p101)* offers many attractions for children, including an indoor ice rink, a bowling alley, playground, and cinema.

Whale skeleton at the Museo Nacional de Historia Natural

DIRECTORY

Information and Tickets

El Mercurio
🆆 emol.com

Puro Teatro
🆆 puroteatro.cl

Revolver Magazine
🆆 revistarevolver.cl

La Tercera
🆆 latercera.com

Ticketmaster
🆆 ticketmaster.cl

Bars and Clubs

Bar The Clinic
Avenida Brasil 258.
City Map 3 A4.
Tel (02) 2697-2578.
🆆 bartheclinic.cl

Bar Constitución
Constitución 62
City Map 3 B4.
Tel (09) 4469-8275.
🆆 barconstitucion.cl

Club la Feria
Constitución 275.
City Map 3 B3
Tel (09) 4984-0948.
🆆 clublaferia.cl

Flannery's Geo Pub
Encomenderos 83.
City Map 5 A4.
Tel (02) 2233-6675.
🆆 flannerys.cl

Havana Salsa
Calle Dominica 142.
City Map 3 B3.
Tel (02) 2737-1737.
🆆 havanasalsa.cl

Ópera Catedral
José Miguel de la Barra, esq. Merced.
City Map 3 A4.
Tel (02) 2664-3048.
🆆 operacatedral.cl

Las Urracas
Avenida Vitacura 9254.
Tel (02) 2224-8025.
🆆 lasurracas.com

Contemporary Music

Bar El Clan
Bombero Nuñez 363.
City Map 3 B3.
Tel (02) 2735-3655.
🆆 elclan.cl

La Batuta
Jorge Washington 52.
Tel (02) 2274 7096.
🆆 labatuta.cl

La Casa en el Aire
Antonio López de Bello 0125
City Map 3 B3.
Tel (02) 2735-6680.
🆆 lacasaenelaire.cl

Club de Jazz
Avenida Ossa 123.
Tel (02) 2830-6208.
🆆 clubdejazz.cl

Confitería Torres
Alameda 1570.
City Map 2 D3
Tel (02) 2668-0751.
🆆 confiteriatorres.cl

Espacio Riesco
El Salto 5000, Huerchuraba.
Tel (02) 2470-4460.
🆆 espacioriesco.cl

Estadio Nacional
Avenida Grecia 2001.
Tel (02) 2238-8102.

Estadio San Carlos de Apoquindo
Camino Las Flores 13000.
Tel (02) 2412-4400.

Teatro Caupolican
San Diego 850.
City Map 2 E5.
Tel (02) 2699-1556.
🆆 teatrocaupolican.cl

Classical Music, Dance, and Theater

Teatro Bellavista
Dardignac 0110.
City Map 3 B4.
Tel (02) 2735-2395.
🆆 teatrobellavista.cl

Teatro La Comedia
Merced 349.
City Map 2 F2.
Tel (02) 2639-1523.
🆆 teatroictus.cl

Teatro a Mil
Juana de Arco 2012, Oficina 11. **City Map** 4 F3.
Tel (02) 2925-0300.
🆆 fundacionteatro amil.cl

Teatro Mori Bellavista
Constitución 183.
City Map 3 B3.
Tel (02) 2777-5046.
🆆 centromori.cl

Teatro Oriente
Avenida Pedro de Valdivia 099.
City Map 4 E2.
Tel (02) 2777-9849 or (02) 2924-8403.
🆆 teatrooriente.cl

Teatro Universidad de Chile
Avenida Providencia 043, Plaza Italia.
City Map 3 B4.
Tel (02) 2978-2480.
🆆 ceacuchile.com

Spectator Sports

Estadio Monumental
Avenida Marathon 5300.
Tel 600 4202222.
🆆 colocolo.cl

Hipódromo Chile
Avenida Hipódromo Chile 1715.
Tel (02) 2270-9200.
🆆 hipodromo.cl

Participation Sports

Club Providencia
Avenida Pocuro 2878.
Tel (02) 2426-6400.
🆆 clubprovidencia.cl

Mall Sport
Avenida Las Condes 13451.
Tel (02) 2429-3030.
🆆 mallsport.cl

El Muro
Avenida Américo Vespucio 1647.
Tel (02) 2475-2851.
🆆 gimnasioelmuro.cl

Entertainment for Children

Museo Interactivo Mirador
Punta Arenas 6711.
Tel (02) 2828-8000.
🆆 mim.cl

SANTIAGO STREET FINDER

The map given below shows the different areas of Santiago covered by the Street Finder maps – Plaza de Armas and Santiago Centro; West of Santiago Centro; and Northeast of Santiago Centro. The map references given in the Santiago section of the guide for sites of interest, historic attractions, shopping areas, and entertainment venues refer to the maps on the following pages. Map references

are also provided for Santiago hotels (see pp276–7) and restaurants (see pp290–92). The first figure in the map reference indicates which Street Finder map to turn to, and the letter and number that follow refer to the map's grid. There is also an index of street names on page 113. The symbols used to represent sights and useful information on the Street Finder maps are listed in the key below.

The tree-shaded Plaza Caupolicán on Cerro Santa Lucía (see p74)

Key

- Major sight
- Other sight
- Other building
- Railroad station
- M Metro de Santiago
- Bus station
- Funicular
- i Visitor information
- Hospital
- Police
- Church
- Expressway
- Pedestrian street

Scale of Maps 1–5

0 meters 250
0 yards 250

Vehicles parked near an equestrian statue, adjacent to Avenida Libertador Bernardo O'Higgins

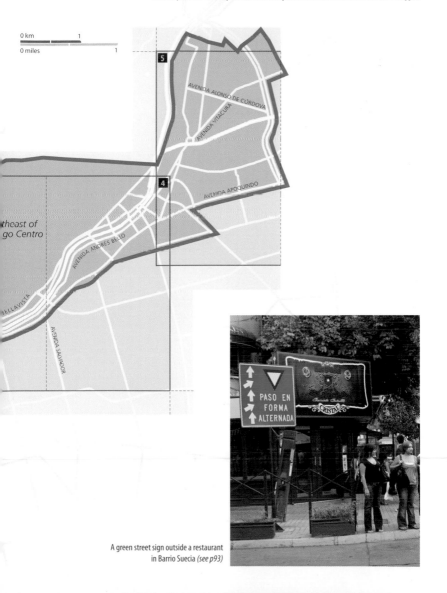

0 km   1
0 miles   1

AVENIDA ALONSO DE CÓRDOVA

AVENIDA VITACURA

AVENIDA APOQUINDO

5

4

theast of
go Centro

AVENIDA ANDRES BELLO

BELLAVISTA

AVENIDA SALVADOR

A green street sign outside a restaurant
in Barrio Suecia *(see p93)*

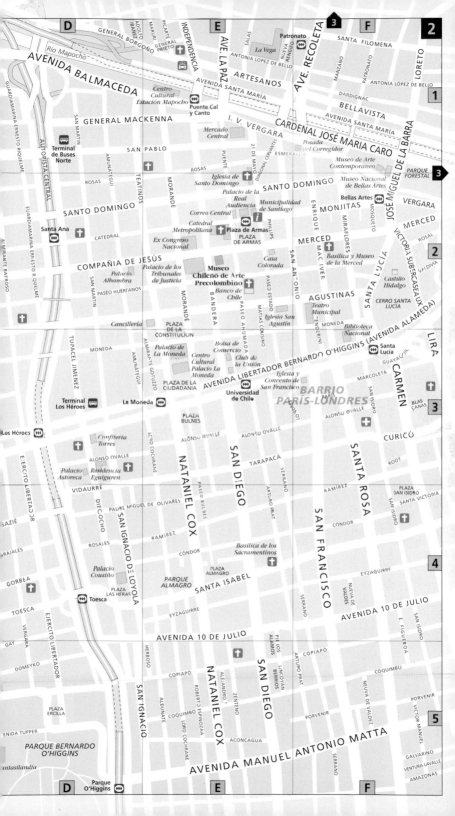

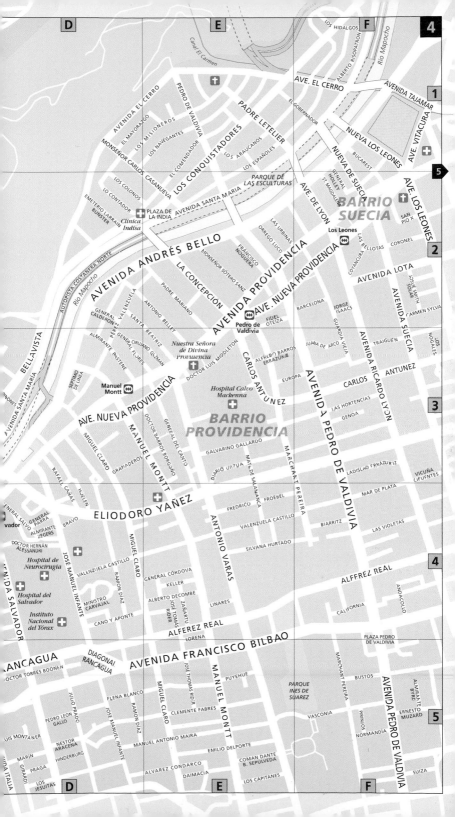

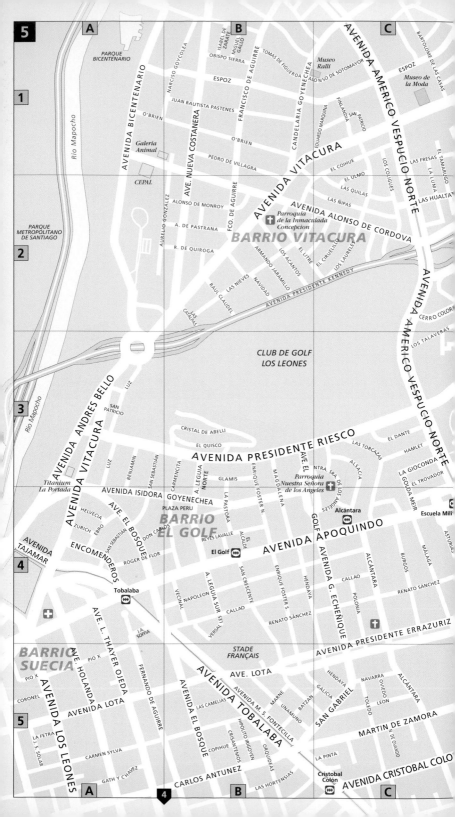

Street Finder Index

CHILE AND EASTER ISLAND REGION BY REGION

Chile and Easter Island at a Glance

With perhaps the greatest latitudinal extent of any country on the planet, Chile is home to a huge level of geographical diversity. Its almost endless coastline is the source of some of the world's finest fish and shellfish, while the land rises rapidly eastward to form the towering Andes. In between, it has the world's driest desert, some of its most productive vineyards, and a lushly forested Lake District studded with volcanoes, fjordlands, and ice fields. The land is inhabited by a polite, congenial people whose rich heritage can be experienced in traditional settlements, as well as in cities such as Valparaíso.

Street murals, with their "surprise around every corner" quality, are major contributors to the bohemian air of Valparaíso *(see pp122–31)*. This port-city's maze of hillside neighborhoods is also where Nobel Prize-winning poet Pablo Neruda once lived.

Palafitos, stilted fishermen's houses that once symbolized the Lake District and Chiloé archipelago, were mostly destroyed in the tsunami of 1960, but quite a few remain in and around the city of Castro *(see pp220–21)*.

Robinson Crusoe Island *(see pp268–9)*

EASTER ISLA
AND ROBIN
CRUSOE ISL
(See pp258–6

0 km   200
0 miles   200

Easter Island

Hanga Roa

0 km   10
0 miles   10

The *moai* of Easter Island *(see pp258–67)*, symbols of Polynesian culture, stand on ceremonial platforms such as Ahu Tahai. Many remain in their original quarry site at Rano Raraku.

◀ Panoramic view of the valley in Coyhaique, Northern Patagonia

Arica

Calama

**NORTE GRANDE
AND NORTE CHICO**
(See pp160–89)

Copiapó

Laguna Céjar, in the Salar de Atacama *(see p179)*, is proof that the world's driest desert can still boast wildlife-rich lagoons and grasslands. Visitors can float effortlessly in the saline waters of this lake.

Valparaíso

SANTIAGO
(See pp54–113)

Rancagua

CENTRAL VALLEY
(See pp118–59)

oncepción

emuco

**LAKE DISTRICT
AND CHILOÉ**
(See pp190–225)

Parque Nacional Queulat *(see p233)* is home to forests of southern beech and to the hanging glacier, Ventisquero Colgante. The latter is reached by a swinging pedestrian bridge over the rushing meltwaters of the Río Guillermo.

The spectacular Parque Nacional Torres del Paine *(see pp246–9)* in Southern Patagonia gets its name from the iconic granite peaks, shaped by glacial ice, that dominate the landscape. The park is rich in Patagonian flora and fauna, and is especially known for its robust populations of guanaco.

Coyhaique

**NORTHERN
PATAGONIA**
(See pp226–39)

**SOUTHERN
PATAGONIA AND
TIERRA DEL FUEGO**
(See pp240–57)

Punta Arenas

Tierra del Fuego
(see pp254–5)

CENTRAL VALLEY

The country's agricultural heartland, the Central Valley is carpeted by lush vineyards and rich arable lands that grow large amounts of fruit for local use and export. From the east, the arid Andes sweep down to the flat valley, which is dotted with wineries and old estates. The terrain yields in the west to coastal mountains and the Pacific littoral, where fishing villages alternate with luxury resorts.

Inhabited since pre-Columbian times, Central Valley is considered Chile's oldest region and a bastion of its traditions. Its original settlers were the Mapuche, who resisted assimilation into the Incan Empire *(see p46)*. The Spanish arrived in 1541, founding Santiago at the foot of the Andes, Valparaíso on the coast, and, later, towns across the valley floor. Central Valley became the center of Colonial Chile: the womb from which the country's north and south grew, its wealthiest area, and the political hub. The hacienda system, by which old families controlled vast tracts of land, evolved here, spawning Chile's legendary *huaso*. Mining of silver, nitrates, and copper brought later wealth.

In modern times, agriculture, in particular viticulture, remains the greatest source of income here. The dry temperate climate and long summers make the region ideal for the production of fine wines. The valley's world-class wineries, open for tours and tastings, are part of a tourism sector that offers an array of other activities for locals and visitors alike. These include skiing and snowboarding at mountain resorts, surfing along big-wave beaches, and white-water rafting and horse riding in national parks. Forested spa retreats pepper the Andean foothills and beach resorts and idyllic fishing villages line the coast. The cities boast some of Chile's best fine arts and decorative-arts museums, complemented by ornate parks, lush plazas, and fine seafood restaurants. Easily accessible from these cities are well-preserved haciendas and mines, and towns full of Colonial charm.

Colorful street art, characteristic of the historic city of Valparaíso, a UNESCO World Heritage Site

◄ View of the beach from Casa Museo Isla Negra, the home and final resting place of Pablo Neruda

Exploring Central Valley

Most of the region's attractions are clustered around the northern part of the valley, and to a lesser extent in the south, with renowned vineyards in areas such as Casablanca and Colchagua valleys in the central lowlands. The region's main cities are the historic port of Valparaíso and Viña del Mar, which is characterized by French palaces and ornate museums. Easily accessed from both these urban centers are Pablo Neruda's house at Isla Negra and the surfers' haven Pichilemu. Away from the coast, in the eastern mountains, resorts such as Portillo promise some of Chile's best skiing runs, while Termas de Jahuel and Termas de Cauquenes are renowned for their thermal pools. In the south, national parks including Reserva Nacional Altos de Lircay and Parque Nacional Laguna del Laja offer a gamut of activities.

People relaxing on a stretch of sandy beach in Tomé

Sights at a Glance

Artifacts and paintings at Casa Museo Isla Negra

Getting Around

Comfortable buses connect Central Valley and Santiago. The Pan-American Highway, or Ruta 5, runs through the region, linking its main urban centers. The majority of wine routes and the more remote sights in the Andes mountains can only be visited by car or via organized tours. Mountain spa and ski resorts usually arrange transfers to and from Santiago.

For hotels and restaurants in this region see pp277–8 and pp292–4

Key

- Highway
- Main road
- Minor road
- Untarred main road
- Untarred minor road
- Main railway
- Minor railway
- Regional border
- International border
- △ Peak

Ingeniero
Santa María
Río del Sobrante
Petorca

PAPUDO 9
ZAPALLAR 8
CACHAGUA 7
Maitencillo
Concón
VIÑA DEL MAR 2
VALPARAÍSO 1
QUINTAY 3
ALGARROBO 4
**CASA MUSEO
ISLA NEGRA** 5
San Antonio
San Juan

VALPARAÍSO
San Felipe
**PARQUE
NACIONAL
LA CAMPAÑA** 14
**LOS
ANDES**
62
**A TOUR OF
WINERIES IN
CASABLANCA
VALLEY**
15
CARTAGENA 6
Pomaire Talagante
78

TERMAS DE JAHUEL 13
10 CH60 11 12 **CRISTO
REDENTOR**

**SKI CENTERS
LA PARVA,
EL COLORADO,
VALLE NEVADO** 16

SANTIAGO
68
G25

**ANTIQUE WINERIES
OF PIRQUE**
San José
de Maipo
66

18 **CAJÓN DEL
MAIPO**

PACIFIC
OCEAN

METROPOLITAN
Longovilo
La Compañía
Coipue

RANCAGUA 19
VALLE DE CACHAPOAL 20
Rengo

21 **SEWELL**
22 **EL TENIENTE**
23 **TERMAS DE
CAUQUENES**

LIBERTADOR

PICHILEMU 27
Los Lobos
Cahuíl

**A TOUR OF WINERIES
IN COLCHAGUA VALLEY** 28
**SANTA
CRUZ** 25
Morza

San
Fernando

26 **HACIENDA
LOS LINGUES**
Chimbarongo

**RESERVA NACIONAL
RÍO DE LOS CIPRESES** 24

LAGO VICHUQUÉN 30
La Capilla

**VALLE DE
CURICÓ** 29
Curicó
Molina
Camarico
5

Los Quenes
Upeo
El Bolsico

Lagunas
de Teno

Volcán
Tinguiririca
14,107 ft

Huaquén

Carrizal
Constitución

MAULE
Talca

WINERIES OF MAULE 32
San Javier
Lago
Colbún

31 **PARQUE NACIONAL
RADAL SIETE TAZAS**

33 **RESERVA NACIONAL
ALTOS DE LIRCAY**

Chanco
Sauzal
126

Pelluhue
Cauquenes

34 **TERMAS DE PANIMÁVIDA**
Linares
Los Rabones
CH115

Cerro
Campanario
13,284 ft

126 128
Cobquecura
Santa
Cruz
Colmuyao
Vegas de Itata

Pocillas
Parral

San Carlos

Laguna
del Maule

Río Itata

Río Cato

Río Ñuble

5

TOMÉ 38
Talcahuano
152

CHILLÁN 35
San
Miguel
N55 Recinto

CONCEPCIÓN 37
Santa Clara
Chiguayante
Coronel
BÍO BÍO
Pemuco

36 **NEVADOS
DE CHILLÁN**

Isla Santa
María
Golfo de
Arauco

Llico
Yumbel
Yungay

Volcán Chillán
10,538 ft

LOTA 39
Arauco
Diuquín

**SALTOS
DEL LAJA** 40

Río Laja

Polcura

Laguna de
la Laja

Volcán Antuco
11,761 ft

160
Los Cambuchos
Los Ángeles

Lebu
180
Mulchén

41 **PARQUE NACIONAL
LAGUNA DEL LAJA**

Cañete Cayucupil

Río Bío Bío

Volcán
Copahue
9,776 ft

Río Renaico

Lago
Lanalhue

Lago
Lleulleu

Quidico Tirúa

| 0 kilometers | 50 |
| 0 miles | 50 |

For keys to symbols *see back flap*

❶ Valparaíso

Founded in 1543, the hillside city of Valparaíso emerged as the South Pacific's greatest port in the late 19th century. During this time, European immigrants flocked to the city, creating a cultural melting pot of raffish sailor bars and solemn Protestant churches. Valparaíso rises abruptly from a narrow strip of coast to cover over 45 steep hills, each a dense jumble of winding streets lined with colorful houses, post-Colonial edifices, and 19th-century museums. The city is a UNESCO World Heritage Site, and much of its rich architecture is beautifully preserved, even as it bursts with trendy restaurants, bars, and boutique hotels.

0 meters 300
0 yards 300

Sights at a Glance

Historic Buildings and Streets
② Edificio de la Aduana
③ Plaza Echaurren
⑥ Plaza Sotomayor
⑨ Palacio de la Justicia
⑩ Calle Prat
⑪ Calle Esmeralda
⑫ Plaza Aníbal Pinto
⑬ Palacio Baburizza
⑭ Paseo Gervasoni
㉒ Congreso Nacional

Churches and Cathedrals
⑮ Iglesia Luterana
⑯ Iglesia Anglicana San Pablo
㉑ Iglesia de los Sagrados Corazones
㉓ Iglesia y Convento de San Francisco

Museums
① Museo Marítimo Nacional
⑤ Museo del Mar Lord Thomas Cochrane
⑱ La Sebastiana
⑲ Palacio Lyon
⑳ Museo a Cielo Abierto

Sites of Interest
④ Bar Inglés and Bar La Playa
⑦ Street Art
⑧ Muelle Prat
⑰ Cementerios Católico and Disidentes

For hotels and restaurants in this region see pp277–8 and pp292–4

Valparaíso's harbor and urbanized hillsides

Getting Around

Valparaíso consists of numerous hillside districts and a lower coastal section called El Plan. This coastal stretch can be explored on foot or by local buses and *trolebuses (see p129)*. However, most of Valparaíso's attractions are concentrated on the hillsides, which can be accessed from the lower section via funiculars *(see pp130–31)* and steep stairways. Cerro Concepción and Cerro Alegre are Valparaíso's main restaurant and hotel zones. An efficient metro system skirts Bahía de Valparaíso and links the city to neighboring Viña del Mar *(see pp132–3)*.

VISITORS' CHECKLIST

Practical Information
Road Map B6. 75 miles (120 km) NW of Santiago. 263,500. Plaza Sotomayor 233, piso 1; (032) 2336264; 9am–6pm Mon–Fri, 9am–5pm Sat. Glorias Navales (May 21); Carnaval Cultural de Valparaíso (end Dec). **W** ciudaddevalparaiso.cl

Transport

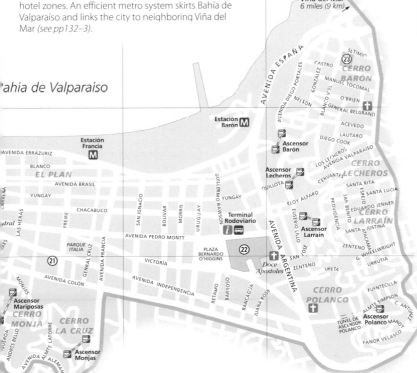

Bahía de Valparaíso

Viña del Mar
6 miles (9 km)

Bust of naval officer Arturo Prat at the
Museo Marítimo Nacional

① Museo Marítimo Nacional

Paseo 21 de Mayo 45, Cerro Artillería.
City Map B2. **Tel** (032) 2437651.
Open 10am–5:30pm Tue–Sun.
🌐 museonaval.cl

Chile's excellent Museo
Marítimo Nacional is housed
in a building dating from 1893.
It has 17 exhibition rooms,
including salons dedicated to
Chile's foremost naval heroes –
Lord Thomas Cochrane, Arturo
Prat, and Bernardo O'Higgins –
and to Chile's key 19th-century
naval battles. Exhibits include
antique sabres and swords,
pocket revolvers, bayonets,
military plans, and models of
battleships. Items salvaged
from Prat's schooner, *Esmeralda*,
such as the clock which stopped
at the precise time the ship
sank during the Battle of Iquique
(1879), are also displayed.

② Edificio de la Aduana

Plaza Wheelwright 144. **City
Map** B2. **Tel** (032) 2134712.
Open hours vary.

Built in 1855, the pink-painted
Edificio de la Aduana (Customs
Building) is a rare example of
post-Colonial architecture. The
institution's most famous
employee was the Nicaraguan
Modernist poet Rubén Darío,
who worked here in the 1880s
while writing his seminal work,
Azul (1888). Guided tours visit a
small museum, which displays

objects from the building's
history. Edificio de la Aduana
overlooks **Plaza Wheelwright**,
named for American industrialist
William Wheelwright, who
played a major role in building
Chile's railroads and steamship
fleet. His statue, raised in 1877,
adorns the plaza.

③ Plaza Echaurren

Calle Cochrane, esq. Calle Serrano.
City Map B3.

The birthplace and historic heart
of Valparaíso, Plaza Echaurren
marks the spot where Spanish
explorer Juan de Saavedra first
made landfall in 1543. Today, it is
fronted by crumbling yet elegant
mid-19th-century structures
such as the beautiful old market
building of Mercado Puerto.

Overlooking the plaza is the
Iglesia de la Matriz, notable
for its octagonal steeple. This
adobe edifice was constructed
in 1837 on the site of the city's
first church.

④ Bar Inglés and Bar La Playa

City Map B3. Bar Inglés:
Cochrane 851. **Tel** (032) 2214625.
Open 10am–midnight Mon–Sat.
Bar La Playa: Serrano 567. **Tel** (032)
2454-8795. **Open** 10–3am Mon–Wed,
10–5am Thu–Sun.

Two popular public bars, **Bar
Inglés** and **Bar La Playa** evoke
Valparaíso's halcyon days as the
greatest port-city in the South
Pacific. Bar Inglés was founded
by English immigrants in 1926.

Well-stocked shelves of liquor behind the
counter at Bar La Playa

Historic buildings overlooking the
palm-lined Plaza Echaurren

Polished wood and brass
embellish its appealing interior,
which is hung with colossal
wall mirrors, whirling ceiling
fans, and forlorn portraits of
Britain's royal family.

Located in the city's old port
area, Bar La Playa was opened
in 1934 as a raffish meeting
spot for local working girls, sailors,
and ship-workers, who would
pass their time here between
shifts. Today a bohemian drinking
den, it is still one of the most
popular bars in the city.

⑤ Museo del Mar Lord Thomas Cochrane

Calle Merlet 195, Cerro Cordillera.
City Map B3. **Tel** (032) 2213124.
Ascensor Cordillera. **Open** Dec–
Mar: 10am–6pm Tue–Sun; Apr–Nov:
10am–1pm & 3–8pm Tue–Sun.

Located on a hilltop, Casa de
Lord Cochrane was built in
1842 for Lord Thomas Cochrane,
although the British naval officer
never actually lived here. Open
to visits, this house is a fine
example of post-Colonial
architecture with thick adobe
walls and heavy oak doors that
open inward on to a Spanish
patio, adorned by a cast-iron
drinking well. The sweeping
front terrace, lined with cannon
rows, offers glorious views of
Valparaíso's bay. Occasional
art exhibitions are hosted
in the museum. At the back
are sloping gardens with
eucalyptus trees and shaded
reading benches.

⑥ Plaza Sotomayor

Calle Cochrane, esq. Avenida Tomás Ramos. **City Map** B3.

Valparaíso's main square is the stately Plaza Sotomayor, a large open space that holds parades on Glorias Navales or Navy Day *(see p41)*. The plaza is centered around the **Monumento a los Heroes de Iquique**, raised in memory of the crew of the *Esmeralda*, killed in the 1879 Battle of Iquique. The battle saw *Esmeralda*, the Chilean navy's oldest ship, fight the Peruvian fleet's most powerful vessel, *Huascar*, for 4 hours. Although the former was sunk, and her captain, Arturo Prat, killed, the battle was a turning point in the War of the Pacific *(see p49)*. Prat's bronze effigy crowns the monument and his body lies buried in a crypt here.

Towering over the southern end of Plaza Sotomayor is the elaborate facade of the Neo-Gothic **Comandancia Jefe de la Armada**. Built in 1910, its design was inspired by the Hôtel de Ville in Paris, and its interiors were multi-functional, serving both as a summer residence for Chile's presidents and as the city's mayors and regional governor's office. Expropriated by the Chilean navy in the mid-1970s, it has since functioned as Chile's naval headquarters.

The Ministry of Culture, a Modernist building dating from 1936, is open daily to the public and hosts art exhibitions. Adjacent to this edifice, the Compañía de Bomberos, built in 1851, is the site of the oldest volunteer fire service in Latin America.

Monumento a los Heroes de Iquique, dominating the Plaza Sotomayor

⑦ Street Art

As artsy as it is gritty, Valparaíso is renowned for its street art. Political-style graffiti and colorful murals are found along the winding streets up Cerros Bellavista, Concepcion, Allegere, and in the edgier Cerro Polanco neighborhood - the site of the first ever Latin American Graffiti Mural Festival. One of the largest murals encompasses the surface of several buildings and belongs to Chilean artist Inti. To explore the best of outdoor masterpieces, contact Valpo Street Art Tours (www.valpostreetart.com).

⑧ Muelle Prat

Avenida Errázuriz, in front of Plaza Sotomayer. **City Map** C3.

A busy pier, Muelle Prat is the departure point for half-hour tours of Valparaíso's bay by water-taxi. Boats wend a sinuous trail between gigantic cruise ships docked in the bay and the

Chilean navy's battleships stationed offshore, before hitting open water. The tour offers tremendous views of the city's hillsides, densely built-up with rows of brightly colored houses.

Cruise ships and boats lining the waterfront at Muelle Prat

⑨ Palacio de la Justicia

Plaza Justicia. **City Map** B3. **Closed** to the public.

Built in 1939, the Palacio de la Justicia is Valparaíso's appeals court. The edifice has a sober, rectilinear facade, with a 10-ft (3-m) high statue of Justitia (Lady Justice) at its entrance. The figure is curiously anomalous in that she wears no blindfold, her customary symbol of objectivity, and her scales of truth dangle forlornly at her side, rather than at the end of her outstretched arm. According to legend, an angry merchant had the statue placed here to protest against a perceived injustice.

The imposing Neo-Gothic facade of the Comandancia Jefe de la Armada

Plaza Aníbal Pinto, dominated by the yellow-and-green Librería Ivens building

⑩ Calle Prat

City Map B3.

A narrow thoroughfare through the city's financial district, Calle Prat links Plaza Sotomayor and the monumental 1929 **Reloj Turri** (Turri Clock Tower), the city's Big Ben. Looming over both sides of the road are grand buildings of stone and black marble, constructed at the turn of the 20th century. Among these is the old Bank of London building, today the Banco de Chile (No. 698), which houses a monument built to commemorate British soldiers killed in World War I. Another evocative edifice here is Valparaíso's stock exchange, **La Bolsa de Valores**, the oldest stock exchange in South America. The old bidding wheel still stands inside the building's cavernous, domed interior.

⑪ Calle Esmeralda

City Map C3.

An extension of Calle Prat, Calle Esmeralda starts at the Turri Clock Tower, close to Ascensor Concepción (see pp130–31) and ends at Plaza Aníbal Pinto. The street's most beautiful construction is the **El Mercurio** building, home to the popular El Mercurio de Valparaíso newspaper. The ornate exterior of the edifice is crowned by a bronze statue of Mercury pointing skyward.

Adjacent to El Mercurio, a stairway climbs up to the mystical **Cueva Chivito**, a natural rock cave, which according to local lore was once inhabited by the devil.

⑫ Plaza Aníbal Pinto

End of Calle Esmeralda. **City Map** C4.

Uniting Valparaíso's financial district and the commercial downtown area, Plaza Aníbal Pinto is a small, chaotic square fronted by beautiful buildings and the old **Bar Cinzano** (see p293). A sepia-tinted bar, the café was founded in 1896 and features live tango shows.

On one side of the plaza is the striking **Librería Ivens** building. Founded in 1891, it is one of the city's oldest bookshops. At the entrance to this building

is the plaza's attractive public artwork – a street fountain sculpted as Neptune in 1892.

⑬ Palacio Baburizza

Paseo Yugoslavo s/n, Cerro Alegre. **City Map** B3. **Tel** (032) 2252332. 🚋 Ascensor El Peral. **Open** 10:30am–7pm Tue–Sun. 🆆 **museobaburizza.cl**

An elegant Art Nouveau mansion, the Palacio Baburizza was constructed in 1916 for Italian saltpeter tycoon Ottorino Zanelli. It was subsequently purchased by Pascual Baburizza, a Croatian immigrant and nitrates magnate, in 1925. Today, the structure houses Valparaíso's fine arts museum, whose displays include the Baburizza family's collection of 19th- and 20th-century European art.

The palace is situated on the summit of Cerro Alegre, from where it overlooks the lovely Paseo Yugoslavo. A leafy promenade and viewing point, the street offers breathtaking vistas of neighboring hillsides, the city's port, financial districts, and the blue Bahía de Valparaíso.

Now reopened after having been restored to something that perhaps even exceeds its original elegance, the museum features a new wing that showcases Chilean landscapes as depicted by expatriate painters. It also boasts original furnishings and an extraordinary Art Deco bathroom. The garden annex includes a café and a well-stocked museum shop.

The sprawling Art Nouveau Palacio Baburizza

⑭ Paseo Gervasoni

Cerro Concepción. 🚡 Ascensor Concepción. **City Map** C3.

Ascensor Concepción spills out on to Paseo Gervasoni at the top of Cerro Concepción. A romantic cobbled promenade and vantage point edged with wildflowers, the *paseo* affords splendid views across the Bahía de Valparaíso to Viña del Mar in the north. Along the street are the elegant Café Turri *(see p293)*, the old Danish consulate building dating from 1848, and **Casa Mirador de Lukas**. The last is a 1900 house that holds a lovely museum dedicated to the life and works of Chile's best-loved cartoonist, Renzo Antonio Pecchenino Raggi (1934–88), popularly known as Lukas.

🏛 **Casa Mirador de Lukas**
Paseo Gervasoni 448, Cerro Concepción. **Tel** (032) 2221344. **Open** 11am–6pm Tue–Sun.
🅰 📷 🏠 🌐 lukas.cl

Entrance to Casa Mirador de Lukas, Paseo Gervasoni

⑮ Iglesia Luterana

Abtao 689, Cerro Concepción. **City Map** C4. **Tel** (032) 2975476. **Open** 10am–1pm Mon–Fri. ✝
🌐 iluterana.cl

Built by the city's German community in 1898, the Iglesia Luterana was South America's first Protestant church to be allowed a steeple and bell tower. Its beautifully austere facade tapers upward toward a slender, 115-ft (35-m) high steeple, which crowns Cerro Concepción and is visible from the city's lower sections. Inside, the nave fills

Soaring bell tower of the Protestant Iglesia Luterana

with natural light and a sculpture of Christ on the cross, which is carved from a single pine trunk, hangs above the altar. A grand organ, brought from England in 1884, stands opposite the altar.

⑯ Iglesia Anglicana San Pablo

Pilcomayo 566, Cerro Concepción. **City Map** B4. **Tel** (032) 2213296. **Open** 10:30am–1pm Tue–Fri.
🌐 saintpaulchile.cl

The Neo-Gothic Iglesia Anglicana San Pablo was built in 1858 by British engineer William Lloyd. This church was established by Valparaíso's English community, but only after the city's Catholic archbishop imposed many conditions on what he considered a temple to a rival faith. Among the most curious was that this church's doors be smaller than those of the city's Catholic churches – and to this day visitors enter not via a grand portal, but by one of the two

small side doors. The church's simple stone and wood interior houses a pipe organ donated in memory of Britain's Queen Victoria in 1903.

⑰ Cementerios Católico and Disidentes

Dinamarca s/n, Cerro Panteón. **City Map** C4. Cementerio Católica: **Open** 8:30am–5pm daily. Cementerio Disidentes: **Open** 9am–5pm daily.

Spectacularly located high up on an overhanging hillside, the **Cementerio Católico** and **Cementerio Disidentes** are poignant evocations of this port-city's halcyon days in the 1800s as a melting pot of different cultures and creeds. The Cementerio Disidentes is the site of the simple, sometimes austere, graves of the city's non-Catholic communities, including American Mormons, English Anglicans, and German Lutherans. Many of the gravestones are engraved with tales of war and shipwreck. Opposite the Cementerio Disidentes, a grand portal enters the Cementerio Católico, otherwise known as Cementerio N°1. Valparaíso's most illustrious sons and daughters lie here in grand, marbled mausoleums. Among the luminaries buried are members of the Edwards-Ross family, owners of the *El Mercurio de Valparaíso* newspaper; José Francisco Vergara, founder of the town Viña del Mar; and Renzo Pecchenino, a popular Chilean cartoonist.

El Mercurio de Valparaíso

The oldest newspaper in continuous circulation in the entire Spanish-speaking world, *El Mercurio de Valparaíso* was founded in 1827 by Chilean journalist Pedro Felix Vicuña and the American typographer Thomas Well. Since the 1880s, it has been under the uninterrupted stewardship of Chile's eminent Edwards-Ross family, who continue to aspire to the newspaper's founding ideal that it be "adequate enough to moderate the extreme passions that divide men."

Facade of the El Mercurio building

La Sebastiana, former residence of Chilean poet Pablo Neruda

⑱ La Sebastiana

Ferrari 692, Cerro Florida. **City Map** C5. **Tel** (032) 2256606. 🚠 Ascensor Espiritu Santo. **Open** Mar–Dec: 10:10am–6pm Tue–Sun; Jan & Feb: 10am–7pm Tue–Sun. 🎧 🏠 📷 📷 🌐 fundacionneruda.org

A must-see for devotees of Pablo Neruda *(see p91)*, La Sebastiana is the last of three houses bought by the poet in Chile. Neruda and two of his friends acquired the shell of the house in 1961 and named it for its architect and first owner, Sebastian Collado. They made extensive renovations to the structure, which resulted in an anarchic architecture that mirrored the city itself – the house became a jumble of narrow, twisting stairways and myriad nooks and crannies, painted in a range of colors.

In 1991, the structure was restored and converted into a museum that preserves the house as it was when Neruda lived there. It contains strange and wonderful objects bought by the poet, such as a Parisian carousel pony in the living room and an unfitted wash-basin from England in the study. Pablo Neruda's rich imagination is also evident in the American oakwood stairway rescued from a demolition site, and a floor mosaic of uncut pebbles shaped into an antique map of Patagonia and Antarctica.

Like Neruda's other houses in Santiago and Isla Negra, La Sebastiana is open for audio-guided tours on a first-come, first-served basis.

⑲ Palacio Lyon

City Map C4. Museo de Historia Natural de Valparaíso: Condell 1546. **Tel** (032) 2544840. **Open** 10am–6pm Tue–Sat, 10am–2pm Sun. 🎧 📷 🌐 **mhnv.cl** Galeria Municipal de Arte Valparaíso: Condell 1550. **Tel** (032) 2293-9567. **Open** 10am–7pm Tue–Sun.

Built in 1887, Palacio Lyon houses the **Museo de Historia Natural de Valparaíso**, the city's natural history museum and Chile's second-oldest state museum. A construction of stone, cast iron, and glass, this edifice evokes the 19th century as a golden age of exploration, scientific discovery, and public education. Displays include exhibits from the early 1900s that feature Chile's marine flora and fauna, stuffed animals from around the world, and rows of curiosities including bovine conjoined twins conserved in tanks of formaldehyde. The crypt in the basement features contemporary artworks by Chile's finest artists.

⑳ Museo a Cielo Abierto

Cerro Bellavista. **City Map** C4. 🚠 Ascensor Espiritu Santo.

A fascinating outdoor museum on Cerro Bellavista, the Museo a Cielo Abierto comprises a maze of winding streets and passageways painted with giant, colorful street murals by some of Chile's best-known contemporary artists. There are about 20 murals, ranging from highly abstract works to humorous depictions of daily life in the city, and a self-guided tour takes about an hour. There are many steps along the way, as well as steep inclines, so be sure to wear comfortable shoes. It is also wise to bring a bottle of water. The greatest concentration of murals can be found on Calle Ferrari and on Pasaje Santa Lucía. The latter is a steeply stepped passageway and a whirl of kaleidoscopically vibrant motifs and figures.

The museum features works by well-known Chilean artists, including the surrealist Roberto Matta, Gracia Barrios, of the Grupo Signo, and Nemesio Antúnez, who in 1956 founded the famous Taller 99, an artists' collective. Unfortunately, both weather and vandalism have damaged many of the works, but the murals are currently undergoing restoration.

Detailed murals painted on walls along Calle Ferrari, part of the Museo a Cielo Abierto

㉑ Iglesia de los Sagrados Corazones

Avenida Independencia 2050–2084.
City Map D5. **Tel** (032) 2746728.
Open daily.

Dating from 1874, the Iglesia de los Sagrados Corazones was the first church built in the Americas for the French Order of the Sacred Hearts. Most of its striking architectural elements, including the elegant clock tower, the wooden altar, pulpit, and confessional boxes, were brought from France. There is a stunning pipe organ made by Aristide de Cavalle-Coll, the most famous French organ maker of the time. Stained glass, a replica of the glass in the Church of Santa Gúdula in Belgium, adorns the church's upper reaches and thousands of tiny gold-painted stars decorate its vaulted ceiling.

Adjacent to the church, the **Colegio de los Sagrados Corazones** dates from 1837 and is Chile's oldest private high school. Several former presidents were educated here.

Manicured lawns fronting the entrance to the Congreso Nacional

㉒ Congreso Nacional

Avenida Pedro Montt s/n. **City Map** E4. **Tel** (032) 2250-5000.
Open 9:30am–12:30pm & 3–5pm Mon–Fri. reserve 24 hrs in advance. **camara.cl**

In 1988, General Pinochet was obliged to return the country to democracy after 14 years of dictatorship (see p52). In doing so, he chose Valparaíso, rather than Santiago, as the seat of the country's new National Congress. Two years later, the starkly modern Congreso Nacional building, built on one of Pinochet's boyhood homes, was inaugurated. The structure has met with divided opinion since its construction – some see it as a powerful symbol of democracy and of decentralized political power, while others question its aesthetic appeal. Tours of its halls and salons guide visitors through the rich allegory and symbolism of this building's architecture. The tours, in Spanish and English, cover the National Senate, the Deputy chambers, and the Salón de Honor – the ceremonial hall where international statesmen including Mikhail Gorbachev and Bill Clinton, former Russian and US presidents respectively, have addressed dignitaries.

㉓ Iglesia y Convento de San Francisco

Blanco Viel s/n, Cerro Barón.
City Map F3. **Tel** (032) 2225-8735.
Closed for restoration.

Established in 1846, the Iglesia San Francisco is one of Chile's most impressive examples of redbrick architecture. The

Towering steeple crowning the Iglesia y Convento de San Francisco

church, designated a national monument in 1983, features an ornate facade topped with a distinct, rising bell tower, which used to be illuminated at night to guide ships to Valparaíso's port. The interior of the church is a study in beautiful simplicity, comprising modest whitewashed walls and a Spanish-tiled floor beneath an arched, dark-wood ceiling.

Entered from the side of the church, the Convento de San Francisco was established as a boarding house for visiting priests. In 2013, as both church and convent were undergoing a restoration, a fire struck the site, setting the work back for several years.

The Trolebuses

Valparaíso's fleet of electric trolebuses was imported from the US between 1946 and 1952, and includes the world's oldest trolleybuses still in service. Under the Pinochet regime, trolleybus systems deteriorated as funds for government-run transportation were cut. In 1982, some of the city's businessmen acquired the assets for the trolebuses, and then completely renovated them. Today, these vehicles ply between Avenida Argentina and Edificio de la Aduana (see p124). Extremely low on noise and air pollution, they offer an easy and charming way to see the city.

Green trolebuses waiting for passengers on Avenida Argentina

Funiculars of Valparaíso

Valparaíso's funiculars are the cheapest, easiest, and most fun way of traveling between the city's residential hillsides and the port and financial districts of its El Plan (Lower Town). An antique form of transport, the funiculars were introduced between 1883 and 1912. Fifteen of the original twenty six still survive, though only eight are currently in service. They rattle up and down Valparaíso's steep hills past dense rows of houses and spill out on to dramatic promenades with beautiful city and ocean vistas. Many also access historic sights and tourist attractions, and together the funiculars themselves constitute a national historical monument.

Steep staircases accompanying the track of Ascensor Cordillera

Ascensor Concepción was Valparaíso's first funicular. Very popular with visitors, its wooden cars connect the financial district with Cerro Concepción, a hillside of historical buildings, narrow alleyways, and hotels and restaurants. The funicular spills out on to the romantic Paseo Gervasoni promenade and its gorgeous vistas.

Ascensor Polanco is a wonderful curiosity. It is one of three urban elevators in the world whose ascent is totally vertical. It is accessed via a 500-ft (150-m) long tunnel, and rises 262 ft (80 m) through a yellow wooden tower to an upper station that is connected by a footbridge to Cerro Polanco.

Ascensor Espíritu Santo connects the city center with colorful Cerro Bellavista. Like all of Valparaíso's funiculars, it was once powered by steam and coal and now runs on electricity. Its upper station opens on to the Museo a Cielo Abierto and also provides easy access to the La Sebastiana museum.

Ascensor Barón climbs Cerro Barón on the eastern side of Valparaíso. It has the city's largest wooden cars and its first electric motors. Its upper station house is home to a small museum.

Ascensor El Peral is one of the busiest funiculars, linking Plaza Sotomayor with the hotels and restaurants of Cerro Alegre. The funicular spills out on to the picturesque Paseo Yugoslavo promenade.

Ascensor Artillería

This funicular's wooden cars climb and descend parallel tracks between the port area near Edificio de la Aduana and Cerro Artillería. At the hilltop, a Victorian promenade offers fantastic port views, and the former machinist's house contains a museum and the Café Arte Mirador. From a window table in the café, it is possible to watch the giant wheels of the funicular turning.

Ascensor Reina Victoria is one of the city's steepest funiculars and an access point to the colorful Cerro Concepción and Cerro Alegre.

Pacific Ocean

0 meters 750
0 yards 750

The Funiculars

① Ascensor Villaseca
② Ascensor Artillería
③ Ascensor Cordillera
④ Ascensor San Agustín
⑤ Ascensor El Peral
⑥ Ascensor Concepción
⑦ Ascensor Reina Victoria
⑧ Ascensor Espíritu Santo
⑨ Ascensor Florida
⑩ Ascensor Mariposas
⑪ Ascensor Monjas
⑫ Ascensor Polanco
⑬ Ascensor Larraín
⑭ Ascensor Lecheros
⑮ Ascensor Barón

❷ Viña del Mar

Founded in 1874, Viña del Mar (Vineyard of the Sea) has its origins in a Colonial hacienda whose vineyards faced the ocean. The area became a city after the 1906 earthquake compelled Valparaíso's elite to relocate here. Its flatter topography was ideal for building the French-style garden palaces that were then fashionable and the town became a resort for the rich. Today, it is Chile's Ciudad Jardín (Garden City) – adorned with green spaces, great beaches, and fine palaces that house stunning museums.

Medieval tower and turrets of the stately Castillo Wulff

🏛 Plaza José Francisco Vergara

Avenida Valparaíso, esq. Avenida Libertad.

Viña del Mar's elegant central square, Plaza José Francisco Vergara, is named for the city's founder, whose bronze statue stands on a marble plinth in a corner of the square. The plaza is decorated with pools, statues, and fountains, and lushly shaded by Chilean palms, Lebanese cedars, and Argentine ombus.

Further grandeur is added by the Hotel O'Higgins. Built in 1930, the Neo-Classical **Teatro Municipal** is the most impressive structure in the square. Its facade of Corinthian columns hides a reception hall that is adorned with marble statues.

🏛 Palacio Vergara

Errázuriz 563–596. **Tel** (032) 2185723. **Closed** for restoration. 📷 🎫 ♿
🎭 Quinta Vergara: **Open** 7am–6pm daily. 📷 🌐 **quintavergara.cl**

Constructed between 1906 and 10 for José Francisco Vergara's family, Palacio Vergara now houses the Museo Municipal de Bellas Artes. The palace is built

in a Venetian Neo-Gothic style with a stunning facade and an ornate interior that houses over 150 artworks. These include religious pieces from the 15th to 18th centuries; works by Chile's 19th-century masters; 20th-century Surrealist and Cubist paintings; and works of art donated by the Vergara family. The themed salons include a Salon Dorado ballroom, with Rococo mirrors, gold-and-silk wall tapestries, and Italian-marble statues.

Surrounding the palace are the parklands of the **Quinta Vergara**, once the Vergara family's private gardens. These are planted with exotic trees and decorated with Classical statues. Dominating the grounds, the Anfiteatro Quinta Vergara is a strikingly contemporary amphitheater that hosts the annual Festival Internacional de la Canción de Viña del Mar (see p40).

⏰ Reloj de Flores

Balmaceda, esq. Avenida Marina.

Planted in 1962 on a grassy slope facing the ocean, the Reloj de Flores (Flower Clock)

symbolizes Viña del Mar's status as the Garden City. The dial is a circular flower-bed planted with numerous bright Chilean flowers. The clock includes wooden hands that were brought from Switzerland.

🏰 Castillo Wulff

Avenida Marina 37. **Tel** (032) 2185751.
Open 10am–1:30pm & 3–5:30pm Tue–Sun.

Located on the city's coastal avenue, Castillo Wulff was constructed for German industrialist Gustavo Adolfo Wulff in 1908. A national monument and architectural landmark, the edifice is built in the style of a typical medieval castle and features turrets, ramparts, a round tower, and a central courtyard. The courtyard stairs climb to a lookout point with marvelous ocean vistas. The tower out the back offers a fantastic view of the sea through its glass floor. It also hosts art exhibitions.

🏛 Museo de Arqueología e Historia Francisco Fonck

4 Norte N 784. **Tel** (032) 2686753.
Open 10am–2pm & 3–6pm Mon, 10am–6pm Tue–Sat, 10am–2pm Sun.
📷 🎫 🏠 🌐 **museofonck.cl**

Housed in an old mansion, the Museo de Arqueología e Historia Francisco Fonck features displays of pre-Hispanic objects collected from across Chile and Latin America. Rooms at this archaeological museum are dedicated to the major pre-Columbian civilizations of Chile as well

Neo-Classical facade of the Teatro Municipal

as of Mexico, Peru, Ecuador, and other Latin American countries. Each salon boasts a rich selection of objects from the era it represents. Its standout collection was brought from Easter Island (*see pp258–67*) in 1951. It includes rare artifacts, has informative panels in English and Spanish, and delves into the religious beliefs behind the erection of its famous *moai*. An original *moai*, one of the few on mainland Chile, stands at the entrance.

🏛 Palacios Rioja and Carrasco

Palacio Rioja: Quillota 214. **Tel** (032) 2184693. **Closed** for restoration. 🅿️ 📷 on request. Palacio Carrasco: Avenida Libertad 250. **Tel** (032) 2184432. **Closed** for restoration.

Constructed after the 1906 earthquake, both **Palacio Rioja** and **Palacio Carrasco** are national monuments. The Neo-Classical Palacio Rioja was inspired by Paris's Versailles Palace and built for tobacco baron Fernando Rioja in 1907. It is now a decorative arts museum that conserves the Rioja family home as it was a century ago. The visit includes a tour of its sumptuous rooms, including

the ornate dining room, which has Corinthian columns and an orchestra balcony, and the magnificent central hall, which is embellished with classic Greek statues and pillars. A garden of exotic trees with paths and benches encircles the palace.

Built between 1912 and 1923 in the Beaux-Arts style, Palacio Carrasco houses the city's cultural center and hosts occasional art exhibitions. At present there is no confirmed date for the reopening of either the Rioja or the Carrasco palaces.

🌿 Jardín Botánico Nacional

5 miles (8 km) SE of Viña del Mar **Tel** (032) 2672566. **Open** 9am–7pm daily. 🆆 jbn.cl

A 151-acre (61-ha) oasis of greenery, the National Botanic Garden is located 5 miles (8 km) southeast of the city along Camino El Olivar. The park was created by a French landscape artist, George Duboi, who was commissioned by Pascual Baburizza. Its well-kept grounds are home to over 3,000 plant species that are native to Chile – a fantastic example of the country's varied ecosystems. It also has several walking trails.

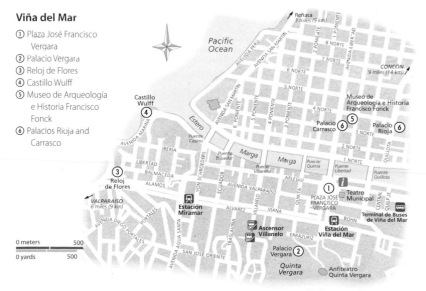

Easter Island *moai* outside the Museo Francisco Fonck

🏖 Reñaca

3 miles (5 km) N of Viña del Mar. 🏖 🚌📷🚗

A gorgeous stretch of golden sand, Reñaca is a popular holiday spot for the residents of Santiago during the summer months. This beach is overlooked by a number of hotels, and several bars and clubs operate at its southern end.

Environs

Some 6 miles (10 km) north of Reñaca, **Concón** is a small town with several good beaches, such as upscale Playa Amarilla and rustic Playa La Boca, a long, crescent-shaped beach popular with surfers. A surf school and numerous seafood restaurants front Playa La Boca. In summer, riders on horseback cross its sands to dunes and coastal forest.

Viña del Mar

① Plaza José Francisco Vergara
② Palacio Vergara
③ Reloj de Flores
④ Castillo Wulff
⑤ Museo de Arqueología e Historia Francisco Fonck
⑥ Palacios Rioja and Carrasco

Pacific Ocean

Reñaca 3 miles (5 km)

CONCÓN 9 miles (14 km)

Museo de Arqueología e Historia Francisco Fonck

Palacio Carrasco ⑥ ⑤ Palacio ⑥ Rioja

Castillo Wulff ④

VALPARAÍSO 6 miles (9 km)

Reloj de Flores ③

Estación Miramar

Ascensor Villanelo

PLAZA JOSÉ FRANCISCO VERGARA ① Teatro Municipal

Terminal de Buses de Viña del Mar

Estación Viña del Mar

Palacio Vergara ②

Quinta Vergara

Anfiteatro Quinta Vergara

0 meters 500
0 yards 500

Calm waters along the rock-encrusted coastline of Quintay

❸ Quintay

Road Map B6. 29 miles (47 km) S of Valparaíso. 🚌 850. 🚐

The fishing village of Quintay is an idyllic spot. Buses drop off visitors at its small plaza, from where sandy lanes wend down to the *caleta*. This is a horseshoe-shaped fishermen's harbor edged by a rocky beach and weatherboard seafood restaurants. Sea otters and birds congregate on the beach and fishermen unload their catch here from wooden boats.

Overlooking the *caleta* is the **Ballenera de Quintay**, Chile's biggest whaling station until its closure in 1967. Now a whaling museum, it includes the station's old and somewhat eerie whaling platform onto which the carcasses of 1,600 blue whale – the world's largest animal – were dragged year after year.

Quintay has two main beaches. From the plaza a 10-minute walk through cool pine and eucalyptus forest leads to the breathtakingly picturesque **Playa Chica**, a wave-pummeled beach ringed by high, rugged cliffs and wildflowers. North of the town centre, **Playa Grande** is a long stretch of golden sand, spoiled slightly by condominiums. For activities in Quintay, diving

schools at the *caleta* run scuba-diving and kayaking excursions. These are ideal for beginners and enthusiasts alike.

🏛 **Ballenera de Quintay**
Caleta de Quintay. **Tel** (032) 2362267. **Open** 9:30am–6:30pm daily. 🏛
W **fundacionquintay.cl**

❹ Algarrobo

Road Map B6. 43 miles (70 km) S of Valparaíso. 🚌 8,600. 🚐
W **vivealgarrobo.cl**

The largest town along the section of Pacific coast south of Valparaíso, Algarrobo is a family-oriented resort that gets crowded in summer with families arriving from Santiago.

Beach umbrellas lining a popular beach in Cartagena

This town boasts excellent tourist services and has some 14 separate beaches where activities include scuba-diving, windsurfing, and horse riding. Its most popular beach, **Playa San Pedro**, is close to the town center and faces calm waters, ideal for swimming. **Playa Grande** is a more dramatic big-wave beach. South of the town center is **Playa El Canelo**, a stretch of fine sand washed by aquamarine waters, which backs onto thick pine forest. **Playa El Canelillo** is secluded and quieter. Reached by boat from Algarrobo, the **Isla de Pájaros Niño** is a rocky islet visited each September to April by nesting colonies of Humboldt penguins. Boats skirt the islet's shore, moving past birdlife such as pelicans, cormorants, and gulls.

❺ Casa Museo Isla Negra

See pp136–7.

❻ Cartagena

Road Map B6. 62 miles (100 km) S of Valparaíso. 🚌 19,000. 🚐 ℹ Municipalidad, Plaza de Armas; (035) 2200736. W **cartagena-chile.cl**

The delightful hillside town of Cartagena has narrow winding streets and colorful houses hanging from a hilltop overlooking a bay. The best time to visit is late spring or early autumn, when the beaches are not as crowded as they are during summer.

From the lushly palm-shaded Plaza de Armas in Cartagena's upper town, twisting streets and stairways wend down to **Playa Chica**, south of the plaza, and to **Playa Grande**, north of the plaza. Set on a hillside east of Playa Chica is the home and tomb of Vicente Huidobro (1893–1948), a great Chilean poet who lived for several years in Cartagena. Sadly rundown, the spot is still a popular point of pilgrimage for Chilean poets and artists. The house is under private ownership and closed to public view.

ⓐ Cachagua

Road Map B6. 45 miles (73 km) N of Valparaíso. ⌗ 1,700. ▥

A beautiful, rustic beach-town, Cachagua arrives as a welcome change along a stretch of coastline dominated by upscale resorts and condominiums. The town has a eucalyptus-shaded plaza from which sandy lanes flanked by thatched houses descend to the long, dramatic **Playa Grande**, Cachagua's main beach. Horse riding and surfing are popular activities here.

Visible from Playa Grande, the **Monumento Natural Isla Cachagua** is a rocky islet that is refuge to a wide variety of birdlife, including nesting colonies of Humboldt penguins from September to April. Boat trips take visitors near the islet and offer a chance to observe this rare birdlife from a close range. Also of interest at Cachagua is **Playa Las Cujas**, a sheltered, rocky beach, popular with divers and anglers.

The long and scenic coastal walkway at Papudo

Humboldt penguins at Isla Cachagua

ⓑ Zapallar

Road Map B6. 50 miles (80 km) N of Valparaíso. ⌗ 2,700. ▥ ⓘ Municipalidad, Germán Riesgo 399; (033) 2742000. ▣ **turismozapallar.cl**

An exceptionally picturesque coastal town and an erstwhile high-end destination, Zapallar is small, secluded, and ringed by steeply forested coastal mountains. The town sits on a wooded hillside that sweeps dramatically down to rocky cliffs and a half-moon shaped sandy beach. A number of weatherboard holiday villas dot the coastal mountains around Zapallar.

Since the late 19th century, this town has been a favorite summer destination for the wealthy citizens of Santiago. From Zapallar's beach, a 4-mile (6-km) long coastal path skirts clifftops and has wide ocean vistas. Boat launches make daily departures in summer, taking birdwatchers and holiday-makers southward to the Monumento Natural Isla Cachagua.

A sandy path up the hillside from the beach leads to Zapallar's white-sand plaza, fronted by a clapboard theaterhouse. This dates from 1908 and was originally the town church. From the plaza, a number of lanes climb uphill to Zapallar's commercial center, with its shops, eateries, and tourist information.

ⓒ Papudo

Road Map B6. 56 miles (91 km) N of Valparaíso. ⌗ 4,900. ▥ ⓘ Chorrillos 9, 2nd Floor; (033) 2325100. ▣ Wed & Sun. ▦ Feria Internacional de Integración Papudo (early Feb). ▣ **municipalidadpapudo.cl**

Less exclusive than the neighboring beach-towns of Zapallar and Cachagua, Papudo is a small and unpretentious seaside town with great walks. A sweeping coastal boulevard runs parallel to the two main beaches: **Playa Grande**, a long open beach popular with surfers; and the smaller, sheltered **Playa Chica**, which is frequented by families. A number of attractive seaside walks strike out from both beaches, crossing sections of cliffs along the coast that are pitted with caves and caverns. On fine days, horses are available for those who wish to ride along the shoreline.

Among the buildings that line the main coastal boulevard, visitors will find the **Iglesia Nuestra Señora de las Mercedes**, a church and national monument built in 1918. Farther on, the honey-colored **Chalet Recart**, site of Papudo's town hall, is one of several alpine-chalet buildings that front the coast here.

The beach and town of Zapallar, sheltered by forested hills

❺ Casa Museo Isla Negra

Attracted by its location facing the Isla Negra beach, Pablo Neruda bought the original building from a Spanish sailor in 1939. Neruda extended the house, creating a structure whose long, thin shape mirrored the geography of Chile, and filled it with over 3,500 weird and wonderful objects from across the globe. Today, the house is a museum and remains exactly as it was when the poet lived here with his third wife, Matilde Urrutia, prior to his death in 1973.

Isla Negra Beach
Named for its isolation and wild black rocks, Isla Negra beach is associated with the poet's love for the sea.

Main entrance and Visitors' Center

③

②

①

Living Room
Ship figureheads, stained glass, and wooden angels adorn this space. Neruda encrusted its floor with seashells to massage his feet.

KEY

① **Narrow wooden corridors** like those on old ships run along the house. Neruda lined this one with African facemasks.

② **Neruda's bedroom**

③ **Dining room**

④ **Seashell Collection** Neruda's collection of seashells occupies an entire room. The long rapier-like tusk of a narwhal whale is also exhibited here.

The Bar
The house bar conserves Neruda's comprehensive collection of surreal bottles. An array of colors, shapes, and sizes are displayed.

For hotels and restaurants in this region see pp277–8 and pp292–4

The reception area
Neruda entertained guests, including other writers, in this reception area. Eclectic collections fill its space.

VISITORS' CHECKLIST

Practical Information
Road Map B6. 56 miles (90 km) S of Valparaíso; Poeta Neruda s/n, Isla Negra. **Tel** (035) 2461284. **Open** 10am–6pm Tue–Sun (Jan–Feb: to 7pm). 🐾 🎫 in English & Spanish, on a first-come, first-served basis (audio guides in numerous languages). 📷 💻 🏠 w **fundacionneruda.org**

Transport
🚌

The Stable
This was built for a papier-mâché horse. Neruda called it "the world's happiest horse"

★ Neruda's Study
Crammed with miscellanea, Neruda's study displays model ships, butterfly collections, astrological charts, portraits, and an antique washbasin.

★ Neruda's Tomb
Two years after the museum's 1990 inauguration, Neruda was re-buried at Isla Negra. His third wife, Matilde Urrutia, is buried alongside him.

The convent building dedicated to Santa Teresa de Los Andes

⓾ Los Andes

Road Map B6. 87 miles (141 km) NE of Valparaíso. 🚗 64,100. 🚌 ℹ Avenida Santa Teresa 333; (034) 2902525. 🚍 Wed, Sat, Sun. 🎭 La Festival Nacional Folclórico "El Guatón Loyola" (mid-Sep). 🌐 **turismoaconcagua.cl**

Ringed by the vineyards of Aconcagua valley, at the foot of the Andean cordillera, Los Andes was founded in 1791 as a staging post on a Colonial trade route. Today, it is the first stop for many travelers making the road crossing of the Andes from Argentina to Chile's Central Valley. There are two museums of interest here. The **Museo Arqueológico de los Andes** is a Colonial house with pre-Columbian displays. The **Museo Histórico Religioso del Antiguo Monasterio del Espiritu Santu** is a convent building dedicated to Santa Teresa de Los Andes, Chile's first saint. Visitors can wander about the convent's old workrooms, sleeping quarters, cloistered courtyard, and orchard. Next door, the Capilla Espiritu Santo is a Neo-Gothic chapel and shrine to the saint. The Neo-Classical headquarters

of the regional government, built between 1888 and 1891, overlooks Los Andes' pretty Colonial plaza. At the edge of town, the Cerro de la Virgen is a hilltop lookout point with fine views.

🏛 Museo Arqueológico de los Andes
Avenida Santa Teresa 396–398. **Tel** (034) 2420115. **Open** 10:30am–6pm Tue–Sun. 🚗 🎟

🏛 Museo Histórico Religioso del Antiguo Monasterio del Espiritu Santu
Avenida Santa Teresa 389. **Tel** (034) 2421765. **Open** 9:30am–12:30pm, 3–5:30pm Mon–Fri, 10am–5:30pm Sat & Sun. 🚗 🏠

⓫ Portillo

Road Map B6. 126 miles (203 km) E of Valparaíso; Renato Sánchez 4270, Las Condes. **Tel** (02) 2263-0606. 🚌 from Santiago airport: Sat only. **Taxi** from Santiago. **Open** mid-June–Sep. 🚗 🚹 🏠 🏠 🌐 **skiportillo.com**

Spectacularly located at 10,000 ft (3,000 m) above sea level, Portillo is South America's oldest ski resort. It has 17 runs for skiers and snowboarders of all levels. Expert and extreme skiers will find fantastic opportunities on slopes that descend from an altitude of 10,900 ft (3,270 m). Challenges include 50-degree descents, countless off-piste routes, heli-skiing and night-skiing. Views from the slopes are tremendous, embracing surrounding peaks and the Laguna del Inca, a lake that freezes in winter. The ski centre is a self-contained resort with

packages that include hotel lodging, lift tickets, and facilities such as a cinema and a heated outdoor pool. Visitors can also choose to stay in cheaper mountain lodges or backpackers' lodges. There is a lively après-ski scene and excellent family-oriented services including babysitting and a ski camp for children aged 4–6 years.

Cristo Redentor on the border between Chile and Argentina

⓬ Cristo Redentor

Road Map B6. 130 miles (210 km) E of Valparaíso; Camino Cristo Redentor. **Taxi** from Santiago. **Open** Dec–Mar.

The gigantic Cristo Redentor (Christ the Redeemer) marks one of the world's great frontier passes: the crossing of the central Andes between Chile and Argentina. Set against a backdrop of the snow-swathed Andes, the figure stands at a dizzying 12,539 ft (3,823 m) above sea level. The 23-ft (7-m) high statue of Christ is set on a 20-ft (6-m) high granite plinth weighing 8,800 lb (4,000 kg). Sculpted in 1904 in Buenos Aires, the Cristo Redentor was conveyed by train to the foot of the Andes, dismantled into various parts, and hauled up the mountains by mules. Its erection marked a historic signing of peace between Chile and Argentina following decades of border disputes that pushed both countries to the brink of war. Tour buses and private cars that pass the Chilean customs post reach the monument by taking the

Wooden benches lining the tree-shaded plaza at Los Andes

Chilean palms (*Jubaea chilensis*) at Parque Nacional La Campana

Camino Cristo Redentor, a gravel turn-off en route to the **Túnel del Cristo Redentor**, a 2-mile (3-km) long tunnel crossing of the Andes.

⓭ Termas de Jahuel

Road Map B6. 87 miles (140 km) NE of Valparaíso; Jahuel s/n, San Felipe. **Tel** (02) 2411-1720. **Taxi** from Los Andes. 🏊 ♿ ✏️ 🖥️ 🏠 📷 🌐 jahuel.cl

Set on the slopes of the arid Andean foothills, overlooking the fertile Aconcagua valley, Termas de Jahuel is a modern, luxurious spa retreat that accepts both day and overnight guests. On offer are sophisticated natural therapies. The spa's signature massage treatment is an olive-oil therapy that uses organically grown plants. There is also an outdoor pool edged by palms, jasmine, and orange groves.

Jahuel's thermal properties were recognized in Colonial times when travelers crossing the Andes came to rest here. Today, guests reside in a Colonial-style pavilion or an exclusive boutique hotel with en suite thermal baths. The resort's activities include horse riding and mountain-biking. Trails climb to a plateau with fine views of the high-altitude Aconcagua Valley wine district. Facilities include playrooms for children, tennis courts, and international and Chilean restaurants.

⓮ Parque Nacional La Campana

Road Map B6. 37 miles (60 km) E of Valparaíso; Paradero 43, Avenida Granizo 9137. **Tel** (033) 2441342. 🚌 from Santiago & Valparaíso. **Open** 9am–5:30pm Sat–Thu, 9am–4:30pm Fri. 📷 ♿ ⚠️ 🌐 conaf.cl

A UNESCO-recognized area, La Campana harbors a wilderness habitat that is considered exceptional for its biodiversity. The park's signature flora is a relict population of Chilean wine palms (*Jubaea chilensis*), the world's southernmost palm. The rich bird life here includes numerous songbirds, and types of eagle, hawk, and falcon. Among mammals and reptiles, there is the vizcacha, a

Mountain vizcacha at La Campana

large burrowing rodent, as well as iguanas, snakes, and lizards. The park is named for its dominant natural feature, Cerro La Campana (The Bell Peak). From the entrance in the Granizo sector, **Sendero El Andinista** is a popular 9-mile (14-km) day-hike that reaches the summit of this peak. Charles Darwin once enjoyed 360-degree views from here – with the Andes to the east and the Pacific Ocean to the west. Less visited, the park's northern Ocoa sector has its largest, densest concentrations of Chilean palms, which may live for several hundred years. The sector can be accessed via the 5 mile- (7-km) Sendero Amasijo, which is connected to the 3-mile (5-km) Sendero Los Peumos that starts at the entrance of Granizo sector.

Darwin and La Campana

In August 1834, English naturalist Charles Darwin began a 2-night ascent of Cerro La Campana on foot and horseback. Accompanied by two cowboys, Darwin climbed the hill's northern flank and made camp at the Agua del Guanaco spring. Writing later in the *Voyage of the Beagle*, he noted, "the atmosphere was so clear the masts at anchor in the Bay of Valparaíso… could be distinguished as little black streaks." The group reached the summit on the second morning. Here, Darwin

Charles Darwin, English naturalist and pioneer

exclaimed, "never has time seemed as short as at that moment. Chile lay at our feet as an immense landscape limited by the Andes and the Pacific Ocean." A plaque at the summit commemorates this ascent.

⑮ A Tour of Wineries in Casablanca Valley

One of Chile's newer wine-growing regions, Casablanca Valley is fast winning an international reputation for its excellent white wines. Located between Santiago and the port-city of Valparaíso, this valley has a maritime-influenced climate of ocean breezes and cool temperatures that is ideal for the production of white varietals such as chardonnay and sauvignon blanc. Overlooked by the snowcapped Andes, the wineries feature grand estates and boutique bodegas that welcome group tours and private visits. Casablanca Valley is also home to Chile's first 100 percent organic winery.

② Viña Casas del Bosque
Established in 1993, this highly rated larger winery was the first in the valley to produce merlot. It has a gourmet restaurant and offers rides across its vineyards, as well as the opportunity to harvest the grapes.

Tips for Drivers

Starting point: Casablanca.
Length: 15 miles (24 km). Allow 2 days for the full tour; it is best to hire a car.
Getting there: Tour agencies in Santiago and Valparaíso organize day-tours of the valley. Visitors arriving by car take the R68 highway that links these two cities and runs through the heart of the valley. Many buses depart daily from Valparaíso for Casablanca, from where taxis can be hired to reach nearby wineries.
Where to eat: Restaurants at the Indómita, Matetic, Casas del Bosque, and Viña Mar wineries.
Tours and tastings: Tours, in English and Spanish, last 1–2 hours. Reserve 1–2 days in advance for private tours.
www.casablancavalley.cl

③ Viña Kingston
Named for the American family that owns it, Viña Kingston is a contemporary bodega where winemaking is done by hand. They specialize in pinot noir and syrah.

① Viña Catrala
This tiny premium winery focuses on quality rather than quantity. Tastings take place in scenic surroundings amid vineyards.

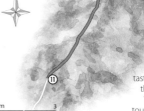

⑪ Matetic Vineyards
Apart from organice wine tastings in a subterranean salon, the modern boutique Matetic Vineyards offers personalized tours and horseback and bicycle rides through its vineyards.

Lo Orozco

Valparaíso 19 miles (30 km)

F-50

R-844

F-852

R68

F-830

Casablanca

F-830

F-74-G

Lo Orrego

F-90

F-962-G

F-940

0 km 3

0 miles 3

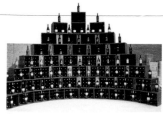

⑤ Estancia El Cuadro
The wine museum at this winery displays antique wine-making machinery. Along with tastings, guests enjoy rodeo shows and horse-drawn carriage rides.

Los Perales

Γ-864-G

La Vinilla Norte

I-870

F-910-G R68

Santiago
47 miles
(75 km)

④ Viña William Cole
Founded in 1999, the family-run Viña William Cole specializes in premium wines. It runs small group tours, where resident wine experts lead the tastings.

⑥ Viña Veramonte
Tours at this large, modern winery take in the entire wine-making process. Its tastings pair wines with fruit, cheese, and chocolates amid the oak barrels of the winery's barrel room.

Key
 Highway
 Tour route
━━━ Other road

Key Facts about Casablanca Valley Wines

 Location and Climate
Casablanca Valley is located in the Central Valley, close to the Pacific coast. The influence of the ocean and the Humboldt Current lends the valley a cool climate that is ideal for producing superior white wines.

Grape Varieties
The valley excels in cool-climate white varieties. The zesty sauvignon blanc has aromas of citrus fruits, grasses, and pines. Creamier chardonnays recall honey and tropical fruit flavors. Pinot noir, a red grape, also flourishes here.

Good Vintages
2003, 2004, 2007, 2008, 2010, 2013, 2014.

⑦ Viña Emiliana
This fully organic and biodynamic winery has been visited by the likes of Britain's Prince Charles. Visitors can arrange wine tastings, bicycle tours, and chocolate pairings.

⑨ House Casa del Vino
This contemporary restaurant serves regional dishes with wines from their own winery. Tours available.

⑩ Viña Mar
Located atop a hillock, the award-winning Viña Mar is an eye-catching winery built to resemble a Venetian villa. A favorite with tour groups, it has a great gourmet restaurant and souvenir shop.

⑧ Viña Indómita
Among Casablanca Valley's most visited wineries, Viña Indómita is housed in a Moorish-style building and features a state-of-the-art wine-making facility. It is popular for pinot noir and sauvignon blanc.

The El Colorado snowboard park, encircled by the lofty Andes mountains

🕧 Ski Centers La Parva, El Colorado, Valle Nevado

Road Map B6. **Taxi** from Santiago.
Open Jun–Oct: 9am–5pm daily. 🎿
🎿 🏠 🎿 El Colorado: 22 miles (36 km) E of Santiago. **Tel** (02) 2964-2010.
W elcolorado.cl La Parva: 25 miles (42 km) E of Santiago. **Tel** (02) 2889-9210. 🚶 **W** laparva.cl Valle Nevado: 34 miles (55 km) E of Santiago. **Tel** (02) 2477-7701. **W** vallenevado.com

Lying adjacent to one another in the central Andes are three ski resorts that are a big attraction with locals and visitors alike. Closest to Santiago, **El Colorado** is the most economical option of these three ski complexes. It has a ski school and a backpackers' lodge, and is particularly popular with beginners and snowboarders.

Located north of El Colorado, **La Parva** is ideal for a day visit and a number of the capital's wealthy residents own condominiums here. The resort caters to both beginners and experts and offers good off-piste skiing. Services include ski schools, restaurants, and hotels.

Chile's biggest, most modern ski center, **Valle Nevado** sits east of La Parva. It has drops for all levels of experience, breathtaking off-piste skiing across Andean slopes, and heli-boarding and heli-skiing at 14,760 ft (4,500 m) above sea level. It also boasts one of South America's biggest skiing surfaces and a snowboard park. Each spring, the resort hosts a round of the annual Nokia Snowboarding World Cup.

World-class facilities available at the complex include three hotels – one with ski-in, ski-out access – and a heated outdoor pool with mountain vistas. Family-oriented services here include a children's snow park.

🕧 Antique Wineries of Pirque

Road Map B6. 🚌 from Santiago.
🎿 🍷 reservations required. 🚶
🏠 Viña: Cousiño-Macul: Avenida Quilín 7100, Peñalolén. **Tel** (02) 2351-4100. 🚇 Línea 4, Estación Quilín.
Open 11am–4:15pm Mon–Fri, 11am–12:15pm Sat & Sun. **W** cousino macul.com Viña Concha y Toro: Avenida Virginia Subercaseaux 210, Pirque. **Tel** (02) 2476-5000 (book 24 hrs in adv). 🚇 Línea 4, Estación Plaza de Puente Alto. **Open** 10am–5pm daily. 🚶 🎥 📷 **W** conchaytoro.com

In the Pirque area of the Maipo valley are two of Chile's oldest wine estates, both offering tours and tastings. Founded in 1856, the **Viña Cousiño-Macul** is the oldest family-run bodega in Chile. Antique wine-making machinery is displayed at the estate's museum. Tastings take place in a romantic candlelit 19th-century cellar.

The second of Pirque's wineries, **Viña Concha y Toro**, is also the biggest in Chile. Established in 1883, it is the largest exporter of wine in all of Latin America. Guided tours take visitors through the estate's grounds, which include a stately 19th-century home and 80-year-old vineyards, as well as state-of-the-art production facilities.

🕦 Cajón del Maipo

Road Map B6. 20 miles (33 km) SE of Santiago. 🚌 from Santiago. 🚹 Comercio 19788, San José del Maipo; (02) 2861-1275. 🎿 🚶 ⚠️ **W** cajondelmaipo.com

Offering a gamut of outdoor activities, Cajón del Maipo is a popular weekend destination from Santiago. Trekking, camping, mountain-biking, and skiing are big draws for the adventurous. Rafting trips on the Río Maipo are popular between September and April.

Independent visitors usually make their base at **San José del Maipo**, the largest of several small towns in the area. Founded in 1791, San José del Maipo is an attraction in its own right, for its Colonial church and adobe houses.

🏕 Reserva Nacional Río Clarillo

25 miles (40 km) SW of San José del Maipo. **Open** Apr–Nov: 8:30am–6pm daily; Dec–Mar: 8:30am–7pm. 🎿 🚶
🏠 **W** conaf.cl

Located southwest of Cajón del Maipo, this area of stunning natural beauty is spread over some 40 sq miles (102 sq km). The reserve is ideal for bird-watching, hiking, horse riding, and rafting excursions.

🎿 Lagunillas

11 miles (17 km) NE of San José del Maipo. **Tel** (09) 8329-2616. **Open** Jun–Oct. 🎿 **W** skilagunillas.cl

The ski resort of Lagunillas has 13 slopes attracting skiers of all levels of experience during the

Río Maipo slicing through the landscape of Cajón del Maipo

winter months. It is also one of the few ski centers where night skiing is possible.

Santuario de la Naturaleza Cascada de las Animas

9 miles (14 km) SE of San José del Maipo; 31087 Camino al Volcán, San Alfonso. **Tel** (02) 2861-1303. cascada.net

An adventure-tourism resort and sanctuary, the 14-sq-mile (36-sq-km) Santurio de la Naturaleza Cascada de las Animas protects an area of rugged mountains, rivers, and waterfalls. It lures visitors with adrenaline-charged activities that include white-water rafting on the Río Maipo, hiking and horse riding in the high Andes, and zip-lining over Cajón del Maipo. Hikes range from short nature trails to multi-day guided tours through mountain circuits. The most popular trek, **Cascada de las Animas**, finishes at three 160-ft (50-m) high waterfalls. Hikers can cool off with a dip in the pool at the foot of the cascades. The sanctuary organizes horse rides, ranging from 2-hour excursions to mountain plateaus to an 11-day circuit of the alpine lakes of the central Andes or a 14-day ride across the Andes to Argentina.

The sanctuary also provides transport to and from Santiago for guests and offers many holiday package options. Accommodation options include well-equipped

Visitors relaxing in the thermal pools at Termas Valle de Colina

log-cabins set in the forest, a full-service guesthouse, and a scenically located campsite.

Monumento Natural El Morado

26 miles (43 km) E of San José del Maipo. **Open** Oct–Mar: 8:30am–6pm daily. cajondelmaipo.com

A relatively compact reserve, Monumento Natural El Morado embraces the 16,597-ft (5,060-m) high **Cerro El Morado**. This snowcapped peak is best viewed on the 3-hour trek departing from the park entrance for **Laguna El Morado**, an alpine lake from where a trail reaches the base of the electrifying **Glaciar San Francisco**. This glacier swathes the lower slopes of the park's second-highest peak, the 14,255-ft (4,345-m) high Cerro San Francisco. South of this peak, the **Baños Morales** area

has hot spring pools that attract weekend visitors from Santiago.

Termas Valle de Colina

37 miles (60 km) SE of San José del Maipo. **Tel** (02) 2985 2609. **Open** Oct–May: daily. termasvalledecolina.cl

A rustic hot springs resort, Termas Valle de Colina sits at the eastern end of Cajón del Maipo. It comprises a series of natural clay pools that bubble and steam on the slopes of a mountain overlooked by snowcapped peaks. Access to the pools is difficult, as the road that reaches the resort is closed to public transport. The Santiago-based Expediciones Manzur (*see p328*) runs round trips over weekends to the pools. Horses can be hired at the resort, and rides to the Argentine border, around 6 hours away, can be arranged with advance notice.

Key

═══ Minor road

– – Trail

Costumed *huasos* gathering for the annual rodeo championship at Rancagua

⓳ Rancagua

Road Map B7. 54 miles (87 km) S of Santiago. 🚶 222,000. 🚉 🚌 ℹ️ Germán Riesgo 350; (072) 2731-8310. 🎠 El Campeonato de Rodeo (early Apr). 🌐 **rancagua.cl**

Founded in 1743, Rancagua lies deep in *huaso* country and plays host to the Campeonato Nacional de Rodeo (*see p35*), which is held here each year. Steeped in history, Rancagua was the site of one of Chile's bloodiest conflicts – the 1814 Battle of Rancagua, in which the patriot militia led by Bernardo O'Higgins (*see p157*) fought against vastly superior Spanish forces. The **Monumento a Bernardo O'Higgins** dominating the city's central plaza – focal point of the battle – is an equestrian memorial honoring Chilean soldiers who were killed at this spot.

Just north of the plaza, the **Iglesia de la Merced** is an adobe church built in 1778. O'Higgins directed his troops from its bell tower, which was rebuilt in 1857. It suffered significant damage in the earthquake of 2010, though, and is undergoing restoration.

Located south of the plaza, the Paseo del Estado is an old Colonial street lined with fine historic structures. The highlight here is the **Museo Regional de Rancagua**, housed in two buildings that date from 1790 and 1800 respectively. The

museum has engaging exhibits on religious art and on the Central Valley's weaving traditions and mining heritage. It also re-creates typical Colonial-era living quarters. At the southern end of Paseo del Estado, another large Colonial building houses Rancagua's **Casa de la Cultura**. Built in the early 1700s, it was the base for Spanish forces during the Battle of Rancagua. Today, it is a cultural center fronted by shaded gardens and hosting art exhibitions.

🏛️ **Casa de la Cultura**
Avenida Cachapoal 90. **Tel** (072) 2226076. **Open** 8:30am–1:30pm, 3–5pm Mon–Sat.

🏛️ **Museo Regional de Rancagua**
Paseo del Estado 685. **Tel** (072) 2221524. **Open** 10am–6pm Tue–Thu (to 5pm Fri), 9am–1pm Sat & Sun. 🌐 **museorancagua.cl**

The ore-crushing and grinding plant at El Teniente

⓴ Valle de Cachapoal

Road Map B7. 60 miles (96 km) S of Santiago. **Taxi** from Rancagua. 🌐 **winesofchile.org**

Located in Chile's agricultural heartland, Valle de Cachapoal is renowned for its production of two excellent red wine grapes, the cabernet sauvignon and the distinctive carménère (*see p289*). Most of the valley's wineries are nestled in its cool eastern sector and are open for tours and tastings. The ultra-modern **Viña Altair**, inaugurated in 2001, features a contemporary design that uses gravity rather than pumps, and offers moonlit tours of its vineyards. More traditional wineries include the **Viña Chateau Los Boldos**, built in the Spanish Colonial style.

Valle de Cachapoal lies in prime *huaso* territory and customized wine tours here include rodeo shows and horse rides through the mountains. Although the valley can be covered on a day trip from nearby Rancagua, overnight travelers will find accommodations at Hacienda Los Lingues (*see p150*), a family-run Colonial estate.

㉑ Sewell

See pp148–9.

㉒ El Teniente

Road Map B7. 49 miles (79 km) SE of Santiago; Carretera al Cobre. **Tel** (072) 2952692. 🚌 from Santiago & Rancagua. 🎫 9am–7:30pm Sat & Sun. 🌐 **vts.cl**

The biggest subterranean copper mine in the world, El Teniente comprises over 1,500 miles (2,400 km) of underground tunnels. In operation since the early 1800s, the mine produces around 485,000 tons (440,000 tonnes) of copper-ore each year. Guided excursions offered by tour operators take visitors through a maze of tunnels, past giant ore-crushing machinery. Also visible is an

The river valley at Reserva Nacional Río de los Cipreses, surrounded by jagged Andean peaks

underground cave of glittering crystal that miners discovered while digging for copper.

㉓ Termas de Cauquenes

Road Map B7. 73 miles (117 km) S of Santiago. **Tel** (09) 4246-1351. **Taxi** from Rancagua. **Open** 7:30am–6:30pm daily. 🐾 🖊 🔄 🆆 **htdc.cl**

Nestled in the Andean foothills at 2,526 ft (770 m), Termas de Cauquenes has entertained such luminaries as English naturalist Charles Darwin (1809–82) and the revered Chilean hero Bernardo O'Higgins. This historic spa complex is set amid dense eucalyptus forests with numerous guided walks leading to a lookout point, an appealing place from where condors can be seen circling in the air. The 19th-century

Neo-Gothic bathhouse of the spa is cathedral-like in size and ambition, with a soaring ceiling, stained-glass walls, and a mosaic floor between rows of private bathrooms. All rooms have exquisite Carrara-marble tubs dating from the 19th century. Overnight guests to this accessible resort are housed in a Colonial-style hotel constructed around a Spanish courtyard with climbing vines and an elegant central fountain.

The resort also welcomes day visitors, who can luxuriate in the spa's thermal baths and enjoy a range of relaxing therapeutic treatments. Facilities include a heated outdoor pool, an outdoor playground for children, and a gourmet restaurant.

Logo of the national reserve

㉔ Reserva Nacional Río de los Cipreses

Road Map B7. 81 miles (131 km) S of Santiago; Camino Chacayes s/n. **Taxi** from Rancagua. **Tel** (072) 2204610. **Open** 8:30am–5:30pm daily. 🐾 🖊 🔄 🅿 🆆 conaf.cl

Created in 1985, Reserva Nacional Río de los Cipreses protects over 142 sq miles (367 sq km) of Andean wilderness, comprising river canyons and forests of mountain cypress. The reserve's popular northern sector has an administration center with displays on the area's wildlife. Starting at the center, paths cross the scenic Cajón Alto Cachapoal, from where the short **Sendero Tricahues** trail leads to a wildlife observation point. Here, colonies of the burrowing parrot, loro tricahue, can be seen nesting in the canyon wall.

The reserve's less-visited central and southern sectors can be reached by longer hikes and horse rides departing from the administration center. These trace the **Cajón Río Cipreses** that forms the spine of the reserve. Along the way, visitors traverse cypress forests and pass grazing guanaco herds. It is also possible to see pre-Hispanic petroglyphs and enjoy dramatic Andean vistas including views of the soaring 15,941-ft (4,860-m) high Volcán Palomo.

Interior of Termas de Cauquenes, with decorative tiles and stained glass

㉑ Sewell: The City of Stairs

Clinging to Cerro Negro at 7,215 ft (2,200 m) above sea level, Sewell, or The City of Stairs, was established by the American Braden Copper Company in 1905 as a camp for workers of the nearby El Teniente mine. By 1960, it was a thriving metropolis, with around 15,000 inhabitants, a bank, a courthouse, a town hall, recreational clubs, and Chile's most advanced hospital. A UNESCO World Heritage Site, Sewell was slowly abandoned from the 1970s to 1999, but now remains an eerily beautiful preserved city of multistoried wooden buildings.

Plaza Morgan, once Sewell's main commercial square

★ El Teniente Club
Once a recreational club for Sewell's US management, El Teniente Club is housed in a building featuring a neat Classical facade, a stuccoed ballroom, and a swimming pool.

Site Plan of Sewell

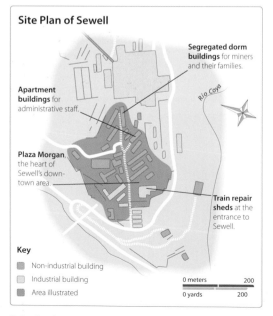

Segregated dorm buildings for miners and their families.

Apartment buildings for administrative staff.

Río Coya

Plaza Morgan, the heart of Sewell's downtown area.

Train repair sheds at the entrance to Sewell.

Key

▨ Non-industrial building

☐ Industrial building

▨ Area illustrated

0 meters   200
0 yards   200

KEY

① Warehouse

② Residential building for hospital staff

③ Hospital

④ Bank

⑤ Shops and bakery

Escalera Central
A steep central stair-
case, the Escalera
Central is the back-
bone of the abandoned
city. Access paths and
secondary stairs stem
from it in a herring-
bone pattern.

★ Iglesia de Sewell
Sewell's restored church
dates from 1928. The Christ
on the Cross above the altar
is cast in copper excavated
from the El Teniente
mine *(see pp146–7).*

★ Museo de la Gran Minería del Cobre
Occupying the attractive Modernist building
of the old Industrial School, the Museo de la
Gran Minería del Cobre displays historical
and geological exhibits from Sewell's past.

Palitroque
Bowling Alley
The preserved
interior of this
bowling alley
features wooden
bowling lanes
and pins.

1914 First
school and
social center
founded

1967 State acquires majority share in company;
toxic fumes from sulphuric plant cause workers
and families to abandon Sewell for Rancagua

1915 Camp is named for Braden
executive Bartin Sewell

1998 Sewell declared
a national monument

1999 Temporary
workers move to
Rancagua; Sewell
opens to tourists

| 1900 | 1920 | 1940 | 1960 | 1980 | 2000 | 2020 |

1928 Iglesia de
Sewell built

1971 El Teniente
mine becomes
fully nationalized

1982 Only
temporary workers
inhabit Sewell

1905 Camp for miners
set up by the US Braden
Copper Company

Iglesia de Sewell

2006 Sewell designated a
UNESCO World Heritage Site

㉕ Santa Cruz

Road Map B7. 113 miles (182 km) SW of Santiago. 🚗 20,000. 🚌 ℹ️ Plaza de Armas s/n. 🎭 La Fiesta de la Vendimia (Mar). 🌐 **portalsantacruz.cl**

One of the larger towns of the Colchagua Valley *(see pp152–3)*, Santa Cruz was founded in the 19th century. The town's most notable Colonial building is the Municipalidad (Town Hall), a reddish arcaded house. Santa Cruz's outstanding highlight is the private **Museo de Colchagua**, owned by alleged arms dealer Carlos Cardoen. It houses over 5,000 objects relating to Chilean history. Displays range from rare objects that belonged to former president Bernardo O'Higgins to the Gran Rescate exhibit, showcasing objects relating to the rescue of 33 miners trapped in San José in August 2010, and 19th-century carriages.

Santa Cruz is the starting point for winery tours to Colchagua. A popular tour option is via the 1920s wine-themed steam train, **Tren Sabores del Valle**, which departs from San Fernando in the valley's north and ends at Santa Cruz in the south. At Santa Cruz visitors depart for two winery coach tours.

🎞️ **Museo de Colchagua**
Avenida Errázuriz 145 **Tel** (072) 2821050. **Open** 10am–7pm daily. 📷 🎥 2 days' notice required. 📷 🌐 **museocolchagua.cl**

🚂 **Tren Sabores del Valle**
Plaza de Armas 298. **Tel** (072) 2823199. **Open** Sat. 📷 🌐 **rutadelvino.cl**

A wealth of historical exhibits at the Museo de Colchagua, Santa Cruz

㉖ Hacienda Los Lingues

Road Map B7. 78 miles (125 km) S of Santiago; Panamericana Sur Km 124.5, San Fernando. **Tel** (02) 2431-0510. **Taxi** from Santa Cruz. **Open** daily. 🍴 📷 🎥 📷 🌐 **loslingues.com**

One of Chile's oldest, most prestigious estates, Hacienda Los Lingues dates from the end of the 16th century when it was gifted by King Philip III of Spain to Don Melchor Jufré del Águila. For over four centuries, it has remained in this Spanish nobleman's family, the current generation of which lives on the hacienda.

Overnight guests stay in sumptuous Colonial rooms that preserve the original architecture and furnishings. Antique family portraits hang from walls, and the sensation of staying at an old aristocratic home rather than simply at a luxury hotel is tangible. Visitors can also opt for the more economical day tour of the hacienda, which visits the courtyard, parks, wine cellar, stables, and the 1790-built chapel. Dating from 1760, the stables breed thoroughbred Aculeo horses, whose lineage can be traced to Moorish Spain. Day tours also feature a gourmet lunch, rodeo show, and horseback rides.

㉗ Pichilemu

Road Map B7. 161 miles (259 km) SW of Santiago. 🚗 12,500. 🚌 ℹ️ Angel Gaete 365; (072) 2976530. 🎭 Wed & Sat. 🎭 La Semana Pichilemina (Feb). 🌐 **pichilemu.cl**

Central Valley's surf capital, Pichilemu is a haven for surfers, bodyboarders, and hippies. Before the boarders arrived, Pichilemu was a luxury coastal resort, built in the 1900s by Chilean speculator Agustín Ross-Edwards. It was the site of Chile's first casino, but went into decline with the rise of Viña del Mar *(see pp132–3)* in the north. However, Pichilemu retains many charming vestiges of its aristocratic past. The old casino building is now occupied by a cultural center.

Today, Pichilemu is a small laid-back town that boasts several beaches, including the main **Las Terrazas** stretch, which has surf schools and is popular with novice boarders, owing to its small waves. About 3.5 miles (6 km) south of the town center, the **Punta de Lobos** beach's long, 8-ft (2-m) high leg breaks attract expert surfers. A stop on the international surfing circuit, Punta de Lobos has excellent infrastructure. Located between the two is **Infernillo**, with its extremely dangerous lefts. It is recommended only for experienced surfers.

Crowds on one of Pichilemu's black-sand beaches

History of Wine in Chile

Chilean wine-making began in the 16th century when Catholic missionaries brought vines from Spain to make wine for religious rites. By the 19th century, a secular demand for wine had blossomed in the nation's capital, Santiago, and it became fashionable in elite circles for families to plant vineyards at their country estates. High-quality vines were introduced from France for the first time and Chile set up its first wineries. In the 1980s, economic liberalization sparked a new age of progress: foreign wine-makers and consultants, led by Spain's Miguel Torres in the Valle de Curicó and France's Michel Rolland in the Colchagua Valley, built ultra-modern wineries. Chile rediscovered its signature carménère grape and a new wine-tourism industry emerged.

Grapes were hand-plucked from vines and carried aloft in casks of native rauli wood.

Chile's first vineyards were planted in the Central Valley at the foot of the Andes.

Since the 1500s women have picked and de-stemmed grapes – female hands were deemed less likely to spoil grapes. This is still true today for premium wines.

Wine-Making in Colonial Times

Chile's first wines came from the Spanish país grape and were harvested on lands gifted to conquistadores by the Spanish Crown. Descendants of the first Spanish immigrants would clamor for more wine to whet their appetites.

Antique wine-making machinery in Chile was made of wood and operated by hand. It included wine presses, pumps, and corking machines.

Steel tanks have replaced wooden vats in the fermentation process. Each has a capacity of 50,720 quarts (48,000 liters).

Chile's world-class premium wines are aged for up to two years in $1,000 barrels of French oak.

Modern Wine-Making in Chile

After independence, Chile turned to France for inspiration, introducing grapes such as merlot and pinot noir that are, today, emblematic of Chilean wine-making. Chile became the first New World country, ahead of California and Australia, to produce high-quality wines.

The avant-garde Clos Apalta winery follows a vertical design and plunges underground to a depth of 115 ft (35 m). Its modern technology uses the flow of gravity, rather than pumps, to make the wine.

New vineyards are founded at high altitudes and at the edge of the Pacific, as the frontiers of Chilean wine-making continue to expand. Organic vineyards are also gaining ground.

㉘ A Tour of Wineries in Colchagua Valley

Chile's premier wine-making region, Colchagua Valley starts at the Andean foothills and sweeps westward toward the Pacific coast. The valley's fertile floor and rolling hills are home to many wineries that specialize in red wine; nearly all are open for tours and tastings. They feature various architectural styles ranging from ultra-modern designs to Colonial-style estates. Among the valley's key attractions is the Tren Sabores del Valle, a steam train that chugs through the vineyard landscape.

The historic Tren del Vino chugging across the Colchagua Valley

⑧ Viña Los Vascos
Owned by the French Rothschild family, this winery runs small group tours. It is notable for its cabernet sauvignon and carmenere that is aged in French oak barrels.

⑦ Viña MontGras
At the grand Colonial-style Viña MontGras, guests make and label their own wines. In early March visitors can take part in the valley's annual grape harvest festival, the Fiesta de la Vendimia.

Poblacíon

Peralillo

Los Olmos

I-50

Pal

Santa Cruz

Key

▬ Highway

▬ Tour route

▬ Minor road

— Railway track

⑥ Santa Cruz
Located at the center of Chile's leading wine-making region, Santa Cruz is the springboard for Colchagua's wineries. The town also serves as the terminal for the Tren Sabores del Valle.

Tips for Drivers

Starting point: San Fernando, 27 miles (43 km) E of Santa Cruz *(see p150)*.
Length: 47 miles (75 km). The tour needs at least 2 days.
Getting there: Ruta 5 runs from Santiago to San Fernando, which is linked to Santa Cruz by the Carretera del Vino, or I-50. Tours are arranged by Ruta del Vino and Red del Vino.
Ⓦ rutadelvino.cl
Ⓦ reddelvino.com
Stopping off points: Viña Lapostolle *(see p277)* has a luxury hotel and gourmet restaurant. Viña Viu Manent is also a good place to stop for lunch.
Ⓦ colchaguavalley.cl

Chile's award-winning wine valley

Owing to its excellent conditions, and technology, the Colchagua Valley produces more world-class wines than any other region in Chile and has been the recipient of innumerable awards.
- Viña Casa Silva – the Best South American Producer in London's 2000 Wine & Spirit Competition.
- Viña MontGras – the Best Chilean Wine Producer in the UK's International Wine & Spirit Competition in 2002.
- In 2005, the international *Wine Enthusiast* magazine labeled the valley as the Best Wine Region in the World.
- *Wine Spectator* magazine voted Viña Lapostolle's Clos Apalta wine as the World's Best Wine in 2008.
- *Asociación de Agricultores Orgánicos Centro-Sur* chose Lapostolle's Cuvée Alexandre Carmenère wine as the Best Organic Wine in 2011.

Wine bottles from Colchagua Valley

Key Facts about Wines Of Colchagua Valley

Location and Climate
Set in Chile's fertile Central Valley, the sweeping Colchagua Valley features a climate similar to that of the Mediterranean regions, with dry, hot summers and cold, rainy winters.

Grape Varieties
Common red grape varieties planted in the valley include Chile's signature grape, cabernet sauvignon, and others such as syrah, merlot, carménère, and malbec. The long summers allow grapes to develop rich aromas suggestive of red fruits, berries, and spices. Viognier, the only white wine grape to flourish here, has a sweet floral aroma.

Good Vintages
(reds) 1995, 1997, 2002, 2005, 2007, 2009, 2010, 2011, 2013.

① Viña Casa Silva
Colchagua's oldest winery, the family-run Viña Casa Silva is housed in a Colonial-style building. Tours include tastings, carriage rides through vineyards, polo matches, and rodeo shows.

0 km 5
0 miles 5

Santiago
90 miles (145 km)

San Fernando

I-50

Cunaco
Placilla
Nancagua

④ Viña Montes
Designed along feng shui principles, this winery grows only premium and icon wines. Tours include tractor-drawn trailer rides to a hilltop that offers spectacular panoramas.

② Viña Viu Manent
Founded in 1935, this winery is housed in a romantic, Spanish-style hacienda. It offers vineyard carriage rides and has an excellent handicrafts shop and an equestrian club that gives riding lessons.

⑤ Viña Lapostolle
A state-of-the-art winery, Viña Lapostolle has a gravity-induced facility that descends six levels beneath the ground. Open to tours, its organic vineyards produce the award-winning Canto de Apalta wine, manufactured exclusively at this winery.

③ Viña Las Niñas
Colchagua's smallest winery, Viña Las Niñas is run by three generations of women from a single French family. Activities include picnics, walks, and bike rides amid lushly planted vineyards.

Verdant banks and forested slopes surrounding Lago Vichuquén

㉙ Valle de Curicó

Road Map B7. 37 miles (60 km) S of Santa Cruz; Curicó. ⊞ from Santiago. ⊞ from Santa Cruz.

One of the less-visited wine valleys of central Chile, the Valle de Curicó carries one significant advantage for wine enthusiasts – personalized, unhurried tours and tastings hosted by wine experts. Valle de Curicó produces fine white wines, especially sauvignon blanc, as well as cabernet sauvignon reds – some from 80-year-old vines. Its wineries include the Spanish-owned Miguel Torres estate, the San Pedro, and Millamar vineyards. The wineries are visited on customized tours arranged by **Ruta del Vino Curicó**, which also organizes private tours.

☒ Ruta del Vino Curicó
Prat 301-A, Curicó. **Tel** (075) 2328972.
Open 9am–2pm & 3:30–7:30pm
Mon–Fri. ⓦ **rutadelvinocurico.cl**

㉚ Lago Vichuquén

Road Map B7. 60 miles (96 km) SW of Santa Cruz. ⊞ from Curicó. ⓘ Manuel Rodríguez 315, Vichuquén; (075) 2400516. ⊞⊡⌂⌗⛰
ⓦ **turismovichuquen.cl**

Central Valley's most beautiful lake, Lago Vichuquén is an intensely blue tongue of water ringed by green, pine-swathed hills. The lake and its surrounds attract bird life, including species of swan, heron, and duck. In Colonial times, the rich suggestiveness of this area led to its notoriety as a

supposed meeting place of sorcerers and witches. Today, it attracts bikers, anglers, wind-surfers, water-skiers, horse-riding aficionados, and nature-watchers.

Some 4 miles (7 km) east of the lake is the historic settlement of Vichuquén, built by the Spanish in 1585 on the site of an old Incan colony. Today, it preserves warrens of winding Colonial streets lined with orange trees and fronted by adobe houses. Both Vichuquén and its lake can be included on wine-tour itineraries of the Valle de Curicó.

㉛ Parque Nacional Radal Siete Tazas

Road Map B7. 78 miles (125 km) SE of Santa Cruz. ⊞ from Curicó, changing at Molina. **Open** 8:30am–5:30pm daily. ⊞⛰ from Curicó. ⛶⟋⊡ ⛵⛰ⓦ **conaf.cl**

This national park is named for its most striking natural feature, the

Velo de la Novia in the Parque Nacional Radal Siete Tazas

Siete Tazas (Seven Bowls). Located in the western section of the park, these are seven connected rock pools formed by the erosive waters of the Río Claro that plunges down a narrow gorge here. Nearby are two breathtaking waterfalls: the 131-ft (40-m) high **Velo de la Novia** and the 82-ft (25-m) high **Salto de la Leona**. The trail linking Salto de la Leona with the Siete Tazas passes transition forest that features both Central Valley flora and temperate rain forest common to the Lake District farther south. A short distance from the pools, the Sector Parque Inglés has scenic walking, horse riding, and mountain-biking trails. The **Sendero El Bolsón** offers visitors a full day's hike to a refuge; beyond, an unsigned trail continues to Reserva Nacional Altos de Lircay. Nature-watching, swimming, and kayaking are popular activities here.

㉜ Wineries of Maule

Road Map B7. 47 miles (76 km) S of Santa Cruz.

Offering an authentic Ruta del Vino that takes in eight of the region's wineries, Maule is one of Chile's top wine producing regions. The area around the city of Talca is renowned for its reds, but there are also a few refreshing white wines being produced here.

On the south side of the international highway to Argentina, **Viña Corral Victoria** doesn't provide tours, but its restaurant pours its own carménère – the only wine its vineyard produces – and a selection from other Maule wineries. Serving traditional Chilean dishes focused on beef, it's open for lunch only.

Only 9 miles (15 km) south of Talca, the town of San Javier is home to **Viña Balduzzi**, a family-run winery that welcomes drop-ins for tours and tastings. They produce a range of reds and whites, including a superb sauvignon blanc, but the truly premium wines are the cabernet sauvignon and the syrah.

To the west of San Javier, on the highway to Constitución,

Gillmore Winery focuses on reds, with cabernet sauvignon, cabernet franc, and merlot, plus blends. It's open for tours and tastings on short notice, but call ahead. It also has its own exclusive lodge and spa that specializes in wine-based therapies.

Located 2.5 miles (4 km) east of San Rafael, **Via Wines** is based on the Fundo Las Chilcas. It is known for both its sustainable approach and its terrific syrah and sauvignon blanc. Advance booking is mandatory for the organic winery tour.

Outdoor pool at the spa resort Termas de Panimávida

🏛 **Gillmore Winery**
Camino a Constitución Km 20.
Tel (073) 1975539. **Open** 10am–noon & 1–5pm Mon–Sat. 🔲 gillmore.cl

🏛 **Via Wines**
K-409. **Tel** (02) 2355-9900.
Open 9am–5pm Mon–Sat.
🔲 viawines.com

🏛 **Viña Balduzzi**
Avenida Balmaceda 1189,
San Javier. **Tel** (073) 2322138.
Open 9am– 6pm Mon–Sat.
🔲 balduzzi.com

🏛 **Viña Corral Victoria**
Km 11, Camino San Clemente,
Talca. **Tel** (02) 2437 4569.
🔲 corralvictoria.cl

㉝ Reserva Nacional Altos de Lircay

Road Map B7. 42 miles (67 km) E of Talca; Ruta Internacional Pehuenche, Cruce Vilches Alto. 🚍 from Talca.
Open 8:30am–1pm & 2–6pm daily.
🔲 conaf.cl

Conserving a wilderness area of southern-beech forest and rugged river-canyon country, Reserva Nacional Altos de Lircay offers activities such

as mountain-biking, hiking, and horse riding. From the administration center at the park entrance, there are several short nature-watching paths. Birdlife seen on these trails includes Andean condors and, in forests, the loro tricahue (an endangered native parrot), and Magellanic woodpeckers.

The two most popular hiking trails also strike out from the park entrance. The **Sendero Laguna del Alto** is an 8-hour return trek of moderate difficulty that climbs through southern-beech forests to the blue Laguna del Alto, which is ringed by craggy mountains. The **Sendero Enladrillado** is a 7-hour return trek, also of medium difficulty, that ascends through native woods to the Enladrillado, a soaring 7,544-ft (2,300-m) high platform of hexagonal basalt. A stunning vantage point, it overlooks a deep river canyon and has 360-degree vistas of an area that includes the peaks of three volcanoes – Cerro Azul, Volcán Quizapú, and Descabezado Grande (The Big Beheaded). Named for its truncated peak, the latter can be climbed on

a 5-day long trekking circuit. Tour agencies such as Trekking Chile (see p311) organize these treks.

㉞ Termas de Panimávida

Road Map B7. 55 miles (88 km) SE of Talca; Panimávida s/n, Linares. **Tel** (073) 2211743. 🚍 from Linares. **Open** 9am–9pm daily. 🎿 ♿ 🚲 🖥 📷 📶 🔲 termasdepanimavida.cl

Set in pastoral farmlands in the Andean foothills, the spa resort of Termas de Panimávida occupies an old Colonial-style edifice surrounded by gardens with statues. On offer are large indoor and outdoor thermal pools, heated to temperatures of 97–104°F (36–40°C), as well as children's pools. Therapeutic treatments here include massages, hot rooms, and Jacuzzis, as well as wine therapies and herbal, Turkish, and mud baths.

Some 3 miles (5 km) to the south, **Termas de Quinamávida** is a spa with similar facilities and services. Its therapies also include steam treatments in cactus wood baths. The resort is closer to the mountains and is a picturesque, modern complex of honey-colored buildings set in century-old eucalyptus and pine forests.

♨ **Termas de Quinamávida**
Camino Linares-Colbún Km16.
Tel (073) 2627100. **Open** 8am–1pm & 3–8pm daily.
🔲 termasdequinamavida.cl

Volcán Quizapú and Descabezado Grande, Reserva Nacional Altos de Lircay

Crates of fruit and vegetables at stalls near Mercado Chillán

❺ Chillán

Road Map D1. 252 miles (405 km) S of Santiago. 🏔 180,000. 🚌
ℹ️ 18 de Septiembre 455; (042) 222-3272. 🎭 Conmemoración Natalicio Bernardo O'Higgins (Aug).
🌐 **municipalidadchillan.cl**

The birthplace of Chile's founder Bernardo O'Higgins, Chillán is centered on a main square fronted by a Modernist cathedral that is supported by 11 giant parabolic arches made from reinforced concrete. Built after the 1939 earthquake, the cathedral has a tunnel-like interior. Above its altar, on a wooden cross pulled from the quake's rubble is a figure of Christ sculpted in Italy.

Also of interest is the **Escuela de México** primary school, whose interior contains two giant murals painted in 1941–2 by Mexican artists David Alfara Siqueiros and Xavier Guerrero. Siqueiros' allegorical *Muerte al Invasor* (Death to the Invader) combines the bold Cubist and Impressionist styles to symbolize the Mexican and Chilean peoples' independence struggle. Guerrero's Realist *De Mexico a Chile* (From Mexico to Chile) depicts, among many scenes, a Mexican woman pulling a Chilean baby from rubble.

Chillán's indoor food market, **Mercado Chillán**, is a delight for foodies. Eateries here serve regional specialties.

🏛 Escuela de México
Ave. O'Higgins 250. **Tel** (042) 221-2012. **Open** 10am–1:30pm & 3–6pm Mon–Fri, 10am–6pm Sat & Sun. 📷

🍴 Mercado Chillán
5 de Abril, Isabel Riquelme, esq. El Roble. **Open** 8am–8pm Mon–Fri, 8am–5pm Sat, 8am–2pm Sun. ♿

❻ Nevados de Chillán

Road Map E1. 51 miles (82 km) E of Chillán. **Tel** (042) 2206100. **Open** daily. 🎿🚠💻🍴🎿⛰
🌐 **termaschillan.cl** 🌐 **nevados dechillan.com**

This year-round resort is best known for skiing, but it also features a state-of-the-art thermal spa complex. The winter ski resort sits on the slope of Volcán Chillán and has 28 runs, including the longest one in South America. Expert skiers can enjoy the excellent off-piste skiing here. The spa complex has thermal pools and outdoor hot springs that rise from natural geothermal fissures. Treatments include massages, mud baths, aromatherapy, and hydrotherapy. There are several hotels, including the ski area's Hotel Nevados de Chillán and the posher Gran Hotel Termas de Chillán.

❼ Concepción

Road Map D1. 322 miles (518 km) SW of Santiago. 🏔 229,000. ✈️ 🚌 🚌
ℹ️ Aníbal Pinto 460; (041) 2741337.
🎭 Aniversario de Concepción (mid-Nov). 🌐 **concepcion.cl**

A vibrant university city, Concepción was founded in 1550 as a frontier settlement on the banks of Río Bío-Bío, and in Colonial times acted as the springboard for Spanish attacks on the Mapuche-held Lake District south of this river.

Much of Concepción's architectural heritage was destroyed in the 19th century by earthquakes and tsunamis, leaving behind a rather bland metropolis. The outstanding historical highlight is the **Mural Historia de Concepción**, a 3,000-sq-ft (280-sq-m) mural in the regional government headquarters, the Edificio Gobierno Regional. Painted in the Socio-Realist style in 1945 by Chilean artist Gregorio de la Fuente, this mural is a stunning visual description of this region's turbulent history from pre-Hispanic times onward.

Opposite this building, **Plaza España** is the city's lively bar and restaurant zone. To its north, **Plaza Independencia** is the historic square from where Bernardo O'Higgins proclaimed Chile's independence in 1818 (*see p48*).

Earthquake of 2010
In the early hours of February 27, 2010, an earthquake measuring 8.8 on the Richter scale struck central Chile, destroying homes and buildings, and flattening motorways across the region. The quake's epicenter was Concepción, one of Chile's most densely populated cities. Towns in its vicinity were the worst hit, but there was also widespread damage, reaching as far as the capital Santiago, 322 miles (518 km) away. In total, over 500,000 homes were destroyed or severely damaged and an estimated 500 people killed. The city has been rebuilt.

Detail from the Mural Historia de Concepción at Edificio Gobierno Regional

❸❽ Tomé

Road Map D1. 293 miles (472 km)
SW of Santiago. ▲ 43,700. 🚌 ℹ️
Municipalidad, Mariano Egaña 1115;
(041) 2406410. 🎉 La Semana de
Tomé (early Feb). 🖥️ tome.cl

A tranquil seaside town, Tomé
was founded in 1875 as a port
for shipping wine and maize
from the Central Valley. Tomé
later became Chile's main textile
port. Its sandy beaches still
attract visitors from the world
over, but the 2010 earthquake
and tsunami did severe damage
here. Four blocks from the town
center, **El Morro** is the most
popular stretch of white sand.
Within walking distance of the
center, **Playa Bellavista** is a
family-oriented beach fronted by
good restaurants. Some 3 miles
(5 km) north of the center, **Playa
Cocholgüe** features high sand
dunes and waves for surfers.

Holidaymakers relaxing on a beach at the
coastal town of Tomé

❸❾ Lota

Road Map D1. 333 miles (537 km)
SW of Santiago. ▲ 49,000. 🚌
ℹ️ Municipalidad, P. Aguirre Cerda
200; (041) 2870682. 🎫 mines.
🖥️ lotasorprendente.cl

For 150 years, Lota lay at the heart
of the Central Valley's coal-mining
industry. Its mines were owned
by the Cousiño family, who oversaw their investment from a grand
villa in town. An earthquake in
1960 destroyed the villa, but its
magnificent gardens, occupying
a promontory overlooking the
ocean, are open for visits. At their
entrance, the **Museo Histórica
de Lota** has historical displays
on the Cousiño family. Closed in
1997, the mines can be seen on

The cascading white curtain of Salto del Laja

tours, booked at the museum.
Former miners act as guides
to its underground galleries.
Visitors descend into the tunnels
in a metal cage elevator. Tours also
include the *Pueblito Minero*, a
re-creation of miners' houses that
were used as a prop in the Chilean
movie *Underground (Subterra)*.

🏛️ **Museo Histórica de Lota**
Avenida El Morro s/n, Lota Alto.
Tel (041) 2870934. **Open** daily. 🎫 🎫
🖥️ lotasorprendente.cl

❹⓿ Saltos del Laja

Road Map D1. 298 miles (480 km) SW
of Santiago. 🚌 from Chillan & Los
Angeles. **Open** daily. 🎫 🖥️ 🎫 🎫
🎫

Natural marvels at the southern
end of the Central Valley, the
Saltos del Laja are four waterfalls
plunging into a rocky canyon
ringed by green forest. Vapor-
drenched trails lie at the base
and top of the falls. At 167 ft
(51 m), **Salto del Laja** is the
highest fall in the chain,
forming a curtain of white
water. Facilities around the
falls include hotels and camps.

❹❶ Parque Nacional Laguna del Laja

Road Map E1. 348 miles (561 km) S
of Santiago. **Open** Dec–Apr: 8:30am–
8pm daily; May–Nov: 8:30am–6:30pm
daily. 🎫 🎫 🎫 🎫 🖥️ conaf.cl

This compact park protects
Chile's northernmost
distribution of araucaria and
mountain cypress. Its most
grand natural feature is the
9,771-ft (2,979-m) high Volcán
Antuco, whose summit is
reached by an undemanding
8-hour return trek. The trail has
great views of the glacier-hung
Sierra Velluda range, just beyond
the park's boundaries. A small
ski center (www.skiantuco.cl)
operates on the volcano's slopes
between June and October. The
park's namesake lake, the green
Laguna del Laja, was formed
by a 1752 eruption of the
volcano. An easy trail skirts this
lake and leads to two gorgeous
falls: **Salto las Chilcas** and
Saltos del Torbellino. Along
the trails, hikers can see plenty
of birdlife – the park is refuge to
over 50 bird species, including
the Andean condor.

Bernardo O'Higgins

Born in Chillán, Bernardo O'Higgins (1778–1842)
was the illegitimate son of Ambrosio O'Higgins,
a lieutenant-general in the Spanish army, and a
local girl. His father rose to be Viceroy of Peru, the
most powerful position in the Spanish Empire,
and Bernardo was educated in Europe, where
he adopted liberal ideas and met revolutionaries
intent on Spain's overthrow in Latin America.
By 1814, O'Higgins was heading Chile's
independence struggle, and eventually became
the post-Independence leader *(see pp47–8)*.

Statue of
O'Higgins

Regional Arts and Crafts

The craft traditions of Central Valley date from pre-Columbian times and range from woodcarvings and weavings to ceramics and wickerwork. High-quality handicrafts can be browsed and bought at crafts markets across the region and at tiny villages, each famed for a century-long tradition in a particular craft. Pomaire, for instance, is known for its pottery, while Chimbarongo produces fine baskets. Visits to these hamlets reveal streets of crafts stalls and workshops where skilled artisans can be observed plying their trade. Most craftspeople in these villages and in other parts of Central Valley are represented by the non-profit Artesanías de Chile.

A range of handicrafts exhibited at a crafts stall in Chillán

Pottery

Villages located close to Santiago in the Central Valley have a long-standing tradition of making ceramics. Talagante is famous for its attractive porcelain creations. Pomaire, 31 miles (50 km) southwest of Santiago, dedicates itself almost exclusively to red-clay pottery, the source of which are the clay-rich hills that surround this hamlet. Well-stocked pottery shops and busy workshops line both sides of Pomaire's main street.

Red-clay crockery displayed at a pottery shop in Pomaire

The *metawe* (jug), shaped to resemble a duck, is part of the Mapuche tradition of using pottery for ritualistic ends. The duck is the Mapuche symbol for female fertility and the *metawe* is used in many rites-of-passage ceremonies for women.

Cerámica Artesanal de Los Andes refers to the decorative ceramics crafted in Los Andes. These feature motifs from the Acanagua valley, for instance grapevines, or broader Chilean themes such as rodeos and haciendas. Potters shape their designs by hand at workshops such as Cerámica Cala *(see p302)*.

Some figurines feature Christmas motifs

Polychromatic figurine depicting a peasant woman

Talagante figurines are porcelain miniatures that portray characters from daily Chilean life such as a washerwoman or an organ-grinder. Artists in Talagante, 27 miles (43 km) southwest of Santiago, make these multicolored figurines by hand. They continue a tradition begun by two sisters who lived here in the early 1900s.

Crin Figurines

Skilled craftswomen from Chile's Central Valley weave multicolored miniatures using horse hair or crin. These are delicately woven figurines, each carefully dyed in a kaleidoscope of bright colors. Among the most popular items are ornamental figures of women, witches, butterflies, birds, huasos, and huasas. Crin products are found at markets and stalls throughout Central Valley, especially in the Maule area.

Crin statuettes of women in brightly colored Colonial attire are popular.

Butterflies, among the most decorative items made of *crin*, reflect a fusion of fine craftsmanship with beautiful coloring.

Textiles

Mapuche women use llama and sheep wool, or the more expensive alpaca wool, to weave ponchos, blankets, rugs, and scarves on rustic looms. These are then colored with natural vegetable dyes to create aesthetic and complex designs.

The Poncho, or *chamanto*, is a rectangular cloth with a horizontal opening for the head. It has been donned by Chileans since pre-Columbian times. Today, it is an essential garb for *huasos* and is functional for horse riding and rodeos.

Multicolored blankets with abstract patterns

Weaving

Artisans use wicker, straw, and reeds to weave baskets, furniture, decorative articles, and hats. Wicker from willow twigs is the most commonly used raw material. These are first soaked in water to separate the bark, and then dried before the fibers can be woven into intricate objects.

Basketry and wickerwork shops in Chimbarongo, 95 miles (153 km) south of Santiago, showcase the skill of local craftsmen.

Hats woven from straw are traditionally worn by *huasos*. The wide brim provides protection from the sun on Chile's open plains. These are also a crucial component of festive Chilean clothing and make excellent souvenirs.

Woodwork

Mapuche woodwork and carvings are central to the group's culture. Craftsmen use ancient techniques to carve both decorative and utilitarian objects. These are crafted from solid blocks of wood from the surrounding forests of raulí, pellín, and coigüe. The artisan's tools usually leave a characteristic tracing on the object's surface.

Simple Mapuche tray made with native wood

Handcrafted cutlery with intricate carvings

NORTE GRANDE AND NORTE CHICO

The north is Chile's vast desert region – an epic landscape of sand dunes, sun-baked ochre earth and white-sand cliffs. The land rises from the coast to the arid altiplano, where camelids roam, pink flamingoes fly, and pointed volcanoes overlook brilliant blue lagoons. Port-cities line the coast, while indigenous hamlets and oasis villages with adobe churches bring the desert to life.

The ever-changing Atacama desert blankets much of the arid Norte Grande (Big North) and the semi-arid Norte Chico (Little North). The original inhabitants of this area belonged to the Diaguita, Aymara, and El Molle cultures, important pre-conquest societies ruled in the past by the Tiwanaku (AD 500–1000) and Incan (1450–1540) empires. The latter was supplanted by Spanish conquistadores and colonizers, who coveted the metal and mineral wealth of the desert, particularly gold, a symbol of power among the pre-Hispanic peoples. Swashbuckling pirates of this time sacked Colonial cities such as La Serena for silver. Even after independence, Chile waged war for the desert's nitrates (see p49).

Today, mining in the Atacama is the bedrock of Chile's economy and many port-cities have prospered from the growth in this industry. However, the north also has many oasis hamlets that hold colorful crafts markets and Quechua-speaking villages that herd llamas on the altiplano and celebrate festivals rooted in Incan culture.

Norte Grande and Norte Chico are best experienced on road trips to the high-altitude wilderness of shimmering lagoons and to lunar valleys, hot springs, and salt lakes. Giant petroglyphs and stone fortresses can be seen on the hillsides by day, while stargazing is a huge nighttime attraction. On the coast, old cities have great beaches and splendid port architecture.

A flock of Andean flamingoes on the Laguna Chaxa

◄ The stark landscape of the Valle de la Luna in the Atacama desert

Exploring Norte Grande and Norte Chico

Chile's northernmost region of Norte Grande is a desert stretch, with the oasis village of San Pedro de Atacama serving as the gateway to the dazzling Salar de Atacama salt pan and the pre-Incan ruins of Aldea Tulor, while the northeastern corner has Chile's highest, Parque Nacional Lauca. The coast is lined with large cities, including Arica, famed for its colorful crafts markets and mummies, the old nitrate capital of Iquique, and the historic city of Antofagasta. Easily reached from these cities are the giant petroglyphs at Cerro Pintados and the massive telescope that draws stargazers to the Cerro Paranal Observatory. South of Río Copiapó, the scrubland of Norte Chico is punctuated by the pretty orchard town of Ovalle and the *pisco* distilleries and vineyards of Pisco Elqui. La Serena, a beach town with quasi-Colonial buildings, marks the desert's southern border.

Moorish designs and furnishings at the Casino Español, Iquique

Sights at a Glance

Villages, Towns, and Cities
- ❶ *Arica pp164–5*
- ❸ Putre
- ❻ *Iquique pp170–71*
- ⓫ La Tirana
- ⓬ Pica
- ⓮ Calama
- ⓰ Chiu-Chiu
- ⓲ Caspana
- ⓴ San Pedro de Atacama
- ㉗ Antofagasta
- ㉚ Copiapó
- ㉛ Caldera
- ㉟ *La Serena pp184–5*
- ㊱ Vicuña
- ㊴ Montegrande
- ㊵ Pisco Elqui
- ㊷ Ovalle

Resorts and Spas
- ㉑ Termas Baños de Puritama
- ㊻ Termas de Socos

National Parks, Reserves, and Natural Monuments
- ❹ *Parque Nacional Lauca pp168–9*
- ❺ Reserva Nacional Las Vicuñas
- ❾ Parque Nacional Volcán Isluga
- ㉜ Parque Nacional Pan de Azúcar
- ㉝ Parque Nacional Nevado Tres Cruces
- ㊶ Paso del Agua Negra
- ㊸ Reserva Nacional Pinguino de Humboldt
- ㊹ Monumento Natural Pichasca
- ㊺ Monumento Nacional Valle del Encanto
- ㊼ Parque Nacional Bosque Fray Jorge

Areas of Natural Beauty
- ㉓ Salar de Tara
- ㉔ Salar de Atacama

- ㉕ Valle de la Luna
- ㉖ Valle de la Muerte
- ㉞ Laguna Verde

Archaeological Sites and Ruins
- ❼ Humberstone and Santa Laura
- ❽ El Gigante de Atacama
- ⓭ Cerro Pintados
- ⓱ Pukará de Lasana
- ㉒ Aldea de Tulor

Sites of Interest
- ❷ Iglesia de San Gerónimo de Poconchile
- ❿ Mamiña Hot Springs
- ⓯ Chuquicamata
- ⓳ Geisers de Tatio
- ㉘ La Portada
- ㉙ Cerro Paranal Observatory
- ㊲ Cerro Mamalluca Observatory
- ㊳ Observatorio del Pangue

The eroded arch of La Portada off the coast of Antofagasta

Key
- ▬▬ Highway
- ▬ Main road
- — Minor road
- = = = Untarred minor road
- — Minor railway
- — Regional border
- ▬ International border
- △ Peak

For hotels and restaurants in this region see pp278–9 and pp294–5

0 km 100
0 miles 100

PUTRE
3
Azapa
4 PARQUE NACIONAL LAUCA
ARICA **1**
2
5 RESERVA NACIONAL LAS VICUÑAS
IGLESIA DE
SAN GERÓNIMO
DE POCONCHILE
Codpa
Cuya
Enquelga Isluga
Camiña Colchane
TARAPACÁ **9**
Pisagua PARQUE NACIONAL VOLCÁN ISLUGA
5
HUMBERSTONE EL GIGANTE DE ATACAMA
AND SANTA LAURA **8**
10 MAMIÑA HOT SPRINGS
IQUIQUE **6 7** LA TIRANA
11 12 PICA
13 CERRO PINTADOS

Lagunas
1
5
Ollagüe
Volcán Ollagüe
19,255 ft
Quillagua Volcán San Pedro
20,206 ft
Tocopilla
PUKARA
DE LASANA
CHUQUICAMATA **15** CASPANA
17
14 CHIU- **16 18 19** GEISERS DE TATIO
CALAMA CHIU
1
21 TERMAS BAÑOS DE PURITAMA
SAN PEDRO DE ATACAMA **20**
Mejillones **23** SALAR DE TARA
VALLE DE LA MUERTE **26 22** Toconao
ALDEA DE TULOR **25 24** SALAR DE ATACAMA
LA PORTADA **28** VALLE DE
ANTOFAGASTA **27** LA LUNA
Socaire Laguna Lejía
Laguna Miscanti
ANTOFAGASTA Laguna Miñeques
Cerro Rincón
18,353 ft
Volcán Socompa
19,786 ft
CERRO PARANAL **5** Salar de
OBSERVATORY **29** Punta Negra

PACIFIC
OCEAN

Paposo
Bahía Volcán Azufre
Nuestra Señora Catalina 18,635 ft
Taltal

PARQUE NACIONAL
PAN DE AZÚCAR **32**
Isla Pan de Azúcar
Caleta Pan de Azúcar Diego de El Salvador
Chañaral Almagro
Inca de Oro Potrerillos
5 ATACAMA Laguna
Santa **34** LAGUNA VERDE
CALDERA **31** Rosa
Bahía Inglesa Volcán Ojos del Salado
30 COPIAPÓ 22,609 ft
Bahía Copiapó Tierra **33**
Amarilla PARQUE NACIONAL
Punta NEVADO
de Díaz Juntas TRES CRUCES
Carrizal Bajo
5
Huasco Cerro del Potro
Vallenar 19,127 ft
Alto del Carmen
RESERVA NACIONAL Cerro del Toro
PINGUINO DE HUMBOLDT Domeyko 20,931 ft
43
La Higuera CERRO MAMALLUCA
LA SERENA OBSERVATORY
Coquimbo **35 37** Hurtado
MONTEGRANDE
OBSERVATORIO DEL PANGUE VICUÑA **36 39** PASO DEL
OVALLE **44 40** AGUA NEGRA
PARQUE NACIONAL **47 42** PISCO ELQUI
BOSQUE FRAY JORGE MONUMENTO
TERMAS DE SOCOS **46 45** NATURAL PICHASCA
MONUMENTO NACIONAL
VALLE DEL ENCANTO
5
COQUIMBO
Salamanca
Los Vilos

Getting Around

The international airports at Arica,
Iquique, and Antofagasta have
direct air links with Santiago's
airport and with each other. Domestic flights serve the airports at
Calama, Copiapó, and La Serena.
Long-distance buses ply the Ruta
5 highway, commonly known as
the Pan-American Highway, and
connect the region's main towns
and villages. Remote areas in the
desert and altiplano, including
archaeological sites and national
parks, can be reached only by
organized tour *(see pp310–11)*
or by a 4WD vehicle.

For keys to symbols *see back flap*

❶ Arica

The coastal city of Arica has palm-lined plazas and a vibrant indigenous flavor whose roots lie in the large mestizo, Aymara, and Quechua Peruvian populations. The city was part of Peru before its secession to Chile after the War of the Pacific (1879–83), and grand Peruvian-era buildings, including some by France's Gustave Eiffel, dot this compact grid of streets and plazas. Indigenous crafts and markets add color, alongside sweeping beaches and outstanding archaeological highlights. Arica is also popular as a base for trips to Chile's altiplano, to the giant geoglyphs in the bordering Valle Azapa, and to Parque Nacional Lauca.

Latticed facade of Arica's Catedral de San Marcos

🎌 Morro de Arica

Camino Al Morro, off Colón.
Open 8am–8pm daily. Museo Histórico y de Armas:
🏛 💿 on request; in Spanish. 📷

This 360-ft (110-m) high cliff towers above the city center and marks the end of Chile's coastal cordillera. It stands as a symbol of national glory, marking the site where, in 1880, Chilean forces stormed Peruvian fortifications to win possession of Arica in the War of the Pacific.

Located on the summit, the **Museo Histórico y de Armas** houses objects of war and other treasures. A monument to the unknown soldiers of Chile and Peru and a 33-ft (10-m) high bronze of Christ, raised as a symbol of peace between both countries, also adorn the cliff's summit.

🏛 Museo de Sitio Colón 10

Avenida Colón 10. **Tel** (058) 2205041.
Open Jan & Feb: 10am–7pm Tue–Sun (Mar–Dec: to 6pm).

In 2004, during excavations for a residential project, construction workers found a host of mummies and skeletons from the pre-Columbian Chinchorro culture. Although many similar finds are already displayed at the museum in Azapa, archaeologists decided to leave them in situ, under glass, on the slope just before the Morro, where they now represent an unmissable sight.

🏛 Catedral de San Marcos

San Marcos 260. **Open** 8:30am–9pm Mon–Fri, 11am–1pm Sat, 9am–1pm & 7:30–9pm Sun. 🎗

Built by French engineer Gustav Eiffel, Arica's cast-iron, Neo-Gothic cathedral was prefabricated in France and assembled in Arica in 1876. Its latticed facade is a rich chocolate color, while the interior is notable for a delicate tracery that supports the cathedral's columns – a design flourish Eiffel used to replace the flying buttresses usually seen in Gothic churches. The bell near the entrance is from 1729 and belonged to the basilica that earlier stood on this site. Above the altar is a 17th-century sculpture of Christ.

🏛 Ex-Aduana

Manuel González. **Tel** (058) 2209501.
Open 9am–5:30pm Mon–Thu, 9am–6:30pm Fri, 10:30am–2pm Sat.

Another building designed by Gustav Eiffel, the city's former customs house (officially called the Casa de la Cultura) was prefabricated in France and erected in Arica in 1874.

This squat, brick building has an attractive pink-and-white striped exterior. Its interior, with cast-iron pillars and spiral staircase, houses art exhibitions. Photographs show pre-urban Arica, including shots of Morro de Arica with thousands of penguins.

🏛 Terminal Pesquero

Avenida Commandante San Martín.
💿 5–8pm daily (boat tours).

In Arica's port area, Terminal Pesquero (Fishermen's Port) is a smelly but colorful experience. Boisterous water birds and sea lions vie over discarded scraps, while fishermen clean and gut the day's catch at stalls. Boat tours of the bay depart from here.

🎗 Beaches

🏖 📷 🏖 🌊

Arica has four main beaches. Just south of the center, **Playa El Laucho** and the pretty **Playa La Lisera** have calm waters ideal for bathing; the former also has bars and restaurants. North of the center, **Playa Chinchorro** is popular for its big waves and amusement rides. Farther on, the rustic **Playa Las Machas** has more surfer waves.

Playa El Laucho, a view from the summit of Morro de Arica

Chinchorro Mummies

The Chinchorro populated Norte Grande during 6000–2000 BC and their mummies, buried in the Atacama desert, are the oldest in the world. The Chinchorro method of mummification was complex – it entailed the removal of the skin, extraction of the internal organs and extremities, and filling in of cavities with mud, ash, and resinous substances. The mummies were then buried in the extended position in collective tombs, which comprised adults, children, and fetuses.

The mummy of a Chinchorro woman

Poblado Artesanal

Hualles 2825. **Open** 10am–1:30pm & 3:30–7pm Tue–Sun.

Arica's craftspeople's village is the place to buy Quechua crafts such as weavings of alpaca and llama wools, ceramics, jewelry, and leatherware. A walled space, the colony is built in the image of an altiplano village and includes workshops and lodging for local craftspeople.

Museo Arqueológico San Miguel de Azapa

Camino Azapa, Km12. **Tel** (058) 2026403. **Open** Jan & Feb: 9am–8pm daily; Mar–Dec: 10am–6pm daily. **masma.uta.cl**

Arica's outstanding museum of archaeology displays objects from up to 10,000 years ago and includes the world's oldest known mummies, the Chinchorro mummies. These comprise a man, woman, and two children buried in mass graves by the Chinchorro people between 4,000 and 8,000 years ago. The site also includes a display of severed heads, part of a "cult of the head" that existed between 500 BC and AD 500; utensils carved by the Tiwanaku people (AD 500–1000) to make

Painted ceramics arrayed on wooden shelves at the Poblado Artesanal

hallucinogens; and ancient petroglyphs. There are also mummies of an Incan fisherman and a baby.

Geoglifos de Cerro Sagrado

Alto Ramírez, Valle Azapa.

The great stone mosaic on the Cerro Sagrado hillside is the most eye-catching of several enormous geoglyphs in the Valle Azapa. A mosaic of anthropomorphic and zoomorphic motifs, it depicts giant human figures – adult and child as well as mammoth lizards and llamas. The latter are composed in dynamic form, as if scaling up or bounding across this barren hillside. The geoglyphs date from this region's Incan period (AD 1450–1500), when farmers settled this green valley.

Arica City Center

1 Morro de Arica
2 Museo de Sitio Colón 10
3 Catedral de San Marcos
4 Ex-Aduana
5 Terminal Pesquero

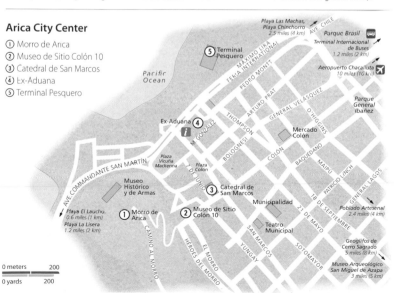

Putre's plaza, with views of the Chilean altiplano

❷ Iglesia de San Gerónimo de Poconchile

Road Map B1. 22 miles (35 km) E of Arica; Poconchile. 🚌

Located in the village of Poconchile, Iglesia de San Gerónimo is the oldest of northern Chile's early Colonial churches. It was built by Spanish priests in 1580, on a site along the old Camino del Inca (Inca Road), and served to evangelize the Aymara people of this area. The church's dazzlingly white exterior is faithful to the classic Spanish Colonial style – a thick adobe perimeter wall marks the boundary of this sacred site and twin bell towers flank its entrance. The restored interior is wooden and painted white. At the back of the church, a desert cemetery contains old graves marked by pebbles and simple wooden crosses.

❸ Putre

Road Map B1. 90 miles (149 km) NE of Arica. 🏔 1,366. 🚌

The largest of the high-altitude settlements close to Arica, Putre is an oasis town ringed by the pointed peaks of several snow-swathed volcanoes. At 11,500 ft (3,500 m) above sea level, it is a stopover for travelers seeking acclimatization before continuing onward to higher altitude highlights such as the adjacent Parque Nacional Lauca and the more distant Reserva Nacional Las Vicuñas. Putre's roots lie in pre-Incan Chile, but the present town was founded

by the Spanish around 1580 as a resting place for muleteers transporting silver from the mines of Potosí, in modern-day Bolivia, to the Pacific coast. The town's most attractive structure is the heavily restored Colonial church fronting the plaza. This edifice dates from 1670 and stands on the site of the original temple that was destroyed by earthquake, and which, according to Spanish chronicles, was completely clad in silver and gold. The rest of Putre is a compact grid of cobbled streets lined with relatively new concrete-and-zinc buildings and old Spanish adobe houses. A selection of hotels and restaurants dot this pleasant altiplano town; tour agencies are found on Calle Baquedano.

Ñandu, Reserva Nacional Las Vicuñas

❹ Parque Nacional Lauca

See pp168–9.

❺ Reserva Nacional Las Vicuñas

Road Map B1. 143 miles (230 km) E of Arica. 🛈 CONAF, Guallatire. 🎫 tours from Putre and Arica. 🚐 🌐 **conaf.cl**

Spectacular and remote, the Reserva Nacional Las Vicuñas protects a vast wilderness of giant volcanoes, high-altitude tablelands, abandoned Aymara settlements, and diverse indigenous fauna. This reserve has a steppe landscape that rises from 13,120 ft (4,000 m) above sea level at its lowest elevation to 18,370 ft (5,600 m) at its highest. It is overlooked by three 20,000-ft (6,000-m) volcanoes – Volcán Acotango, Volcán Capurata, and Volcán Guallatire. Vicuñas, for whose protection this park was founded in 1983, can be seen bounding across the puna; ñandus, ostrich-like birds, sprint over open plains; pink flamingoes congregate on the banks of high lagoons; and vizcachas (large chinchilla-like rodents) scurry over rocks. In the central sector of the reserve, the llama-herding hamlet of **Guallatire** has lodgings, the CONAF ranger post, and a 17th-century church. South of this hamlet, the **Monumento Natural Salar de Surire** is a dazzlingly white salt plain. Three different species of flamingo nest on its shores in the summer months, and on its western bank a CONAF *refugio* offers rustic accommodations.

The snow-bound peak of Volcán Guallatire at Reserva Nacional Las Vicuñas

Pukarás and the Camino del Inca

Northern Chile's pre-Incan fortresses, built between AD 1000 and 1450, are known as *pukarás*. In the 11th century, the reigning Tiwanaku Empire, whose seat was in present-day Bolivia, collapsed, returning autonomy to Norte Grande's Aymara and Atacameño peoples. However, the peace of empire was replaced by intermittent warfare as local warlords rose to compete for resources. To protect ancestral trading routes, the warlords built *pukarás* on strategic hillsides. The *pukará's* role as a powerbase continued until the 1450s, when Incan forces sacked them and incorporated their routes into the Camino del Inca (Inca Road), a 3,720-mile (6,000-km) highway that ran the length of the Incan Empire.

A long perimeter wall marked the *pukará's* boundary and was its first line of defense.

Pukarás occupied strategic positions on hillsides in rocky canyons and oasis valleys.

Pukará Architecture

In peacetime, pukarás were used by warlords to wield authority over surrounding aldeas (villages). In wartime, they became defensive fortresses, where villagers relocated for their own safety. Accordingly, pukarás at Lasana (see p175) and Quitor (see p178) include not only defensive fortifications but domestic neighborhoods as well.

Family quarters in the fortress could be circular or square, with drystone or stone-and-mud walls. Smaller storehouses adjoined them for stocking timber, maize, and other provisions.

Narrow stone passages connected the *pukará's* maze of fortifications and its residential neighborhoods. The latter comprised numerous houses, storehouses, patios, communal squares, and animal pens for llamas.

Pukarás climbed hillsides in terraces. The hill's crest was an ideal vantage point for spotting enemy approach; its steep slopes a further defense against attack.

❹ Parque Nacional Lauca

Northern Chile's most scenic sanctuary, Parque Nacional Lauca protects around 532 sq miles (1,378 sq km) of altiplano wilderness. The park features a tiered ecology that starts at 10,500 ft (3,200 m) in its western zone and rises to over 20,700 ft (6,300 m) in the east. The accessible, high-altitude attractions include brilliantly colored lakes, snowy volcanoes, lava islands, stretches of high tableland, and tiny Aymara villages. There is also an abundance of wildlife. Over 140 bird species find refuge in this area, key among them the ostrich-like ñandu and three species of flamingo, which feed and nest on lakeshores. Wild populations of vicuña and viscacha are also easily spotted.

Llareta, a cushion plant found at high altitudes

Jurasi Thermal Baths
These hot springs are scenically situated within a rocky gorge. They include many small baths of bubbling hot water, a large pool, changing rooms, and toilets.

Exploring the Park

Parque Nacional Lauca can be reached via hired vehicles, organized tours, or the Arica-Bolivia international bus, whose route passes through this area. Within the park, the CH-11 international highway runs east to west, and walking trails link the popular sites of Parinacota, Lago Chungará, and Lagunas Cotacotani. There are CONAF stations at Las Cuevas, Parinacota, and Lago Chungará. The last of these has refugio accommodation and Parinacota has a visitors' center.

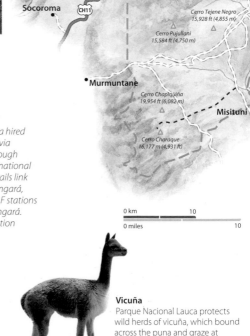

PAMPA GUARIPUJO

NEVADOS DE PUTRE

Cerro Larancagua
17,716 ft (5,400 m)

Las Cuevas

CH11

PARQUE NACIO
LAUCA

Putre

Cerro
Villañuhumani
16,404 ft (5,000 m)

Socoroma   CH11

Cerro Tejene Negro
15,928 ft (4,855 m)

Cerro Pujullani
15,584 ft (4,750 m)

Murmuntane

Cerro Chapiquiña
19,954 ft (6,082 m)

Misituni

Cerro Charaque
16,177 m (4,931 ft)

0 km · · · · · 10
0 miles · · · · · 10

KEY

① **Las Cuevas** marks the start of the altiplano and is ideal for wildlife sightings.

② **Cerro Choquelimpe** reaches a height of 16,191 ft (4,935 m) and can be explored on a 4-hour hike. The summit offers fantastic views of lakes and volcanoes.

Vicuña
Parque Nacional Lauca protects wild herds of vicuña, which bound across the puna and graze at lakeshores. Vicuña numbers in the park have increased from barely 1,000 in the 1970s to over 20,000 today.

For hotels and restaurants in this region see pp278–9 and pp294–5

★ Volcán Parinacota
The twin peaks of Volcán Parinacota and Volcán Pomerape form a glorious backdrop to Lago Chungará. At a height of 20,762 ft (6,330 m), dormant Volcán Parinacota is a target for climbers, who scale its summit on 2-day expeditions.

Laguna Cotacotani
Visible from the CH-11, this area is a network of jade-green lagoons patterned with black lava flows and cinder cones. The banks can be explored on scenic trails.

★ Parinacota
A small Aymara hamlet, Parinacota is visited for its handicrafts market and a 17th-century church, where frescoes depict the tortures of hell.

★ Lago Chungará
At 14,990 ft (4,570 m), Lago Chungará is one of the world's highest lakes. It is stunningly beautiful: metallic-blue and ringed by snowy volcanoes. Colorful birdlife feeds on its shores.

Key

▬▬ Main road

= = Untarred minor road

– – Trail

– – Park boundary

▬·▬ International border

For keys to symbols *see back flap*

❻ Iquique

Originally part of Peru, Iquique was annexed by Chile during the War of the Pacific (1879–83) and it subsequently emerged as Chile's nitrate capital. Opulent buildings and streets from the nitrate-era stand testament to the city's decadent golden past, a period when Iquique is said to have consumed greater quantities of champagne per capita than any other city in the world. Backed against a vast sand dune, this important port is the springboard for excursions to nearby national parks, nitrate ghost towns, and oasis villages.

The Iquique skyline seen from Playa Cavancha

🏛 Palacio Astoreca

O'Higgins 350. **Tel** (057) 2526890. **Open** 10am–6pm Mon–Fri, 11am–2pm Sat. 📷 for group visits only.

One of Iquique's extravagant mansions, Palacio Astoreca is a beautiful 27-room house that was built in British Georgian style for a nitrate magnate in 1903. It was constructed with Douglas fir that was shipped from the US. The house retains vestiges of a glorious past that include silk wallpaper, a grand staircase, and a stained-glass skylight in its reception hall. Today, this grand building serves as Iquique's cultural center, and hosts occasional art exhibitions and workshops. Permanent exhibitions include re-creations of nitrate-era living quarters with original Art Nouveau furnishings. On display is a collection of seashells of varying sizes from around the world.

🏛 Teatro Municipal

Calle Thompson 269. **Tel** (057) 2544734. **Open** 9am–6pm daily. 📷

Built in 1890 at the height of the nitrate boom, Iquique's Teatro Municipal is housed in a magnificent wooden structure, whose Neo-Classical facade is ornamented with female stone figures symbolizing theatrical elements such as costume and dance. The foyer, topped by a cupola, has a ceiling painted with cherubic allegories of music, dance, painting, and theater, as well as depictions of famed literary and musical masters including Shakespeare, Chopin, and Mozart. A domed ceiling crowns the auditorium and is painted with more theatrical motifs, including musical instruments and theater masks symbolizing

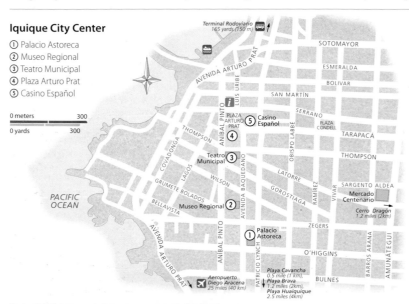

Iquique City Center

① Palacio Astoreca
② Museo Regional
③ Teatro Municipal
④ Plaza Arturo Prat
⑤ Casino Español

0 meters   300
0 yards   300

Terminal Rodoviario
165 yards (150 m)

SOTOMAYOR
ESMERALDA
BOLIVAR

AVENIDA ARTURO PRAT
LUIS URIBE
SAN MARTÍN
SERRANO
ANIBAL PINTO
PLAZA ARTURO PRAT
⑤ Casino Español
PLAZA CONDELL
OBISPO LABBÉ
TARAPACÁ
THOMPSON
④
Teatro ③ Municipal
COVADONGA
LAGOS
WILSON
LATORRE
GOROSTIAGA
RAMÍREZ
VIVAR
SARGENTO ALDEA
GRUMETE BOLADOS
AVENIDA BAQUEDANO
BELLAVISTA
Museo Regional ②
Mercado Centenario
Cerro Dragón
1.2 miles (2km)
ZEGERS
PACIFIC OCEAN
① Palacio Astoreca
ANIBAL PINTO
PATRICIO LYNCH
O'HIGGINS
BARROS ARANA
AMUNATEGUI
AVENIDA ARTURO PRAT
✈ Aeropuerto Diego Aracena
25 miles (40 km)
Playa Cavancha
0.5 mile (1 km),
Playa Brava
1.2 miles (2km),
Playa Huaiquique
2.5 miles (4km)
BULNES

Interior of the Teatro Municipal, displaying luxurious furnishings

comedy and tragedy. Adjacent to the stage, stairs descend to the bowels of this edifice, where century old wooden pulleys and wheels still serve as stage machinery.

🎭 Plaza Arturo Prat

Between Calle Aníbal Pinto & Avenida Baquedano. 🔲 🖺 🎪

Iquique's main square, Plaza Arturo Prat is located in the heart of the city's historic center. Dominating the plaza is the city's emblematic landmark, the flamboyant **Torre Reloj**. Built from Douglas fir by the English community in 1877, this clock tower is made up of three tapering tiers that are painted white and rise to 82 ft (25 m). The tower's arched base features a bust of Arturo Prat, considered Chile's greatest naval hero. He captained the *Esmeralda* schooner that was sunk by the Peruvian battleship *Huáscar* at the Battle of Iquique during the War of the Pacific. This battle ended with the death of Prat and much of his crew, but proved to be the turning point in a war that secured possession of Iquique for Chile and dominion over this area's lucrative nitrate deposits.

The historic Torre Reloj at Plaza Arturo Prat

🏞️ Cerro Dragón

Popular with the parapente (paragliding) enthusiasts, the massive Cerro Dragón

sand dune looms high above the city and acts as a launching point for paragliders. After a running start off the dune, soar above the city and get propelled by the currents before landing on the beach. Paragliding here makes for a truly memorable experience.

🎭 Casino Español

Plaza Prat 584. **Tel** (057) 2333911. **Open** 10am–4pm Mon–Sat. 🎪
W casinoespanoliquique.cl

Constructed by the city's Spanish community in 1904, the Casino Español occupies a Moorish-style wooden edifice with an arched, Arabesque facade. Its domed interior recalls the Moorish palaces of Andalusian Spain with every inch of floor, wall, and ceiling space decorated with glittering Moorish motifs, patterns, and inscriptions. Arabesque archways and columns divide the salons, and kaleidoscopically glazed tiles decorate floors overlooked by Spanish stained glass, mirrors, and statues. There is also a public restaurant, the walls of which are embellished with eight giant oil paintings by well-known Spanish artist Antonio Torrecilla. Completed in 1907, these depict scenes from Miguel de Cervantes' famous novel *Don Quijote de la Mancha* (1605).

🏛️ Museo Regional

Baquedano 951. **Open** 9am–5:30pm Tue–Fri, 9:30am–6pm Sat. 🎪
Set in the former courthouse, this regional museum traces the emergence of Iquique, and its growth as a port city, through a series of photographs while giving an insight into the nitrate industry. The exhibits include several masked Chinchorro mummies and elongated skulls.

🏖️ Beaches

Along Avenida Arturo Prat.
Located within walking distance south of the city center, **Playa Cavancha** is Iquique's most popular beach for swimming. Further south lies **Playa Brava**, accessible via shared taxis, a favourite among sunbathers, but with treacherous rip currents. While it is possible to ride some waves towards the northern end of Playa Cavancha, serious surfers make their way further south to the exhilarating breaks of **Playa Huaiquique**.

Shops selling a variety of goods at Iquique's duty-free Mall Zofri

❼ Humberstone and Santa Laura

Road Map B2. 30 miles (48 km) E of Iquique; Ruta A16, Km3. **Tel** (057) 2760626. ▦ from Iquique. **Open** 9am–7pm daily. 🎫 Tue–Sat; on request. ♿ 🏠 🅦 **museodelsalitre.cl**

In the 1930s, British investors built the towns of Santa Laura and Humberstone to provide housing and leisure for the workers and management of the area's nitrate mines. By 1960, the advent of artificial nitrates had closed the mines, leaving these two towns eerily abandoned. Today, these UNESCO-protected nitrate ghost towns have become popular visitor attractions. The more-visited Humberstone is a silent grid of named roads, empty plazas, creaking street signs, and shells of deserted buildings and facilities. These include quarters that once housed 3,700 employees, a hospital and school, an outdoor pool, sports fields, a marketplace, a church, clock tower, and a theater that could seat up to 800 people. Each of these desolate structures is signposted with panels bearing historical information that help visitors explore the town independently. Adjacent to these buildings stands the rusting machinery of the town's nitrate mine.

About one mile (1.5 km) east of Humberstone, the smaller ghost town of Santa Laura, feels all the more abandoned for receiving fewer visitors. Its hulking processing facilities – which include giant chimneys and mills – are perfectly preserved.

Empty quarters for workers at the nitrate ghost town of Humberstone

❽ El Gigante de Atacama

Road Map B1. 50 miles (80 km) NW of Iquique.

Located 9 miles (14 km) east of the town of Huara, this 283-ft-(86-m-) tall geoglyph is the world's largest image of a human being. It rests on the west slope of Cerro Unitas hill, along the Huara-Colchane road. Although there is no public transport to its location, tours of Humberstone from Iquique generally stop here.

❾ Parque Nacional Volcán Isluga

Road Map B1. 155 miles (250 km) NE of Iquique. ℹ CONAF; (057) 238 3537. ▦ from Iquique to Colchane: 10 miles (16 km) from park. **Open** 8:30am–7:30pm daily. 🚫 ▣ 🏠 🚻 ⛰ 🅦 **conaf.cl**

Isolated from northern Chile's beaten track, Parque Nacional Volcán Isluga protects around 674 sq miles (1,741 sq km) of altiplano wilderness that embraces brilliantly hued lagoons, forgotten Aymara villages, and soaring volcanoes, including the 18,209-ft (5,550-m) high Volcán Isluga. The park's highlights are in its eastern sector, accessible via the paved A-55 international highway that connects Iquique with neighboring Bolivia. Close to the park entrance, **Isluga** is an Aymara village with a beautiful 17th-century church as well as the Pukará de Isluga, a ruined fortress d ating from pre-Columbian times. Also located in the eastern sector, the Aymara village of Enquelga is the gateway to the park's hot springs. This sector has two pristine lakes: Laguna Arabilla has a walking trail along its shore, while Laguna Parinacota is popular for sightings of wildlife such as pink flamingoes, camelids, and the taruca, a mid-sized Andean deer.

❿ Mamiña Hot Springs

Road Map B2. 78 miles (125 km) E of Iquique; Mamiña. ▦ from Iquique. 🚫 ▣ 🏠 🚻 ⛰ 🅦 **termasdemamina.cl**

Located 8,860 ft (2,700m) above sea level, these hot springs have been used to cure afflictions ranging from eczema to anxiety and respiratory illnesses since the age of the Incas. They comprise a number of hot springs such as **Baños de Ipla** that has sodium-rich waters and **Baños Barros Chinos**, famous for its mud baths. Adjacent to the springs is the village of Mamiña, with stone houses, terraced fields, and Incan ruins. The village's restored **Iglesia de San Marcos**, dating from 1632, is unique among Andean churches for its twin bell towers.

One of the thermal swimming pools at Mamiña Hot Springs

⓫ La Tirana

Road Map B2. 45 miles (72 km) SE of Iquique. 🏔 1,300. 🚌 🎭 Festival de La Tirana (mid-Jul).

A somnolent oasis village with adobe houses, La Tirana springs to life each July for the lively Festival de La Tirana, a religious celebration, drawing over 200,000 devotees to the village from across Chile.

The origins of the village can be traced to the 1500s when an Incan princess, notorious for killing Christians, ruled the area. The princess, who was known as La Tirana (The Tyrant), eventually fell in love with a Portuguese prisoner and converted to Christianity, only to have her irate subjects kill them both on their wedding day. In 1540, a Jesuit missionary found the cross marking the princess's grave and ordered the construction of a church on the site. Named the Iglesia de la Virgen del Carmen de la Tirana in honor of Chile's patron saint and the Incan princess, the church became the progenitor of the cult of La Tirana. The **Santuario de la Tirana** comprises the present-day wooden church, a sweeping plaza adorned with effigies of the Virgin and the princess, and the Museo de la Virgen de la Tirana, which displays costumes and masks from the Festival de La Tirana. Inside the church is a polychrome shrine to the Virgin.

🏛 **Santuario de la Tirana**
Open 9.30am–1pm & 3.30–8pm Mon–Fri, 9am–8pm Sat & Sun. 🏛 📷
🌐 fiestadelatirana.cl

Festival de La Tirana

Chile's biggest religious event, Festival de La Tirana has its roots in pre-Columbian rituals and offers a peek at Andean culture. It venerates the Virgen del Carmen via costume and dance. On its first day, dancers enter La Tirana's church to percussion and brass bands and ask the Virgin's permission to dance. They then embark on four days of frenetic dancing that culminate on the Day of the Virgin, when a hoisted image of the saint leads a mass procession through the village. On the final day, they visit the church to bid farewell to the Virgin, before exiting on their knees.

Costumed performer at the Festival de La Tirana

A fruit-laden tree in one of Pica's orange and lemon groves

⓬ Pica

Road Map B2. 71 miles (114 km) E of Iquique. 🏔 6,200. 🚌 ℹ️ Balmaceda 299, (09) 4275-2311. 🎭 La Fiesta de San Andrés (end Nov). 🌐 pica.cl

Called the Flower in the Sand, Pica is an oasis village famed for its orchards. Regional and local varieties thrive in Pica's micro-climate, and fruit trees and adobe houses line its sleepy streets. Facing the main plaza, the beautiful Iglesia de San Andrés was built in 1886. Its polychrome interior holds a life-size representation of the Last Supper carved from wood. Just east of the plaza, the **Museo de Pica** displays millennia-old preserved Chinchorro mummies *(see p165)*. At the edge of town, the warm waters of **Cocha Resbaladero** thermal pools have attracted visitors since the 16th century.

🔆 **Cocha Resbaladero**
Balneario Cocha Resbaladero. **Tel** (057) 2741173. **Open** 8am– 8pm daily 📷 📷

🏛 **Museo Municipal de Pica**
Balmaceda 178. **Tel** (057) 2741665. **Open** 9am–2pm & 3.30–5.30pm Mon–Fri.

⓭ Cerro Pintados

Road Map B2. 59 miles (96 km) SE of Iquique; El Cruce de Geoglifos de Pintados, La Panamericana. **Tel** (057) 2751055. **Open** 10am– 4pm daily. 📷

The barren hillsides of Cerro Pintados are etched with more than 420 gigantic geoglyphs. Dating from AD 500–1450, when this region was part of a caravan route to the Pacific coast, the geoglyphs comprise huge geometric shapes as well as anthropomorphic and zoomorphic figures including depictions of fish, llamas, and the ñandu, a native ostrich-like bird. These are accessible via a 3-mile (5-km) long path that skirts the base of the hillsides.

The facade of La Tirana's Iglesia de la Virgen del Carmen de la Tirana

⓮ Calama

Road Map B2. 242 miles (390 km) SE of Iquique. 🏠 165,000. ✈ El Aeró-dromo El Loa de Calama. 🚌 **ℹ** J. J. Latorre 1689; (055) 2531707. 🎭 Aniversario de la Ciudad de Calama (end Mar). **W** mascalama.cl

The industrial city of Calama is the base for visits to the great copper mines of Chuquicamata. An oasis city in the driest zone on the planet's driest desert, Calama has its roots in pre-Columbian Chile, and derives its name from the Atacameño word *kara ama*, meaning water haven. In the 1920s, Calama boomed as a service town and provider of debauched diversion to pit workers. Today, the city is fairly unremarkable, its single daytime attraction being the **Parque El Loa**, a riverside tourist park featuring a replica of the Colonial church at Chiu-Chiu. The grounds are also the site of the city's Museo Arqueológico y Etnografico Parque El Loa, which houses artifacts belonging to this area's pre-Incan oasis villages.

🎋 Parque El Loa

Avenida Bernardo O'Higgins s/n. **Tel** (055) 2531771. **Open** 10am–7pm daily. 📷

⓯ Chuquicamata

Road Map B2. 10 miles (16 km) N of Calama; Entrada al Campamento, J.M. Carrera. **Tel** (055) 2322122. 📧 2pm Mon–Fri. Note: book in advance by email (visitas@codelco.cl); passport needed to gain entry. **W** codelco.cl

Visited only by guided tour, Chuquicamata is the world's biggest open-pit mine. This huge copper quarry is about 2 miles (3 km) wide, 3 miles (5 km) long, and an impressive 2,300 ft (1,000 m) deep. The mine is to copper what Saudi Arabia is to oil – any blip in the production process here strikes panic in world copper markets. Chile's biggest state company, Codelco, oversees the mine. It employs 20,000 workers, operates 24 hours per day, and is the single biggest contributor to Chile's state coffers, bankrolling the country's

An altar at the Iglesia San Francisco de Chiu-Chiu

public health and education systems. Each year this massive hole in the Andes mountains is gouged ever deeper, a phenomenon brought into stunning perspective on 1-hour coach tours of the site. Tours pass refineries, and crushing and smelting plants to a viewpoint that overlooks the open pit. Here, visitors can peer into the depths of Chuquicamata, and see from a distance the giant 394-ton (400-tonne) dump trucks, with 10-ft- (3-m-) high wheels, that ascend and descend its terraced walls like worker ants. It is advisable to wear comfortable shoes and clothes that cover the arms and legs.

A stepped quarry and gravel roads at the copper mine of Chuquicamata

⓰ Chiu-Chiu

Road Map B2. 22 miles (36 km) NE of Calama. 🚌 🎭 Festival de Nuestra Señora de Lourdes (mid-Feb).

Founded by the Spanish around 1610, Chiu-Chiu is an oasis village of whitewashed adobe houses and cactus-wood doors. Visited on tours from Calama, or more usually from San Pedro de Atacama *(see p178)*, the village conserves one of Chile's oldest, most beautiful churches, the **Iglesia San Francisco de Chiu-Chiu**. This whitewashed adobe church was built in 1674 in the Spanish Colonial style, with two bell towers, walls over 3 ft (1 m) thick, and a well-preserved interior of mini altars and polychrome statues of saints and virgins. The church's small grounds, protected by a thick perimeter wall, contain a tiny cemetery.

One block from the main plaza of Chiu-Chiu is the **Museo Geológico de Chiu-Chiu**, housing some interesting rock and fossil exhibits.

🏛 Museo Geológico de Chiu-Chiu

Tel (09) 9703-8988. **Open** 10am–1pm & 3–6pm Thu–Mon. **w** sanfranciscochiuchiu.com

⓱ Pukará de Lasana

Road Map B2. 28 miles (45 km) N of Calama; Pueblo Lasana, Valle Lasana. **Open** 9:30am–5pm daily.

The stone ruins of the pre-Inca Pukará de Lasana occupy a natural promontory that overlooks the green Valle Lasana from within a rocky canyon. The people of the Atacameño civilization (400 BC–AD 1400) erected this fortress from a pre-existing village during a period of war in the 11th century. Today, the well-preserved ruins are a hilly maze of perimeter walls, roofless houses, storehouses, patios, narrow passageways, and fortifications. Incan forces sacked this site in 1447, and converted it into a strategic administrative center for control of the valley. They abandoned it in the 16th century on the arrival of the Spanish to this region.

⓲ Caspana

Road Map C2. 52 miles (84 km) E of Calama. ☐ 480. ☐ La Virgen Candelaria (early Feb).

One of the oasis villages that dot the high mountain pass between Calama and San Pedro de Atacama, Caspana is spectacularly situated 11,870 ft (3,260 m) above sea level in a steep gorge irrigated by a tributary of the Río Salado. The village is an adobe jewel, with monochrome stone-and-mud houses that were inhabited by the Atacameño people before the arrival of the Incas and Spanish. Today, it subsists on farming, and sinuous rows of green terraces can be seen along the contours of the lower slopes of the gorge. These are planted with root vegetables, grown to be sold at the market in Calama.

At the edge of the village, the adobe and cactus-wood **Iglesia San Lucas** dates from 1641 and backs on to a small cemetery. The village's **Museo Etnográfico** has archaeological and ethnographic exhibits. The tiny village plaza offers shaded benches and lovely vistas of the rocky gorge, pale houses, and verdant terraces.

▥ Museo Etnográfico
Los Tres Alamos s/n. **Tel** (055) 2340112. **Open** 10am–1pm & 2–6pm Tue–Fri, 2–6pm Sat & Sun. ☐ ☐
ⓦ mascalama.cl

Jets of steam rising from the Geisers de Tatio

⓳ Geisers de Tatio

Road Map C2. 74 miles (119 km) E of Calama; Camino a Tatio. **Open** daily. ☐

A natural spectacle, the Geisers de Tatio shoot skyward in columns of white vapor at an altitude of 14,200 ft (4,320 m) above sea level. There are some 40 geysers and 70 fumaroles here, each a scar on the surface of a flat geothermic basin that is ringed by rust-colored mountains and pointed volcanoes. Their origin lies in the contact of a cold river with hot, magmatic rock deep underground. This contact causes jets of vapor to stream upward through fissures in the earth's crust and to exit here, in white-vapor streams that rise to a height of 33 ft (10 m) and reach a temperature of 185°F (85°C). It is best to visit the geysers on 4WD excursions that depart from San Pedro de Atacama at 4am, reaching the geysers at around daybreak, when they are at their most impressive. Visitors who make this early trip will be able to view the geyser field at its most elemental; hear it groan, grumble, spit, and ultimately, both audibly and visibly, exhale. Half-day trips to the Geisers de Tatio end with a dip in sulfur-rich hot springs. Full-day excursions continue to Calama, visiting Caspana, Chiu-Chiu and the Pukará de Lasana, before returning to San Pedro de Atacama.

Terraced cultivation around the village of Caspana

The awe-inspiring landscape of the Atacama desert ▶

Entrance to the Museo Arqueológico Gustavo Le Paige, San Pedro de Atacama

⑳ San Pedro de Atacama

Road Map C3. 304 miles (490 km) SE of Iquique. 🏔 3,900. 🚌 ℹ Toconao esq Gustavo Le Paige. 🎭 La Celebración de San Pedro (end Jul). 🌐 **sanpedroatacama.com**

Lovely San Pedro de Atacama is northern Chile's most popular tourist destination. A small oasis village of clay-colored adobe houses and dirt streets, this is the picturesque springboard for trips into a region of stunning natural highlights and rich archaeological interest, and as such is a magnet to adventure-hungry visitors. Its location is a geological basin at 7,990 ft (2,436 m) above sea level, overlooked from its west by the Domeyko mountains and from its east by the younger Andes range. Both basin and mountains are part of a tiered ecology that rises to over 19,700 ft (6,000 m) at its highest altitude and features jaw-dropping highlights such

The adobe church, Iglesia San Pedro de Atacama

as dazzlingly white salt lakes, lunar valleys, Chile's biggest volcanoes, smoking geyser fields, high-altitude lagoons and hot springs, and the ruins of pre-Incan forts and villages. These can be visited on 4WD tours, mountain-bike rides, and horseback excursions.

An important settlement in pre-Incan Chile, San Pedro de Atacama retains a beguiling, authentic charm despite the year-round presence of tourists and the large number of accommodations, from backpacker hostels to luxury hotels, which line its narrow streets. The **Iglesia San Pedro de Atacama** overlooks its pretty, tree-lined plaza. A brilliant white adobe edifice with interesting cactus-wood doors, the church dates from the early 1600s. Standing opposite it, the **Casa Incaica** was supposedly built for Chile's founder Pedro de Valdivia in 1540 and is the town's oldest house. The superb **Museo Arqueológico**

Gustavo Le Paige houses archaeological objects such as stone paraphernalia sculpted with images of animalistic deities, which the decadent Tiwanaku (AD 500–1000) used to make hallucinogens. Tour agencies line the town's main street, Caracoles.

Environs
Reached on horseback or by mountain bike from San Pedro de Atacama, the **Pukará de Quitor** comprises ruins of a red-stone pre-Incan fortress, built in the 12th century during a period of war. The ruins sprawl across a steep hillside which overlooks the stunning San Pedro river canyon and consist of an outer wall, narrow passageways, living quarters, grain storehouses, herding pens, and communal squares. A walking trail climbs to the top of the fortress for wonderful views of the canyon, volcanoes, and the Valle de la Muerte.

From Pukará de Quitor, determined visitors can continue 3 miles (5 km) north to **Catarpe**, site of the ruins of a *tambo* (Incan administrative center). These are less intact than the *pukará*, but the journey to them traverses breathtakingly wild canyon country.

🏛 **Museo Arqueológico Gustavo Le Paige**
Gustavo Le Paige 380. **Tel** (055) 2851002. **Closed** for restoration until 2019. 🎫 📷 ♿ 📷

🏯 **Pukará de Quitor**
2 miles (3 km) N of San Pedro de Atacama; Avenida Pukará. **Open** 8:30am–6:30pm daily. 📷 📷

Hedges and pepper trees lining the main plaza at San Pedro de Atacama

For hotels and restaurants in this region see pp278–9 and pp294–5

㉑ Termas Baños de Puritama

Road Map C3. 19 miles (30 km) NE of San Pedro de Atacama; Camino al Tatio, Km32. 🚌 from San Pedro de Atacama. **Open** 9:15am–5:30pm daily. 🅿️

A half-day excursion from San Pedro de Atacama, the Termas Baños de Puritama are terraced hot springs that tumble down a narrow canyon. At 77–86°F (25–30°C), these natural volcanic pools are perfect for bathing. There are changing rooms nearby, and wooden footbridges link the stepped, interconnected pools.

People in the secluded thermal pools at Termas Baños de Puritama

㉒ Aldea de Tulor

Road Map C3. 6 miles (9 km) SW of San Pedro de Atacama; Ayllu de Tulor, RN Los Flamencos. **Open** Dec–Mar: 8:30am–7:30pm daily; Apr–Nov: 9am–6pm daily. 🚗 📷 📸

Excavated as recently as 1982, after desertification had left it buried beneath sand for 1,500 years, Aldea de Tulor comprises the 2,800-year-old red-clay ruins of one of Chile's first sedentary settlements. The Atacameño abandoned this site in AD 500 owing to the encroaching desert. Today the walls of their settlement and its doorways, passageways, and large honey-comb-like patterns of rooms lie partially or fully exposed to view. Most visitors choose to reach Tulor from San Pedro de Atacama independently on horseback or by mountain bike, crossing the Atacama desert in the shadows of impressive volcanoes.

Neolithic settlement of adobe mud brick, preserved at Aldea de Tulor

㉓ Salar de Tara

Road Map C3. 62 miles (100 km) E of San Pedro de Atacama; Reserva Nacional Los Flamencos. ℹ️ Control de CONAF. 🆆 conaf.cl

Adventurous travelers make the arduous yet memorable excursion from San Pedro de Atacama to the Salar de Tara, a salt lake located 14,100 ft (4,300 m) above sea level. Tough roads lead to this breathtaking white spectacle decorated by jewel-like lakes and green vegetation with abundant fauna. Its birdlife includes Chile's three species of flamingo, which rest on the shores of the lagoons, horned coots (*Fulica cornuta*) and Andean geese (*Chloephaga melanoptera*). Herds of vicuña can be seen grazing at the edge of the salt pan.

㉔ Salar de Atacama

Road Map C3. 6 miles (10 km) S of San Pedro de Atacama; RN Los Flamencos. **Taxi** from San Pedro de Atacama. ℹ️ Control de CONAF, Sector Soncor. 📷 🆆 conaf.cl

Occupying 1,160 sq miles (3,000 sq km) of surface area, Salar de Atacama is Chile's largest, and the world's third-largest, salt flat. It lies 7,700 ft (2,350 m) above sea level in a great geological depression between the Domeyko and Andes mountain ranges. The *salar* formed when lakes that originally filled this basin evaporated, leaving a thick coat of silver-gray salt crystals on the flat earth. Not blindingly white like other salt pans in this region, the Salar de Atacama is nevertheless a vision of color and beauty, with salt-water lagoons of intense hues decorating its surface. **Laguna Céjar** is a brilliantly blue lake whose high salt and lithium content allows bathers to float weightlessly on its surface. **Laguna Chaxa** has shallow waters, a volcanic backdrop, sure flamingo sightings, and brilliant sunsets.

Environs

Lying 13,100 ft (4,000 m) above sea level, just east of the Salar de Atacama, are the arrestingly beautiful **Laguna Miscanti**, **Laguna Miñeques**, and **Laguna Lejía**, famous for their birdlife. Also east of the *salar* are **Toconao**, **Peine**, and **Socaire**, oasis villages with early Colonial churches, pre-Incan ruins, and petroglyphs.

The beautiful Salar de Atacama

Sweeping sand dunes and volcanoes at the Valle de la Luna

㉕ Valle de la Luna

Road Map B3. 12 miles (19 km) SW of San Pedro de Atacama; Sector 6, Reserva Nacional Los Flamencos. **Taxi** from San Pedro de Atacama. 🖼️ 📖 📷

This lunar valley is a stark landscape of otherworldly rock formations, salt caves, natural amphitheaters, and vast sand dunes. Set 7,870 ft (2,400 m) above sea level in the Cordillera de Sal (Salt Mountain Range), it is explored via a well-marked circuit. This path includes **Las Tres Marias**, eroded rock sculptures that resemble three praying women, and the **Duna Mayor**, the greatest of this valley's massive sand dunes. Most tours climb the Duna Mayor at dusk for stupendous views of the Andean peaks and volcanoes washed in indigo, orange, and red tones. The vistas include Volcán Licancabur and Volcán Láscar; the latter being one of Chile's most explosive peaks.

㉖ Valle de la Muerte

Road Map B3. 6 miles (10 km) W of San Pedro de Atacama; Camino a Calama. **Taxi** from San Pedro de Atacama. 🖼️

An otherworldly spectacle of huge sand dunes and red-rock pinnacles, Valle de la Muerte (Valley of Death) was thrust upward from the earth's crust 23 million years ago during the violent upheaval that created the Andes. This valley's death

tag is no misnomer – though rich in mineral deposits, it is one of the driest, most inhospitable places on the planet and no known life exists here. Guided tours to Valle de la Luna stop briefly en route at Valle de la Muerte. Travelers with more time can join horseback excursions, including full-moon rides, as well as trekking expeditions from San Pedro de Atacama. Treks feature sand-boarding runs down the valley's great dunes.

㉗ Antofagasta

Road Map B3. 194 miles (313 km) SW of San Pedro de Atacama. 🚶 632,000. ✈️ Aeropuerto Cerro Moreno. 🚌 🚆 ℹ️ Avenida Prat 384; (055) 2451818. 📅 El Día del Aniversario de Antofagasta (mid-Feb). 🌐 **municipalidadantofagasta.cl**

A historic port-city, Antofagasta is the sea outlet for the metals and minerals mined in the Atacama desert. Founded in 1869 as part of Bolivia, it was absorbed by Chile in the War of the Pacific (1879–83) and used to ship silver, nitrates and, from 1915, copper from the great Chuquicamata mine *(see p174)*. Chile's most progressive city by the 1930s, it appears today as a somewhat grimy place, but there is still some historic charm.

Set in the city center, the Neo-Gothic cathedral dates from 1917 and faces the Plaza Colón. The clock tower adorning the plaza was donated in 1910 by the city's English community and is a tangible reminder of British

influence in Antofagasta. Just north of the plaza, the former Customs House, dating from 1869, is home to the **Museo Regional de Antofagasta**. The museum's collection of over 9,000 objects includes fossils from the region, objects salvaged from the old nitrate mines, and period furniture.

At the end of the same road is **Ex-Estación El Ferrocarril de Antofagasta a Bolivia**, the city's former train station. Built in 1873 using British capital, this was the terminus for the Antofagasta-Bolivia railway. Designated a National Historic Landmark in 1981, it conserves Scottish steam trains, English clocks, and red telephone boxes. Trains carrying copper from the Chuquicamata mine still pass through this station on their way to the port. Also near the port is the **Muelle Histórico Salitrero** (Nitrates Wharf), which dates from 1872, and the Terminal Pesquero, Antofagasta's rustic fish market. The roof of the market forms the perch for dozens of pelicans.

Facing the Pacific Ocean, some 5 miles (8 km) south of the city center, are the massive stone remnants of a silver refinery dating from 1888–92. Known as the **Ruinas de Huanchaca**, this fascinating and intact site occupies a desert hillside in stepped terraces, and features a steep central staircase, a round tower, narrow passageways, and rows of stone storehouses. The Casino Enjoy Antofagasta, opposite the ruins, runs tours (including night tours)

Ruinas de Huanchaca, with Antofagasta's tower blocks in the background

for visitors. The casino's glitzy architecture mirrors the ruins with a round tower and terraced facade that lends a quasi-Aztecan symmetry to this site.

A small on-site museum displays geological, archaeological, and anthropological objects, including antique silver-refining machinery.

🏛 Ex-Estación El Ferrocarril de Antofagasta a Bolivia
Bolívar 255. **Tel** (055) 2546300.
Open 8:30am–7pm daily. 📷
🌐 estacionantofagasta.cl

🏛 Museo Regional de Antofagasta
Balmaceda 2786. **Tel** (055) 2227016.
Open 9am–5pm Tue–Fri,
11am–2pm Sat & Sun. 🈺 📷
🌐 museodeantofagasta.cl

🎭 Ruinas de Huanchaca
Avenida Angamos 01606. **Tel** (055) 2417860. 🚌 from Antofagasta. **Taxi** from Antofagasta. **Open** 10am–1pm & 2:30–7pm Tue–Sun. 🈺 📷

❷❽ La Portada

Road Map B3. 10 miles (16 km) N of Antofagasta: Ruta 5, Lado Norte. 🚌 from Antofagasta. **Open** daily. 🈺 📱 🏛

La Portada (The Gateway) is a natural sedimentary arch that faces dramatic coastline. The arch, eroded over seven million years, is visible from a parking area immediately to its north; however, descending from the seismically unstable headlands to the beach is prohibited. Visitors can explore the small CONAF-run museum on the cliff that overlooks the arch.

❷❾ Cerro Paranal Observatory

Road Map B3. 75 miles (120 km) S of Antofagasta; Cerro Paranal, Ruta B-710. **Tel** (055) 2716931. **Taxi** from Antofagasta. **Open** 2pm Sat. 📷 mandatory; book in advance.
🌐 eso.cl

One of the world's most advanced astronomical facilities, the Cerro Paranal Observatory is housed in a futuristic complex of brilliant-white buildings, sharp lines, and curved domes.

The VLT (Very Large Telescope) at Cerro Paranal Observatory

Stargazing in the Atacama Desert

Chile's Atacama desert boasts some of the world's clearest night skies and most hi-tech astronomical observatories. Open to visits, these include the facilities at Cerro Mamalluca (see p186) and Cerro Paranal. The latter is the location of the gigantic VLT, previously the world's most powerful telescope. In 2013, this awe-inspiring instrument was eclipsed when ALMA, a multi-billion-dollar facility, opened on a 16,400-ft (5,000-m) high plateau near San Pedro de Atacama. Financed by North American, European, and Asian governments in cooperation with Chile, ALMA is the single biggest astronomical project on the planet. It comprises a mind-boggling 50 antennae, each 39 ft (12 m) in diameter, that act as a single telescope and offer vision 10 times sharper than the Hubble Space Telescope. ALMA astrophysicists can, for the first time, see planets and super-massive black holes formed 10 billion years ago.

It stands at 8,500 ft (2,600 m) above sea level atop Cerro Paranal and is overseen by the European Southern Observatory (ESO). Its star attraction is the **Very Large Telescope** (VLT). One of the world's most powerful optical instruments, the VLT comprises four separate telescopes that combine to form one gigantic lens measuring 650 ft (200 m) in diameter. This lens can define objects four billion times fainter than any that are visible to the naked eye – that is the equivalent of distinguishing car headlights from the surface of the moon. Fascinating 2-hour guided tours follow a presentation on astronomy with visits to the VLT and its control room. Some scenes from the James Bond film *Quantum of Solace* were shot here.

Stargazing facilities at the Cerro Paranal Observatory

Shoreline of La Piscina, a stretch along the Bahía Inglesa, south of Caldera

❸⓿ Copiapó

Road Map B4. 351 miles (566 km) S of Antofagasta. 🏙 171,000. 🛫 🚌 🛈 Sernatur, Los Carrera 691; (052) 2212838. 🎭 Festival de la Virgen de la Candelaria (Feb). 🌐 **municipalidadcopiapo.cl**

Capital of Chile's Atacama (III) region, Copiapó is a low-key city whose attractions are linked to its silver-mining heritage. Silver was first found here in 1832 by the muleteer Juan Godoy. His statue stands in a plaza fronting the Iglesia de San Francisco, an 1872 church with ornate paintings. Chile's first (and now defunct) railway was built in 1851 to take silver from Copiapó to the port at Caldera. Flash floods and mudflows in early 2015 damaged some of the lovely wooden buildings from the 1800s on Avenida Manuel Matta.

Copiapó is centered around a plaza, which is fronted by a wooden cathedral from 1851. The Neo-Classical design of this edifice features an unusual three-tiered bell tower. Set at the city's western end is its grandest mansion, the **Palacio Viña de Cristo**, built in 1860 in the Georgian style for a silver baron. The **Museo Mineralógico** and **Museo Regional de Atacama** recount the Atacama region's history and mineral wealth.

🏛 **Museo Mineralógico**
Colipi 333. **Tel** (052) 2206606.
Open 9am–5pm Tue–Sun. 🐾 🎫

🏛 **Museo Regional de Atacama**
Atacama 98. **Tel** (052) 2212313. **Open** 9am–5:45pm Mon–Fri, 10am–12:45pm & 3–5:45pm Sat, 10am–12:45pm Sun. 🐾 Sun free. 🎫 with reservation only. 🌐 **museodeatacama.cl**

❸❶ Caldera

Road Map B4. 50 miles (80 km) W of Copiapó. 🏙 16,000. 🚌 🛈 Plaza Carlos Condell; (052) 2316076. 🚢 Sat. 🎭 La Fiesta de Recreación (mid-Jul). 🌐 **caldera.cl**

The colorful harbor town of Caldera grew in the late 1800s as a port for shipping silver brought in by the railway from Copiapó. Today, it has a picturesque waterfront of sparkling ocean and sandy beaches where pelicans congregate. On the waterfront, the **Terminal Pesquero** is the fishermen's harbor and market, where small ma-and-pa eateries serve fresh seafood specialties. Located next to it, the **Museo Paleontológico** is housed in Caldera's recycled railway station, built in 1850, and displays mammoth marine fossils. Its standout exhibit is a fossilized skull of a bearded whale that lived 10 million years ago. Once home to an Italian immigrant family, the red Neo-Classical mansion, **Casa Tornini**, was built in the 1890s. Guided tours in English,

German, and Spanish take in the appealing original furniture owned by the family. Occasional art exhibitions are also held here.

Environs
Just south of Caldera is northern Chile's most beautiful beach, named **Bahía Inglesa** (English Bay) for the swashbuckling English pirates who dropped anchor here in the 17th century. This long sweep of bleach-white sand is fronted by a turquoise ocean of calm, sheltered waters and blissfully little construction save a smattering of upscale hotels and restaurants.

🚍 **Bahía Inglesa**
4 miles (6 km) S of Caldera. 🚌
🛈 next to Hotel Rocas de Bahía.
🌐 **bahiainglesachile.com**

🏛 **Casa Tornini**
Paseo Gana 210. **Tel** (052) 2317930.
Open Jan & Feb: noon–8pm daily; Mar–Dec: 11:30am–4:30pm. 🐾 🎫 mandotry. ♿ 📷

🏛 **Museo Paleontológico**
Centro Cultural Estación Caldera, Wheelwright s/n. **Tel** (052) 2535604. **Open** 10:30am–1pm & 4–7pm Tue–Fri, 11am–2pm & 4–8pm Sat & Sun. 🐾 🎫 ♿ 📷

❸❷ Parque Nacional Pan de Azúcar

Road Map B4. 120 miles (194 km) NW of Copiapó; Ruta C-120, Km27 de Chañaral. **Taxi** from Copiapó. 🐾 🎫 🚿 🏔 🌐 **conaf.cl**

Created in 1985 to protect 169 sq miles (438 sq km) of coastal desert, this park has long white beaches, sheltered coves, and

Desert scenery in the Parque Nacional Pan de Azúcar

A flock of birds on Laguna Santa Rosa, in the Parque Nacional Nevado Tres Cruces

vertiginous sand cliffs. The striking coastline plays refuge to magnificent, easily sighted marine fauna. Dolphins, southern sea lions, gulls, Humboldt penguins, cormorants, and pelicans populate the shoreline. Coastal attractions include the offshore **Isla Pan de Azúcar**, a refuge to penguins and other seabirds, that is reached by boat excursion; and **Caleta Pan de Azúcar**, a picturesque fishermen's hamlet with campsites and cabins. Farther inland the flora and fauna includes guanacos, foxes, condors, and over 20 species of cactus. Scenic highlights include the Quebrada del Castillo and Quebrada Pan de Azúcar canyons, and the Mirador and Las Lomitas viewpoints that offer vistas of desert, coast, and the blue ocean.

❸ Parque Nacional Nevado Tres Cruces

Road Map B4. 94 miles (151 km) E of Copiapó. **Tel** (052) 2213404. ℹ️ CONAF, Laguna del Negro Francisco. **Open** 8:30am–6pm daily 🚗 from Copiapó. 🏕️ 🏔️ 🌐 conaf.cl

This remote but stunning national park conserves some 228 sq miles (591 sq km) of altiplano wilderness typified by colored lakes, snowy volcanoes, and abundant native fauna. Most visits focus on the northern sector, where **Laguna Santa Rosa**, an intensely blue saltwater lake, fills a depression ringed by the snowy peaks of the Nevados Tres Cruces massif. Next to the lake, the white Salar de Maricunga is Chile's southernmost salt flat.

Accessed via a 4WD route from Laguna Santa Rosa, the park's southern sector is less visited. Its greatest natural feature is **Laguna del Negro Francisco**, a lake with mirror-like waters which reflect the pointed cone of Volcán Copiapó and the giant wings of flapping flamingoes. Chile's three flamingo species are present on the lakeshore here, part of a wildlife bonanza that features some 30 bird species and easily sighted mammals, including vicuñas, guanacos, vizcachas, and Andean foxes. Walking trails circle around Laguna Santa Rosa and Laguna del Negro Francisco, where a 12-bed CONAF *refugio* offers lodging and hot showers.

❸ Laguna Verde

Road Map C4. 164 miles (265 km) NE of Copiapó. Along the CH31 toward the San Francisco border pass to Argentina. ℹ️ Sernatur, Los Carrera 691, Copiapó; (052) 2212838. 🚗 from Copiapó 🏔️ Volcán Ojos del Salado. **Open** Oct–Mar.

Located high in the Andes, at 13,780 ft (4,200 m) above sea level, Laguna Verde is a breathtaking lake of green and turquoise tones that change hue according to the light and time of day. On the lake's western shore, rustic hot springs provide blissful relaxation. Mighty volcanoes, including El Muerto, Peña Blanca, Incahuasi, Barrancas Blancas, and Vicuñas, encircle the area. Their snowy peaks and the brown, red, and ochre tones of their flanks complete an artist's palette of sharply contrasting colors. However, most of these peaks are challenging and hard to climb.

At 22,615 ft (6,893m), **Volcán Ojos del Salado** towers over the southern basin of Laguna Verde. This is the world's highest active volcano, as well as Chile's highest peak. The climb to its summit is physically challenging but technically undemanding.

Climbing Ojos del Salado requires permits from Chile's foreign ministry. There are shelters at several levels.

The turquoise waters of the Laguna Verde lake

35 La Serena

Founded in 1544, La Serena is Chile's second-oldest city and one of its biggest coastal resorts. Soon after it was established, the city was destroyed in an Indian attack, resettled in 1549, and later sacked by pirates, most famously by England's Bartholomew Sharp. Today, at La Serena's historical heart, the bell towers of Colonial churches ring out amid contemporary Spanish-style architecture. On the coast are golden beaches and rolling white waves, with modern buildings lining the avenues. At the mouth of Río Elqui, La Serena is also the gateway to the lush Valle del Elqui.

The granite fountain at the center of Plaza de Armas

Plaza de Armas

Museo Histórico Gabriel González Videla: Matta 495. **Tel** (051) 2217189. **Open** 10am–6pm Mon–Fri, 10am–1pm Sat. on request, in Spanish only. **museohistoricolaserena.cl**

La Serena's central plaza marks the site of the city's second founding by conquistador Francisco de Aguirre (1507–81). Located here is the limestone Catedral de La Serena as well as the Neo-Colonial Tribunales de la Justicia (Law Courts) and Municipalidad (City Hall). Both date from the 1930s and have extravagant red-and-white exteriors. A Modernist fountain by the sculptor Román Rojas adorns the center of this square. On a corner of the plaza is the **Museo Histórico Gabriel González Videla**, housed in the 19th-century family home of the former Chilean president whose name it bears. The first floor displays personal objects of the late president, and a regional historical museum occupies the floor upstairs.

Catedral de La Serena

Plaza de Armas. Museo Sala de Arte Religioso: Los Carrera 450. **Tel** (051) 2216956. **Open** 9am–1pm & 3–6pm Tue–Sun.

The Neo-Classical facade and proud, prow-like tower of La Serena's cathedral stand majestically over the Plaza de Armas. Built from limestone under the direction of French architect Juan Herbage in 1844, this cathedral preserves the tomb of conquistador Francisco de Aguirre. The building itself stands on the site of a previous cathedral destroyed in 1680 by English pirate Bartholomew Sharp, who sacked the city over three days before razing it to the ground. Beautiful stained-glass windows from France ornament the cathedral's walls. Located on the building's grounds, the **Museo Sala de Arte Religioso** displays religious art and objects from the 17th to 19th centuries.

Catedral de La Serena

Iglesia de San Francisco

Balmaceda 640. **Tel** (051) 2224477. **Open** 8am–1pm & 4–9pm Tue–Fri. Museo de Colonial Iglesia San Francisco: **Open** 10:30am–1pm & 3–6pm Mon–Fri, 10am–2pm Sat & Sun.

Built between 1585 and 1590, the Iglesia de San Francisco is the oldest of La Serena's stone churches, and the only one of the city's temples to escape destruction at the hands of the pirate Sharp. The church is crowned by a bell tower and cupola, and its exterior walls are flamboyantly carved with Baroque motifs: a design that is considered mestizo for its South American influences. Adjacent to the church, the **Museo de Colonial Iglesia San Francisco** holds a collection of religious art and imagery dating from the arrival of the Franciscan Order to Chile in the 16th century, including a Bible penned in 1538.

Museo Arqueológico

Cordovez, esq. Cienfuegos. **Tel** (051) 2672210. **Open** 9:30am–6pm Tue–Fri, 10am–1pm & 4–7pm Sat, 10am–1pm Sun. on request, in Spanish only. **museoarqueologicalaserena.cl**

Entered via an 18th-century Baroque portal, La Serena's archaeological museum displays pre-Columbian objects from Norte Chico, Norte Grande, and Easter Island. Artifacts include petroglyphs carved by the Molle civilization (AD 1–700) and ceramics painted by the Diaguita between AD 1000 and 1536. The most remarkable exhibits include a 1,500-year-old mummy dug up in the Atacama desert close to Chiu-Chiu *(see p174)*, and a 10-ft (3-m) tall *moai* from Easter Island.

The baroque entrance to the city's Museo Arqueológico

For hotels and restaurants in this region see pp278–9 and pp294–5

Desierto Florido

Glory-of-the-sun in the Desierto Florido

Every 4–5 years, the sparse rainfall on a section of the Atacama causes dormant seeds beneath the sands to explode into a profusion of life and color in a phenomenon called the Desierto Florido (Flowering Desert). When this happens, the monochrome desert floor turns overnight into a carpet of flamboyant flowers of vibrant blues, purples, yellows, and reds that attracts a rich bird and insect life, as well as thousands of visitors from across Chile. It is impossible to predict the year of the Desierto Florido, only that it occurs between September and November. It last happened in 2015.

⯐ Museo Mineralógico

Benavente 980. **Tel** (051) 2204096. **Open** 9:30am–12:30pm & 2–5pm Mon–Fri. 🛈 non-Chileans only. 📷 on request, in Spanish only.

Set in the Universidad de La Serena, the museum of mining and metallurgy features over 2,000 mineral and rock samples collected by Polish mineralogist Ignacio Domeyko, who arrived in Chile at the height of its 19th-century mining boom. Displays include samples from each of Chile's major mining zones and exhibits of all their minerals, from gold to magnesium, which glitter and shine in glass display boxes. The most compelling exhibits are great boulder-sized, multicolored crystallized rock samples, and a meteorite that crashed into the Atacama desert in 1861. Displays also include mineral samples collected from Europe, Asia, and Africa.

The modern city blocks and sandy beach at La Serena

VISITORS' CHECKLIST

Practical Information
Road Map B5. 435 miles (700 km) S of Antofagasta. 🚗 198,000. 🛈 Sernatur, Matta 461; (051) 2225199. 🎉 Aniversario de La Serena (end Aug).
🌐 **turismolaserena.cl**

Transport
✈ Aeropuerto La Florida. 🚌

Avenida del Mar
🚡 🖊 📷 🏛 🚡

La Serena's 4-mile (6-km) long coastal boulevard is the city's thriving restaurant and bar zone. The avenue, lined by sandy beaches and big white waves on one side and by modern hotels, apartment blocks, bars, and restaurants on the other, is a frenzy of day and night time activity in summer. In the off-peak season, it offers dramatic sea walks, especially at sunset. A 20-minute walk from the center, west along the city's main Avenida Francisco de Aguirre, leads to **El Faro Monumental**, a lighthouse marking the northern end of Avenida del Mar. Beaches around this area are rustic, with big waves that attract surfers. Just south of the lighthouse are the main bathing beaches, **Playa 4 Esquinas** and **Playa Canto del Agua**, with plenty of bars and restaurants.

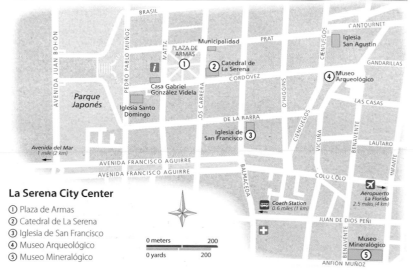

La Serena City Center

① Plaza de Armas
② Catedral de La Serena
③ Iglesia de San Francisco
④ Museo Arqueológico
⑤ Museo Mineralógico

0 meters 200
0 yards 200

Painted facade of Iglesia de la Inmaculada Concepción, Vicuña

⊕ Vicuña

Road Map B5. 39 miles (63 km) E of La Serena. 🚗 25,000. 🚌 ℹ️ Gabriela Mistral, esq. San Martín; (051) 2670308. 🎉 Fiesta de la Vendimia (Feb). **W** turismovicuna.cl

Set in the valley of Río Elqui, Vicuña is a small town of adobe houses ringed by rippled mountains. The birthplace of Chile's Nobel-prize-winning poet, Gabriela Mistral (see p30), it is a popular pilgrimage site for writers and artists. The **Museo Gabriela Mistral** displays personal items of the celebrated poet, including books, paintings, and awards. At the center of town, sculptures inspired by Mistral's works adorn Vicuña's plaza. Overlooking the plaza is the landmark **Torre Bauer**, an incongruous yet charming red Bavarian tower. It was constructed in 1905 at the behest of Vicuña's former mayor of German descent, Alfonso Bauer. Adjacent to the tower, the cabildo (town hall) dates from 1826 and houses a small, historically

themed museum as well as an information office for visitors. Also bordering the plaza, the **Iglesia de la Inmaculada Concepción** was built in 1909 and has a luminous interior with beautiful frescoes on the ceiling. The font here was used to baptize Mistral in 1889.

Located two blocks east of the plaza, the **Museo Casa El Solar de los Madariaga** is a restored adobe house from 1875 with period furnishings, photographs, and artifacts. At the edge of town is **Planta Capel**, Chile's biggest pisco distillery. Guided tours take visitors to its vineyards, plant facilities, and a pisco museum, and end with tastings.

🏛 Museo Casa El Solar de los Madariaga
Gabriela Mistral 683. **Tel** (051) 2411220. **Open** Dec–Mar: 10am–2pm & 3–7pm Wed–Mon; Apr–Nov: 11am–1pm & 3–6pm Wed–Mon. 🎥 📷 on request; in Spanish, English, & French. **W** solardelosmadariaga.cl

🏛 Museo Gabriela Mistral
Gabriela Mistral 759. **Tel** (051) 2411223. **Open** Jan–Feb: 10am–7pm daily; Mar–Dec: 10am–5:45pm Mon–Fri, 10:30am–6pm Sat, 10am–1pm Sun. 🎥 **W** mgmistral.cl

🏛 Planta Capel
Camino a Peralillo s/n. **Tel** (051) 2554336. **Open** Jan–Feb: 10am–7:30pm daily; Mar–Dec: 10am–6pm daily. 🎥 📷 ♿ 🚻 📶 📷 **W** centroturisticocapel.cl

⊕ Cerro Mamalluca Observatory

Road Map B5. 6 miles (9 km) NE of Vicuña. ℹ️ Gabriela Mistral 260, Vicuña; (051) 2670330. 🎥 📷 mandatory; reservations & departures at information center in Vicuña (summer: 8:30pm–2:30am; winter: 7:30pm–1:30am). 📷 📷 **W** turismoastronomico.cl

One of the greatest attractions of visiting Valle del Elqui is stargazing at the fascinating Cerro Mamalluca Observatory. A large complex of huge telescopes and white domed buildings that sit like giant golf balls on the mountainside. The facility is seen on guided tours that are conducted in English and Spanish and last up to 2 hours. Visitors can spot the Milky Way, star constellations thousands of light years away, planets, nebulae and clusters, as well as blue and red stars, with the lens of powerful telescopes. Other highlights include watching the rings on Jupiter and Saturn, and craters on the surface of the moon, all of which appear with a photographic clarity in one of the clearest night skies in the world.

⊕ Observatorio del Pangue

Road Map B5. 11 miles (17 km) S of Vicuña. **Tel** (051) 2412584. **W** odp-i.blogspot.co.uk

Run by French and Chilean astronomers, Observatorio del Pangue conducts intimate nightly tours of the stars. The tour is conducted by the astronomers at 8:30pm every night, with a maximum of 10 people.

Part of the Cerro Mamalluca Observatory complex near Vicuña, Valle del Elqui

A statue honoring poet Gabriela Mistral in Montegrande

⑨ Montegrande

Road Map B5. 63 miles (101 km) E of La Serena. 🚍 600. 🚌 from La Serena & Vicuña.

The tiny Andean village of Montegrande lies at the eastern end of Valle del Elqui at 3,600 ft (1,100 m) above sea level. Here, the valley narrows to a width of just 1,312 ft (400 m) and is surrounded by the steep slopes of the pre-cordillera, behind which the snowcapped peaks of the Andes form a backdrop.

Montegrande was also the hamlet where poet Gabriela Mistral spent her childhood, having moved here from Vicuña with her mother and stepsister when she was three years old. The small house in which Mistral grew up is preserved as the **Museo de Sitio Casa-Escuela Gabriela Mistral**. The house doubled as the village school when Mistral lived here and has furniture and personal belongings of the poet.

Prior to her death from cancer in 1957, Mistral had requested that she be laid to rest in her "beloved Montegrande"; her tomb lies on the crest of a low hill near the village plaza. Facing this small tree-lined plaza is a church. Built in 1879, it is crowned by a tall bell tower. Mistral took her first communion in its decorative interior.

🏛 **Museo de Sitio Casa-Escuela Gabriela Mistral**
Open 9am–1pm & 2–7pm Mon–Fri. ♿

⑩ Pisco Elqui

Road Map B5. 65 miles (105 km) SE of La Serena. 🚍 700. 🚌 from La Serena & Montegrande. 🌐 **piscoelqui.com**

Set 4,100 ft (1,250 m) above sea level, Pisco Elqui is one of the prettiest villages of Valle del Elqui. It was originally christened La Unión by the Spanish, but renamed in 1936 as part of a government initiative to boost the area's most famous commodity, *pisco*. Among the best-known distilleries here is the **Destilería Pisco Mistral**, formerly the Solar de Pisco Tres Erres. This facility has been making *pisco* for over a century. Guided tours take visitors to its *pisco* museum and to the production, barrelling, and bottling salons, and end with tastings.

Destilería Pisco Mistral
O'Higgins 746. **Tel** (051) 2451358.
Open Jan–Feb: noon–7pm daily; Mar–Dec: 11am–5pm Tue–Sun.
🚗 📷 hourly. ✍ 💻 📷
🌐 destileriapiscomistral.cl

㊶ Paso del Agua Negra

Road Map B5. 115 miles (185 km) E of Vicuña.

A spectacular drive from Vicuña, Ruta 41 snakes up into the arid mountains, rising up to the highest, 15,633-ft- (4,765-m-), Andean border crossing between Chile and Argentina. The drive is made particularly spectacular by the presence of *penitentes* (enormous snow pinnacles sculpted into unearthly shapes by the fierce wind), named after the hunched forms of penitent monks.

Sprawling *pisco* vineyards on the slopes of Pisco Elqui

Pisco

First developed by Spanish settlers in the 16th century, *pisco* is an aromatic, fruity brandy made from distilled Muscat grape wine. Chile's unrivaled national drink, it is commonly consumed as *pisco sour*, a refreshing aperitif made by mixing *pisco*, lemon juice, and sugar. It is also drunk neat and as *piscola*, a fashionable highball cocktail that mixes *pisco* with cola and is a favorite among nightclubbing Chileans. Travelers can taste *pisco* in its many guises during visits to distilleries in the Valle del Elqui.

Bottled *pisco* produced at Planta Capel in the Valle del Elqui

㊷ Ovalle

Road Map B5. 53 miles (86 km) S of La Serena. 🚗 98,100. 🚌 ℹ️ Victoria, esq. Independencia; (053) 2622108. 🅿️ 🏠 🏕️ 🗺️ La Fiesta de Vendimia (Mar). 🚃 **W** **ovalleencantonativo.cl**

Little visited, Valle del Limarí is a fertile area of orchards and farms that feeds much of the arid Norte Chico. The valley's largest settlement is Ovalle, a small city ringed by monochrome peaks. Farmers from the valley sell their produce at **Feria Modelo de Ovalle**, the city's great food market. On any day, the floor space is stacked with rows of spices, mounds of goat's cheese, fruit pyramids, and hanging fish. In the city center, the **Iglesia de San Vicente Ferrer** faces Ovalle's tree-lined plaza. Built in 1888, it has a strikingly tall bell tower and an ornate interior. The city's big draw is the outstanding **Museo del Limarí** which exhibits pre-Hispanic items from the local area and features Chile's most impressive displays of Diaguita ceramics (AD 1000–1536).

Environs

Ovalle is a springboard for visits to Valle del Limarí's wineries and villages. West of the city is the picturesque oasis village of **Barraza**, with narrow adobe streets and a church that dates from 1681. The upright tombs of former priests are encased in its adobe walls. Also in the western sector are the wineries **Viña Tabalí** and **Viña Casa Tamaya**, which open for tours and tastings.

One of the historic lava caves at Monumento Natural Pichasca

🏛️ **Museo del Limarí**
Covarrubias, esq. Antofagasta, Ovalle. **Tel** (053) 2433680. **Open** 10am–6pm Tue–Fri, 10am–2pm Sat & Sun. 🖼️ Sun free. 📷 on request. ♿ **W** **museolimari.cl**

🍷 **Viña Casa Tamaya**
Camino Quebrada Seca Km 9, Ovalle. **Tel** (053) 2686014. **W** **tamaya.cl**

🍷 **Viña Tabalí**
Hacienda Santa Rosa de Tabalí, Ruta Valle del Encanto. **Tel** (02) 2477-5535. **Open** 10am–6pm Mon–Fri; on request Sat & Sun. 🖼️ 📷 **W** **tabali.com**

㊸ Reserva Nacional Pinguino de Humboldt

Road Map B5. 54 miles (87 km) N of La Serena. **Tel** (051) 2244769. ℹ️ CONAF, park entrance. **W** **conaf.cl**

Named after the Humboldt penguins that breed here, this 2,195 acres (888 ha) reserve consists of three islands off the rocky coast. It is a popular day trip from La Serena. Almost 10,000 pairs of this vulnerable penguin species nest in the reserve, particularly on Isla de Choros. Zodiac offers boat tours that make landings on the more accessible Isla Damas. Visitors are advised to stick to the established paths and not to disturb the birds. While on the boat, visitors can hear and smell the sea lion colony that also call this area home. Pods of bottle-nosed dolphins and sea otters also make an occasional appearance.

㊹ Monumento Natural Pichasca

Road Map B5. 34 miles (55 km) NE of Ovalle, Valle del Limarí. **Tel** (053) 2620058. 🚌 from Ovalle to 3 miles (5 km) before entrance. **Open** 9am–5:30pm daily. 🖼️ 📷 from Ovalle. 📷 **W** **conaf.cl**

Rich in palaeontological and archaeological finds, the Monumento Natural Pichasca is

The tree-shaded Plaza de Armas at Ovalle

a site with petrified forests of fossil-ized tree trunks, gigantic dinosaur fossils, and 11,000-year-old rock paintings in ancient lava caves.

The area was also a refuge for hunter-gatherers around 8000 BC. Tours begin at a visitors' center that has displays on the area's fauna, flora, palaeontology, and archaeology. From here, a 2-mile (3-km) long walking trail explores the site, which also includes life-size replicas of the gigantic dinosaurs that once roamed this region.

45 Monumento Nacional Valle del Encanto

Road Map B5. 16 miles (25 km) SW of Ovalle; D45, Valle del Encanto. from Ovalle to 3 miles (5 km) from entrance. **Open** Jan–Feb: 8:30am–8pm daily; Mar–Dec: 8:30am–6:30pm daily. from Ovalle.

An ancient ceremonial and hunting ground, this site has Chile's finest collection of El Molle petroglyphs, dating from around AD 700. Viewed from a marked circuit, there are more than 30 petroglyphs, etched onto rockfaces using sharp stones. Most are line drawings depicting human, zoomorphic, abstract, and geometric shapes. The human portraits are most interesting: entire families are shown in various poses with fingers pointing upward at the sun or downward, at Mother Earth. The shamans and deities in these carvings are crowned with tiaras and headdresses. The petroglyphs are best seen at noon, when the sharp midday light shows them at their most impressive.

Another highlight of the site is the *piedras tacitas* – slabs of flat rock gouged with large patterns of identical, circular, and deep holes that were probably used as mortars for grinding food and for ceremonial purposes, including the preparation of hallucinogens. There are also smaller, earlier depressions known as cupules, the purpose of which was decorative.

46 Termas de Socos

Road Map B5. 24 miles (38 km) SW of Ovalle; Panamericana Norte, Km370. **Tel** (53) 2631490. **Open** 8:30am–7pm daily (spa).

Encircled by rugged canyons in the Valle del Limarí, Termas de Socos is a family-owned spa retreat open to day and overnight visitors. Its amenities include massage treatments, thermal baths, and an exterior pool that is ringed by cacti as well as pepper and eucalyptus trees. There is a rustic but refined feel to this place – poolside vistas rise to rocky canyons, wild honey grows in the spa's gardens, hummingbirds abound, and guests are accommodated in comfortable rooms.

For budget travelers, there is a separate campsite with its own thermal baths. Staff run trips to Monumento Nacional Valle del Encanto and Parque Nacional Bosque Fray Jorge.

At night, guests can gaze at the stars from this spa's canyon-top observatory.

47 Parque Nacional Bosque Fray Jorge

Road Map B5. 56 miles (90 km) W of Ovalle; Km26 de la Ruta Patrimonial. **Tel** (051) 2244769. **Open** 9am–4pm daily. CONAF, park entrance. **conaf.cl**

The highlight of this UNESCO biosphere reserve is a relictual Valdivian rain forest – a remnant of the temperate rain forest that cloaked all Norte Chico prior to

Boardwalk through the forest at Parque Nacional Bosque Fray Jorge

the southward advancement of the Atacama desert, some 30,000 years ago.

The densest forest occurs on the western slopes of the coastal mountains that reach as high as 1,837 ft (560 m). It owes its continued existence to the high rainfall that hits the mountain peak each year – around 47 inches (120 cm) per year compared with just 4 inches (10 cm) on the semi-arid lowlands directly to the mountain's east. The park is at its most impressive between October and December, when, after heavy rainfall, the forest floor is carpeted with flowers.

A vehicle route and a 6-mile (10-km) long walking trail strike west from the park entrance, where a CONAF center has displays on the area's flora. Overlooking the Pacific, a short boardwalk traverses the lush forest. At mid-morning visitors can see the mist-shrouded rain forest.

A veranda with cane furnishings at the Termas de Socos

LAKE DISTRICT AND CHILOÉ

Named for the string of blue lakes that spreads across its entirety, Chile's Lake District features emerald forests, smoldering volcanoes, bubbling thermal springs, and tumbling rivers and waterfalls. Immediately south of the district, and separated from it by a narrow channel, lies enchanting Chiloé, an island archipelago of misty bays, quaint *palafitos*, and historic Jesuit churches.

The Lake District is bounded to its north by the Río Bío-Bío and to its south by the Canal Chacao, the sea-channel that links it to the Chiloé archipelago. In pre-Columbian times, the Lake District was populated by Mapuche communities, and Chiloé by the seafaring Chono.

The Spaniards arrived in 1552 and established what are today the region's largest cities, including Valdivia, Villarrica, and Osorno. However, much of the area remained a Mapuche stronghold even after independence, when Chile launched the Araucanian wars *(see p49)* to supress all indigenous resistance. Subsequently, the area opened up to European immigrants, notably German settlers, who greatly influenced the architecture, art, and cuisine of the urban centers they established in the Lake District.

By the late 19th century, railroad construction had sparked agriculture, forestry, and port industries, with the city of Temuco emerging as the Lake District's main commercial center. In the Chiloé archipelago, fishing, in particular salmon farming, has become the bedrock of the economy. Today, a booming tourism sector has brought added prosperity to both the Lake District and Chiloé.

The region's national parks are a favored destination for outdoor activities, including skiing down volcano slopes and horse riding through ancient araucaria (monkey-puzzle) forests. These parks are accessible from lakeshore towns that also offer splendid examples of Teutonic-style architecture, while the Chiloé archipelago fascinates with its rich mythology, distinct cuisine, and vibrant festivals.

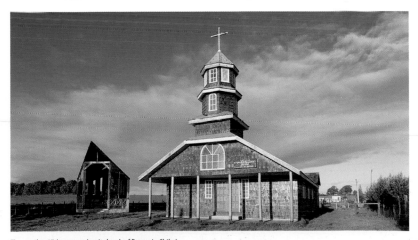

The wooden 17th-century Jesuit church of Degan in Chiloé

◀ Colorful fishing boats at Ancud, Chiloé

Exploring the Lake District and Chiloé

The Andean foothills in the Lake District's eastern section embrace lake, volcano, and forest scenery in reserves such as Parque Nacional Conguillío, Parque Nacional Vicente Pérez Rosales, and Parque Nacional Villarrica. Lakeshore towns and cities provide ideal stopovers: Pucón is the area's adventure-tourism capital, Frutillar and Puerto Varas its German heartland, and Temuco and Villarrica its historic Mapuche towns. West of the mountains, the land dips, crossing a central valley to the Pacific coast, to Valdivia, a beautiful port-city encircled by historic fortresses. Farther south, a short ferry ride from the city of Puerto Montt leads to the Chiloé archipelago, where Jesuit churches alternate with wooden *palafitos*.

Rafting on Río Petrohué, Parque Nacional Vicente Pérez Rosales

Sights at a Glance

Villages, Towns, and Cities

- ① *Temuco pp194–5*
- ⑦ Villarrica
- ⑧ Pucón
- ⑭ Licán Ray
- ⑮ Coñaripe
- ⑯ Panguipulli
- ⑱ *Valdivia pp206–7*
- ㉒ Osorno
- ㉖ Puerto Octay
- ㉗ Frutillar
- ㉘ Puerto Varas
- ㉚ *Puerto Montt pp216–17*
- ㉝ Calbuco
- ㉞ Ancud
- ㊱ *Castro pp220–21*
- ㊳ Dalcahue
- ㊴ Curaco de Vélez
- ㊵ Achao
- ㊶ Chonchi
- ㊷ Quellón

Resorts and Spas

- ③ Termas de Malalcahuello
- ④ Ski Center Corralco
- ㉔ Termas de Puyehue

National Parks, Reserves, and Natural Monuments

- ② Parque Nacional Tolhuaca
- ⑤ *Parque Nacional Conguillío pp198–9*
- ⑪ Parque Nacional Huerquehue
- ⑫ Santuario Cañi
- ⑬ *Parque Nacional Villarrica pp202–3*
- ⑳ Santuario de la Naturaleza Carlos Anwandter
- ㉓ Parque Nacional Puyehue
- ㉙ *Parque Nacional Vicente Pérez Rosales pp214–15*
- ㉛ Parque Nacional Alerce Andino
- ㊲ Parque Nacional Chiloé

Areas of Natural Beauty

- ⑥ Nevados de Sollipulli
- ⑨ Lago Caburgua
- ⑩ Ojos del Caburgua
- ⑰ Reserva Biológica Huilo-Huilo
- ㉑ Lago Ranco
- ㉕ Lago Llanquihue
- ㉜ Cochamó Valley
- ㉟ Monumento Natural Islotes de Puñihuil
- ㊸ Parque Tantauco

Sites of Interest

- ⑲ Forts around Valdivia

Castro's *palafitos* lining the water's edge, Chiloé

Getting Around

The well-paved Pan-American Highway (Ruta 5) runs through the Lake District, making traveling by bus the best way to explore the area. Long-distance buses link major cities, while smaller micros connect lakeshore towns with major national parks, although a sturdy car, preferably a 4WD, is needed to reach some parts of the Andean foothills. Daily flights connect Santiago to the airports at Temuco and Puerto Montt. From Puerto Montt, ferries take buses across the Canal Chacao to Chiloé. Frequent bus and ferry services link sites in the archipelago.

For hotels and restaurants in this region see pp279–80 and pp295–7

Tijeral
Angol
Trintre
Collipulli
PARQUE NACIONAL TOLHUACA 2
SKI CENTER CORRALCO
Victoria
Volcán Lonquimay 9,481 ft **4**
Traiguen
ARAUCANÍA
Curacautín
3 TERMAS DE MALALCAHUELLO
Tirúa
Lautaro
5 PARQUE NACIONAL CONGUILLIO
TEMUCO 1
General López
Volcán Llaima 10,253 ft
Caroline
Melipeuco
Puerto Saavedra
Río Quepe Freire
Cunco
6 NEVADOS DE SOLLIPULLI
Puerto Domínguez
LAGO CABURGUA
9
11 PARQUE NACIONAL HUERQUEHUE
Gualpín
OJOS DE CABURGUA
Lago Villarrica **10**
VILLARRICA 7
8
12 SANTUARIO CAÑI
Mehuín
Lanco
PUCÓN
Curarrehue
LICÁN RAY 14
13 PARQUE NACIONAL VILLARRICA
SANTUARIO DE LA NATURALEZA CARLOS ANWANDTER 20 Máfil
CH203
Lago Calafquén
15
COÑARIPE
PANGUIPULLI 16
T39
Neltume
VALDIVIA
Riñihue
17 RESERVA BIOLÓGICA HUILO-HUILO
18 Enco
Puerto Fuy
FORTS AROUND VALDIVIA 19
207
Paillaco
Volcán Mocho Choshuenco 7,923 ft
Futrono
La Unión
Río Bueno
5
LAGO RANCO
T85
21
San Pablo
Volcán Puyehue 7,319 ft
LOS LAGOS
Pucatrihue
TERMAS DE PUYEHUE
23 PARQUE NACIONAL PUYEHUE
OSORNO 22 CH215
Volcán Casablanca 7,349 ft
Maicolpué
U40
Entre Lagos
24
Puyehue
Purranque
PUERTO OCTAY
Volcán Osorno 8,700 ft
Lago Todos Los Santos
Volcán Tronador 11,660 ft
Bariloche
26
LAGO LLANQUIHUE 25
Petrohué
29 PARQUE NACIONAL VICENTE PÉREZ ROSALES
FRUTILLAR 27
Llanquihue
CH225
Ralún
PACIFIC OCEAN
PUERTO VARAS 28
Volcán Calbuco 6,568 ft
32 COCHAMÓ VALLEY
PUERTO MONTT 30
31 PARQUE NACIONAL ALERCE ANDINO
Maullín
Río Maullín
Seno de Reloncaví
La Arena
Canal Chacao
Pargua
33 CALBUCO
Bahía Puñihuil
34 ANCUD
Golfo de Ancud
MONUMENTO NATURAL ISLOTES DE PUÑIHUIL 35
Degán
Quemchi
PARQUE NACIONAL CHILOÉ 37
Quicaví
DALCAHUE
38
CURACO DE VÉLEZ
39
CASTRO 36
Rilán
40 ACHAO
CHONCHI 41
Aituy
Queilen
5
ISLA GRANDE DE CHILOÉ
42 QUELLÓN
Golfo de Corcovado
PARQUE TANTAUCO 43 Inio

0 km   50
0 miles   50

Key
Highway
Major road
Minor road
Untarred minor road
Main railway
Minor railway
Regional border
International border
△ Peak

For keys to symbols *see back flap*

❶ Temuco

Set in the former Mapuche heartland, Temuco traces its origins to a fortress settlement established during the 19th century – the city itself was officially founded in 1881. The construction of the railroad and European immigration in the 20th century brought about rapid growth. Today, Temuco is a commercial hub with busy plazas and museums. Famous for colorful markets attended by Mapuche traders and artisans, the city is also an ideal base for exploring the natural beauty of the surrounding countryside.

Urban Temuco from the crest of Cerro Ñielol

🏛 Museo Regional de la Araucanía
Avenida Alemania 084. **Tel** (045) 274 7948. **Open** 9:30am–5:30pm Tue–Fri, 11am–5pm Sat, 11am–2pm Sun. 🚻 📷 🌐 museoregionalaraucania.cl

Housed in a 1924 mansion, this museum records the often bloody history of Chile's Araucanía region (*see map, p193*) through a collection of some 3,000 archaeological, ethnographic, and historical objects. Among them is one of the country's most impressive collection of Mapuche objects, including stunning 19th-century weavings and an array of elaborate silver jewelry, heavy necklaces and belts. Also on display are conquistador firearms, 17th- century religious objects, pioneer-era photographs of Temuco, and a life-size reconstruction of a *ruca* (communal thatched house).

🌿 Monumento Natural Cerro Ñielol
Avenida Arturo Prat s/n. **Tel** (045) 2298222. **Open** 8am–9pm daily. 📷 on request. 🚻 📷 📱

A protected hillside, Cerro Ñielol harbors a species-rich temperate rain forest that once covered the Araucanía region. Walking trails explore native evergreen woods of coigüe and arrayan, and lagoons that provide refuge for an abundant birdlife. One of the trails leads to **La Patagua del Armisticio**, a site commemorating the signing of an armistice in 1881 between the Mapuche and the Chilean government, by which the Mapuche ceded territory for the founding of Temuco. The hill's crest offers extraordinary panoramic city vistas.

🏛 Plaza Teodoro Schmidt
Avenida Arturo Prat, esq. Lautaro.

Shaded by lime, oak, and palm trees, Plaza Teodoro Schmidt is best known as the site of the city's **Feria Arte**. This important crafts fair, held each year in February, features wood-carvings, ceramics, and weavings made by artisans from across the country.

🛒 Mercado Municipal
Between Calles Diego Portales, M. Rodríguez, Aldunate, & Avenida M. Bulnes. **Open** Oct–Mar: 8am–8pm Mon–Sat, 8:30am–3pm Sun; Apr–Sep: 8am–6pm Mon–Sat, 8:30am–3pm Sun. 📷

A sprawling indoor market, Mercado Municipal combines the grandeur of early 20th-century European architecture with the vibrancy of modern Chile. The market building dates from 1930 and features a central fountain under an English-style cast-iron roof. At the heart of the market, local craftsmen sell high-quality woollens, weavings, and woodcarvings. The market is also the best place in Temuco to feast on shellfish and seafood specialties.

🏛 Plaza Aníbal Pinto
Avenida Arturo Prat, esq. Claro Solar. 📱

The city's main plaza is planted with native trees and exotic palms, and centered on the **Monumento a la Araucanía**, a bronze-and-stone sculpture that pays homage to this area's principal colonizers. The figure of a robed *machi* (female Mapuche shaman) crowns the monument and is flanked by four other figures – a Mapuche hunter with a spear; a Spanish conquistador with a Christian cross; a 19th-century soldier; and a settler farmer. A stylized rock-face symbolizing the Andes forms the base of the monument.

The arched entrance to Temuco's bustling Mercado Municipal

Fruit and vegetable stalls at the Feria Libre Aníbal Pinto

Feria Libre Aníbal Pinto

Ave. Aníbal Pinto, esq. Balmaceda.
Open 7am–5pm daily.

Temuco's rustic open-air market
is a high-energy nexus of
feverish trading and stimu-
lating smells. Traders here sell
pungent cheese, herbs, spices,
vegetables, and fruit, including
piñones (araucaria nuts),
cochayuyo (dried seaweed),
and *merquen* (smoky, spicy
chilli powder), a staple part of
the Mapuche diet. Mapuche
women travel in from outlying
districts to sit in groups selling
flour, eggs, and *mote* (husked
wheat). Small restaurants in the
center of the market serve local
specialties such as *pastel de
choclo (see p287)* and seafood
dishes. More stalls stocking
traditional *huaso* hats, stirrups,
and spurs ring this market's
outer limits.

Museo Nacional Ferroviario Pablo Neruda

Avenida Barros Arana 0565. **Tel** (045)
2973941. **Open** Oct–Mar: 9am–6pm
Tue–Fri, 10am–6pm Sat & Sun, Apr–
Sep: 9am–6pm Tue–Fri, 10am–6pm
Sat, 11am–5pm Sun.
tacb.cl

Chile's national railway museum
occupies the old headquarters
of the country's national railroad, a UNESCO World Heritage

The Presidential Train at Museo Nacional
Ferroviario Pablo Neruda

Site. Its great attraction is
the old **Casa de Máquinas**
(Locomotive Hall), a cavernous
oval construction built 1929–43
for the maintenance of
locomotives. Today, the hall
preserves rows of old trains,
such as the Presidential
Train, built in Germany in
1920 and used by all Chilean
presidents between 1924 and
2004, barring General Pinochet.
Tours of the train's sumptuous
interior include the presidential
quarters, linked to the First Lady's
bedroom via a hidden door.
The old Administrative Hall
features photographic displays.

The museum is named for
Temuco's most celebrated son,
Pablo Neruda (see p91), whose
father was a lifelong employee
of the railways. Neruda's many
odes to Chile's railroad adorn
plaques throughout this large
and beautifully curated museum.

Temuco City Center

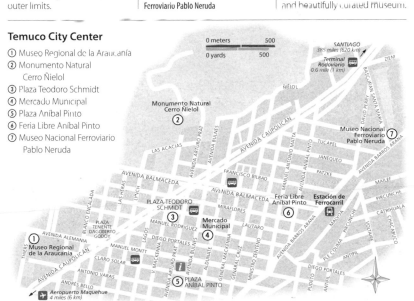

❷ Parque Nacional Tolhuaca

Road Map E1. 81 miles (130 km) NE of Temuco; Acceso 1, road via village of Inspector Fernández. **Tel** (02) 2840-6830. 🚌 from Temuco. ℹ️ CONAF office near southeastern entrance to park. **Open** 8:30am–7pm daily. 🥾 ⛰️ 🅦 conaf.cl

Set in the far north of the Lake District and distant from the region's more traveled routes, Parque Nacional Tolhuaca conserves a highly scenic area of the Andean foothills, where altitudes vary from 3,280 ft (1,000 m) to 5,974 ft (1,821 m) above sea level. The park encompasses wild temperate rain forest famous for the prehistoric araucaria (*Araucaria araucana*), also called the monkey-puzzle tree. Attractive trails through the pristine forests offer great bird-watching; among the more easily observed species are the Chilean parakeet (*Microsittace ferruginea*), several types of duck, and the Andean condor. Swimming, fishing, and hiking are also popular activities in this park. Tolhuaca's most hiked trail, the **Sendero Salto Malleco**, skirts the northern shore of Lago Malleco, the park's dominant feature, before crossing native forest to the stunning 164-ft (50-m) high Salto Malleco waterfalls.

Another picturesque hike edges along the **Laguna Verde**, which lies 4,264 ft (1,300 m) above sea level and is ringed by small waterfalls and spindly araucaria woods. Other treks in the area include the **Sendero Lagunillas** and the **Sendero Mesacura**. The first is an undemanding climb to a set of mountain lagoons, where 360-degree views encompass the 9,206-ft (2,806-m) high Volcán Tolhuaca. The second passes through dense forest. Both are full-day hikes and require advance planning.

Just south of the park lie the thermal pools of **Termas Malleco**. Located in a canyon, the natural sauna created by the rocks and sulfurous steam provide the ideal spot to relax after a long hike. Formerly known as Termas de Tolhuaca, Malleco has refurbished the facilities of what was once a worn-down hot springs resort. It is now open for both day use and overnighters (for more activities, check website; www.termasmalleco.cl).

The distinctive monkey-puzzle tree, *Araucaria araucana*

The spa Termas de Malalcahuello, at the foot of Volcán Lonquimay

❸ Termas de Malalcahuello

Road Map E1. Ruta Bioceánica 181-CH, Km86, Región de la Araucanía, Malalcahuello. **Tel** (09) 6617-4605. 🚌 from Temuco. **Open** 9am–9pm daily. 🥾 ♿ 🧖 🧖 🅦 malalcahuello.cl

The serene location for the modern spa complex of Termas de Malalcahuello is a lushly forested valley at the foot of the 9,400-ft (2,865-m) high Volcán Lonquimay. Both day and overnight visitors are welcome here. On offer are three indoor thermal pools, each filled with mineral-rich water that bubbles up from deep beneath the earth's crust – the temperature of the water ranges from 37°C (99°F) to 43°C (109°F). Floor-to-ceiling windows surround the pools and offer bathers dreamy views of the fertile Lonquimay valley and the snow-covered peak of its volcano. There is also a broad sun-terrace overlooking the valley.

Therapeutic treatments at the resort include wine, honey, and hot-stone massages, as well as herbal and mud baths, and steam rooms. Accommodation options at the complex include a mountain lodge-style hotel, log cabins, and family-sized bungalows. Local bus services and private transfers connect the Termas de Malalcahuello to the nearby Ski Center Corralco.

❹ Ski Center Corralco

Road Map E1. Volcán Lonquimay, Camino a RN Malalcahuello. **Tel** (02) 2206-0741. 🚌 **Open** mid-Jun–Sep: 9am–5pm Fri–Sun; Oct–mid-Jun: 9am–5pm daily. 🅿 🅿 🖳 📷 📧 ⓦ corralco.com

The scenic Ski Center Corralco is one of Chile's newest resorts. Skiers can descend Volcán Lonquimay on seven pistes that have a maximum drop of 3,018 ft (920 m). The off-piste opportunities are best suited to experts. There are snowboarding runs as well, some with steep drops, and Nordic skiing circuits. Summer activities include trekking, horse riding, and mountainbiking. The resort also offers a ski school, mountain lodge, and equipment rental.

❺ Parque Nacional Conguillío

See pp198–9.

Ice-hiking on the steep slopes of Nevados de Sollipulli

❻ Nevados de Sollipulli

Road Map F2. Nevados de Sollipulli Dome Camp, Camino hacia Carén Alto. **Tel** (045) 2276000. 🅿 📷 ⓦ sollipulli.cl

There are few places in Chile where travelers can witness nature's powerful geological forces more clearly than at **Volcán Sollipulli**, part of the Nevados de Sollipulli range, close to Chile's border with Argentina. This volcano's ancient crater, and the 5-sq-mile (12-sq-km) glacier that fills it, are two of the primal elements that are responsible for the formation of the great Andes mountain range.

Visitors can climb to the crater on a day-long hike that passes through dense forests of araucaria, with sweeping vistas of the Andean peaks, crystalline rivers, and countless parasitic craters. There is also a 2-day trekking circuit, which includes ice-hikes on the glacier. All hikes start at the **Nevados de Sollipulli Dome Camp**. Situated next to a forested lake on the volcano's northeastern face, this camp comprises six superbly equipped, centrally heated domes. Among the many luxuries found here are hot tubs in the open air.

Volcán Sollipulli among the majestic Nevados de Sollipulli

❺ Parque Nacional Conguillío

One of the Lake District's great natural attractions, Parque Nacional Conguillío stretches over 235 sq miles (609 sq km) of volcanic wilderness crowned by the smoking cone of the 10,253-ft (3,125-m) high Volcán Llaima. A diverse, spectacular landscape surrounds this colossal peak and features ancient araucaria forests, rolling sierras, crystalline lakes, and deep valleys scarred by jagged lava flows. The park abounds with rich wildlife, including pumas, smaller wildcats, red and gray foxes, woodpeckers, hawks, and condors. Splendid hiking trails, skiing down volcanic slopes, and boat trips across serene lakes draw a large number of visitors to the park throughout the year.

Magellanic woodpecker in Parque Nacional Conguillío

Laguna Captrén
This shallow lake was formed when lava flows from Volcán Llaima obstructed the Río Captrén. Upright trunks of a submerged forest pierce its surface.

PARQUE NACIONAL CONGUILLÍO

Centro de Esquí Las Araucarias

Refugio Llaima

Volcán Llaima
10,253 ft (3,125 m)

Temuco
74 miles (120 km)
Curacautín
17 miles (28 km)

R-925-S

Lag
Cap

Centro de Esquí Las Araucarias
Functioning on Volcán Llaima's western slope, this popular ski center is surrounded by thick araucaria forest. Services include a snowboarding park, accommodations, a ski-school, and an equipment rental shop.

KEY

① **Laguna Verde**, named for its intense green color, is a small lake with a walking path linking its shore to the park's main road.

② **The Salto del Truful Truful** waterfall cascades amid solidified lava flows and rocks.

★**Volcán Llaima**
The glacier-swathed cone of this active volcano dominates the park's land-scape. Seasoned climbers can make the guided ascent to its summit.

★ Lago Conguillío
The beautiful Lago Conguillío, the park's biggest lake, was created when lava flow blocked Río Captrén. Bordered by forests, its shores offer fantastic vistas. Lakeside services include shops, cabins, campsites, and boat trips.

VISITORS' CHECKLIST

Practical Information
Road Map E1. 74 miles (120 km) E of Temuco. 🛈 Oct–Apr: CONAF, Sector del Lago Conguillío. **Open** Apr–mid-Dec: 8:30am–1pm & 2:30–6pm daily; mid-Dec–Mar: 8:30am–9:30pm daily. 🅿 🍴 from Temuco. 🚻 💻 📷 🏠 ♿ ⚠
🆆 conaf.cl

Transport
🚌 from Temuco. **Taxi** from Melipeuco & Curacautín.

Exploring the Park

Parque Nacional Conguillío comprises two sectors separated from each other by Volcán Llaima. The western sector, Sector Los Paraguas, offers winter skiing, while the bigger eastern sector, Sector del Lago Conguillío, has great hiking trails including the popular Sendero Sierra Nevada. This sector is served by the gateway towns of Melipeuco in the south and Curacautín in the north. Heavy snowfall usually makes this sector impassable between May and September.

★ Sendero Sierra Nevada
The park's most popular trail, the Sendero Sierra Nevada climbs to pure araucaria forests and offers splendid views of Volcán Llaima, Lago Conguillío, and the snowy Sierra Nevada.

The Wrath of Volcán Llaima

Smoldering Volcán Llaima is one of Chile's two most explosive volcanoes; the other being Volcán Villarrica *(see p202)*. Over 40 eruptions have been recorded since 1640, and Volcán Llaima's boiling lava has shaped most of Parque Nacional Conguillío's landscape. The eruptions in 2008–09 created 9,800-ft (3,000-m) high smoke columns, forced the evacuation of villages, and dumped ash on Argentina. Over the years, lava flows blocked rivers, turning forests into lakes. Today, lava fields scar the earth where lush forests once stood, and dense woods are still visible in the water.

Volcán Llaima spewing lava, smoke, and ash

Key

═══ Minor road
‑ ‑ Trail
━ ━ Park boundary
△ Peak

❼ Villarrica

Road Map D2. 54 miles (87 km) SE of Temuco. 🚗 33,500. 🚌 ℹ️ Pedro de Valdivia 1070; (045) 2206619. 🎭 La Semana de la Chilenidad (mid-Feb). 🌐 **villarrica.org**

Originally founded in 1552 by the Spanish, Villarrica (Rich Town) was named for the abundant gold and silver deposits discovered here. In 1598, the town was razed in a Mapuche uprising and only resettled in 1883. Today, it is a laid-back, family-oriented destination on the western shore of a sapphire lake of the same name and at the foot of the majestic 9,341-ft (2,847-m) high Volcán Villarrica. Lago Villarrica, a big attraction in its own right, boasts a charming *costanera* (lakefront promenade), and an attractive black sand beach, **Playa Pucará**.

Villarrica's Mapuche heritage finds expression at the **Museo Arqueológico Municipal Mapuche** where pre-Columbian exhibits include ceramics and weaponry. Next to it, the **Centro Cultural Mapuche** features a Mapuche crafts market in the summer months. At the edge of town, the **Mirador Canela** is a lookout point with great views of the lake and volcano.

The snowcapped Volcán Villarrica rising above the landscape

low-slung buildings that serve the booming tourism industry. Nestled in an area of natural beauty, Pucón is a base for trips to nearby hot springs and national parks, and visitors heading out to these areas will find the city's CONAF office helpful. Pucón is also the starting point for many adrenaline-charged activities such as white-water rafting on Río Trancura; horse riding in Huerquehue and Villarrica national parks; hikes up Volcán Villarrica; kayaking and sport fishing on nearby lakes; light-aircraft trips over Volcán Villarrica; cultural tours to Mapuche settlements, and rock climbing, mountain biking, parachuting, paragliding, and zip-lining excursions. Pucón has two black-sand beaches where swimming and water sports are possible. The main beach, **Playa Grande**, is overlooked by forested peaks. To its west, the smaller **La Poza** beach faces a protected inlet. In summer, boat rides from La Poza are a popular way of

Exhibit, Centro Cultural Mapuche

touring Lago Villarrica. Amid the fun-filled adventure, beaches and the best dining scene in Lake District, visitors will find a small concession to culture – **Museo Mapuche**, a private collection of 19th-century Mapuche silverware and pre-Colonial stone artifacts.

Environs

To the east of Pucón are a number of *termas*, ranging from luxurious spa complexes to rustic hot springs. These are usually visited as day trips, either with a tour operator or in a hired car or taxi.

Among the best is **Termas de Huife**, concealed within native forest. This offers smart log cabins on the banks of Río Liucura, thermal pools, therapeutic treatments, and activities such as horse riding. Located in the same valley, **Termas Los Pozones** is a great economical choice. Nestled in the shadow of craggy peaks, it has seven stone-walled pools on the forested banks of Río Liucura.

🏛️ **Museo Mapuche**
Caupolicán 243. **Tel** (045) 2441963. **Open** 11am–1pm & 4–6pm Tue–Sun. 🚫 ✏️ 📷

♨️ **Termas de Huife**
20 miles (33 km) E of Pucón; Camino Pucón-Huife Km33, Valle del Liucura. **Tel** (045) 244 1222. 🚫 ♿ ✏️ 🖥️ 📷 ↩️ 🌐 **termashuife.cl**

♨️ **Termas Los Pozones**
22 miles (35 km) E of Pucón; Valle del Liucura. **Tel** (09) 8474-0218. 🚫 ♿ ✏️ 🖥️ 📷 ⚠️ 🌐 **termaslospozones.cl**

🏛️ **Museo Arqueológico Municipal Mapuche**
Pedro de Valdivia 1050. **Tel** (045) 2415706. **Open** 9am–1pm & 2:30–6pm Mon–Fri. 🚫 ✏️

❽ Pucón

Road Map E2. 69 miles (112 km) SE of Temuco. 🚗 22,000. 🚌 ℹ️ O'Higgins 483; (045) 2293002. 🎭 Ironman (mid-Jan). 🌐 **destinopucon.com**

On the eastern shore of Lago Villarrica, Pucón is the Lake District's adventure-tourism capital. It was founded in 1883 as a fort settlement at the foot of Volcán Villarrica; and today its compact grid of smoothly paved streets is full of mostly

Boats for rent on the black-sand Playa Grande at Pucón

For hotels and restaurants in this region see pp279–80 and pp295–7

❾ Lago Caburgua

Road Map D2. 76 miles (122 km)
SE of Temuco via Pucón.

Ringed by forested mountains, Lago Caburgua is a crystalline lake with this region's only white-sand beaches. Thermal activity in the depths of the lake make its waters warmer than those of the district's other lakes. Popular beaches here are **Playa Negra**, a black-sand beach, and **Playa Blanca**, a stretch of white, crystallized sand. Boat tours of the lake depart from Playa Negra, from where paddle-boats can also be rented. A scenic lakeside walk links these two beaches.

❿ Ojos del Caburgua

Road Map D2. 73 miles (117 km)
SE of Temuco via Pucón. Camino Internacional 7, Km17 or Km20.
Open 9am–9pm daily.

The waters of Lago Caburgua flow southward and underground for 3 miles (5 km) before gushing out to form the Ojos del Caburgua (Eyes of Caburgua). This necklace of aquamarine rock pools lies at the base of cascading waterfalls and is shrouded in pristine forest. Travelers to the site access the pools at a signposted entrance on the main road from Pucón. A second entrance lies 2 miles (3 km) north on the same road and offers a more intimate view of the pools, falls, and forest. This approach is marked solely by a wooden roadside statue of Christ on the cross.

⓫ Parque Nacional Huerquehue

Road Map E2. 94 miles (152 km) SE of Temuco via Pucón; Camino a Caburgua. from Pucón. CONAF Pucón, Lincoyán 336; (045) 2443781.
Open 8:30am–5pm Mon–Fri.
conaf.cl

Created in 1967, the compact Parque Nacional Huerquehue protects around 48 sq miles (124 sq km) of native forest that includes 2,000-year-old araucaria

Forested slopes surrounding Lago Tinquilco, Parque Nacional Huerquehue

woods. The park has some of the Lake District's best short treks and offers spectacular views of Volcán Villarrica and its surroundings. A must-do trail is the 4-mile (7 km) **Sendero Los Lagos**, which traverses forests of Chilean yew and beech, skirts five different lakes, and two waterfalls. Along the way there are breathtaking vistas of the volcano and of Lago Tinquilco, the park's largest body of water. The trail ends at Lago Chico, a small alpine lake surrounded by cliffs crowned by araucaria. Another spectacular hike is the 10-mile (16-km) round trek to **Cerro San Sebastián**. One can spot up to eight volcanoes from the height of 6,562 ft (2,000 m) on a clear day.

Between hikes, visitors can enjoy swimming in the lakes and nature-watching. Birdlife abounds

One of the falls plummeting into the rock pools of Ojos del Caburgua

in this area, the highlight being the different species of eagle. Among the mammals here are the puma; the pudú (*Pudu pudu*), the world's smallest deer; and the brown-gray mouse opossum (*Dromiciops gliroides*), one of the southern Andes' few surviving marsupials.

⓬ Santuario Cañi

Road Map E2. 83 miles (133 km) SE of Temuco via Pucón; Camino Termas de Huife, Km21, Pichares. **Tel** (09) 9837-3928. **Open** 9am–6pm daily.
santuariocani.cl

Protecting a lush swathe of temperate Valdivian rain forest, Santuario Cañi is home to some of Chile's oldest stands of araucaria. A single trail climbs through forests of southern beech (*Nothofagus*) to reveal hidden mountain tarns and, at higher elevations, pure forests of araucaria. Together, these habitats harbor a rich variety of birdlife and many shy mammals that are usually difficult to spot, including the puma and pudú. The steep 6-mile (9-km) trail ends at a lookout point about 5,084 ft (1,550 m) above sea level. This has 360-degree views of the area's four volcanoes – Lanín, Villarrica, Quetrupillán, and Llaima – as well as its three biggest lakes – Caburgua, Villarrica, and Calafquén. Travelers on overnight treks can stay at rustic *La Loma* and camping grounds.

⓲ Parque Nacional Villarrica

Conserving 243 sq miles (629 sq km) of stunning wilderness, Parque Nacional Villarrica extends from south of Pucón to Chile's frontier with Argentina. The smoking, snow-swathed cone of the grand 9,341-ft- (2,847-m-) high Volcán Villarrica forms the park's centerpiece, crowning a landscape that embraces two other volcanoes, several small lakes, steep gorges, and dense forests of southern beech and araucaria. The park provides shelter to a rich wildlife, including the rare Chilean shrew opossum.

Major eruptions in February and March of 2015 had closed the park until late 2016. Although the park has reopened, volatile volcanic activity leaves it vulnerable to future closures.

Spindly araucaria flourishing on the slopes of Volcán Villarrica

Centro de Ski Pucón
Volcán Villarrica's northern face is the stunning location for this popular ski resort. However, recent eruptions have put the ski season at risk.

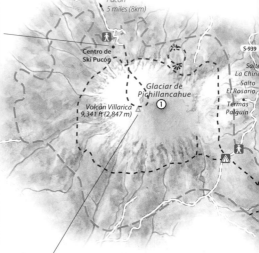

KEY

① **Glaciar de Pichillancahue**, the park's largest glacier, is a sweeping body of blue ice with waterfalls cascading down its front wall. It is reached by the main walking trail in the park's western sector.

② **Volcán Quetrupillán** is a dormant, snowcapped volcano. Its name means mute devil in the Mapuche tongue.

③ **Lago Quilleihue** is a tranquil lake reached by a hiking trail through thick araucaria forest.

Pucón
5 miles (8km)

Centro de Ski Pucón

Glaciar de Pichillancahue

Volcán Villarrica
9,341 ft (2,847 m)

S-939

Salte
La Chine
Salto
El Rosario
Termas
Palguin

★ **Volcán Villarrica**
The trek to Volcán Villarrica's crater features a physically challenging but technically undemanding hike through icy glaciers and a slide down the slopes via snow tunnels. The route has reopened for trekkers after the 2015 volcanic activity.

House of the Devil

The Mapuche of the area refer to Volcán Villarrica as Rucapillán, or House of the Devil – an apt description for one of Chile's most explosive peaks. The volcano erupted 18 times in the 20th century alone. A major explosion in 1971 almost destroyed the nearby village of Coñaripe *(see p204)*. It last erupted in 2015, and remains constantly active. Its crater smokes, hisses, and belches, and is one of only four craters on the globe that has an active lava lake.

Bubbling and flaming lava in Volcán Villarrica's crater lake

Exploring the Park

Parque Nacional Villarrica has three sectors, each with hiking trails and a ranger station. The westernmost sector, accessible from the gateway town of Pucón, features the park's major highlights, including the magnificent Volcán Villarrica. The two sectors to the east are remote, yet beautiful; the park's wildest sector is in the area bordering Argentina.

PARQUE NACIONAL VILLARRICA
Cerro Quinquili 6,634 ft (2,022 m)
② Volcán Quetrupillán 7,743 ft (2,360 m)
Laguna Blanca
Laguna Azul
CH-199
ARGENTINA
Laguna Abutardes
Lago Quilleihue ③
CHILE
Paso Mamuil Malal
Volcán Lanín 12,290 ft (3,746 m)

0 km 5
0 miles 5

Volcán Lanín

Shared by Chile and Argentina, the snow-topped Volcán Lanín is southern Chile's biggest volcano. The hike from Laguna Abutardes to Lago Quilleihue offers fabulous vistas of this volcano.

★ Laguna Azul

A mirror-like sheet of water edged by a forested flank of the majestic Volcán Quetrupillán, Laguna Azul can be reached by the 9-mile (15-km) long Los Venados trail that starts at the ranger station in the Quetrupillán sector.

For keys to symbols *see back flap*

Boardwalk past a waterfall at the Termas Geómetricas, near Coñaripe

⑭ Licán Ray

Road Map E2. 70 miles (113 km) SE of Temuco. 🚐 2,100. 🚍 𝒊 General Urrutia, esq. Cacique Marichanquin; (045) 2431516 (Dec–Mar only). 🎭 La Semana de Licán Ray (Feb).

Small and tranquil, Licán Ray is the main resort on the hauntingly beautiful **Lago Calafquén**. The village is a quiet oasis, except in February when the people of Santiago arrive in large numbers to holiday by Lago Calafquén's mist-shrouded warm waters.

There are two beaches at this miniature retreat – **Playa Grande** and the more picture-sque **Playa Chica**, which is ringed by rolling forested peaks that sweep down to a shore of black volcanic sand. A wooded peninsula divides these two beaches and is crossed by walking paths that ascend to lookout points with great vistas. Catamaran tours of the lake

depart from Playa Chica. At the village center, the main plaza is edged by sandy sidewalks and artisans' fairs.

⑮ Coñaripe

Road Map E2. 83 miles (134 km) SE of Temuco. 🚐 1,500. 🚍 🅆 coñaripe.com

On the eastern shore of Lago Calafquén, and away from the region's more traveled routes, Coñaripe is a tiny village with a soporific air and a couple of black-sand beaches. The area around the village offers ample opportunities for adventure sports, including white-water rafting on the Río San Pedro, and horseback, mountain-bike, and trekking trips. Coñaripe has many accommodation options for overnight guests; budget-travelers in particular will enjoy the well-equipped campsites by the beaches.

Environs

The hills around Coñaripe are dotted with more than a dozen thermal springs which are scenic, relaxing, and well worth visiting. They range from very basic, rustic pools to modern hotel-and-spa complexes. One of the best among these is the **Termas Geómetricas**. Nestled within a forested ravine, this stylish spa comprises 60 thermal fountains that gush into bubbling bathing pools through a network of wooden water channels. Visitors simply walk across the ravine on a 1,476-ft (450-m) long catwalk, and descend via wooden stairs to the pool of their choice.

The **Termas Coñaripe** is a good choice for an overnight stay. This modern hotel and spa made of glass and wood offers indoor and semi-covered pools, and outdoor thermal pools. Guests can also slather around in mud baths and enjoy walks and horseback rides to nearby waterfalls and lagoons.

A rough road leads to Parque Nacional Villarrica (see pp202–3), some 11 miles (18 km) to the north.

🔥 **Termas Coñaripe**
9 miles (15 km) SE of Coñaripe; Camino Coñaripe-Liquine, Km15. **Tel** (045) 2324800. 🈳 🈂 💻 🈶 🈁 🅆 **termasconaripe.cl**

🔥 **Termas Geómetricas**
10 miles (16 km) NE of Coñaripe. **Tel** (09) 7477-1708. **Open** day visits only; 11am–8pm Sun–Thu, 10am–11pm Fri & Sat. 🈳 🈂 🅆 **termasgeometricas.cl**

Tour boats on Lago Calafquén, moored by the forest-lined Playa Chica at Licán Ray

For hotels and restaurants in this region see pp279–80 and pp295–7

⑯ Panguipulli

Road Map E2. 90 miles (145 km)
SE of Temuco. 🚹 16,000. 🚌 ℹ️
Bernardo O'Higgins s/n, in front of
Plaza A. Prat; (063) 2310436. 🎭 La
Semana de las Rosas (mid-Feb).
🆆 sietelagos.cl

Overlooking the tranquil waters
of its lake, Panguipulli is a popular
stop for visitors heading on to the
Reserva Biológica Huilo-Huilo. A
pleasant lakeshore destination of
brightly painted clapboard houses
on hillside streets, the town's
biggest attraction is the landmark
Iglesia Capuchina. A twin-tow-
ered wooden construction, the
church was built by German
Capuchin missionaries in 1947
and stands on the site of a
German mission from the 1890s.
The building is fronted by a latticed facade that is painted red,
yellow, and black – the colors
of the German national flag.
Religious statues brought from
Germany adorn the church's interior. Overlooking the altar is a large
high-relief, sculpted from native
raulí and mañío woods, depicting
Christ's ascension to heaven.

Environs
Panguipulli and its namesake
lake lie at the heart of Chile's
Seven Lakes region. These lakes
– Calafquén, Pallaita, Pullinque,
Ruñihue, Neltume, Panguipulli,
and Pirihueico – are linked to
each other by rivers, which
together comprise a single
hydrological system. A chain of
beautiful and generally uncrowd-
ed villages face the shores of
these lakes. Although it's possible
to spend the night in Panguipulli,
Pucón (see p200) is the main
springboard for day trips into
the Siete Lagos area.

⑰ Reserva Biológica Huilo-Huilo

Road Map E2. 130 miles (210 km)
SE of Temuco; El Portal, Camino
Internacional Panguipulli-Puerto Fuy,
Km56. **Tel** (02) 2887-3510. 🚌 from
Panguipulli. 🏇 🚲 💻 📷 🚠
🆆 huilohuilo.com

Run by a private foundation
dedicated to sustainable
tourism, Reserva Biológica Huilo-

Iglesia Capuchina, with its twin towers rising above Pangiupulli

Huilo preserves 232 sq miles
(600 sq km) of temperate rain
forest that was once the target
of large-scale logging. Within
the reserve boundaries, there is
some truly compelling scenery.
By far the most impressive is the
Volcán Mocho-Choshuenco,
which is in fact two volcanoes
bridged by a large glacier.
The surrounding landscape
comprises glacial lakes, rivers,
and Andean prairies.

Visitors to the reserve
first need to choose a
base from which to
explore this area. There
is a range of lodging
options, from an upscale
mountain lodge in
the woods, to more
inexpensive accom-
modations in the
small towns of Neltume and
Puerto Fuy. These were built in
the 1930s to house employees
of the logging companies.
Puerto Fuy is situated near the
beautiful Lago Pirihueico and is
the starting point for fly-fishing,
kayaking, and boating trips.

The reserve's lodge, **La
Montaña Mágica** (The Magic
Mountain), is worth a visit
even for non-guests. It rises
above the forest like a fantasy
castle from a Grimm Brothers'
fairy tale, and has a cascading
waterfall that plunges down
its side. The interior is constructed
almost entirely from native
woods. Next door is the
whimsical **Nothofagus
Hotel** that looks like a giant
treehouse. Activities at the
reserve are mostly guided and
arranged at La Montaña Mágica

Chilean firebush at the
Huilo-Huilo reserve

or at the administration center
close to the reserve's main
entrance. These include horse
rides across forest, prairie,
and mountain terrain, and
wildlife observation of reintro-
duced fauna – such as the
camelid species, guanaco
that once roamed freely
here. Travelers looking for
more rugged activities will
also find zip-lining, mountain-
biking, and trekking
excursions.

Hiking trails range
from a gentle walk
through indigenous
forest that ends at the
gushing, 115-ft (35-m)
high **Salto del Huilo-
Huilo** waterfall, to
the thrilling full-day
trek to the crater of
Volcán Mocho. The premises
also houses the stunning **Museo
de los Volcanes**, which displays
Chile's most extensive collection
of silver Mapuche items within
a pyramid-like interior.

The whimsical La Montaña Mágica at
Reserva Biológica Huilo-Huilo

⑱ Valdivia

A waterfront city, Valdivia is named for its founder, the Spanish explorer Pedro de Valdivia. Established in 1552, the colony spread along the banks of three rivers – Río Cau Cau, Río Calle Calle, and Río Valdivia, the last of which links this port-city to the Pacific Ocean. Valdivia was a prized possession of the Spanish, who guarded it with military forts for over 200 years until its defenses were breached in the War of Independence (1810–26). In 1960, a massive earthquake devastated Valdivia, but today, it is a vibrant city whose lush riverside is fronted by fine museums and 19th-century Teutonic architecture.

Boats docked along the Río Valdivia, near the lively Mercado Fluvial

🍴 Mercado Fluvial

Avenida Arturo Prat s/n.
Open 10am–8pm daily.
Located on the banks of Río Valdivia, Mercado Fluvial, the city's bustling fish market, is a colorful snapshot of coastal Chilean life as well as the prime industry that sustains it. Traders clean the day's catch for customers, while live crabs scuttle about in huge crates and bobbing sea lions bellow for scraps by the water's edge. In this scuffle over discarded odds and ends are hundreds of screaming seabirds. Inexpensive seafood eateries serving local specialties edge the market.

🏛 Centro Cultural El Austral

Yungay 733. **Tel** (063) 2213658.
Open 10am–1pm & 3–7:30pm Tue–Sun. 🎥 📧 🌐 cculturalvaldivia.cl
In a large, beautifully restored house, Valdivia's Centro Cultural El Austral dates from the period of German settlement in the Lake District. Built in the 1870s for a pioneer family, it was made entirely from local wood in the German chalet style and features a striking Bavarian steeple. The interiors reflect typical living quarters of early German settlers. Dazzlingly furnished, the rooms feature Art Nouveau chandeliers, extravagant wall mirrors, and stately 19th-century European furniture. Other rooms in the building showcase works by contemporary artists.

🏛 Museo de Arte Contemporaneo

Los Laureles s/n, Isla Teja. **Tel** (063) 2221968. **Open** Jan–Feb: 10am–2pm & 4–8pm Tue–Sun; Mar–May & Sep–Dec: 10am–1pm & 2–6pm Tue–Sun. 🎥

A recycled brewery building with a strikingly modern glass facade is the post-Industrial

Valdivia City Center

① Mercado Fluvial
② Centro Cultural El Austral
③ Museo de Arte
   Contemporaneo
④ Museo Histórico y
   Antropológico Mauricio
   Van de Maele

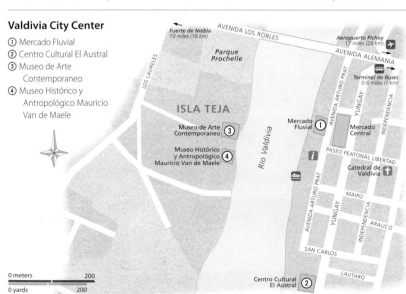

0 meters 200
0 yards 200

Modern glass exterior of the Museo de Arte Contemporaneo

setting for the city's Museo de Arte Contemporaneo, popularly referred to as MAC. The exhibitions here feature video and installation art as well as paintings, photographs, and sculptures by emerging and established artists, both international and Chilean.

The collection is spread over two floors of abandoned industrial workspace, which is characterized by bare cement flooring and cast-iron columns. These still bear the scars of the devastating earthquake that hit this area in 1960.

🏛 Museo Histórico y Antropológico Mauricio Van de Maele

Los Laureles s/n, Isla Teja.
Tel (063) 2212872. **Open** Jan & Feb: 10am–8pm daily; Mar–Dec: 10am–1pm & 2–6pm Tue–Sun.
🌿 🏛 **W** museosaustral.cl

Adjacent to the Museo de Arte Contemporaneo is the 19th-century mansion and former home of the founder of Chile's first brewery, Karl Anwandter (1801–89). Today, the edifice houses the Museo

VISITORS' CHECKLIST

Practical Information
Road Map D2. 100 miles (162 km) SW of Temuco. 🏙 154,000. *i* Arturo Prat 555; (063) 2239060. 🎭 La Noche Valdiviana (3rd Sat of Feb), Festival Internacional de Cine Valdivia (mid-Oct). **W** valdivia.cl

Transport
✈ 🚌 🚎

Histórico y Antropológico Mauricio Van de Maele, whose collection is displayed in a series of themed salons, each depicting different periods in local history, from pre-Columbian times to the 20th century. Each salon has a multilingual information panel with historical details about the period it represents.

Rooms include the **Sala de Platería Mapuche**, which has exhibits of Mapuche tools and textiles. The stunning jewelry display here portrays the indigenous Mapuche's belief in silverware as a symbol of power and prestige.

Dedicated to Thomas Cochrane (1775–1860), the **Sala Lord Cochrane** displays some of his personal belongings. This buccaneering British naval officer led Chile's naval forces during the 1820 attack on Valdivia that ended Royalist resistance in the area.

The museum also re-creates a Colonial-period lounge, embellished with ornate wall hangings, Damask tapestry, and a Venetian mirror.

🔟 Forts Around Valdivia

Road Map D2. 11 miles (18 km) SW of Valdivia. 🚌 🏞 🏰

In the mid-1600s, the Spanish Crown constructed 17 forts near Valdivia. Overlooking Corral bay, these provided formidable defense against naval and pirate attacks, and made the much-valued port-city impregnable. It was only in 1820, that an attack led by Lord Thomas Cochrane, from a beachhead rather than from sea, finally breached Valdivia's defenses. Only three of the original 17 stone forts remain.

Located at the mouth of Río Valdivia, **Fuerte de Niebla** was constructed in 1671 and reinforced in 1767. It now houses the Museo de Sitio Castillo de Niebla, which exhibits antique artillery and maps of the area.

South of Niebla, **Fuerte de Mancera** was founded in 1645 on a small island in Corral bay. Most of the additions seen today date from renovations carried out in 1762. The grounds around the fort, a popular picnic site, afford sweeping views out to sea. Farther south of Mancera, across Corral bay, **Fuerte de Corral** was built in 1645 and is the area's first and most robust fort. Daily re-enactments of Cochrane's raid are staged here during summer.

The collective ruins of these forts include secret supply tunnels, dynamite storehouses, chapels, barracks, and cannon rows. Visitors can enjoy spectacular vistas from the water-taxis that depart regularly from Niebla to Corral and Mancera.

🏛 Fuerte de Corral
Calle Blanco s/n. **Open** Jan & Feb: 8:30am–9:30pm daily; Mar–Dec: 8:30am–5pm daily.

🏛 Fuerte de Mancera
Isla Mancera. **Tel** (063) 2212872. **Open** Jan & Feb: 10am–8pm daily; Mar–Dec: 10am–1pm & 2–6pm Tue–Sun. **W** museosaustral.cl

🏛 Fuerte de Niebla
RP350, Km17. **Tel** (063) 2282084. 🚌 **Open** Dec–Mar: 10am–7pm Tue–Sun; Apr–Nov: 10am–5:30pm Tue–Sun. **W** museodeniebla.cl

Period furnishings at the Museo Histórico y Antropológico Mauricio Van de Maele

⑳ Santuario de la Naturaleza Carlos Anwandter

Road Map D2. 13 miles (21 km) N of Valdivia. 🚇 from Valdivia. 🛈 CONAF Valdivia; (063) 2245200. 🗹

Over 23 sq miles (60 sq km) of wildlife-rich wetlands are protected by the Santuario de la Naturaleza Carlos Anwandter. The origin of these wetlands lies in the aftermath of the 1960 earthquake, when a tsunami submerged the area's forests and cattle pastures. The new ecosystem attracted a variety of birdlife and was recognized as a nature sanctuary in 1981.

Over 100 species of birds, such as herons, pelicans, and black-necked swans, can be seen here. It is also possible to spot river otters and the coipú, a large aquatic rodent.

㉑ Lago Ranco

Road Map E2. 77 miles (124 km) SE of Valdivia. 🚹 2,200. 🚌 from Valdivia. 🛈 Linares & Concepción; (063) 2491348. 🅦 **municipalidad lagoranco.cl**

Located on the southern shore of the eponymous silver-gray lake, Lago Ranco is a small and quiet village of gravel streets and weatherboard houses. These old, weather-beaten structures encircle the forested shoreline of what is possibly the Lake District's most beautiful body of water. Ringed by craggy Andean peaks, the lake's

Neo-Gothic arches and stained-glass windows at Osorno's cathedral

crystalline, warm waters are perfect for a swim. The village's cultural attraction, **Museo Tringlo Lago Ranco**, displays archaeological and anthropological exhibits including ancient ceramics.

🏛 Museo Tringlo Lago Ranco
Ancud s/n. **Tel** (063) 2491348. **Open** Dec–Mar: 10am–1pm & 3–5pm Mon–Sat. 🗹 🗹 on request (Spanish only).

㉒ Osorno

Road Map D2. 66 miles (107 km) S of Valdivia. 🚹 144,000. 🚉 🚌 🛈 O'Higgins 667; (064) 2234104. 🚢 Mon, Fri. 🎉 Festival Nacional de la Leche y la Carne (Jan).

Founded in 1558 by García Hurtado de Mendoza, then governor of Chile, the city of Osorno is located at the center of Chile's cattle heartland. The

country's biggest cattle market, the Feria Ganadera de Osorno, is held here on Mondays and Fridays and is worth visiting.

Although primarily an agricultural city, Osorno offers many attractions. Most striking of these is the Neo-Gothic **Catedral San Mateo Apóstol** with its massive facade of reinforced concrete and ogival filigree. Built in 1960, it towers over the city's central plaza.

South of the cathedral is the **Calle Juan Mackenna**, lined with a row of Teutonic-style wooden houses dating from the 19th century, when German settlers arrived at Osorno. Those at numbers 939, 1011, 1027, 1068, and 1095 are designated national monuments.

A block west of the houses, an elegant 1929 Neo-Classical building is the setting for the **Museo Histórico Municipal**. Its displays trace the city's history chronologically; exhibits include Mapuche pottery and Colonial-era weapons.

Osorno is a convenient base for visits to the nearby Parque Nacional Puyehue. It is a good idea for travelers heading on to the national park to first visit Osorno's CONAF office for information.

🏛 Museo Histórico Municipal
M.A. Matta 809. **Tel** (064) 223 8615. **Open** 9:30am–5:30pm Mon–Thu, 9:30am–5pm Fri, 2–6pm Sat.

㉓ Parque Nacional Puyehue

Road Map E2. 116 miles (187 km) SE of Valdivia; Aguas Calientes. **Tel** (064) 1974572. 🚌 from Osorno. 🛈 Centro de Informacion Ambiental, Aguas Calientes; (064) 1974572. **Open** 9am–1pm & 2–6pm daily. 🗹 🏔 🅦 **parquepuyehue.cl**

Famed for its hot springs, Parque Nacional Puyehue is one of Chile's most popular and remote national parks. It covers 412 sq miles (1,067 sq km) of wilderness that encompasses two volcanoes, around 200 craters, and large swathes of evergreen Valdivian rain forest. Close to the park's entrance, in its Aguas Calientes

Sweeping views of the dramatic landscape at Parque Nacional Puyehue

For hotels and restaurants in this region see pp279–80 and pp295–7

The busy outdoor thermal pool at Aguas Calientes, Parque Nacional Puyehue

㉔ Termas de Puyehue

Road Map E2. 114 miles (183 km) SE of Valdivia; Ruta 215, Km76, Puyehue. **Tel** (064) 2331425. 🚌 from Osorno. **Open** 8am–8pm Mon–Fri, 8am–9pm Sat & Sun. 🐾 ♿ 🏊 🖥 📷 🔄 **ⓦ puyehue.cl**

A five-star spa resort, the Termas de Puyehue is the ideal place to soothe aching limbs after long treks in the nearby Parque Nacional Puyehue. Hidden within forests at the edge of the park, this luxurious, yet accessible, mountain lodge and spa receives both day and overnight guests. It is possible to relax in the therapeutic waters of three large thermal pools – covered, semi-covered, and outdoor – whose temperatures range from a comfortable 22°C (72°F) to a warm 41°C (106°F). There are hot rooms and hydrotherapy pools, and a tempting variety of indulgent treatments that include honey, algae, and herbal massages, as well as sulfur-rich mud baths. The spa has a daily program of children's activities and a well-equipped playroom. Other facilities include two gourmet restaurants, a small art gallery, and outdoor tennis courts. Visitors can enjoy exhilarating horse rides to the forested shore of the nearby Lago Puyehue, where the spa arranges several water sports for its guests.

sector, the **Termas Aguas Calientes** is a rustic hot-springs resort featuring sulfur-rich outdoor rock pools that are edged by forest and tumbling rivers. In the park's Antillanca sector, **Volcán Casablanca**, rising to a height of 6,529 ft (1,990 m), has one of the Lake District's least demanding ascents. The base is the starting point for several trails, both easy and challenging, that wind through native forests of lenga, ulmo, and coigue trees. The park is home to a rich and varied birdlife, including hummingbirds, condors, and kingfishers. Hikers can also hear the distinctive chirp of the endemic, onomatopoeically named chucao (*Scelorchilus rubecula*). Among the park's mammals are pumas, foxes, the native and endangered huemul, as well as the tiny, tree-dwelling mouse opossum.

Volcán Casablanca is also the location for the highly rated **Centro de Ski Antillanca** which operates on the volcano's western wall. This popular ski resort attracts a large number of skiing enthusiasts. Offering excellent off-piste skiing, it features 17 slopes for all levels, snowboard runs, and a maximum drop of 1,640 ft (500 m). The slopes afford panoramic views of the blue skyline pierced by the snowcapped cones of surrounding volcanoes. Services available include an equipment rental shop, a ski-school, and a snow park for children. Summertime activities at Antillanca

feature mountain-biking, horse riding, caving, and trekking on the volcano, as well as kayaking and fishing excursions. Snowmobile rides through virgin forest are an added draw during the winter months.

In the less trodden northern sector of the national park, the 7,334-ft (2,236-m) high **Volcán Puyehue** offers a difficult 2-day ascent, and is for experienced hikers only. The stunning trails here pass geysers, steaming fumaroles, and gurgling hot springs.

Kingfisher, Parque Nacional Puyehue

🚡 Centro de Ski Antillanca
Volcán Casablanca. **Tel** (064) 2612070. **Open** Jun–Oct: 8am–5:30pm daily. 🐾 🏊 🖥 📷 🔄 ⓦ **antillanca.cl**

🛁 Termas Aguas Calientes
Km4 Camino Antillanca. **Tel** (064) 2331785. 🐾 ⓦ **termasaguascalientes.cl**

Entrance to the popular hot-springs resort, Termas de Puyehue

㉕ Lago Llanquihue

Road Map D2. 99 miles (160 km) SE of Valdivia.

Resembling a small sea in its size, the breathtakingly beautiful Lago Llanquihue is South America's third-largest natural lake. It covers a surface area of 338 sq miles (875 sq km), plunges to a depth of 1,148 ft (350 m), and its crystal blue waters are bound by Volcán Osorno and Volcán Calbuco. The Mapuche believed this lake and its dominions to be a realm of monsters and evil spirits. The Spanish discovered it in 1552, but it was not until the arrival of German immigrants in the 19th century that Europeans finally colonized the lake's shores. Since then, Llanquihue has been the German heartland of the Lake District and is today fronted by steepled Bavarian towns. Of these, Puerto Octay has the most authentically Teutonic feel, while Frutillar is famous for its beaches and classical music festival, and Puerto Varas offers great restaurants and nightlife.

㉖ Puerto Octay

Road Map D2. 99 miles (160 km) SE of Valdivia. 3,500.
German Wulf s/n; (064) 2391860. Festival de la Leche (Jan).
w turismopuertoctay.cl

Set on the northern shore of Lago Llanquihue, Puerto Octay was founded in 1852 by German immigrants who were attracted

Volcán Osorno, overlooking the azure waters of Lago Llanquihue

by its location on a sheltered bay. The town grew into an important lake port and staging post on the trade route between Osorno and Puerto Montt. Today, it is a charming holiday destination with a stunning natural setting and streets of well-conserved Germanic architecture. Wooden houses and civic buildings from the settler era front streets such as Avenida Pedro Montt, Calle G. Wulf, and Calle Amunategui. Occupying an old settler's house, the excellent **Museo El Colono** exhibits period objects. Another noteworthy building is the landmark 1907-built **Iglesia Parroquial**, constructed in a simple Gothic style.

Puerto Octay faces the peaks of three volcanoes – Calbuco, Puntiagudo, and Osorno. Each is visible from the town's main

beach, **Playa La Baja**, a stretch of volcanic black sand fringed by eucalyptus and pine forests. Puerto Octay's hilltop cemetery, which holds the graves of the original German settlers, offers even more magnificent views of the lake and its surrounding volcanoes.

🏛 Museo El Colono

Avenida Independencia 591. **Tel** (064) 2391523. **Open** 10:15am–1pm & 3–5pm daily. on request.
w museoelcolono.jimdo.com

㉗ Frutillar

Road Map D2. 105 miles (170 km) SE of Valdivia. 10,000.
Philippi & O'Higgins. Wed, Fri. Semana Musical de Frutillar (late Jan–early Feb). **w** frutillar.com
w semanasmusicales.cl

Said to be the Lake District's loveliest town, Frutillar was founded in 1856 by German colonists on the western shore of Lago Llanquihue. The town's charming district Frutillar Bajo (Lower Frutillar) has stunning views of Volcán Osorno, whose perfect snowcapped cone seems to float ethereally above the far shore of the sapphire lake.

A mix of hotels, crafts markets, restaurants, and old Germanic architecture line the long sandy shores of Frutillar Bajo. The **Museo Colonial Alemán** is in landscaped gardens and re-creates the pioneer era with life-size buildings that include a mill, farmhouse, and blacksmith's forge. Period

The tower of Iglesia Parroquial rising above Puerto Octay, on the banks of Lago Llanquihue

For hotels and restaurants in this region see pp279–80 and pp295–7

objects furnish these buildings and multilingual information panels provide historical detail.

On the waterfront, the **Teatro del Lago Sur** is a striking, multi-million dollar contemporary theater venue and site of the Semana Musical de Frutillar, a ten-day-long festival featuring opera, jazz, and classical music. At the town's northern edge, the **Reserva Forestal Edmundo Winkler** preserves Valdivian rain forest. A short walking path here climbs to a lookout point with lake and volcano vistas.

🏛 **Museo Colonial Alemán**
Avenida Vicente Pérez Rosales, esq. Arturo Prat, Frutillar Bajo. **Tel** (065) 2421142. **Open** Jan & Feb: 9am–7:30pm daily; Mar–Dec: 9am–5:30pm daily. 🐦 📷 **W** museosaustral.cl

🌿 **Reserva Forestal Edmundo Winkler**
Calle Caupolicán s/n, Frutillar Bajo. **Open** 8am–7pm Mon–Fri (winter: to 5pm). 🌿

❼ Puerto Varas

Road Map D2. 118 miles (190 km) S of Valdivia. 🏔 27,900. 🚌 Puerto Montt. 🚐 ℹ Del Salvador 320; (065) 236 1146. **W** puertovaras.org

Fronting the southern shores of Lago Llanquihue, Puerto Varas is the biggest town on the lake. It was founded

Traditional German buildings at the Museo Colonial Alemán, Frutillar

in 1854 by German immigrants, and pioneer-era homes can still be seen on streets such as Prat, Miraflores, and Decker. The tourist information office offers a walking tour brochure, the Paseo Patrimonial, which encompasses 28 different houses. The town's most remarkable Teutonic building, the **Iglesia Sagrado Corazón de Jesús**, was built in 1915–18 as a to-scale replica of a church in Germany's Black Forest. Made entirely from wood, its Baroque interior boasts two cupolas, built to

the maximum height possible without metal supports. The town is popular for various adventure sports such as white-water rafting, horse riding, and kayaking. Visitors can also trek to Volcán Osorno, and hike in Parque Vicente Pérez-Rosales. Another option is to rent bikes and ride to Ensenada and then visit the Petrohué waterfalls.

During winter, the locals also celebrate the seasonal rains with the the traditional Rain Festival. The most popular of the town's black sand beaches is **Playa de Puerto Chico**, with views of Volcán Osorno.

🏛 **Iglesia Sagrado Corazón de Jesús**
Verbo Divino, esq. San Francisco. **Open** hours vary. 🔔 8pm.

German Immigrants of the Lake District

An original settler house in Frutillar

In 1845, the Chilean government passed the Badlands Law, a regulation that aimed to loosen Mapuche control over the Lake District via colonization. Some 150 German Catholic families accepted Chile's invitation to populate the area; a trickle that became a torrent as more Germans sought to escape poverty and authoritarian rule at home. Between 1846 and 1875, 66 ships made the 5-month journey from Hamburg in Germany to Valdivia (*see pp206–7*). Families of artisans and farmers settled first in Valdivia and, as thousands more arrived, in Osorno (*see p208*), and finally in the area around Lago Llanquihue. Here, German settlers founded three lakeshore towns – Puerto Octay, Frutillar, and Puerto Varas – that became the German heartland of the region. German immigration fizzled out in the 1880s, but the towns around Lago Llanquihue continued to thrive as main stops on the route from Osorno to Puerto Montt (*see pp216–17*).

The Teutonic-style Iglesia Sagrado Corazón de Jesús at Puerto Varas

㉙ Parque Nacional Vicente Pérez Rosales

Created in 1926, Parque Nacional Vicente Pérez Rosales is one of Chile's most breathtaking parks. Its landscape of lost-world beauty encompasses volcanoes, crystalline lakes and lagoons, gushing waterfalls, and evergreen forest. Its crowning glory is the perfect cone of the active Volcán Osorno. Two more great volcanoes – Tronador and Puntiagudo – pierce the skyline here. They, along with Lago Todos Los Santos and Saltos de Petrohué, protect an abundant bird and mammal life, and offer activities such as boat rides, horse riding through forests, lava treks, and volcano skiing.

Key

     Parque Nacional Vicente Pérez Rosales

★ Volcán Osorno
The park's most striking feature, Volcán Osorno is the focus of many hikes and horseback rides. A paved road climbs its flank to Estación Base, site of a spectacular viewpoint, as well as a modern ski and snowboard center. Summer activities here include mountain-biking and zip-lining.

Volcán Puntiac
8,195 ft (2,498

Volcán Osorno
8,700 ft (2,652 m)

Lago Todos
Los Santos

Petrohué

Lago
Llanquihue

Río Petrohué

Ensenada

Puerto Varas
28 miles (45 km)

★ Saltos de Petrohué
White-water torrents, emerging from where a lava field splits Río Petrohué, form the gushing Saltos de Petrohué. Walkways gouged from lava rock skirt the rapids and powerboats depart for their swirling base. A number of trails snake through the surrounding forest to jade lagoons.

KEY

① **Laguna Verde** is an intensely green lagoon surrounded by black lava rock and emerald forest. Trails cross lava fields to Lago Llanquihue, the great lake whose waters seep into Laguna Verde.

② **Peulla** is a hamlet with two hotels, which is reached by catamaran. It offers lake-fishing, as well as hikes and horse riding on the slopes of Volcán Tronador.

Río Petrohué
Originating at the Lagos Todos Los Santos, Río Petrohué is one of Chile's most popular rivers for activities such as sport fishing, kayaking, and rafting.

★ Lago Todos Los Santos
This beautiful glacial lake ringed by forested mountains and black beaches is explored on catamarans and small wooden boats. Three volcanoes are visible from the lake.

VISITORS' CHECKLIST

Practical Information
Road Map E2. 28 miles (45 km) NE of Puerto Varas. *i* CONAF, Petrohue, (065) 8821680. **Open** 9am–6pm daily. 🚻 🚮 🛒 📷 🛶 ⛰ 🇼 **conaf.cl**

Transport
🚌 from Puerto Montt & Puerto Varas, via Ensenada & Petrohué.

Key
═══ Minor road
--- Trail
═ ═ Park boundary
▬▬ International boundary
△ Peak

0 km _____ 10
0 miles _____ 10

Exploring the Park

The park's star sights are concentrated in its western sector, which is served by road and local bus, and is linked to the gateway city Puerto Varas (see p211). Located in this sector, the villages of Ensenada and Petrohué have hotel and campsite accommodations. From Petrohué, catamarans make the daily 2-hour crossing to the park's eastern sector, called Peulla, where the eponymous hamlet has two hotels.

Cruce de los Lagos

This spectacular crossing over the Andes, between the lake districts of Chile and Argentina, traverses two national parks and four lakes. The full day journey, beginning at Petrohuè, over both land and lakes ends at Bariloche, Argentina. En route, there are four volcanoes, many waterfalls, and abundant wildlife.

A catamaran crossing the waters of Lago Todos Los Santos

Volcán Tronador
The awesome 11,351-ft- (3,460-m-) high peak of this extinct volcano straddles the border between Chile and neighboring Argentina.

For keys to symbols *see back flap*

③⓪ Puerto Montt

The port-city of Puerto Montt is where the Lake District meets the Pacific Ocean. Founded in 1853 on a hillside overlooking the Seno de Reloncaví, the city grew rapidly around its port, which was used to ship grains and alerce timber. Puerto Montt was badly hit by the 1960 earthquake and much of it was rebuilt thereafter. The salmon industry which employs many locals, was also hit hard by algae-related problems. The city is now used strictly as a transit point by most travelers. It is the departure point for south-bound ferries and cruise ships sailing through Chile's fjords. Apart from the busy fish market and seafront promenade, the town has a few attractions.

Shoppers in downtown Puerto Montt

🚍 Plaza Buenaventura Martínez
Built on the site of the city's foundation, Puerto Montt's main plaza is overlooked by the Neo-Classical **Iglesia Catedral**.

Erected in 1856–96, the cathedral is modeled on Greece's iconic Parthenon, with Doric pillars of alerce adorning the facade and a simple interior. One of these columns conceals

VISITORS' CHECKLIST

Practical Information
Road Map D2. 130 miles
(210 km) S of Valdivia.
🚇 218,000. ℹ San Martín 80;
(065) 2258087. 🎭 La Semana
Puertomontina (mid-Feb).
🌐 puertomontt.cl

Transport
✈ Aeropuerto El Tepual. 🚌 ⛴

the city's founding stone. The San Francisco de Sales, a Neo-Gothic side chapel, is entered from inside the cathedral.

🐟 Angelmó Fish Market
Avenida Angelmó s/n.
Open 8am–11pm daily. 🖼
Located on the waterfront, the raucous Angelmó Fish Market is the city's biggest attraction. A whirl of vibrant colors and aromas, the market is a maze of narrow, guttered passageways along which traders sell fish, spices, algae strings, and local delicacies. Wooden stairs climb to numerous small restaurants that serve some of the best seafood platters in the city. On streets bordering the market, craftspeople sell woolens and woodcarvings made from local alerce.

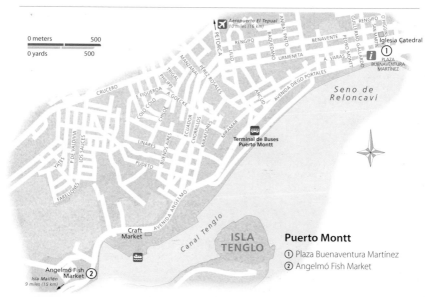

Puerto Montt
① Plaza Buenaventura Martínez
② Angelmó Fish Market

Excursion boats moored at the waterfront of Calbuco

From a jetty behind the market, boats leave for Tenglo and Maillén, islands in the Seno de Reloncaví.

A wooden building on stilts at the colorful Angelmó Fish Market

❸ Parque Nacional Alerce Andino

Road Map E2. 25 miles (40 km) SE of Puerto Montt. 🄵 CONAF, Sector Correntoso, E of Correntoso village. 🚌 **Open** 9am–6pm daily. 🖼 📷 🚫 🗻 🖥 conaf.cl

Covering an area of around 150 sq miles (390 sq km), Parque Nacional Alerce Andino protects the magnificent alerce tree, *Fitzroya cupressoides*. Native and exclusive to southern Chile and Argentina, the alerce is a majestic species that grows up to 230 ft (70 m) in height and can live for up to 4,000 years. The national park also embraces a dramatic landscape of rolling mountains, deep valleys, southern beech forests, and some 50 mountain lagoons. Nature-watching, river kayaking, and trekking are popular activities here. The most hiked trails are two undemanding 2-mile- (2.5-km-) long paths to the Sargazo and Frías lagoons, ringed respectively by 800- and 300-year-old alerce forests. Birdlife abounds along both trails.

❿ Cochamó Valley

The beautiful and serene Cochamó Valley is situated across the Reloncaví fjord from Parque Nacional Alerce Andino. Also known as the Chilean Yosemite, the valley is overgrown with the mighty alerce trees. It is accessible from the village of Cochamó on horseback, as well as on foot. The valley has drawn a great number of rock climbers and trekking enthusiasts with its little-trodden trails and imposing granite domes. The most popular is the 7-mile (12-km) trek to the La Junta spot that is surrounded

Trail through stands of alerce trees at Parque Nacional Alerce Andino

by granite peaks, with the trailhead 3 miles (5 km) east of Cochamó proper.

There are two rustic accommodations in the valley: one catering to climbers and another to horseback-riding adventurers. A number of good accommodations, a couple of rustic restaurants and horseback-riding clothing can be found in Cochamó.

❸ Calbuco

Road Map D3. 32 miles (52 km) S of Puerto Montt. 🄰 12,000. 🚌

The scenic seaside town of Calbuco, named with the Mapuche word for Blue Water, is where Chile's long, thin mainland begins to break up into a medley of archipelagos. Spanish forces founded the town as a fort settlement in 1603 when retreating southward from a Mapuche uprising. The colony later became an important port used to ship alerce trunks felled in nearby forests. Today, it is a small, picturesque stopover whose main attraction is a plaza facing the open sea with dramatic views of islands and three volcanoes. The plaza is fronted by a mustard-colored church that contains a statue of Archangel Michael, brought from Spain by Calbuco's founders.

The town faces the 14 islands of the Calbuco archipelago, where colonies of Magellanic penguins and other seabirds congregate between September and April. Boat trips from Caleta La Vega, Calbuco's fishermen's harbor, visit these colonies.

For keys to symbols *see back flap*

Chiloé

Green, rainy, and dotted with wooden churches, the enchanting archipelago of Chiloé lies south of the Lake District and comprises one large island, Isla Grande, and many smaller ones. In pre-Columbian times, it was occupied by the seafaring Chono, and later by the Huilliche, a sedentary Mapuche sub-group. The Spanish arrived in 1567 and, over the next 200 years, steered Chiloé along a historical course distinct from that of mainland Chile. During this period, Chiloé saw ethnic mixing between the Spanish and indigenous peoples, evolved a unique culture, and was the last Spanish stronghold to fall in the War of Independence. Today, Chiloé's Jesuit churches and numerous coastal towns and villages, distinct in character from their mainland counterparts, can be visited on day trips from the historical regional capital of Castro.

The town of Ancud with its surrounding greenery and waterways

➌➍ Ancud

Road Map D3. 54 miles (87 km) S of Puerto Montt; Isla Grande. 🚐 30,300. 🚍 🚢 from Puerto Montt. 🛈 Libertad 665; (065) 2622 800. 🎭 Festival Costumbrista Chilote (last week of Feb). 🌐 **ancud.cl**

A picturesque fishing town, Ancud is the first stop for most visitors crossing the Canal de Chacao, from the Lake District to Chiloé. The town was set up by the Spanish in 1768 as a fort settlement on the Bahía de Ancud, a tongue of water dotted with fishing boats, edged by algae-strewn beaches and colorful houses, and ringed by emerald hills. This compact town is easily explored on foot. Its coastal Avenida Salvador Allende runs parallel to the bay, which is overlooked by the ruins of **Fuerte San Antonio**. This Spanish fort marks the site where Royalist forces made their last stand in Chile's War of Independence in 1826. An obelisk at the fort commemorates the Spanish Crown's final defeat.

Beneath rocky cliffs nearby is **Playa Arena Gruesa**, a horseshoe-shaped beach and bathing spot.

In the town itself, **Museo Regional de Ancud** in the central plaza displays archaeological and ethnographic exhibits. It includes an ornate collection of 17th- and 18th-century Jesuit artifacts; carved mythical figures from Chilote mythology; and a life-size replica of *Goleta Ancud*, the Ancud-built schooner that carried the first Chilean settlers to the Strait of Magellan in 1843. Adjacent to the museum is the town's cathedral, whose shingled

exterior resembles the facade of a typical Chilote home. Visitors can also explore the scale models of Chiloé's 16 unique churches at Centro de Visitantes Inmaculada.

🏰 **Fuerte San Antonio**
Cochrane esq. San Antonio.
Open 8.30am–9pm Mon–Fri, 9am–8pm Sat & Sun 🐾

🏛 **Museo Regional de Ancud**
Libertad 370. **Tel** (065) 2622413.
Open 10am–5.30pm Tue–Fri, 10am–1:30pm Sat & Sun (Jan & Feb: 10am–5pm Mon–Fri, 10:30am–3:30pm Sat & Sun). 🐾 🎫 10am–noon & 3.30–5pm. 📷 🌐 **museoancud.cl**

➌➎ Monumento Natural Islotes de Puñihuil

Road Map D3. 17 miles (27 km) W of Ancud; off Playa de Lechagua, Bahía Puñihuil, Isla Grande. 🚢 from Bahía Puñihuil: Sep–Apr: 10am–7pm daily. **Tel** (09) 8317-4302.**Open** Sep–Apr: 10am–7pm daily. 🐾 🌐 **pinguineraschiloe.cl**

Three rocky islets of volcanic origin, the Monumento Natural Islotes de Puñihuil are refuge to colonies of Humboldt and Magellanic penguins that nest here each year. These islets are among the world's few places where the vulnerable Humboldt shares the same habitat as its close Magellanic relative. Small-boat excursions depart from Bahía Puñihuil on Isla Grande's northwestern coast to observe the penguins and other fauna. This includes marine otters, which scramble across the black rock at the water's edge; red-legged cormorants, agile flyers that can be seen dive-bombing the water for crustaceans; flightless steamer ducks; and two species of oystercatchers.

A nesting colony of penguins at Monumento Natural Islotes de Puñihuil

For hotels and restaurants in this region see pp279–80 and pp295–7

Myths and Folklore of Chiloé

Folktales and myths have long enriched Chilote life, with stories handed across centuries, from one generation to the next, through oral tradition. Goddesses who protect the land, a lascivious forest dweller who tricks adolescent girls into surrendering their virginity, a serpent that sucks the lifeblood from a household, and witches disguised as owls that are seen as harbingers of death: these are just a few of the benevolent and evil spirits, sorcerers, witches, and monsters believed by the islanders to roam Chiloé. The origin of these tales lies in thousands of years of Mapuche legend and its later blurring with Spanish superstition and Roman Catholic beliefs. In addition, the archipelago's landscape forms an ideal background; the mist-shrouded bays, silent forests, craggy peaks, and frequent bad weather are evocative of fantastical worlds.

El Trauco is a little forest-dwelling man, without toes and heels, who walks with a stick and carries an axe that can fell a tree in just three blows. He roams his domain searching for youthful virgins walking the forest alone. On seeing one, his axe becomes a flute, the woman is mesmerized into submission and left with child. These children are later called to the forest to replace their father when he is absent.

El Basilisco hatches from a hen's egg, but is a snake with a rooster's red crest. Concealing itself beneath floorboards, it feeds on the saliva of its host family as they sleep. The family members develop dry coughs and die before El Basilisco abandons their house.

La Pincoya, a woman of incomparable beauty, appears at midnight to dance frenetically on Chiloé's beaches. A dance facing the sea signals an abundance of fish; facing the beach means scarcity.

El Coo is a witch disguised as an owl-like creature, whose night-time appearance on the windowsill of a Chilote house announces the death of a loved one.

El Camahueto, a single-horned calf born in marshland, emigrates seaward on reaching adulthood. It destroys farmland as it goes, and causes disastrous tidal waves on its submergence into the sea.

◉ Castro

An island gem, Castro is the capital of Chiloé and an inevitable stop on any visit to the archipelago. The third-oldest settlement in Chile, Castro was founded by the Spanish in 1567 on a hill overlooking the mist-swathed Fiordo Castro. It became the southernmost city in the world and the point for Spanish endeavors to conquer the Chiloé archipelago, as well as for Jesuit attempts to evangelize it. Today, it is a picturesque destination of hilly lanes, gorgeous sea views, and historic *palafitos*.

Brightly painted wooden *palafitos* along the shores of Fiordo Castro

🏛 Museo Regional de Castro
Esmeralda 255. **Tel** (065) 2635967.
Open Jan & Feb: 9:30am–6:30pm
Mon–Sat, 10:30am–1pm Sun; Mar–
Dec: 9:30am–1pm & 3–6pm Mon–Fri,
9:30am–1pm Sat. 🅿 🅒 ♿ ✉

This small museum traces Chiloé's history right from the

arrival of hunter-gatherer groups at the archipelago – around 6,000 years ago – to modern times. Historical objects and information panels record the islands' colonization by the Chono and Huilliche communities; the subsequent

Spanish conquest during the 16th century; and the primary role played by Chiloé as a Royalist stronghold during Chile's War of Independence (1810–18). The exhibits on modern history feature photographs of the destruction caused by the 1960 earthquake and tsunami, which battered coastal villages throughout the archipelago.

🏠 Iglesia San Francisco
Plaza de Armas. **Open** 9:30am–
9:30pm daily. 🏠

Chiloé's most iconic landmark, the beautiful Iglesia San Francisco is an extraordinary work of local craftsmanship. A UNESCO-protected building, it was designed by Italian architect Eduardo Provasoli in 1910, constructed entirely from native woods such as cypress, alerce, and coigüe, and finished in flamboyant polychrome fashion. The edifice's striking Neo-Gothic facade is clad with sheets of corrugated tin, painted gold and purple, and features two 130-ft (40-m) high bell towers. For decades, these towers were used to guide ships arriving at the port and today their status as Castro's tallest structures is protected by law. The church's vaulted interior is ornamented with opulent

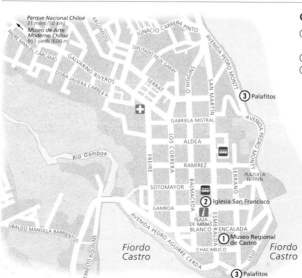

Castro City Center
1. Museo Regional de Castro
2. Iglesia San Francisco
3. Palafitos

0 meters ———— 500
0 yards ———— 500

religious imagery and the altar, pulpit, and confessional boxes are exquisitely hand-carved from native woods by local artisans.

The impressive Neo-Classical facade of Iglesia San Francisco

🏠 Palafitos
Shore of Fiordo Castro.

Castro's *palafitos*, the city's favorite postcard image, are traditional wooden houses built on stilts along the edge of the Fiordo Castro. These picturesque homes are constructed from local woods and painted in vibrant colors. Each *palafito* has two facades: one facing the street and the other overlooking the water. Exquisite examples of vernacular architecture, the *palafitos* were originally built in the 19th century for local fishermen, who would moor their boats in the water before climbing a wooden ladder to their family home.

Prior to the 1960 earthquake, the *palafitos* lined most of Isla Grande's eastern shore. However, their numbers have greatly

VISITORS' CHECKLIST

Practical Information
Road Map D3. 48 miles (77 km) S of Ancud. 🗺 36,300. 🚺 Plaza de Armas. 🎭 Festival Costumbrista Chilote (Feb). 🔲 **municastro.cl**

Transport
🚌

reduced and they are now concentrated on Castro's coastal Avenida Pedro Montt, Calle Lillo, and Calle Ernesto Riquelme, with particularly splendid examples on the northern approach to Castro. Many *palafitos* have been restored and converted into luxurious guesthouses and boutique hotels.

🏛 Museo de Arte Moderno Chiloé
Galvarino Riveros s/n, Parque Municipal. **Tel** (065) 2635454. **Open** only during exhibitions (check website for details). 🔲 **mamchiloe.cl**

Housed in a former grain warehouse, the Museo de Arte Moderno Chiloé sits atop a windswept hillside that offers spectacular views of the city. This excellent contemporary art museum showcases a wide range of styles such as installation, graffiti, and digital art. The permanent collection includes works by well-known Chilean artists Arturo Duclos and Ricardo Yrarrázaval.

Many of the displays at the museum make use of indigenous materials such as sheep's wool and native woods. It also explores local themes that emphasize Chiloé's identity as distinct from that of mainland Chile.

🟥 Parque Nacional Chiloé
Road Map D3. 32 miles (52 km) SW of Castro; Sector Chanquín, Cucao. 🚺 CONAF, Gamboa 424, Castro; (065) 2532501. 🚌 from Castro. **Open** 9am–7pm daily. 🚻 🚣 ⚠ 🔲 **conaf.cl**

The scenic Parque Nacional Chiloé is fringed by the Pacific Ocean on its west and by Chile's coastal mountain range on its east. In between, it protects over 164 sq miles (426 sq km) of indigenous forest, including Chile's southernmost forests of alerce. The park has abundant wildlife and its coastal sections harbor colonies of southern sea lions, Magellanic and Humboldt penguins, and several seabirds.

Most visits to the park focus on the southern sector, where the Cucao village offers rustic accommodations at the park entrance. The village is the trailhead for the **Chanquín-Cole Cole Trail**, which skirts past a stretch of the Pacific coastline, marked by white beaches, big surf, and sand dunes edged by native forest. At the end of the trail, members of a Huilliche community organize horseback rides through the verdant woods.

The park's northern sector, although less visited, has forests of greater size and density. Here, the outstanding 11-mile (18-km) long **Castro-Abtao Trek** crosses through thick alerce forest and ends at the Pacific Ocean.

Windswept landscape of cliffs and dunes fringing the Pacific Ocean at Parque Nacional Chiloé

Local crafts on sale at the market near the harbor, Dalcahue

❸❽ Dalcahue

Road Map D3. 17 miles (28 km) NE of Castro. ⛰ 11,000. 🚌 🚢 Sun. 🎭 La Fiesta del Ajo y de las Tradiciones (mid-Feb). 🌐 dalcahue.cl

Located on the eastern coast of Isla Grande, the town of Dalcahue faces the smaller islands of the Chiloé archipelago. Dalcahue was not founded on any particular date; it evolved from the 1700s onward as a stop on the Jesuits' Circular Mission – annual trips made by the Jesuits across Chiloé.

The town's chief draw is the UNESCO-protected **Iglesia Dalcahue**. This Neo-Gothic structure was built in 1903 on the site of the Jesuits' original mission. Close to it, the **Museo Cultural de Dalcahue** has local historical exhibits. There is also a wooden dining hall on the waterfront that features best of Chilote food.

Dalcahue is also a sales hub for craftsmen from the nearby islands, who arrive daily by boat to offer their wares at the artisans' market.

🏛 **Museo Cultural de Dalcahue**
Avenida Pedro Montt 105. **Tel** (065) 2642375. **Open** Dec–Mar: 9am–5pm daily; Apr–Nov: 8am–5pm Mon–Fri.

❸❾ Curaco de Vélez

Road Map D3. 23 miles (37 km) E of Castro. ⛰ 3,600. 🚌 from Castro. 🚢 from Dalcahue. 🛈 Entrada a Curaco de Vélez, Plazoleta la Amistad. 🎭 Festival Costumbrista Chilote (Feb). 🌐 curacodevelez.cl

From Dalcahue, boats cross the Canal Dalcahue – part of the Mar Interior (Inner Sea) that separates Chiloé from mainland Chile – to reach Isla de Quinchao, an island dotted with tiny coastal villages.

Facing the canal on this island is the pretty village of Curaco de Vélez, the smallest settlement in the Chiloé archipelago. Its origins can be traced to the 1600s, when Jesuit priests first dropped anchor here on their missionary route. Although the town's original Jesuit church was destroyed in a fire in 1971, a wealth of century-old vernacular architecture can still be seen. **Calle Errázuriz** is lined with gray wooden houses clad with alerce tiles in the typical Chilote style. These stand as a testament to Curaco de Vélez's prosperous past, when forestry brought wealth and fine craftsmanship. Today, life in this sleepy village revolves around a small plaza where the **Museo Municipal de Curaco de Vélez** has displays on the town's local history. The plaza backs on to a dramatic sweep of shell-strewn beach facing the narrow stretch of sea. Colonies of black-necked swans dot the water's surface in summer. Isla de Quinchao is also visited for its old Jesuit churches, historic wooden houses, seafood restaurants, and crafts markets.

🏛 **Museo Municipal de Curaco de Vélez**
Calle 21 de Mayo s/n. **Tel** (065) 2667317. **Open** 9am–1:30pm & 2:30–6pm Mon–Fri, 10am–1pm Sun.

❹❀ Achao

Road Map D3. 28 miles (45 km) E of Castro. ⛰ 9,000. 🚌 from Castro & Curaco de Vélez. 🛈 Amunátegui s/n, Plaza de Armas. 🎭 Encuentro Folclórico de las Islas del Archipiélago (Feb).

Nestled on Isla de Quinchao's eastern coast, the small town of Achao makes for a good half-day visit. **Iglesia Santa María de Loreto**, the archipelago's oldest church, is the single surviving structure from the Jesuits' original mission. Built in 1754, the church fronts the town's main plaza and is a completely wooden structure: even the pegs and nails used in its construction are made of wood. The vaulted interior features Baroque columns and a beautifully carved altar and pulpit. The church's Neo-Classical facade is clad in alerce tiles in the traditional Chilote style. Also facing the plaza, the **Museo de Achao** has engaging exhibits on the Chono, the nomadic people who colonized Chiloé in the pre-Columbian era, and colorful displays of Chilote weavings.

🏛 **Museo de Achao**
Amunátegui 014. **Open** Jan & Feb: 10am–5pm daily. 🎟

❹❶ Chonchi

Road Map D3. 14 miles (23 km) S of Castro. ⛰ 4,600. 🚌 🛈 Centenario, esq. Sgto. Candelaria. 🎭 Festival Costumbrista Chilote (Feb).

Referred to as the City of Three Floors for its abrupt topography, Chonchi is actually a hillside village overlooking

Bust of a local naval hero adorning the tree-lined plaza of Curaco de Vélez

Fishing and excursion boats docked at Chonchi's sheltered harbor

a scenic bay on Isla Grande. The town, seen by Jesuit priests as a beachhead from where they could evangelize the archipelago's southern zones, evolved around the Jesuits' Circular Mission in the 17th century.

In the late 19th century, Chonchi reached its commercial peak as a major timber port and wooden buildings still line its gravel streets, particularly on Calle Centenario. Dating from 1883, the **Iglesia de Chonchi** is one of 16 UNESCO-protected churches on the archipelago. Its wooden facade, painted vanilla and powder-blue, hides a vaulted interior decorated with thousands of tiny white stars.

Also of interest, the **Museo de las Tradiciones Chonchinas** is housed in a large family mansion that was built for a rich logging baron in 1910. Inside, the museum re-creates the rooms of a typical pioneer-era Chilote home.

🏛 **Museo de las Tradiciones Chonchinas**
Centenario 116. **Tel** (065) 2671260. **Open** 9am–1pm & 3–6:30pm Mon–Fri, 10:30am–1:30pm Sat. 🚫 📷 ✉
cameras without flash allowed. 📷

㊷ Quellón

Road Map D3. 62 miles (99 km) S of Castro. 🚹 13,000. 🚌 ⛴ 🅸 22 de Mayo 251; (065) 2683500. 🎉 Festival Costumbrista Chilote (Feb.).

A grim, commercial fishing port, Quellón is a departure hub for ferries bound for

destinations along the Carretera Austral. It is also the official point of the great Pan-American highway. Visitors can use Quellon as a jumping-off point to visit the southern sector of Parque Tantauco. However, this requires advance booking.

In the town itself, a sight well worth visiting is the **Museo Inchin Cuivi Ant**, which has exhibits on Chilote technology and history, and sculptural representations of Chiloé's mythological figures (see p219).

🏛 **Museo Inchin Cuivi Ant**
Avenida Juan Ladrilleros 225. **Tel** (065) 2681901. **Open** Dec–Mar: 10am–1pm & 2–8pm Mon–Fri.

㊸ Parque Tantauco

Road Map D3. 45 miles (73 km) SW of Castro. 🚌 ⛴ ✈ 🅸 Panamerican Sur 1826, Castro; (065) 2633805. 🅰
🆆 **parquetantauco.cl**

Created by the business tycoon, and former president of Chile, Sebastián Piñera, this 456 sq mile (1180 sq km) private nature reserve sits in the southwest corner of Chiloé. It is among the world's 35 biodiversity hotspots and is home to a variety of flora and fauna, including Darwin foxes, pudú deer, and the pygmy. The park has an excellent infrastructure with its well-kept trails, camping huts, and designated campsites. However, only a limited number of visitors are allowed at any point of time in the park.

Tantauco is divided into two halves; the northern section can be reached via several weekly buses from Quellon in summer, while the southern section is accessed via a small plane from Castro to the tiny airstrip in the village of Caleta Inio, or by boat from Quellon to Caleta Inio.

Visitors can choose from a two-day loop trek around the Caleta Inio Peninsula or from a three- to eight-day trek within the park. Several tour companies in Castro organize flights and treks into the park.

Festival Costumbrista Chilote

A vibrant celebration of Chilote culture, the Festival Costumbrista Chilote is Chiloé's biggest annual event, and is held across towns and villages in the archipelago in January and February. Festivities feature folk music and dance, craft fairs, and demonstrations of traditional island activities. Visitors can try their hand at shearing sheep, driving oxen, making jams, as well as learn traditional Chilote weaving methods. Food stalls serve Chilote food and drinks, including shellfish empanadas, *curanto* (see p287), *licor de oro* (a fermented cow-milk liqueur), and sweet ulmo honey, made from the native ulmo tree. The festivities involve a number of events held at different times and places, so it is advisable to ask a tourist information office for details.

Costumed children dancing, Festival Costumbrista Chilote

Jesuit Churches in Chiloé

In 1608, Jesuit priests arrived at Chiloé to evangelize the indigenous Huilliche. In the process, they established the Circular Mission and built wooden churches across the archipelago. Their construction represented a new form of religious architecture – the Chilote School – whose roots lay in the Jesuit-church architecture of 17th-century Central Europe. Today, over 60 Jesuit churches survive on the archipelago, some of which were rebuilt in the 18th and 19th centuries following fire or earthquake. Each church shares essential architectural features, though they differ in size and detail. Sixteen constitute a UNESCO World Heritage Site.

A vaulted ceiling covers the central nave, such as in Iglesia de Castro. This elegant feature might be brightly painted or left bare and unadorned.

The interior of the church can be simple and austere or highly decorative.

Two lateral naves flank the central nave. These have flat ceilings.

The altar table stands at the church's northern end. Crafted from native alerce, cypress, and mañío trunks by local artisans, it is often richly carved with Catholic imagery. Brightly painted, wooden saints adorn the space above the altar.

Church Architecture

Chilote churches have similar key characteristics, all of which can be seen in Iglesia de Achao. Most distinctive are the bell tower and symmetrical facade. The shape of the church, with its angled roof, vaulted ceiling, and long nave, suggests an inverted boat. The churches overlook a natural harbor from the coast and face south for protection from northern rains.

Windows are set along the church's portico, bell tower and side walls.

A long central nave stands at the heart of the church. Wooden columns, set in stone and carved from the trunks of native island trees, separate this part from two lateral naves. Only the central nave reaches the back of the church and the altar.

The Jesuits' Circular Mission

Facade of Iglesia de Tenaun

Jesuit priests faced two major obstacles to the evangelization of Chiloé: the exceptional isolation of its islands and of its Huilliche populations. In an effort to overcome these, the Jesuits made round, annual trips of the archipelago by sea. On this Circular Mission, priests disembarked at each indigenous settlement, converted its people, deposited a layman for continued spiritual assistance, and returned the following year. A church was built at each new mission – 200 were built in total – around which villages grew. After the Jesuits' expulsion from the Spanish New World in 1767, Franciscans continued the Circular Mission.

UNESCO-Protected Churches in Chiloé

1. Iglesia de Colo
2. Iglesia de San Juan
3. Iglesia de Dalcahue
4. Iglesia de Castro
5. Iglesia de Nercón
6. Iglesia de Vilupulli
7. Iglesia de Chonchi
8. Iglesia de Ichuac
9. Iglesia de Rilán
10. Iglesia de Aldachildo
11. Iglesia de Detif
12. Iglesia de Chelín
13. Iglesia de Quinchao
14. Iglesia de Achao
15. Iglesia de Caguach
16. Iglesia de Tenaún

Visits and Tours

Many churches grace the center of Chiloé's towns. These are open all day and easily accessible. For visitors arriving in Chiloé by car, the Ruta de las Iglesias is a half-day driving tour of Chiloé's UNESCO-protected churches. Organized tours of selected churches run from Castro and Ancud. Details are available at **rutadelasiglesias.cl**

A cross crowns the tower. It acts as a guiding beacon for fishermen and sailors at sea.

A bell tower rises above the choir at the center of the facade, lending the church a symmetrical design. The tower consists of a rectangular base and a tapering, windowed octagonal tower.

The façade is beautiful for its simplicity and symmetry. It features a gabled roof and is sometimes tiled with alerce shingles.

The choir lies above the entrance, forming a triangular shape when viewed from outside.

The entrance may have a columned and arched arcade in the Neo-Gothic or Neo-Classical style, as seen in Iglesia de Dalcahue. The Jesuits laid out squares in front of entrances for religious processions.

NORTHERN PATAGONIA

Thinly populated Northern Patagonia is home to some of the continent's wildest country, including Chile's most scenic highway, the Carretera Austral. The region embraces icy-blue glaciers and icebergs, rugged Andean pinnacles, and large forest reserves. Scattered hamlets and small towns such as Coyhaique serve as ideal bases for exploring the region's myriad attractions.

The fjords, forests, and steppes of Northern Patagonia were originally inhabited by a handful of Tehuelche hunter-gatherers and Kawéskar fisherfolk. During the age of exploration, few Europeans penetrated the area, apart from Jesuit missionaries based in Chiloé. British seafarers and scientists such as John Byron (1723–86) and Charles Darwin (1809–82) left some of the best early records. Even after independence, Chile was slow to colonize Northern Patagonia. It was not until the early 20th century that a huge land grant for sheep ranching and forestry provided the impetus for economic growth in the region.

The Chilean government's 1903 grant was made to private agricultural companies in and around the budding regional capital of Coyhaique. This initially led to large-scale fires, deforestation, and erosion

that closed up Puerto Aisén, the area's main port, at a time when virtually all transportation was seaborne. Road access began to be established in the 1970s with the construction of the Carretera Austral – a longitudinal road that extends the length of Northern Patagonia and is gradually being paved. The new highway helped promote tourism, encouraged mining and salmon farming, and introduced massive, though controversial, hydroelectric projects.

Northern Patagonia's many national parks conserve large swathes of old native forests, wild rivers, rugged peaks, and plunging waterfalls. Explored via scenic ferry routes and road trips off the Carretera Austral, these are ideal for a gamut of activities, from white-water rafting to fly-fishing and trekking.

Paseo Horn, a pedestrian mall in downtown Coyhaique

◄ The vast Campo de Hielo Norte ice sheet, in the Parque Nacional Laguna San Rafael

Exploring Northern Patagonia

The region is characterized by the absence of large towns, other than the provincial capital of Coyhaique, which is the gateway to the glacier-swathed Parque Nacional Laguna San Rafael and the trekkers' paradise Reserva Nacional Cerro Castillo. Most travelers explore Northern Patagonia on the Carretera Austral, which stretches across the length of the region. Among the attractions accessible via this highway are the top white-water destinations of Río Futaleufú and Río Baker, the forest reserves of Parque Pumalín and Reserva Nacional Lago Jeinemeni, and the orchard-town of Chile Chico. The highway ends near Villa O'Higgins, where an adventurous overland trekking route leads into Argentina. Ferries and catamarans navigate island channels to reach the fishing hamlet of Melinka and the secluded Puerto Edén.

Kayaking on the waters of Lago Bertrand, off the Carretera Austral

Sights at a Glance

Villages, Towns, and Cities
1 Hornopirén
3 Chaitén
4 Futaleufú
5 Palena
6 Melinka
7 Puyuhuapi
10 Puerto Cisnes
11 Coyhaique
12 Puerto Chacabuco
17 Chile Chico
19 Cochrane

21 Caleta Tortel
22 Villa O'Higgins
23 Puerto Edén

Resorts and Spas
8 Puyuhuapi Lodge & Spa

National Parks, Reserves, and Natural Monuments
9 Parque Nacional Queulat
14 Reserva Nacional Río Simpson
15 Reserva Nacional Cerro Castillo

16 Parque Nacional Laguna San Rafael
18 Reserva Nacional Lago Jeinemeni

Areas of Natural Beauty
2 Parque Pumalín
13 Parque Aiken del Sur
20 Río Baker

Rugged landscape rising behind the lakeshore town of Chile Chico

For hotels and restaurants in this region see pp280–81 and pp297–8

Puerto
Montt
Ralún
La Arena
Cochamo
*Parque Nacional
Hornopirén*
🚠 ❶ HORNOPIRÉN
*Isla
Llancahué*
🚠 ❷ PARQUE PUMALÍN
**LOS
LAGOS**
Caleta Gonzalo
Santa
Barbara
*Volcán Chaitén
3,681 ft*
🚠 ❸ CHAITÉN
*Reserva Nacional
Futaleufú*
⚡ ❹ FUTALEUFÚ
Lago Yelcho
Villa Santa Lucia
Puerto
Ramirez
✈ ❺ PALENA
*Golfo de
Corcovado*
*Lago
Palena*
La Junta
*Lago
Rosselot*
✈ ❻ MELINKA
Lago Verde
Lago Rispatrón
ℹ ❼ PUYUHUAPI
🚠 ❽ PUYUHUAPI LODGE & SPA
PARQUE NACIONAL QUELAT ❾
La Tapera
*Parque Nacional
Isla Magdalena*
❿
Villa Amengual
*Archipiélago
de los
Chonos*
**PUERTO
CISNES**
*Reserva
Nacional
Coyhaique*
**PACIFIC
OCEAN**
Puerto
Aisén
RESERVA
NACIONAL
RÍO SIMPSON
PUERTO CHACABUCO ⓬ ⓮ ⓫ COYHAIQUE
⓭
*Cerro
Castillo
7,605 ft*
PARQUE AIKEN DEL SUR
Balmaceda
*Volcán Hudson
6,250 ft*
⓯ RESERVA NACIONAL
CERRO CASTILLO
*Reserva Nacional
las Guaitecas*
AISÉN
Villa Cerro
Castillo
Puerto Ingeniero Ibáñez
Puerto Murta
*Monte San Valentín
13,314 ft*
Puerto
Tranquilo
Lago General Carrera
⓱ CHILE CHICO
⓰
*Lago
Bertrand*
Puerto
Guadal
⓲
RESERVA NACIONAL
LAGO JEINEMENI
**PARQUE NACIONAL
LAGUNA SAN RAFAEL**
Puerto
Bertrand
Estancia Valle
Chacabuco
*Golfo de
Penas*
COCHRANE ⓳
*Lago
Cochrane*
⓴ RÍO BAKER
*Cerro San Lorenzo
12,158 ft*
CALETA TORTEL ㉑
Puerto
Yungay
*Reserva
Nacional
Katalalixar*
Campo de Hielo Norte
VILLA O'HIGGINS ㉒
*Lago
O'Higgins*
Campo de Hielo Sur
PUERTO EDÉN ㉓
MAGALLANES
*Isla
Wellington*

0 km   100
0 miles   100

Key

▬▬ Main road

━━ Minor road

═ ═ ═ Untarred minor road

━━ Regional border

▬▬ International border

△ Peak

For keys to symbols *see back flap*

Boats at Hornopirén's quay, surrounded by dramatic fjord scenery

❶ Hornopirén

Road Map E3. 581 miles (936 km) S of Santiago. 🚶 2,500. 🚌 from Puerto Montt. ⛴

Scenically set on the edge of a serene fjord, Hornopirén is named for the towering, 5,150-ft- (1,570-m-) high Volcán Hornopirén that looms over the town. Hornopirén has been prosperous since the 19th century, despite being hard hit by the Volcán Chaitén eruption in 2008. Today, it is the gateway to Parque Nacional Hornopirén, 7 miles (12 km) to the north-west, which offers good wildlife-watching and hiking. Local launches docked at the ferry port take visitors to hot-spring pools nearby. Harborside vendors sell fresh fish.

❷ Parque Pumalín

Road Map E3. 82 miles (132 km) S of Puerto Montt; Caleta Gonzalo. ⛴ from Hornopirén: Jan & Feb only. ℹ Klenner 299, Puerto Varas; (065) 2250079. 🛇🛇🖥🏠🔺 🌐 parquepumalin.cl

The world's largest privately owned nature reserve, Parque Pumalín protects over 1,224 sq miles (3,170 sq km) of temp-erate rain forest in an area of rugged mountains rising out of deep fjords. Established in 1991, the park was the result of the conservation initiatives of its founder, US environmental millionaire and entrepreneur, Doug Tompkins. The project initially faced stiff resistance from some of Chile's

nationalists, who objected to a foreigner's acquisition of such a massive piece of land in the country. However, the park's gradual opening to the public, complete with campgrounds, *cabañas*, and hiking trails, has delighted many Chileans.

Parque Pumalín is a favored destination with hikers, owing to the many trails that start from the main road in the southern part of the park and snake through its stunning landscapes of verdant alerce forests, cascading waterfalls, and pristine fjords. Hikers can choose from three other trails of varying length, as well as two campsites at the third section of Parque Pumalín, located near the village of Amarillo, and a multi-day

trail between South Pumalín and Amarillo. Most of these trails are short but some are truly challenging, and require hikers to climb steep ladders while attached to ropes. There are also many hot springs within the park; some are freely available to the public, while others can be accessed for a fee.

❸ Chaitén

Road Map E3. 100 miles (160 km) S of Puerto Montt. 🚶 4,000. ✈ to Puerto Montt. 🚌 to Puerto Montt and Coyhaique. ⛴ to Coyhaique, Puerto Montt, Quellon and Castro

Located along Chile's Ruta 7, better known as the Carretera Austral, the town of Chaitén was popular for its scenic blend of seaside and sierra until the Volcán Chaitén, barely 6 miles (10 km) away, erupted on May 2, 2008. This catastrophe was followed by massive flooding, which swept many houses off their foundations and buried several others in soggy ash.

A government attempt to relocate the residents proved unpopular, however, and many of them returned to town. In spite of the volcano's presence, the area continues to attract many visitors with its hiking options and the nearby El Amarillo hot springs. Ferries

Cabañas amid the lush vegetation in Parque Pumalín

Kayaking on the calm waters of Río Azul, near Futaleufú

from Puerto Montt and the Chiloé archipelago arrive at Chaitén's port, and many accommodations and other services have reopened.

❹ Futaleufú

Road Map E3. 96 miles (154 km) SE of Chaitén. ⛰ 1,800. 🚌 from Chaitén and Coyhaique. ℹ O'Higgins 536; (065) 2721241. 🌐 **futaleufu.cl**

Nestled in a secluded and picturesque valley close to the Argentine border, the village of Futaleufú is famous for its eponymous river. Popularly called the Fu, Río Futaleufú is one of the world's top destinations for white-water rafting and kayaking. Operators maintain riverside camps for the adventurous who travel to this river to test its Class 4 and 5 rapids, which include the Gates of Hell, Terminator, and The Perfect Storm. Novices can try their hand at calmer sections of the river, or head to the less demanding Río Azul and Río Espolón nearby. Sea kayaking is possible on Lago Yelcho, which merges with the Pacific Ocean via Río Yelcho. Other activities around Futaleufú include hiking, horse riding, mountain-biking and fly-fishing.

The village, as well as a large part of the area east of Río Futaleufú, is part of the 19-sq-mile (49-sq-km) **Reserva Nacional Futaleufú**. This reserve is home to lush forests of lenga, coigüe, and the Chilean cedar, and offers sanctuary to a number of animal species, including the endangered huemul deer.

❺ Palena

Road Map E3. 160 miles (257 km) SE of Puerto Montt. ⛰ 1,700. 🚌 from Chaitén. ℹ O'Higgins 740; (065) 2741221. 🐎 Rodeo de Palena (Jan). 🌐 **municipalidadpalena.cl**

Close to the Argentine border, the village of Palena is named for the river that flows past it. It is notable for the **Rodeo de Palena**, which showcases Chile's huaso heritage. The main event at this rodeo involves costumed huasos on horseback, trying to pin a calf to a padded ring.

The Sendero de Chile (see p306), a web of trails across Chile, passes through Palena en route to the little-known Reserva Nacional Lago Palena, from where the road continues to the Argentine border.

Fly-fishing from a wooden bridge across the meandering Río Palena

❻ Melinka

Road Map D3. 171 miles (276 km) SW of Puerto Montt. ⛰ 1400. ✈ from Puerto Montt. ⛴ from Puerto Montt & Quellón.

Off the mainland west of Palena, the Guaitecas archipelago is made up of several tiny islands. Of these, Isla Ascensión is home to the fishing village of Melinka, the archipelago's main settlement. The village overlooks Golfo de Corcovado, known for its sizable blue whale population; these are often visible from shore. Melinka has some simple, but comfortable lodgings and a few small eateries.

Sailing the Fjords of Northern Patagonia

The 3-day voyage from Puerto Montt (see p216) south to Puerto Natales (see p244) aboard the M/V Edén, operated by Navimag Ferries (see p329), is one of Northern Patagonia's top attractions and an experience in itself. The exhilarating journey passes through innumerable fjords, channels, and thousands of uninhabited islands along the length of Patagonia. From the deck, passengers can admire an electrifying landscape – dense temperate rain forests, serene lakes, massive glaciers, and snowcapped mountains. It is also possible to spot some wildlife, including the odd colony of sea lions. Pods of dolphins occasionally follow the boats, and seagulls and albatrosses soar above in the skies. Entertainment on board includes talks on natural history and screenings of Chilean documentaries. The ferry passes the tiny fishing village of Melinka and the isolated fjord town of Puerto Eden, home to a few remaining indigenous Yamana people.

Tranquil lake in Parque Pumalín

❼ Puyuhuapi

Road Map E4. 269 miles (434 km) SE of Puerto Montt. 🚗 830. 🚌 from Chaiten, Coyhaique & Futaleufu. ℹ️ Otto Übel s/n; (067) 2325244.

Sitting on the edge of a scenic fjord, Puyuhuapi, unlike the newer settlements along the Carretera Austral, was founded by German immigrants from the Sudetenland (later, part of Czechoslovakia) in the 1930s. As a result, a large number of the houses in this area are distinctly Teutonic in style and the traditions of early settlers are still kept alive by the residents. Along with the building of wooden boats, artisanal fishery constitutes the main economic activity of the village.

The village is known for the **Alfombras de Puyuhuapi**, a family-owned factory that produces custom-made carpets for export. Set up in 1945 by German textile engineer Walter Hopperdietzel, the factory (open for tours on request) employs women from the archipelago of Chiloé to weave a range of exquisite hand-knotted woolen carpets. Unique vertical looms are used to create these beautiful rugs.

Puyuhuapi also serves as an ideal base for those who want to explore nearby destinations such as the Parque Nacional Queulat and the adjacent Reserva Nacional Lago Rosselot. Also in the vicinity are the hot springs of the luxurious Puyuhuapi Lodge & Spa. The place also offers activities such as trekking, horseriding, and boat riding.

Guests relaxing in the indoor thermal pool at Puyuhuapi Lodge & Spa

Environs

Located 4 miles (6 km) south of Puyuhuapi, the **Termas Ventisquero de Puyuhuapi** has four thermal pools overlooking the sound, basic changing rooms, and a café.

🏭 **Alfombras de Puyuhuapi**
Aisén s/n. **Tel** (09) 9359-9515. **Open** 10am–1:30pm & 3–6:30pm Mon–Sat. 🔲 🏠 🌐 puyuhuapi.com

♨️ **Termas Ventisquero de Puyuhuapi**
Carretera Austral Sur Km6. **Tel** (09) 7966-6862. **Open** 9am–11pm daily. 🔲 🌐 termas ventisqueropuyuhuapi.cl

❽ Puyuhuapi Lodge & Spa

Road Map E4. 277 miles (447 km) SE of Puerto Montt; Bahía Dorita s/n. **Tel** (02) 2225-6489. 🚌 from reception at Carretera Austral, 9 miles (14 km) S of Puyuhuapi. 🔲 🌐 puyuhuapilodge.com

In a country known for its hot-springs resorts, Puyuhuapi Lodge & Spa is one of the top choices. Located in a secluded and an exceptional spot on the western side of the gorgeous Seno Ventisquero inlet, where the water from the sea, waterfalls, and thermal springs converge, the lodge blends smoothly into the fern- and flower-filled rain forest.

Puyuhuapi Lodge & Spa welcomes overnight guests and day guests during the off season. The complex is made up of charming units, whose facades recall the shingled houses often seen on the islands of Chiloé. Rooms at the lodge boast polished wooden interiors and face the Bahía Dorita. Day visitors have access to three outdoor thermal pools and a café, while hotel guests can also use the heated indoor pool and enjoy a wide range of therapies, body treatments, and massages.

An interesting variety of package options are available for overnight guests. These include outdoor activities such as hiking through the Parque Nacional Queulat, fly-fishing on the nearby rivers, and a visit to the village of Puyuhuapi and its famous carpet factory. Most stays conclude with a day trip south to Parque Nacional Laguna San Rafael (*see p237*), sailing on the high-speed catamaran *Patagonia Express*, which passes through serene fjords and canals. The boat then returns north to Puerto Chacabuco, from where the lodge's guests are transferred to Coyhaique (*see p236*) and its airport at Balmaceda.

Casa Ludwig, a Teutonic-style house characteristic of Puyuhuapi

❾ Parque Nacional Queulat

Road Map E4. 269 miles (434 km) SE of Puerto Montt. ℹ️ CONAF, Sector Ventisquero Colgante, Carretera Austral. 🚌 from Puerto Puyuhuapi & Coyhaique. 🏠 🚻 ♿ ⛰️ 🌐 conaf.cl

Covering some of Northern Patagonia's most rugged terrain, Parque Nacional Queulat stretches from La Junta in the north to Puerto Cisnes in the south, and almost to the Argentine border in the east. Its dense rain forests, limpid lakes, clear trout streams, and steep-sided mountains cover an area of more than 5,800 sq miles (15,000 sq km). Altitudes in the park vary significantly – from sea level to a height of 7,300 ft (2,255 m), where much of the abundant precipitation falls as snow.

Although the national park fronts the Carretera Austral, its trackless backcountry is generally unexplored. However, Queulat's Sector Ventisquero Colgante offers good hiking trails. An eastbound lateral off the Carretera Austral leads to CONAF's office for visitors. From here, a couple of nature trails offer breathtaking views of the **Ventisquero Colgante**, a hanging glacier that in the early 19th century nearly reached the sea. From this mass of solid ice, waterfalls plunge into the jade-colored **Laguna Témpanos** (Iceberg Lake), which, in spite of its name, has no icebergs. The lake can be reached via

Narrow bridge across Río Guillermo at the Parque Nacional Queulat

the **Sendero Río Guillermo**, a 1,969-ft (600 m) long route that crosses a suspension bridge over the river from which it takes its name.

From the lake, a 2-mile (3.5-km) long trail, called the **Sendero Ventisquero Colgante**, climbs through dark and dense temperate rain forest to an over-look. When the sun warms the glacier's face, it is possible to see blocks of ice fall and shatter onto the rock debris below.

Near the park's southern entrance, the **Sendero Río de las Cascadas** is a short path leading to a fascinating natural granite amphitheater. Another road in the southern sector zigzags over the 1,650-ft (500-m) high Portezuelo Queulat pass. An offshoot from this point leads to the **Salto Padre García**, an attractive, tumbling waterfall.

In the northern part of the park, **Lago Risopatrón** is a popular point for fly-fishing. While the park itself has only campgrounds, there are several fishing lodges along the highway, and other accommodations at La Junta and Puyuhuapi.

❿ Puerto Cisnes

Road Map E4. 320 miles (520 km) SE of Puerto Montt. 🗻 2500. 🚌 ℹ️ Sotomayor s/n; (09) 7663-7208.

Sitting at the mouth of the eponymous river, Puerto Cisnes was founded in 1929 as a humble lumber factory. Today it is a pretty fishing village, with colorful boats lining its waterfront. The wooden Neo-Classical **Biblioteca Pública Genaro Godoy**, the village library, is a notable landmark. Its facade is adorned with figurines from Greek mythology. Puerto Cisnes is also the access point to the **Parque Nacional Isla Magdalena**, and local fishermen shuttle visitors to this lushly forested park.

On the Carretera Austral, immediately east of the turnoff to Puerto Cisnes, is the Viaducto Piedra El Gato, a remarkable engineering achievement. Here the highway runs parallel to the river along the face of a nearly vertical granite pitch. There are several viewpoints on each approach to the viaduct that allow motorists to admire the structure and the landscape.

Waterfalls from the Ventisquero Colgante glacier plunging into Laguna Témpanos, Parque Nacional Queulat

Río Simpson, running through the scenic valley between Coyhaique and Puerto Aisén ▶

Cerro Macay rising above one of Coyhaique's tree-lined streets

⓫ Coyhaique

Road Map E4. 286 miles (461 km) SE of Puerto Montt. 🏔 55,400. ✈ 🚌 ℹ Bulnes 35; (067) 2233949. 🅦 **coyhaique.cl**

Capital of Chile's Aisén region, and Northern Patagonia's only sizable city, Coyhaique is a labyrinth of concentric roads that encircle the pentagonal Plaza de Armas and change names on every other block. Despite this bewildering orientation, Coyhaique offers the region's best tourist infrastructure and easy access to destinations such as Lago Elizalde and the Reserva Nacional Río Simpson.

Though Coyhaique has no major attractions, it is the only major town on the Carretera Austral that has a vibrant dining scene. Those who wish to explore the Carretera Austral can find rental cars in town. Visitors who are headed north or south should take the opportunity to withdraw money from the city.

Just beyond the city limits, the **Reserva Nacional Coyhaique** is a 10-sq-mile (27-sq-km) park with hiking trails through forests of coigüe and lenga. It has a campground and offers great panoramas of the city and its environs.

🏕 **Reserva Nacional Coyhaique**
Ruta 7 Norte. **Tel** (067) 2212225.
Open Dec–Mar: 8:30am–9pm daily; Apr–Nov: 8:30am–5:30pm daily. 🚻 🅦 **conaf.cl**

⓬ Puerto Chacabuco

Road Map E4. 37 miles (60 km) W of Coyhaique. 🏔 1,200. 🚌 from Coyhaique. ⛴ from Puerto Montt & Quellón.

Located on the shores of an attractive natural harbor, Puerto Chacabuco is a small but lively port-town, and the center of a thriving fishing industry. It superseded nearby Puerto Aisén as the Aisén region's main port in the 1940s; by this time, deforestation of Patagonia's forests had filled Río Aisén's outlet with sediments that made it impossible to anchor at Puerto Aisén.

Today, Puerto Chacabuco serves as the gateway to nearby sights such as Parque Aiken del Sur and Parque Nacional Laguna San Rafael.

⓭ Parque Aiken del Sur

Road Map E4. 54 miles (87 km) SW of Coyhaique. ⛴ from Puerto Chacabuco. ℹ J.M. Carrera 50, Puerto Chacabuco; (067) 2351115. **Open** reservations required. 🚶 📷 🚻 🅦 **loberiasdelsur.cl**

The privately owned nature reserve and botanical garden of Parque Aiken del Sur covers a densely forested area of 1 sq mile (3 sq km). It has four good hiking trails featuring information panels and viewpoints, as well as an arboretum with a number of helpfully labeled plant species. Parque Aiken is under the same ownership as Puerto Chacabuco's Hotel Loberías del Sur, which organizes guided trips to the park. Tours end with a *parrillada* (barbecue) lunch and folkloric entertainment that includes performances of Chile's national dance, the *cueca (see p28)*.

The plunging Cascada La Vírgen at Reserva Nacional Río Simpson

⓮ Reserva Nacional Río Simpson

Road Map E4. 15 miles (25 km) W of Coyhaique. 🚌 from Coyhaique . ℹ CONAF, Ruta 240, Km37. **Open** 10am–4pm Mon–Sat, 11am–2pm Sun. 🚶 🅦 **conaf.cl**

Straddling both the Carretera Austral and the Río Simpson are the humid wooded mountains of the Reserva Nacional Río Simpson. This reserve protects

Entrance through forested hills to the Parque Aiken del Sur

an area of over 256 sq miles (426 sq km) and is characterized by deep canyons, gushing waterfalls and forests of tepa, coigüe, and lenga. The park is also an important sanctuary for the pudú and the endangered huemul deer.

CONAF's visitor center features a small natural history museum that offers interesting information on native flora and fauna. A short trail leads from the center to the attractive **Cascada La Vírgen** waterfall, which is encircled by wild ferns and shrubs.

⑮ Reserva Nacional Cerro Castillo

Road Map E4. 28 miles (45 km) S of Coyhaique. 🚌 from Coyhaique.

Covering over 517 sq miles (1,340 sq km) of rugged Andean landscape, Reserva Nacional Cerro Castillo is named for the impressive 8,465-ft (2,581-m) high Cerro Castillo, which crowns this reserve. A popular destination for hikers, the reserve offers several nature trails that snake through forests of lenga and around cascading waterfalls and icy glaciers. Wildlife spotted on these hikes includes the huemul, puma, and fox.

The reserve's big attraction is a 4-day trek through dense vegetation that ends at the tiny hamlet of Villa Cerro Castillo. A short distance south from this village is **Alero de las Manos**, a natural rock shelter that is home to spectacular pre-Columbian paintings. Exquisite examples of rock art, these paintings date from 3,000 years ago.

Situated along the northern border of Reserva Nacional Cerro Castillo, **Lago Elizalde** is a narrow lake that stretches for 15 miles (25 km), but is less than a mile (2 km) wide at any point. Verdant woodlands of coigüe and lenga fringe this lake, which is a popular spot for fishing, sailing, and kayaking.

Southeast of the reserve, the port-town of **Puerto Ingeniero Ibáñez** sits at the edge of Chile's

Lago Elizalde in the Reserva Nacional Cerro Castillo

largest lake, Lago General Carrera. While notable for its orchards, the town is frequented by travelers wishing to take the ferry across the lake to Chile Chico.

🏛 Alero de las Manos
3 miles (5 km) S of Villa Cerro Castillo. **Open** 10am–6pm daily. 🅿 📷

⑯ Parque Nacional Laguna San Rafael

Road Map D4. 110 miles (190 km) SW of Coyhaique. ✈ from Coyhaique. 🚢 from Puerto Chacabuco. 🅿 🛶 🛖 **w** conaf.cl

A UNESCO World Biosphere Reserve, Parque Nacional Laguna San Rafael is one of Chile's largest national parks. Almost half of this sprawling 6,726-sq-miles (17,420-sq-km) reserve is covered by the **Campo de Hielo Norte**, the second-largest ice sheet in the southern hemisphere. This sheet embraces the towering Monte San Valentín, which at 13,314 ft (4,058 m) is the highest summit in Patagonia. Campo de Hielo Norte feeds over 18 glaciers including the 200-ft (60-m) high **Ventisquero San Rafael**, which overlooks Laguna San Raphael. From the face of this receding glacier, massive chunks of blue ice spill into the lagoon below.

Several tour operators arrange sailing excursions to the glacier through a maze of fjords and

channels. While boats usually keep a safe distance from the glacier, passengers can enjoy a closer look from inflatable dinghies, or take the plane ride over the park for breathtaking panoramas of the ice field. A road cuts cross-country from Puerto Rio Tranquilo, 135 miles (217 km) south of Coyhaique, through the Valle Exploradores to a water crossing where travelers on a budget can take a boat to the glacier with pre-arranged outfitters. The park is also accessible via car from Puerto Rio Tranquilo.

Famous names associated with this place include that of renowned British naturalist Charles Darwin (1809–82), who visited the glacier during his voyage on board the HMS *Beagle*. John Byron, grandfather of famous British poet Lord Byron, was shipwrecked here in 1742 and gave extensive descriptions of the area.

A mist-swathed glacier in Parque Nacional Laguna San Rafael

⑰ Chile Chico

Road Map E4. 68 miles (110 km)
SE of Coyhaique. 🚐 5,127. 🚌 🚐
🚌 from Puerto Ingeniero Ibañez.
ℹ️ O'Higgins 192; (067) 2411303.
🌐 chilechico.cl

Close to the Argentine border, Chile Chico is part of a fruit-growing belt near Lago General Carrera. The town can either be approached by a scenic and precipitous road from the Carreta Austral, or via an equally exciting ferry ride across the vast, electric blue lake.

Chile Chico dates from 1909, when Argentines crossed over to settle in this area. It was briefly famous in 1917, when the colonizers faced the ranchers in the War of Chile Chico. In 1991, the eruption of Volcán Hudson nearly smothered the area's apple and pear orchards. This past and the area's natural history are documented in the **Museo de la Casa de Cultura**, part of which occupies the grounded *Los Andes* steamer, which once toured the lake.

🏛️ **Museo de la Casa de Cultura**
Calle O'Higgins and Lautaro. **Tel** (067) 2411355. **Open** 9am–1pm & 3–6pm Mon–Fri; hours vary Sat & Sun. **Closed** Dec–Mar: Sun.

⑱ Reserva Nacional Lago Jeinemeni

Road Map E4. 89 miles (143 km) SE of Coyhaique; Blest Gana 121, Chile Chico. **Tel** (067) 2411325. 🚶 ⚠️ 🌐 conaf.cl

Hugging the Argentine border, and accessible only by high-

Broad, mountainous landscape in the Reserva Nacional Lago Jeinemeni

clearance vehicles, the Reserva Nacional Lago Jeinemeni is an enormous 622-sq-mile (1,600-sq-km) sanctuary named for its lake, which is popular with fly-fishers. The reserve is located 32 miles (52 km) southwest of Chile Chico and is linked to Valle Chacabuco by a three-day hiking traverse. In the northeastern sector, a footpath leads to pre-Columbian rock art at the **Cueva de las Manos**.

⑲ Cochrane

Road Map E4. 119 miles (192 km) S of Coyhaique. 🚐 3,382. 🚌 🚐
ℹ️ Dr. Steffen and Esmeralda; (067) 2522115. 🌐 cochranepatagonia.cl

Situated at the western edge of the eponymous lake, the tidy town of Cochrane is the last service center on the Carretera

Austral. Visitors, notably motorists, will find the highway's last gasoline station here. Cochrane is also the gateway to the **Reserva Nacional Lago Tamango**, a major sanctuary for the endangered huemul deer, situated 4 miles (6 km) northeast of town. From the entrance, hiking trails run to Laguna Tamnaguito, Laguna Elefantina, and up Cerro Tamango. It is also possible to hike directly from this reserve to Valle Chacabuco in Parque Nacional Patagonia.

📷 **Reserva Nacional Tamango**
4 miles (6 km) E of Cochrane; CONAF, Río Nef 417. **Tel** (067) 2522164. 🚶 ⚠️ 🌐 conaf.cl

⑳ Río Baker

Road Map E5. 146 miles (235 km) S of Coyhaique. 🚐 from Cochrane and Coyhaique. 🚶 ⚠️

Flowing between Caleta Tortel and Lago Bertrand, the 116-mile (170-km) long Río Baker is Chile's largest river in terms of volume. Owing to its flow, and the mountainous terrain through which it runs, this wild and scenic river has been a prime candidate for a massive hydro-electric project. Part of the river has been dammed, however, the area just south of **Puerto**

The *Los Andes* steamer outside the Museo de la Casa de Cultura at Chile Chico

Bertrand, especially at the stunning confluence of the Baker and the Río Nef, is a paradise for campers, hikers, rafters, fly-fishers, and other recreationists. Rafting trips can be arranged in tiny Puerto Bertrand, north of Cochrane.

㉑ Caleta Tortel

Road Map D5. 172 km (277 miles) SW of Coyhaique. ⚟ 320. 🚌 from Coyhaique.

Located on an inlet off the Río Baker's Fiordo Mitchell, Caleta Tortel is arguably Patagonia's most picturesque village. The settlement was unreachable by road until 2003. It still has no streets as such, but boardwalks and staircases that link its bayside *palafitos* (see p116). These homesteads show the influence of the folk architecture of the Chiloé archipelago (see pp218–25). Most of the buildings are made of guaiteca cypress, the world's southernmost conifer species.

In recent years, the tourism industry has grown, with more basic questhouses and motorised boat trips to **Glaciar Steffens** and **Glaciar Montt**, which is part of Parque Nacional Bernardo O'Higgins. Hiking and horse riding can also be arranged. The village is also an ideal base for visiting the nearby Reserva Nacional Katalalixar, which can also be reached by basic motor launches.

Río Baker, forming a ribbon of blue through the verdant hills of Patagonia

㉒ Villa O'Higgins

Road Map E5. 204 miles (328 km) S of Coyhaique. ⚟ 612. ✈ from Coyhaique. 🚌 from Cochrane. 🚢 from Candelario Mansilla. 🛈 Carretera Austral 267, (067) 2431821. 🌐 villaohiggins.com

Beyond Cochrane, services are nearly non-existent on the last 120 miles (200 km) of the Carretera Austral. There is, however, a free ferry shuttle from Puerto Yungay, near the Río Bravo, which takes visitors to the last stretch of the highway, that terminates at Villa O'Higgins. This village dates from 1966 and is named for the Chilean hero Bernardo O'Higgins (see p157). Since the arrival of the Carretera Austral in 1999, the village has grown due to tourism. Surrounded by wild mountain scenery, and within sight of the **Campo del Hielo Sur** (Southern Icefield), Villa

O'Higgins offers ample hiking trails including part of the Sendero de Chile, an ongoing project that connects major trails across the country. It is a popular destination for cyclists and trekkers who wish to cross over to Argentina's El Chalten. Enthusiasts can take the La Quetru catamaran from Villa O'Higgins across Lago O'Higgins to the border post of Candelario Mansilla, hike for 12.5 miles (20 km), and then take the ferry across Argentina's Lago del Desierto.

㉓ Puerto Edén

Road Map D5. 272 miles (438 km) SW of Coyhaique. ⚟ 275. 🚢 ferry and cruise ship days

On Isla Wellington, in one of the rainiest sectors of the Pacific fjords, the town of Puerto Edén owes its origin to an air force initiative that contemplated a stop for seaplanes between Puerto Montt (see pp216–17) and Punta Arenas (see pp250–51). However, the site soon became the last outpost of Kawéskar hunter-gatherers, who settled here after the air force abandoned it. Today, Puerto Edén is home to the few surviving members of the Kawéskar community, who have re-created some of their traditional shelters. It is possible to purchase a sample of their crafts here. Weather and schedule permitting, the town is a stop for Skorpios cruise ships and Navimag ferries that sail out of Puerto Natales (see p244).

Palafitos and boardwalks at the secluded riverside village of Caleta Tortel

SOUTHERN PATAGONIA AND TIERRA DEL FUEGO

An archipelagic labyrinth and a thin strip of mainland, Southern Patagonia is a dramatic wilderness of emerald fjords, vast ice fields, rugged peaks, and windswept prairies. Separated from the mainland by the Strait of Magellan, Tierra del Fuego stretches across untamed and largely unpopulated territory to Cape Horn, the awe-inspiring tip of South America.

The original inhabitants of Southern Patagonia and Tierra del Fuego were the Ona, Yamana, Tehuelche, and Alacaluf (Kawéskar) communities, who are now extinct or greatly reduced in number. In 1520, Portuguese navigator Ferdinand Magellan became the first European to discover the area. However, permanent settlements were not established until the 19th century, when missionaries, adventurers, and merchants arrived from Spain, Britain, Croatia, and northern Chile. Immigrants also came to work on sheep estancias that emerged across the region.

The late 19th century witnessed a rise in prosperity as a result of large-scale sheep ranching. At the same time, a thriving shipping industry developed, benefitting from the navigable Strait of Magellan, which served as a passage between the Pacific and Atlantic until the opening of the Panama Canal in 1914. Today, sheep farming, along with oil extraction and tourism, are the mainstays of the economy.

Spectacular natural attractions and a wide range of activities draw travelers to the region each year. Sprawling parks offer excellent fly-fishing, trekking, kayaking, horse riding, and mountain climbing. On the coast, whale-watching and trips to penguin rookeries are becoming increasingly popular. Cruise ships take passengers through magnificent channels and past the craggy scenery of Tierra del Fuego, where they can spot sea lions, albatrosses, and flamingos.

Sea lions off a fjord near Puerto Williams, in Tierra del Fuego

◀ The peaks of Los Cuernos rising majestically above Lago Pehoé, Parque Nacional Torres del Paine

Exploring Southern Patagonia and Tierra del Fuego

The region's Magallanes area is known for its fjords, dense forests, and windy steppes. The Campo de Hielo Sur (Southern Ice Field) blankets much of Southern Patagonia and sends forth glaciers that can be visited from Puerto Natales. The town is also a good base to explore the top trekking destination of Parque Nacional Torres del Paine and the archaeological site of Cueva del Milodón. Punta Arenas is the gateway to the national monument of Puerto Hambre and the large colonies of Magellanic penguins at Isla Magdalena. Across the Strait of Magellan, Chilean Tierra del Fuego is the least-visited destination, home to a handful of lodges and southernmost town in the world, Puerto Williams.

Sights at a Glance

Villages, Towns, and Cities

❶ Puerto Natales
❺ Villa Tehuelches
❻ *Punta Arenas pp250–51*
❾ Puerto Hambre
⓫ Porvenir
⓬ Puerto Williams

National Parks, Reserves, and Natural Monuments

❸ *Parque Nacional Torres del Paine pp246–9*
❹ Parque Nacional Bernardo O'Higgins

Areas of Natural Beauty

❼ Seno Otway
❽ Isla Magdalena
❿ Strait of Magellan

Archaeological Sites and Ruins

❷ Cueva del Milodón
⓭ Cape Horn

Key

━━ Main road
═══ Minor road
= = = Untarred minor road
▬▬ International border
△ Peak

Parque Nacional Los Glaciares

Lago Arger

El Calafate

Campo de Hielo Sur

PARQUE NACIONAL ❹
BERNARDO O'HIGGINS

*Cuernos
8,530 ft △ Lago
Nordensk*
△ *Cerro Paine G
10,006 ft*
Lago Pehoé

PARQUE NACIONAL ❸
TORRES DEL PAINE
*Ce
Cas*

*Cerro Balmaceda
6,676 ft* △ CUEVA DE
MILODÓ

*Seno Última
Esperanza*

Puerto Bories

PUERTO NATA

MAGALLANES AND
ANTÁRTICA CHILENA

Puerto
Ramirez

*Cerro Burney △
5,741 ft*

*Reserva Nacio
Alacalufes*

*Cerro Atalaya △
6,069 ft*

*Pirámide △
3,937 ft* *Cerro
Ladrillero
5,462 ft*

Cutter Co

*Isla
Santa Iné*

Boardwalk to the Monumento al Navegante Solitario on Cape Horn

For hotels and restaurants in this region see pp281–3 and pp298–9

The vibrant Punta Arenas to the Strait of Magellan, with Tierra del Fuego in the distance

Getting Around

It is possible to get around Southern Patagonia by air, ship, or long-distance bus. A large number of visitors arrive at the airport in Punta Arenas. Puerto Natales and Puerto Williams also have local aerodromes, the former served by charter flights. Bus services are plentiful and reliable. Some roads are unpaved and gas stations are scarce, so motorists should consider carrying a canister of gas. Ferries and cruise ships go to destinations in Tierra del Fuego.

For keys to symbols see back flap

❶ Puerto Natales

Road Map E6. 1,268 miles (2,040 km)
S of Santiago. 🛈 Pedro Montt 19,
(061) 2412125. 🚂 19,600. ✈ 🚌 🚢
🌐 torresdelpaine.com

Capital of the Última Esperanza
Province of Chile, Puerto Natales
is a windswept town backed by
the Sierra Dorotea range. The
town overlooks the Seno Última
Esperanza (Last Hope Sound) –
so called because this was the
site that Spanish explorer Juan
Ladrilleros considered his last
hope while attempting to
locate the Strait of Magellan in
1557. The region was originally
inhabited by the indigenous
Tehuelche and Kawéskar tribes;
the present town was only
founded in 1911 when a sheep-
ranching boom and the
subsequent establishment of
two mutton processing
factories nearby led to
the influx of Croatian,
British, and German
immigrants, as well as
of people from the
Chiloé archipelago.
Today, the economy of
Puerto Natales is primarily
based on its flourishing
tourism industry.

At the town's center, the
restored **Plaza de Armas**
features a steam locomotive
that stands testament to the
region's flourishing sheep-
ranching days. This rail engine
was used to transport workers
back and forth from the abattoir

Historic locomotive in the Plaza de Armas,
Puerto Natales

**Black-necked swan
at Puerto Natales**

in nearby Puerto Bories. Located
two blocks west of the plaza,
the **Museo Histórico Municipal**
features displays of antique
tools and household items, as
well as photographs of the
vanished Kawéskar and
Aonikenk indigenous
communities. The
town's main road,
Avenida Pedro Montt,
popularly called the
Avenida Costanera, affords
splendid views of glacier-topped
peaks and the turquoise sound,
which is dotted with cormorants,
native black-necked swans, and
other seabirds.

Puerto Natales serves as the
main gateway to Southern
Patagonia's famous Parque
Nacional Torres del Paine. As
a result, the town caters to

numerous travelers who stop
here en route to the park.
Several tour operators offer
activities such as ice trekking,
cruises to a nearby glacier, horse
riding, and kayak trips.

Situated 6 miles (10 km) from
Puerto Natales, **Mirador Dorotea**
is a moderate trek of 2,625 ft
(800 m). After crossing the forest,
at the summit, visitors can enjoy
breathtaking, panoramic views
of Puerto Natales, surrounding
mountains, and the glacial valley.
If lucky, one can also spot majestic condors in the area. The
excursion can also be done on a
horseback, which also comprises
a traditional late afternoon *once*
(high-tea) that includes tea,
coffee, handmade bread, and
jams among other things, with
a local family. A small admission
fee might apply.

Environs

Located 3 miles (5 km) north of
Puerto Natales is **Puerto Bories**,
a small housing community
and site of the Frígorifico Bories,
an old sheep processing plant
founded in 1915. This factory was
part of the Sociedad Explotadora
de Tierra del Fuego, once the
largest sheep-ranching operation
in Patagonia which extended
for some 11,584 sq miles
(30,000 sq km) across Chile and
Argentina. Today, the Frígorifico
Bories is a national monument
and has been converted into
the region's finest hotel. Its
locomotive garage, blacksmiths'

Looking over the rooftops of Puerto Natales to the Sierra Dorotea range

For hotels and restaurants in this region see pp281–3 and pp298–9

A replica of the Pleistocene-era ground sloth outside Cueva del Milodón

workshop, offices, and boiling and tannery facilities have been incorporated into the hotel's design. Most notable is the architectural style of this brick factory, which is reminiscent of post-Victorian England

A short distance northwest of Puerto Prat, **Estancia Puerto Consuelo** was founded by German immigrant Hermann Eberhard. Among the earliest ranches in Chilean Patagonia, the estancia offers spectacular views of Parque Nacional Torres del Paine. Visitors can ride horses, hike in the surrounding countryside, kayak in the series of waterways close by, observe ranch hands at work, and finish with a delicious barbecue.

Ⅲ Museo Histórico Municipal
Manuel Bulnes 285. **Tel** (061) 2411263. **Open** 8am–7pm Mon–Fri, 10am–1pm & 3–7pm Sat. 🖉

❷ Cueva del Milodón

Road Map E6. 15 miles (24 km) NW of Puerto Natales. 🚌 from Puerto Natales. **Open** Oct–Apr: 8am–7pm daily; May–Sep: 8:30am–6pm daily. 🅿 ♿ 🚻 🍴 **w** cuevadel milodon.cl

Arguably the most important paleontological and archaeological site in Southern Patagonia, the Cueva del Milodón is named for the now-extinct ground sloth, or milodón (*Mylodon darwinii*), whose partial remains were discovered here by immigrant Hermann Eberhard in 1895. The slow-moving milodón, measuring up to 10 ft (3 m) in height when on its hind legs

and weighing around 400 pounds (181 kg), roamed Patagonia till the Pleistocene period, about 10,000 years ago. Today, a replica of this sloth dominates the cave entrance. A small visitors' center displays fossil remains of the sloth and other extinct animals such as the dwarf horse and saber-toothed tiger.

❸ Parque Nacional Torres del Paine

See pp246–9.

❹ Parque Nacional Bernardo O'Higgins

Road Map E6. 90 miles (145 km) NW of Puerto Natales. 👤 CONAF, Manuel Baquedano 847, Puerto Natales; (061) 2411438. 🚤 by Turismo 21 de Mayo from Puerto Natales; call (061) 2614420 for details. 🏨 included in catamaran price. **w** turismo21demayo.cl

Created in 1969, Parque Nacional Bernardo O'Higgins is bordered on the east by the mammoth ice field Campo de Hielo Sur and comprises a maze of small islands, fjords, and channels. Covering an area

of 13,614 sq miles (35,260 sq km), it is Chile's largest national park, but the lack of land access also makes it one of the least visited. The park is also reached on a full-day catamaran cruise from Puerto Natales. Retracing the 16th-century voyage of Juan Ladrilleros through the Seno Última Esperanza, the trip offers views of sea lions, cascades, and rugged scenery. The trip includes a visit to the hanging Glaciar Balmaceda and a short trek to the iceberg-laden lagoon of Glaciar Serrano. From the lagoon, kayaks and dinghies navigate up the Río Serrano through a little-known route marked by untrammeled scenery of glaciers, peaks, and dense forest, and ends at Parque Nacional Torres del Paine administration center. This trip can also be made in the opposite direction from Torres del Paine.

❺ Villa Tehuelches

Road Map F6. 96 miles (154 km) SE of Puerto Natales. 🚐 700. 🚌 from Puerto Natales. 🎉 Festival de la Esquila (third weekend of Jan). 🏨

The pocket-sized outpost of Villa Tehuelches was founded in 1967 as a service center for the regional population, with shops, a post office, church, school, and police station. This village is famous for the annual Festival de la Esquila, or Shearing Festival, that draws hundreds of people from across Patagonia and features rodeos, sheep-shearing competitions, and lamb barbecues.

The sleepy village of Villa Tehuelches

❸ Parque Nacional Torres del Paine

Chile's most dazzling national park, Torres del Paine (Towers of Blue) is a UNESCO World Biosphere Reserve. The park is named for the Paine massif, a cluster of metamorphic ridges and needles between the Southern Patagonian Ice Field and the Patagonian steppe. The name itself is a mix of Spanish and indigenous Patagonian words: *paine* being the Tehuelche term for blue, a color frequently seen throughout the area in the form of turquoise glaciers, icebergs, rivers, and lakes. The park is Chile's trekking mecca, with numerous day hikes as well as 3- to 10-day backpacking routes.

Laguna Amarga entrance to Parque Nacional Torres del Paine, Patagonia

★ **Glaciar Grey**
The 2-mile (4-km) wide Glaciar Grey descends from the Southern Ice Field. Boats cruise up to the glacier face; visitors can also trek across the glacier in crampons, or kayak past the icebergs on Lago Grey.

Salto Grande
This waterfall connects Lago Nordenskjold with Lago Pehoé, which drains water from glacier melt-off in the northern sector.

Map labels:
Glaciar Dickson · Lago Dickson · Refugio Dickson · Refugio Los Perros · Rio Los Perros · Southern Ice Field · Campamento Paso · John Gardner Pass · Glaciar Grey · Cuerno Fortaleza 9,186 ft (2,800 m) · Refugio Grey · Cerro Paine Grande 10,006 ft (3,050 m) · Cuerno No 7,874 ft (2,40 · Valle del Francés · Cuerno Principal 8,530 ft (2,600 m) · Campamento Italiano · Lago Grey · Lago Skottsberg · Glaciar Zapata · Rio Pingo · Refugio Paine Grande · Lago Pehoé · Sendero Pingo-Zapata · Refugio Pingo · Laguna Marco Antonio · Rio Grey · CONAF Administration Headquarters

KEY

① **The Circuito Grande** is a lengthy trek that explores all the main attractions of the park.

② **The Lago Sarmiento area** is less frequented by people and more by guanacos, flamingos, and red foxes. There are also ancient rock paintings nearby.

③ **The 3-day W** is the park's most popular hike. It takes in Glaciar Grey, Valle del Frances and Las Torres.

Exploring the Park

The national park is dominated by the Paine massif which includes the Cuernos formation of mountains, the Torres del Paine peaks, and the park's highest summit – the 10,006-ft (3,050-m) high Cerro Paine Grande. Apart from these rugged peaks, there are a number of other microclimates and geological features that form part of the park. These include glaciers, granite spires, beech forests, lakes, and steppe, and can be explored by foot, by vehicle, aboard a catamaran, or on horseback. The park also offers a series of campgrounds and refugios, in addition to several hotels (see pp281–2).

For hotels and restaurants in this region see pp281–3 and pp298–9

Valle Ascencio
The valley leads up to a granite moraine and the last leg of the Torres hike, continuing on to Valle de Silencio.

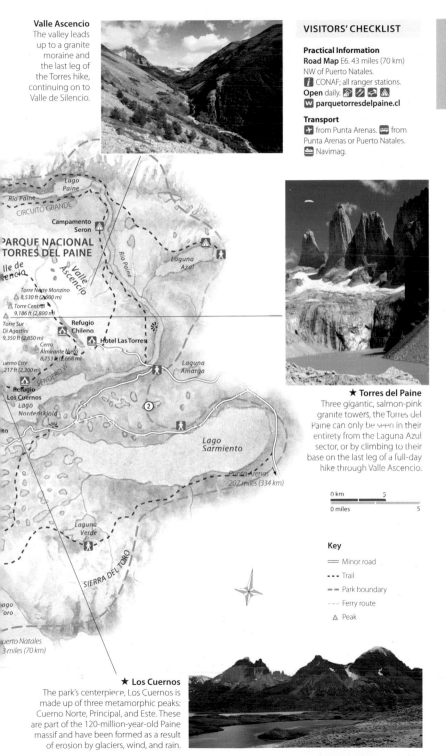

VISITORS' CHECKLIST

Practical Information
Road Map E6. 43 miles (70 km) NW of Puerto Natales.
🛈 CONAF; all ranger stations.
Open daily. 🌐 parquetorresdelpaine.cl

Transport
✈ from Punta Arenas. 🚌 from Punta Arenas or Puerto Natales.
⛴ Navimag.

★ Torres del Paine
Three gigantic, salmon-pink granite towers, the Torres del Paine can only be seen in their entirety from the Laguna Azul sector, or by climbing to their base on the last leg of a full-day hike through Valle Ascencio.

Key
═══ Minor road
--- Trail
▬ ▬ Park boundary
--- Ferry route
△ Peak

★ Los Cuernos
The park's centerpiece, Los Cuernos is made up of three metamorphic peaks: Cuerno Norte, Principal, and Este. These are part of the 120-million-year-old Paine massif and have been formed as a result of erosion by glaciers, wind, and rain.

For keys to symbols *see back flap*

Exploring Parque Nacional Torres del Paine

Access to the park is from Punta Arenas via road, or from Puerto Natales by one of two roads or by inflatable boat along the Río Serrano. There are three separate entrances to the park, all manned by CONAF ranger stations. Within its boundaries, some 155 miles (250 km) of the sanctuary is covered by clearly marked trails. The longest of these is the Circuito Grande, a hike that needs roughly 8 days and takes visitors to the Paine massif, passing by the brilliant lakes of Paine, Dickson and Grey. There are also trails to Lago Paine, the Torres peaks, and the Valle del Francés, which are typically combined into the park's most popular single hike, named the W after its shape.

A herd of guanacos at Parque Nacional Torres del Paine

🧍 CONAF Administration Headquarters

Lago del Toro sector, southern entrance of park. **Tel** (061) 2691931. **Open** 8:30am–8:30pm daily.

The southern road from Puerto Natales is the most beautiful of all routes into the park, and leads to the CONAF Administration Headquarters. This center gives a compulsory talk on park safety and provides general information about the park. It also has educational displays on the flora, fauna, and geological features of the sanctuary. A small kiosk sells maps, books, and sundry items.

🛶 The W

🦆 ⛺

This medium-difficult trail follows the shape of a W, hence its name. The W is the most popular multiday trek because it takes visitors to the three major highlights of the park: the Torres del Paine, the Valle del Francés (French Valley), and Glaciar Grey. Most trekkers begin at the Las Torres (see p281), a ranch-style complex that has campgrounds, hostels, and a hotel, the **Hotel Las Torres**. The 7- to 8-hour roundtrip hike to the iconic Torres del Paine is

strenuous, first traversing the beautiful beech forests of the **Valle Ascencio** and ending with a steep, 45-minute hike up a boulder field to the Torres, three stunning granite towers that rise majestically in front of a glacial tarn.

The W continues southwest from Hotel Las Torres along the shores of the turquoise **Lago Nordenskjold** and skirting the flank of the park's famous two-toned Cuernos.

About 7 miles (11 km) along this route are the hostel and campgrounds of Refugio Los Cuernos. Trekkers may either spend the night here or, if camping, continue onward another 4 miles (6 km) to the **Valle del Francés** and its Campamento Italiano. However, there are no services here. The trail up and into the Valle del Francés is about 5 miles (8 km) long, climbing high into the valley ringed with granite peaks and offering sweeping views of the Patagonian steppe.

From the base of the Valle del Francés, it is some 5 miles (8 km) to the Refugio Paine Grande and campground, and to the docking area for a catamaran that crosses **Lago Pehoé** to the Pudeto sector. From this point, the trail heads north for the final leg of The W, 7 miles (11 km) to Refugio Grey. Visitors to the *refugio* can arrange trekking excursions to Glaciar Grey. Most trekkers return to Lago Pehoé and take the catamaran

Forests of southern beech carpeting Valle Ascencio

Hikers on the Circuito Grande, near Laguna Azul

to Pudeto, from where transportation is available to Puerto Natales. However, it is also possible to walk 11 miles (18 km) of level terrain to the park's administration center.

🗙 Circuito Grande
🏞 ⛰

For a thorough exploration of the park, hikers should consider the Circuito Grande (Big Circuit Trail), which circles the Paine massif. This hike takes about 6 to 8 days depending on individual ability and weather conditions. The trail is usually undertaken in a counter-clockwise direction, starting at the Hotel Las Torres or from the Laguna Amarga ranger station.

The trail from Hotel Las Torres begins with a 4-hour hike through the Valle Ascencio, with its grazing cattle and forest, to Campamento Seron. It then continues for 12 miles (19 km) to Refugio Dickson, which offers direct views of **Glaciar Dickson**.

The trail grows increasingly strenuous from this point. However, the views are far more dramatic, with glaciers, peaks, and beech forest. About 6 miles (9 km) through forest and swampy terrain from Refugio Dickson lies the campground Los Perros. The 7-mile (12-km) climb from here, up to **John Gardner Pass** can be difficult during bad weather. Hikers are advised to wait for a few days as crossing the pass during strong winds can be deadly. The electrifying views of Glaciar

Grey and the **Southern Ice Field** from the pass are the highlights of the route; the vast stretch of ice is breathtaking. Recreational hikers can spend the night at the Campamento Paso, as the next 6 miles (10 km) to Refugio Grey are difficult, with steep, rocky gorges and fallen tree trunks. Hikers then trek from Refugio Grey to Lago Pehoé, for the journey back to Puerto Natales.

🗙 Sendero Pingo-Zapata
🏞 ⛰

This infrequently visited trail is good for bird-watching, and has an easy-medium

Blossoming porcelain orchid in the park

difficulty level. The trail begins at the Lago Grey CONAF station and follows the Río Pingo past prairie, scrub, and views of the western granite walls of the Paine massif. After about 5 hours, visitors arrive at the Campamento Zapata, with a decrepit *refugio*, and a half-hour later to a lookout point with views of the stunning **Glaciar Zapata** and its numerous rows of glacial moraine.

🗙 Glaciar Grey
Although the rate at which it is receding has increased, Glaciar Grey is one of the largest and most easily accessed glaciers in Patagonia. The icebergs that break off from the glacier float to the end of Lago Grey. These can be seen along a short walk on flat beach from the Grey sector's ranger station, near Refugio Grey. At the end of the beach, reached by about a half-hour walk, a peninsula with a viewing platform offers vistas of Glaciar Grey in the distance.

A popular journey here is aboard the catamaran *Grey II*, which leaves Refugio Grey twice daily and sails to the face of the glacier in summer.

Kayaking near the floating icebergs on Lago Grey

⑥ Punta Arenas

The capital of the Magallanes region, Punta Arenas is the jumping off point for cruises to Tierra del Fuego and Antarctica. Set up in 1848, the city was initially a penal colony and a disciplinary center for military personnel. In the late 19th and early 20th centuries, it drew thousands of Europeans escaping World War I and seeking fortunes in sheep ranching, gold and coal mining, and the shipping industry. Today, the best place to begin exploring the town is at the Plaza Muñoz Gamero.

The drawing room at the Museo Regional Braun Menéndez

🏛 Museo Regional Braun Menéndez

H. de Magallanes 949. **Tel** (061) 2242049. **Open** 10:30am–5pm Wed–Mon & hols (May–Sep: to 2pm). ♿ reservation required.
🌐 **museodemagallanes.cl**

Travelers to Punta Arenas can appreciate the staggering wealth of the Braun-Menéndez family –

owners of mammoth ranching operations in the early 20th century – at the Museo Regional Braun Menéndez. Dating from 1903, the edifice is preserved with its original furniture and finery, which was imported from Europe and includes marble fireplaces, French tapestries, crystal chandeliers, and examples of

some of the best European craftsmanship from that time. The museum also features a room dedicated to the ethnographic history of the region.

Just south of the museum is the main square, Plaza Muñoz Gamero, with the Magellan Monument at its center. The ritual here is to kiss the toe of the Tehuelche statue on the monument, for good luck or, as legend goes, so that visitors return to Punta Arenas. Also on the square is **Palacio Sara Braun**, another mansion of the Braun-Menéndez family that is now home to a hotel and the Club de la Unión.

🏛 Museo Regional Salesiano Maggiorino Borgatello

Ave. M. Bulnes & Maipú. **Tel** (061) 2221001. **Open** 10am–12:30pm & 3–6pm Tue–Sun. ♿ ♿ ♿

Founded in 1893, the Museo Regional Salesiano Maggiorino Borgatello charts the history, ecology, and anthropology of the Magallanes region. Visits begin at the lobby, which displays stuffed local fauna, pickled marine life, and geological samples collected by Salesian missionaries of the early 20th century. There are also ethnographic exhibits of Kawéskar and Selk'nam Indians that include tools, clothing, and

Punta Arenas

① Museo Regional
   Braun Menéndez
② Museo Regional Salesiano
   Maggiorino Borgatello
③ Cementerio Municipal
   Sara Braun

VISITORS' CHECKLIST

Practical Information
Road Map E6. 153 miles (247 km)
S of Puerto Natales. 🗺 132,000.
ℹ️ Lautaro Navarro 999. 🖼
Winter carnival (Jul).
ⓦ **puntaarenas.cl**

Transport
✈️ 🚌

black-and-white photographs;
a history of missionary work in the
area and Catholic religious artifacts; and a floor devoted to the
industrial history of Punta Arenas.

Cypress trees and tombs at the Cementerio
Municipal Sara Braun

🏛 Cementerio Municipal Sara Braun

Avenida M. Bulnes & Rómulo Correa.
Open Oct–Mar: 7:30am–8pm daily;
Apr–Sep: 8am–6pm daily.

This antique mausoleum is the
site of many tombs belonging
to Punta Arenas's powerful
families, along with the graves
of immigrants from Croatia and
Scotland. The pathways of the
cemetery feature extravagantly
pruned cypress trees. Located on
the northwest side, is the Indiecito
(Little Indian) statue that represents deceased indigenous groups
and is a totem for good luck.

🏛 Nao Victoria Museum

Off Ruta 9. **Tel** (09) 9640-0772.
Open 9am–6pm daily.
ⓦ **naovictoria.cl**

Located on the banks of Magellan
Strait, this outdoor museum
features lifesize replica ships of
the great explorers of the region.
Visitors can climb aboard Darwin's
HMS Beagle, and Magellan's *Nao
Victoria*. However, the most
impressive exhibit is the replica
of the lifeboat used by Ernest
Shackleton and his men while
navigating the Antarctic Ocean.

Chilean flag fluttering above Fuerte Bulnes,
near Puerto Hambre

➐ Seno Otway

Road Map E6. 40 miles (65 km) N of
Punta Arenas. **Tel** (061) 2610650.
Open mid-Oct–Mar: 8am–6:30pm
daily. ⓦ **turisotway.cl**

A delightful half-day tour from
Punta Arenas is a visit to this
penguin rookery, accessible by
an unpaved road. Every year,
between November and March,
some 2,500 pairs of Magellanic
penguins come to burrow nests
here before heading north to
Argentina or the south-central
Chilean coast.

The 110-acre (45-ha) reserve
features roped walkways and
lookout platforms, and a souvenir
store. On the way to Seno Otway,
it is possible to spot birds such
as the flightless Darwin's rhea.

➑ Isla Magdalena

Road Map E6. 22 miles (35 km) NE of
Punta Arenas. **Tel** (061) 2200200. 🚢
from Punta Arenas; Dec–Feb: 10am
Tue, Thu & Sat (Jan & Feb: 4pm Tue–
Sun). ⓦ **comapa.com**

The 2-hour boat trip to Isla
Magdalena is worth the effort
given that the island hosts

up to 60,000 breeding pairs
of Magellanic penguins. In
addition, each pair produces
two chicks November–March,
bringing the population
on the island to some 240,000
penguins. A roped walkway
runs across the area, and an
old lighthouse acts as a ranger
and research station. Adult
penguins take turns guarding
the nest and fishing, and every
morning and afternoon visitors
can watch the birds waddling
along narrow paths to and
from the sea, passing just
inches from them.

➒ Puerto Hambre

Road Map E7. 36 miles (58 km) S
of Punta Arenas. **Open** 9:30am–
6pm daily. ⓦ **delestrecho.cl**

The first attempt to establish
a settlement on the Strait of
Magellan took place in 1584
when the Spanish captain Pedro
Sarmiento de Gamboa left
several hundred colonists about
20 miles (50 km) south of Punta
Arenas. He called the settlement
Rey Felipe, but it was changed
to Puerto Hambre (Port Hunger)
in 1587 by British captain Thomas
Cavendish, who landed here to
find just one survivor – the rest
had starved or succumbed to
the elements. The traces of
these ruins are now considered
a national monument.

About 2 miles (4 km) to the
south is the national monument
Fuerte Bulnes, set up in 1843 by
colonists from Chiloé who were
later transplanted to present-day
Punta Arenas in 1848. It was
the second, and first successful,
colonization of the strait, and
the site offers an interesting
look into the colonists' lives.

Walking among Magellanic penguins on Isla Magdalena

Fishing boat trawling across the Strait of Magellan

❿ Strait of Magellan

Road Map E7. 62 miles (100 km) S of Punta Arenas. 🚌 from Punta Delgada to Puerto Espora and from Punta Arenas to Porvenir.

A navigable sea route linking the Atlantic with the Pacific Ocean, the Strait of Magellan is named for Ferdinand Magellan, the first European to discover this passage in 1520. Measuring 354 miles (570 km) in length, this strait separates Tierra del Fuego from the Chilean mainland, and, in spite of currents and strong winds, offers a safer route for ships rounding the South American continent than the Drake Passage farther south. Until the opening of the Panama Canal in 1914, the Strait of Magellan served as the principal route for steam ships traveling between Europe and the Americas.

The strait is a breeding and feeding ground for humpback whales, sea lions, and other marine fauna during the summer months. Breeding colonies are easily spotted at Isla Carlos III, near the strait's western entrance. The waters surrounding the island comprise the 259-sq-mile (670-sq-km) **Parque Marino Francisco Coloane**, Chile's first marine reserve. Whale-watching boat trips to Isla Carlos III include a stop at Cabo Froward, the southernmost tip of the Chilean mainland, and the Cabo San Isidro. Located on the southeastern coast of the Brunswick Peninsula, this cape has a lighthouse dating from 1904.

Once used to guide ships through the Strait of Magellan, the lighthouse has now been converted into a comfortable lodge with a small museum that charts the culture and history of the region's indigenous groups such as the Selk'nam and Yamana Indians. It is reachable via a 4-day roundtrip hike from south of Punta Arenas.

⓫ Porvenir

Road Map E6. 25 miles (40 km) SE of Punta Arenas. 🏚 7,615. ✈ 🚌 🚐 (limited bus service).
W **muniporvenir.cl**

Dating back to 1834, but officially established as a town only in 1894, windswept Porvenir first grew as an outpost for miners working in the Baquedano mountain range during a local gold rush

Brightly painted houses in the town of Porvenir

in the mid-19th century. Later, during the 20th-century boom in wool production, the town acted as a service center for the region's sheep estancias that had been established principally by Croatian immigrants. Today, Porvenir is the capital of the Tierra del Fuego province. The town's tin-walled homes are interspersed with buildings erected in the 1930s and its main highlight is the **Museo Municipal Fernando Cordero Rusque**. The museum has displays on local fauna and archaeological and anthropological exhibits on the indigenous cultures that once inhabited the region. Four blocks north of the museum, the **Cementerio Municipal** features antique mausoleums in the shade of cypress trees pruned into cylindrical shapes. Located on the town's main coastal road, Avenida Manuel Senoret, **Parque del Recuerdo** displays antique machinery and vehicles from the 19th century. On the same road, the Plaza de las Américas features a monument constructed to commemorate the Selk'nam Indians, the original inhabitants of the region.

Environs
Located some 4 miles (6 km) north of Porvenir, **Monumento Natural Lagunas de los Cisnes** is known for large flocks of pink flamingos and black-necked swans. Farther south, Lago Blanco is a scenic lake renowned for rainbow trout and brown trout fishing. The lake sits on the northeastern edge of Parque Natural Karukinka. This privately run nature reserve was founded by the Wildlife Conservation Society with funding from Goldman Sachs in 2004 to protect the region's endangered beech forests from exploitation by international timber agencies. A further 62 miles (100 km) south, Bahia Inutil is home to a small seasonal colony of king penguin.

🏛 **Museo Municipal Fernando Cordero Rusque**
Padre Mario Zavattaro 402. **Tel** (061) 2581800. **Open** 8am–5:15pm Mon–Thu, 8am–4:15pm Fri, 11am–4pm Sat, Sun & holidays.
📷 🎥 ♿

The World's Southernmost Prison

Following the military coup of 1973 *(see p52)*, the Pinochet regime sent deposed government leaders to the tiny Isla Dawson in the Strait of Magellan. Characterized by cold, wretched weather and a remoteness that made escape nearly impossible, the island held up to 400 prisoners who were subjected to torture, harsh living conditions, and brutal forced labor. These prisoners were either executed or transferred to other jails in 1974. Many who survived played a major role in the restoration of democracy in Chile. The prisoners' experience was documented in the 2009 film *Dawson: Isla 10*, directed by former exile Miguel Littín. The film was inspired by the autobiographical work of former Minister of Mining, Sergio Bitar, one of Allende's cabinet ministers who was imprisoned on the island from 1973 to 1974.

A poster of the
Dawson: Isla 10

⑫ Puerto Williams

Road Map F7. 182 miles (293 km) SE of Punta Arenas. Museo Martín Gusinde: **Open** 9am–1pm & 3–6:30pm Tue–Fri, 3–6:30pm Sat & Sun. 🚗 2,874. ✈️ 🚢 from Punta Arenas.
🌐 ptowilliams.cl

The solitary town on Isla Navarino, south of mainland Chile, Puerto Williams is the capital of the Magallanes and Chilean Antarctic region, and also the southernmost town in the world. Founded in 1953 as a Chilean naval base, it was later named Puerto Williams in honor of Irish-born officer Juan Williams, who captured the Strait of Magellan for Chile in 1843. The town boasts a stunning backdrop of the granite peaks of Dientes de Navarino, a rugged area that offers some of the most challenging trekking in the south of Chile.

Hikers can choose from the 4- to 5-day Dientes de Navarino circuit, or a 4-hour roundtrip up the Cerro Bandera. The town's main attraction, the **Museo Martín Gusinde**, established in 1974, is dedicated to the Austrian anthropologist and clergyman (1886–1969) who did significant research on the region's indigenous Yamana and Selk'nam Indian communities. The museum features ethnographic exhibits on these groups and has displays on local geology, fauna, and flora. The island is a favored destination for sailors and yachtsmen, who meet at the Club de Yates Micalvi, an old boat retrofitted as a bar.

Located around half a mile (1 km) east of Puerto Williams, a village known as Villa Ukika is home to the handful of surviving members of the Yamana community.

⑬ Cape Horn

Road Map F7. 437 miles (703 km) SE of Punta Arenas. ✈️ from Punta Arenas & Puerto Williams. 🚢 from Punta Arenas & Puerto Williams.

The southernmost "point" of the Americas, Cape Horn, or the Horn as it is often called, actually comprises a group of islands that form the Parque Nacional Cabo de Hornos. Cape Horn was discovered by Europeans during a Dutch sailing expedition in 1616 and named for the town of Hoorn in the Netherlands. From the 18th century until the opening of the Panama Canal in 1914, it served as an important trade route for cargo ships.

The waters around the Cape Horn islands are among the most treacherous in the world due to choppy swells, rogue waves, strong currents, notorious gales, and, in particular, the williwaws, blasts of wind that appear out of nowhere. Inhospitable sailing conditions make it difficult to reach the very tip, and **Isla Hornos**, to its northwest, is usually as far as people can go.

The moss-covered Isla Hornos is home to a naval station, a lighthouse, and a chapel. Shaped to resemble an albatross, the Monumento al Navegante Solitario honors sailors who died while sailing around the Horn. The island has a rich birdlife, including Magellanic penguins, condors, and albatrosses. Dolphins and whales can be seen offshore.

The coastal town of Puerto Williams, overlooked by the jagged peaks of Dientes de Navarino

Visiting Argentina

Visitors to Chile's Patagonia have the option of traveling to the Argentine Patagonia, given that both the countries' star attractions are so close to each other. In just a few hours, travelers to Parque Nacional Torres del Paine can visit the Argentine town El Calafate, a tourism-oriented town that forms the base for visits to the Glaciar Perito Moreno and Los Glaciares National Park. Cruise ship passengers often have the option of stopping over for a day or night in the Argentine port-city of Ushuaia, a phenomenally beautiful town backed by jagged peaks.

Key

▬ Highway

═ Other road

▬ ▪ International border

Sights at a Glance

① Parque Nacional Los Glaciares
② Ushuaia
③ Parque Nacional Tierra del Fuego
④ Cerro Castor

① Parque Nacional Los Glaciares

227 miles (336 km) NW of Puerto Natales; 50 miles (80 km) W of El Calafate. ✈ El Calafate. 🚌 El Calafate. 🛈 Avenida del Libertador 1302, El Calafate; (02902) 491545. 🅿 💼 ⬛
📷 ♻ ⛰ 🆆 losglaciares.com

Created in 1937, Parque Nacional Los Glaciares is an add-on destination favored by most travelers to Parque Nacional Torres del Paine, as there are two border crossings near it. Named for the glaciers that

cascade down from the Southern Ice Field, this reserve is Argentina's second-largest national park and a trekking and climbing mecca. The park, most of it inaccessible, covers 1.6 million acres of rugged mountains, turquoise lakes, glaciers, and thundering rivers. Dominating the whole is the dramatic Fitz Roy massif, a towering cluster of granite

needles. Trekkers to this area can take part in camping-based trips over many days, or on shorter day hikes that last between 2 and 6 hours. Trips begin at the tiny mountain village of **El Chaltén**, a cluster of hotels and restaurants that sprang up in the 1990s along the Río Las Vueltas.

The major crowd-puller at Parque Nacional Los Glaciares is the **Glaciar Perito Moreno**, which flows for some 18 miles (29 km) before making contact with a peninsula that provides visitors with ideal lookout points from which to view the glacial marvel. The glacier is, in fact, one of the few in Patagonia that is not receding, although it cannot grow very far either as its terminus is obstructed by land. Every several years, pressure that has built up from the ice's contact with land causes the glacier to calve in a crashing fury, a sight many travelers aspire to see when visiting this park. Several agencies offer trekking on the glacier with crampons and ropes, along with a selection of nature walks, and boat rides to the neighboring glaciers of Upsala and Spegazzini, and around floating icebergs.

Los Glaciares is accessed from **El Calafate**, a tourism-based town on the shore of Lago Argentino, a 5-hour drive from Puerto Natales, Chile. Old *estancias* (sheep ranches) here have been converted into hotels and restaurants and give visitors a taste of Patagonian gaucho life and culture.

Visitors at the Glacier Perito Moreno, Parque Nacional Los Glaciares

An early morning view of Ushuaia, Argentina's southernmost city

② Ushuaia

351 miles (564 km) SE of El Calafate. 🏔 57,000. ✈ 🚌 ℹ Avenida Prefectura Naval 470; (02901) 432000. 🎭 Festival Música Clásica de Ushuaia (Apr). 🌐 turismoushuaia.com

Hugging the shore of the Beagle Channel with the broken peaks of the Parque Nacional Tierra del Fuego rising majestically behind it, Ushuaia is Argentina's southernmost city. Visited for its natural beauty, Ushuaia is the jumping off point for trips to Antarctica. It is also a wildlife-watching destination and has various boat companies that offer penguin- and sea-lion-spotting tours on the Beagle Channel.

The city is named in the language of the region's first indigenous inhabitants, the Yamana; Ushuaia translates as the Bay Leading West. It was formally established as the capital of Tierra del Fuego in 1904. British missionaries first settled the area in the mid 1800s, and in 1896, President Julio Argentino Roca founded a penal colony here for criminals and political prisoners from the north and Buenos Aires. The colony not only served as a means of hiding away society's most dangerous criminals, it was also a way of establishing a strong Argentine presence in Tierra del Fuego. The sprawling prison was shut down in 1947 and now houses the **Museo Marítimo y Presidio**, a vast collection of historical, nautical, scientific, and cultural exhibits of the area. There are also exhibits of prison-era artifacts and interpretative

displays depicting the life of prisoners and their guards.

Sitting right on the Beagle Channel, Tierra del Fuego's oldest ranch, Estancia Harberton, is located 53 miles (85 km) east of Ushuaia. It was founded in 1887 by the missionary Thomas Bridges, and is now run by the fourth generation of the family. There is an excellent on-site museum dedicated to the marine fauna of Tierra del Fuego.

③ Parque Nacional Tierra del Fuego

8 miles (11 km) N of Ushuaia. 🚌 from Ushuaia. ℹ Ruta Nacional 3, Km 3047; (02901) 421315. **Open** 24hrs daily. 🅿 ♿ 🏪 📷 🏞 🌐 parquesnacionales.gob.ar

Founded in 1960 to protect some 235 sq miles (610 sq km) of southern beech forest and rugged terrain, Parque Nacional Tierra del Fuego was Argentina's first coastal national park. Though most of the park is inaccessible, it is still popular with Ushuaia locals as a recreational area offering picnic grounds, trails, boating, bird-watching, and trout fishing. Short pedestrian paths and longer hikes pass through thick forest and past dark-water *turbales* (peat bogs). Visitors may see guanacos and red foxes, or the island's scourge, the Canadian beaver, which was introduced in the 1940s to harvest pelts. They have now vastly multiplied and represent a huge environmental threat.

Both children and adults enjoy riding the park's **Tren del Fin de Mundo**, a steam locomotive that once took prisoners to

VISITORS' CHECKLIST

Transport
El Calafate: ✈ from Ushuaia and Buenos Aires. 🚌 from Puerto Natales via Cerro Castillo. Ushuaia: ✈ from Santiago; charter flights from Punta Arenas. 🚌 from Punta Arenas via border control at Paso San Sebastian.

the forest to chop wood, during Ushuaia's stint as a penal colony. The train leaves from Estación de Tren, outside the park, for an hour-long journey, passing forest, waterfalls, and rivers.

④ Cerro Castor

16 miles (26 km) NE of Ushuaia; Ruta Nacional 3, Km.3047. **Tel** (02901) 499301. ✈ 🚌 from Ushuaia. **Open** mid-Jun–mid-Oct. 🅿 🎿 🏪 📷 🏞 🌐 cerrocastor.com

Argentina's southernmost ski resort attracts not only locals from Ushuaia, but skiers and snowboarders from Buenos Aires, and Chile too. The base is just 640 ft (195 m) above sea level, with the highest elevation at 3,468 ft (1,057 m), yet Cerro Castor receives prodigious snowfall.

The exclusive and modern retreat comprises the Castor Ski Lodge, with 15 rustic-chic and cozy cabins, four restaurants, and four *refugios* or mountain cafés. The resort offers nearly 1,500 acres (607 ha) of skiable terrain and 2,630 ft (800 m) of vertical drop, a snowpark, and seven lifts. Numerous activities are on offer, including a series of ski and culinary events that extend throughout the season.

Boardwalk to Lapataia bay, Parque Nacional Tierra del Fuego

EASTER ISLAND AND ROBINSON CRUSOE ISLAND

Chile's borders extend over two of the planet's most isolated, remote, and exotic islands. Easter Island, known as Rapa Nui to its inhabitants, is most visited for its *moai* statues, world-renowned icons of archaeology and enigmatic remnants of a vanished society. Closer to the mainland, Robinson Crusoe Island is the site of one of the world's greatest adventure sagas.

Five hours from the mainland by jet, Easter Island is a tiny volcanic triangle whose culture, despite its political link to Chile, is more Polynesian than Latin American. The original settlers island-hopped their way across the Western Pacific and arrived at Easter Island around AD 1000. What they lacked in numbers they made up for with ingenuity and creativity, carving giant monuments that have since made the island famous. Restored to their original platforms, if not their former glory, the *moai* attract tens of thousands of visitors each year. Activities such as hiking, diving, riding, and surfing, not to mention the Polynesian ambience, complement its unique cultural resources.

Visited by few tourists, Robinson Crusoe Island is part of the Juan Fernández archipelago, named for the Spanish navigator who landed here in 1574. The island itself takes its name from the novel *Robinson Crusoe*, which was inspired by the real-life story of 18th-century Scotsman Alexander Selkirk *(see p269)*. The first permanent settlements were set up in the mid-18th century and Chilean authority was established in the early 19th century. The present inhabitants, concentrated in the tiny town of San Juan Bautista, live off lobster fishing and tourism. The town is also the base for exploring endemic forests on the island's north and the trails that were familiar to Selkirk.

Thick forest, home to numerous endemic species, Robinson Crusoe Island

◀ *Moai* statues on the slopes of Rano Raraku, on Easter Island

Exploring Easter Island and Robinson Crusoe Island

The ideal base for exploring Easter Island is Hanga Roa, a sprawling village with some of the island's main sights close by, notably the crater and ceremonial village at Rano Kau. More remote sights, such as the *moais* at Rano Raraku, Playa Anakena, and Península Poike, can be seen on a full-day loop along the island's eastern shores before returning to Hanga Roa. Robinson Crusoe Island is primarily a summer destination, as flights to the island are most frequent in January and February. Here, the village of San Juan Bautista is one of the few bases. The rugged terrain is ideal for hiking, especially along Sendero Salsipuedes and Mirador Selkirk. Limited transportation makes sightseeing time-consuming – though always rewarding.

0 km 5
0 miles 5

Moais at Ahu Nau Nau on Playa Anakena, Easter Island

Sights at a Glance

Villages
1. *Hanga Roa pp262–3*
8. San Juan Bautista

Areas of Natural Beauty
5. Playa Anakena
6. Península Poike
9. Sendero Salsipuedes
11. Mirador Selkirk

Archaeological Sites
2. Rano Kau
3. Ahu Akivi
4. Ana Te Pahu
7. *Rano Raraku pp266–7*
10. Cueva Robinson
12. Plazoleta El Yunque

Spectacular panorama from Mirador Selkirk, on Robinson Crusoe Island

| 0 km | | 3 |
| 0 miles | | 3 |

Getting Around

Both Easter Island and Robinson Crusoe Island are small in area, but getting around each of them is different. Easter Island has a good road system, suitable for cars, motorbikes, and bicycles. However, not all roads are paved and some are potholed. Hanga Roa has a taxi fleet, as well as tour companies that shuttle clients to and from the main sights. Horses can also be rented for excursions. There are many routes suitable for hiking, though camping is not permitted outside Hanga Roa. On Robinson Crusoe Island, there are no roads to speak of. The terrain is usually tackled on hikes, some of which can be challenging. It is possible to hire boats to sights that are not easily accessible by foot.

Key

— Major road

➡➡➡ Untarred major road

▪▪▪ Untarred minor road

- - - Track

– – – Boat route

△ Peak

For keys to symbols see back flap

❶ Hanga Roa

Easter Island's only permanent settlement, Hanga Roa is a sprawling subtropical village housing nearly all of the island's inhabitants. Most of its wide streets are lined with compact homes fronted by gardens. The population is mainly Polynesian but there are also expatriates, many from mainland Chile, who participate in the island's growing tourism industry. The village is a hub for visitors who come to enjoy the area's unique attractions, including a surprisingly sophisticated cuisine that blends fresh ingredients with South Pacific touches.

Well-tended graves with flowers at the Cementerio Hanga Roa

🏛 Iglesia Sagrado Corazón

Tuukoihu, esq. Avenida Te Pito Ote Henua.

Originally a simple structure, the village church of Iglesia Sagrado Corazón underwent a major renovation in 1982, and now stands out from Hanga Roa's other mainly utilitarian buildings. It boasts an attractive facade with bas-reliefs of Rapa Nui imagery, including the Birdman *(see p264)*, and figures of fish, frigate birds, and turtles. On one side, the church is flanked by the crypt of the Capuchin priest and scholar Sebastián Englert (1888–1969), who took an active interest in the island's history and culture. His tomb lies next to that of the island's first missionary, Eugene Eyraud, who died here in 1864.

Within the luminous interior of the church, woodcarvings blend traditional Christian imagery with Rapa Nui symbols – the Birdman here is depicted as an angel. The church is also the center of vibrant Easter Sunday celebrations, with the local priest's arrival on horseback being the high point of the ceremonies. Sunday mass services include chants in the Rapa Nui language, with decidedly Polynesian rhythms.

🛍 Mercado Artesanal

Tuukoihu, esq. Ara Roa Rakei.
Open 9am–7pm daily. 📷

Located opposite the Iglesia Sagrado Corazón, the Mercado Artesanal is Hanga Roa's lively artisans' market. It is the perfect place to purchase local handicrafts, textiles, and ornaments, as well as custom-made souvenir *moai*, which are either carved of wood or made of volcanic tuff. Shoppers are also offered wooden replicas of the ancient inscribed stone tablets known as *rongorongo* and of wooden *moai kavakava*, which are skeletal carvings with prominent ribs. The market is best visited during the early hours of the morning, before the area gets hot and crowded.

Souvenir at the Mercado Artesanal

🪦 Cementerio Hanga Roa

Near Petero Atamu. ♿

Situated at the northern end of the village, Cementerio Hanga Roa officially dates from 1951, although the site has been used for burials since the early 20th century. Lovingly maintained, the cemetery overlooks the Bahía Cook inlet and is surrounded by a wall of volcanic stones. Simple, home-crafted headstones marked with crosses and decorated with artificial flowers dot the cemetery's grounds. This is a good place to appreciate the island's contemporary local history, in addition to its enigmatic pre-European epic.

🗿 Ahu Tahai

Tahai.

North of Hanga Roa's cemetery, Ahu Tahai is the most notable archaeological site within walking distance of the village. It is actually a complex of three *ahus* (stone platforms) that were restored by US anthropologist William Mulloy in the 1960s and 1970s. The central platform, Ahu Tahai proper, has a single standing *moai*. To its north, the *moai* at Ahu Ko Te Riku has a restored topknot and ceramic eyes. To the south, Ahu Vai Ure is crowned with five standing *moai*.

The Ahu Tahai complex also includes the foundations of several *hare paenga* (boat-shaped houses) and a boat ramp. Mulloy, who died in 1978, is buried in the complex next to his wife Emily.

Rapa Nui imagery on the entrance of Iglesia Sagrado Corazón

🏛 Museo Antropológico P. Sebastián Englert

Tahai s/n. **Tel** (032) 2551020.
Open 9:30am–5:30pm Tue–Fri,
9:30am–12:30pm Sat, Sun & holidays.
🅿 ♿ 🖥 📷 W **museorapanui.cl**

Founded in 1973, Museo Antropológico P. Sebastián Englert is named for the benevolent Capuchin priest who spent many years on the island. The museum's displays focus on trans-Pacific navigation and migration and on iconic Rapa Nui artifacts such as the *moai* and *rongorongo* tablets created by this people upon settling on the island. The museum also explores the crisis, probably demographic, that led to the toppling of several *moai* in the 18th century.

The museum's anthropology section offers information on most of Oceania, the geographical region comprising the Pacific islands from New Guinea and Australia to the tiny atolls of Polynesia. Temporary exhibitions focus on the history, culture, and art of Rapa Nui and Oceania.

Biblioteca William Mulloy, named for the pioneer archaeologist, is well stocked with photographs, videos, and literature that document the island's rich history and culture.

Red and white painted birds on the ceiling of Ana Kai Tangata

🏛 Ana Kai Tangata

Near Avenida Policarpo Toro.
An impressive rock-art site, Ana Kai Tangata is a coastal cavern that features painted terns on its ceiling. Legend has it that cannibalism may have been practiced here, and the cave's ambiguous name, according to American archaeologist Georgia Lee, could mean 'cave where men eat', 'cave where men are eaten', or 'cave that eats men.'

Tapati Rapa Nui

Easter Island's biggest annual event for the past 30 years, Tapati Rapa Nui, has filled the streets of Hanga Roa with folkloric music, dance, and competitive events. Celebrated during the first two weeks of February, the festival is a chance for islanders to showcase their skills and crafts, which include stone and woodcarvings, body-painting, and cooking in the Polynesian style. Tapati Rapa Nui focuses on tradition and identity despite the use of imported elements such as drums and guitars.

VISITORS' CHECKLIST

Practical Information
2,340 miles (3,765 km) NW of
Santiago. 🚾 6,600. ℹ Avenida
Policarpo Toro, at Tuu Maheke;
(032) 2100255. 🎭 Tapati Rapa
Nui (first two weeks of Feb).

Transport
✈ Aeropuerto Mataveri.

However, the evidence to support this theory is tenuous. A carved ceremonial skull has been found on this site, but without cut marks on bones that could indicate cannibalistic practices. Ana Kai Tangata is also the starting point of the Sendero Te Ara O Te Ao, a network of trails that climbs to Rano Kau (*see p264*) and Orongo.

Performers with traditional costumes

Hanga Roa

① Iglesia Sagrado Corazón
② Mercado Artesanal
③ Cementerio Hanga Roa
④ Ahu Tahai
⑤ Museo Antropológico P. Sebastián Englert
⑥ Ana Kai Tangata

0 metre — 750
0 yard — 750

PACIFIC OCEAN

Ahu Tahai ④
Bahía Cook
③ Cementerio Hanga Roa
⑤ Museo Antropológico P. Sebastián Englert
⑦ Mercado Artesanal
① Iglesia Sagrado Corazón
Aeropuerto Mataveri
Ana Kai Tangata ⑥
Rano Kau 3 miles (5 km)

For keys to symbols *see back flap*

The water-filled crater of Rano Kau, with the Pacific beyond

❷ Rano Kau

3 miles (5 km) S of Hanga Roa; Sector Orongo. **Open** 9am–7pm daily.

Part of a national park on Easter Island, the water-filled crater of Rano Kau is the island's most striking natural sight – the panorama from its rim, with the seemingly endless Pacific Ocean on the horizon, is one of the most unforgettable sights of the island. Descending into the crater is no longer permitted, but walking around its undulating rim is a true top-of-the-world experience. On the crater's southwest side, the ceremonial village at **Orongo** is a complex of 53 houses that were linked to this island's Birdman sect in the 18th and 19th centuries. The sect gets its name from the Birdman, an influential post whose incumbent was chosen each year in a ritual that culminated in the collection of a sooty tern egg. Visitors to this historic and fragile site are requested not to leave the marked path or enter the houses, which consist of earth and overlapping slabs, with doors so low that entering them would require crawling.

Rano Kau and Orongo are reached by a road that passes by the west end of Mataveri airport and loops around its south side. However, it is also possible to hike there, and back, on the Te Ara O Te Ao footpath that starts at Ana Kai Tangata (*see p263*). The admission fee for Rano Kau, collected by CONAF, is also valid for entry to Rano Raraku (*see pp266–7*).

Environs

Some 2 miles (4 km) northeast of Rano Kau, **Ahu Vinapu** is one of the sites that was once held to be proof of South American influence on Easter Island, because its closely fitted stones superficially resemble Incan sites in Peru. Ahu Vinapu actually consists of three separate platforms, whose *moai* tumbled over in conflicts during the 18th and 19th centuries. The site is also known for the discovery of fossilized palm, believed to be evidence of early island settlement, around AD 1300. Theory holds that the tree became extinct as islanders cleared woods to make space for erecting *moai*.

Large, compact boulders forming the platform at Ahu Vinapu

❸ Ahu Akivi

4 miles (6 km) NE of Hanga Roa; Sector Akivi.

With seven standing *moai*, restored in 1960 by American anthropologist William Mulloy and his Chilean colleague Gonzalo Figueroa García-Huidobro, Ahu Akivi is one of few inland *ahu* (stone platforms) and, unlike most other *ahus*, its *moai* look toward the sea. They also look toward the platform's

Legend of the Birdman

Petroglyph of a Birdman, Orongo

Around the 16th century, Rapa Nui's culture, rooted in ancestor worship, was replaced by a system of beliefs known as *makemake*, after the creator god of that belief. One of this new sect's key customs was an annual competition held to elect the Tangata Manu (Birdman), who held a position of power on the island. Each of the contestants would sponsor an islander, a *hopu*, whose task was to scramble down the 1,300-ft (400-m) slope of Rano Kau, swim through shark-infested waters to the islet of Motu Nui, and retrieve the egg of a sooty tern. The first *hopu* to do so would climb back to Orongo and be greeted by his sponsor, who became that year's Birdman. The Birdman people disappeared with the slave raids of the 1860s and the arrival of Christian missionaries.

ceremonial center and, during both equinoxes, directly into the setting sun.

❹ Ana Te Pahu

4 miles (6 km) NE of Hanga Roa; Sector Ahu Akivi.

Today, much of Easter Island's food is imported from the mainland, but before this became an option, the islanders used lava tube caves called *manavai*, or sunken gardens, to grow their produce. Ana Te Pahu is one such cave. Owing to the total absence of surface streams on Easter Island's porous volcanic terrain, large-scale agriculture has always been a challenge. The humid micro-climate and relatively deep soils in the caves permitted the cultivation of crops such as bananas; these are still grown in Ana Te Pahu and in similar sites around the island. Visitors can easily descend into the cave, but a flashlight is necessary.

❺ Playa Anakena

10 miles (16 km) NE of Hanga Roa; Sector Anakena.

On the northeastern shores of Rapa Nui, Playa Anakena is the island's only broad sandy beach and, with its tall palms and turquoise waters, is almost a caricature of a South Pacific idyll. The beach is a perfect spot for swimming and sunbathing. It

The impressive row of standing *moai* at Ahu Tongariki

also has barbecue pits, picnic tables, changing rooms, and several snack bars that make it the most popular choice with locals for a day's outing.

According to Easter Island's oral tradition, Playa Anakena is the place where the first Polynesian settlers, under chief Hotu Motu'a, landed. Anakena has one thing that no part of Polynesia can match – the seven standing *moai* of **Ahu Nau Nau**, four of them with *pukao* (topknots) that were restored in 1979 under the direction of island archaeologist Sergio Rapu. Two of these *moai* are badly damaged, but the remainder are in excellent condition. Also on the same beach is the smaller **Ahu Ature Huki** with a single *moai*. From Anakena, it is possible to hike around the little-visited north coast, returning to Hanga Roa via two other sites – Ahu Tepeu and Ahu Tahai. However, this is a full day's trip and demands an

early start. Since there is an absence of shade along the shore, visitors are advised to carry plenty of water.

❻ Península Poike

13 miles (21 km) NE of Hanga Roa; Sector Poike.

The peninsula at the island's eastern end takes its name from Volcán Poike, which marks this area's highest point. In pre-European times there was a village here, and petroglyphs from the period include a turtle, a Birdman, and a tunafish. The area also has fascinating land-marks associated with legends of the island. Key among these is a 2-mile (4-km) long westerly "ditch" believed to mark a line of defensive fortifications during a war between rival clans. On the peninsula's southwestern edge is Poike's most stunning asset – **Ahu Tongariki**. With its 15 *moai*, it is the island's largest platform.

Moai of Ahu Nau Nau on the palm-lined Playa Anakena, backed by the Pacific Ocean

❼ Rano Raraku

Among Easter Island's most breathtaking features are the crater lake and *moai*-studded slopes of Rano Raraku. In fact, the southeastern rim and banks of this volcano are the cradle of the island's iconic *moai*. It was here, long before the arrival of Europeans, that Rapa Nui carvers crafted their massive statues from volcanic tuff and, with substantial effort, freed them from the quarry to be transported across the island. Today, nearly 400 of these can still be seen standing or toppled beside their *ahu* (stone platform). While they differ in detail, the *moai* have much in common. The CONAF-built trails around the crater's outer slopes are the only way to explore the area.

A tilting *moai* head on the crater slopes of Rano Raraku

★ Crater Lake

The vast center of Rano Raraku is occupied by a serene lake whose edges are lined with totora reeds. The crater can only be reached through a gap in the western end of this site. Hordes of feral horses often visit this area, and can be seen trampling over the green beds of totora.

★ Hinariru

Located on one of the lower points of the trail, the much-photographed, 13-ft (4-m) high Hinariru is also called the *moai* with the twisted neck, in reference to its bulging base. According to various folktales, Hinariru was the brother-in-law of Hotu Motu'a, legendary leader of the first island settlers, and perhaps also the master who brought the *moai* to the island.

| 0 metres | 200 |
| 0 yards | 200 |

Piropiro

Just west of Hinariru is another 13-ft (4-m) high *moai* known as Piropiro. About 22 ft (7 m) of this *moai's* body is buried beneath volcanic soil.

★ El Gigante
Climbing to the upper slopes of Rano Raraku, the trail reaches El Gigante, which, at 65 ft (20 m), is the largest *moai* ever carved. Still attached to bedrock, its estimated weight is about 270 tons (240 tonnes).

VISITORS' CHECKLIST

11 miles (18 km) E of Hanga Roa.
Taxi from Hanga Roa. 🛈 ranger station and rangers on-site.
Open 9am–7pm daily. 🎫 📷 mandatory. 🆆 **conaf.cl**

Tukuturi
The fenced-off Tukuturi is the singular kneeling, bearded *moai* that apparently mimics the posture of Polynesian ceremonial singers. According to American archaeologist Joanne van Tilburg, it may be the last *moai* ever made, with links to the Birdman cult *(see p264).*

The Eastern Rim
of Rano Raraku is scenic, but has steep drop-offs.

Key

- - - Trail

🔆 Viewpoint

Ko Kona He Roa
The *moai* known as Ko Kona He Roa bears evidence of European contact in the carved image of a three-masted sailing ship roughly etched on its trunk.

Hare Paenga
Immediately east of Tukuturi are the basalt foundations of many *hare paenga*, thatched boat-shaped houses that were reserved for chiefs and priests. Several others are scattered around the crater.

Robinson Crusoe Island

Covering a land mass of only 36 sq miles (93 sq km), Robinson Crusoe Island is a rugged volcanic speck with a rich natural heritage – about 70 percent of its plant species are endemic. Originally known as Isla Masatierra, the island was renamed for Daniel Defoe's 1719 novel *Robinson Crusoe (see p269)*. Today, Robinson Crusoe Island is home to a small fishing community that subsists mainly on lobster exports to Santiago. Much of the island is part of the Parque Nacional Archipélago de Juan Fernández, a UNESCO World Heritage Site. The many hiking trails are a prime draw for adventurous visitors, while rare bird species such as the Juan Fernandez firecrown hummingbird are a bonus for bird-watchers.

The Tsunami of 2010

The massive earthquake of February 27, 2010, unleashed a tsunami that struck the village of San Juan Bautista, demolishing shoreline constructions and claiming eight lives. Most of the island's trails and sights, such as Mirador Selkirk and Plazoleta El Yunque, remained unaffected because they are inland. With the help of *Desafío Levantemos Chile* (Together We Pick Up Chile), services have since recovered.

A colony of native Juan Fernández fur seals basking in the sun

❽ San Juan Bautista

472 miles (759 km) W of Santiago.
🚐 863. ✈ from Santiago. 🚢 from Valparaíso. ℹ Larraín Alcalde s/n.
🎉 Día de la Isla (Nov 22).
🌐 comunajuanfernandez.cl

Robinson Crusoe Island's only permanent settlement, San Juan Bautista is nestled on the curving shoreline of the scenic Bahía Cumberland. Located just south of the village plaza, atop a hill, the small **Fuerte Santa Barbara** dates from 1770. This stone fort was constructed by the Spanish

in response to the presence of the British in the South Pacific. It was rebuilt in 1974, but the fort's several cannons, pointing at the harbor, still stand here.

Next to the fort, the **Cuevas de los Patriotas** (Caves of the Patriots) was where, in the early 19th century, the Spanish held Chilean leaders fighting for independence. At the village's western end, the **Cementerio San Juan Bautista** has tombs of early settlers, and of German sailors who stayed on the island after the scuttling of the *Dresden* in 1915. This battleship had been cornered by the British navy in the Bahía Cumberland.

Since the tsunami of 2010, the **Casa de Cultura Alfredo de Rodt**, named for an early Swiss settler, shares space with CONAF's national park information office.

🏛 Casa de Cultura Alfredo de Rodt/CONAF

Vicente González 130. **Open** 8am–1pm & 2–6pm Mon–Fri.

❾ Sendero Salsipuedes

1 mile (2 km) W of San Juan Bautista.
Tel (032) 2680381. 🏞 🌐 conaf.cl

Starting at Calle La Pólvora, just west of San Juan Bautista, the Sendero Salsipuedes is a nature trail with multiple switchbacks. The path snakes through dense vegetation and verdant forests of acacia, eucalyptus, Montrey cypress, Montrey pine, and the native murtilla before culminating at the jagged Salsipuedes ridge. The views from here are exceptional and include sweeping panoramas of San Juan Bautista and of the blue waters of Bahía Cumberland that surround the village.

❿ Cueva Robinson

2 miles (3 km) NW of San Juan Bautista by boat; Puerto Inglés. 🚢 🌐 conaf.cl

From the Salsipuedes ridge, a steep pathway descends to the

The settlement of San Juan Bautista on the shores of Bahía Cumberland

beach at Puerto Inglés and to the Cueva Robinson, claimed to be the site of Alexander Selkirk's shelter. This precipitous approach can be dangerous, and it is necessary to hire the services of a local guide. While there is no clear evidence that Selkirk inhabited this cave, a replica of his supposed refuge dominates the site. From 1995 onward, American treasure hunter Bernard Keiser spent several years in the area around Cueva Robinson searching for a massive, 18th-century Spanish treasure, allegedly found by the British and then re-hidden here.

Cueva Robinson, Alexander Selkirk's alleged cave house

⓫ Mirador Selkirk

2 miles (3 km) S of San Juan Bautista.
🏞 🚾 conaf.cl

A popular hiking destination, Mirador Selkirk is the saddle from where, in despondency and hope, castaway Alexander Selkirk watched for the ship that would rescue him from his lonely exile. The trek to this lookout starts at the southern end of San Juan Bautista's central plaza and climbs steeply through an eroded zone dotted with blackberry bushes. As the trail gains altitude, it passes through thick endemic rain forest, studded with towering tree ferns, before culminating at the saddle. It is also possible to start the hike from Mirador Selkirk all the way to the airstrip. Visitors can ask the local fishermen to drop them off in the morning and hike back to San Juan Bautista.

Two metal plaques on the saddle, one placed by the Royal Navy in 1868 and the other by a distant relative in 1983, commemorate Selkirk's exile.

This site offers great views of Bahía Cumberland and San Juan Bautista to the east. To the south, the landscape changes dramatically from dense rain forest to desert at Tierras Blancas, where the rugged shoreline provides habitat to the endemic Juan Fernández fur seal, *Arctocephalus philippii*.

Alexander Selkirk

The story of Alexander Selkirk, who was marooned on Isla Masatierra in the 18th century, served as a partial template for Daniel Defoe's novel *Robinson Crusoe* (1719). Selkirk, a Scotsman who had served under the English privateer William Dampier, was abandoned on the island in 1704 by Dampier's former associate Thomas Stradling after Selkirk complained about the seaworthiness of Stradling's vessel, *Cinque Ports*. During his years as a castaway, Selkirk subsisted on feral goats, fish, and wild plants, clothed himself with animal skins, and stayed hidden from Spanish vessels until his rescue in 1709 by the British privateering ship *Duke*, under Woodes Rogers. Ironically, as Selkirk had predicted, the *Cinque Ports* sank within a month and most of its crew tragically drowned.

Castaway Alexander Selkirk, rescued by the *Duke* in 1709

⓬ Plazoleta El Yunque

2 miles (3 km) S of San Juan Bautista.
🏞 🚻 🚾 conaf.cl

Starting at San Juan Bautista's power plant, a short south-bound road turns into a gentle nature trail that leads to the Plazoleta El Yunque, a serene forest clearing with a campsite. The site is also the spot where Hugo Weber, a German survivor of the *Dresden* sinking, built a house whose foundations are still visible.

A steep and challenging hike beginning at the Plazoleta El Yunque traverses dense forest to reach the saddle of El Camote, which offers sweeping views of the island. Farther ahead, a more strenuous hike culminates at **Cerro El Yunque** (The Anvil Hill), which, at 3,002 ft (915 m), is the highest point on Robinson Crusoe Island. CONAF organizes guides for those who wish to undertake this hike.

Cerro El Yunque, rising above the island's forested shoreline

TRAVELERS' NEEDS

WHERE TO STAY

Chile offers lodging options for every preference and budget, ranging from five-star international chains and cutting-edge boutique hotels to campgrounds and hostels. Most of the large chains are located in the capital city and beach resorts. Boutique hotels are generally found in large cities, in and around the temperate wine-growing areas of the country, and in Patagonia. Many boutique hotels in the Lake District have their own hot springs. Chile also has some good estancias – cattle and sheep ranches that have been turned into accommodations. Mid- and upper-range hotels usually offer guests the option of paying in US dollars. Budget lodgings, especially hostels, are worth consideration as their private rooms are sometimes less expensive yet better than comparable quarters in one- or two-star hotels. Prices for all accommodations rise steeply in the main resorts and urban centers during the tourist season.

The idyllic pool on the top floor of The Ritz-Carlton, Santiago *(see p277)*

Gradings

Hotels in Chile are ranked on a scale of one to five stars by the national tourist board. However, this system can be misleading as the grading is dependent on the facilities offered by a hotel, not on the quality of its hospitality. As a result, some two- and three-star options may be better than their four-star competitors, and boutique hotels may be downgraded for lacking amenities such as abundant parking. Nor do *cabaña* (cabin) accommodations, which can be a bargain for families, fit within the traditional categories. Generally, however, international five-star chains live up to their billing.

Prices

Pricing is mainly dependent on three factors – season, location, and the prevailing economic situation, the last of which includes both macroeconomics and the exchange rate between the US dollar and the Chilean peso.

The most costly locations are in the capital city of Santiago, the desert oasis of San Pedro de Atacama, beach resorts such as Viña del Mar and La Serena, lakeside locales such as Pucón and Puerto Varas, and Patagonian national parks such as Torres del Paine. That said, all these areas also have budget options.

Luxury five-star hotels can cost upward of US$300 per night, while exclusive fishing lodges in the southern Lake District and Patagonia are beyond US$500 per night. Luxury chains such as Explora, and even some boutique hotels, sell only multi-day packages. Though prices in the capital are usually not seasonal, rates are highest in the months of January and February – when most Chileans take their vacations – and lower in November–December and March–April. Prices can also rise in July, the winter school holidays, especially at the Andean ski resorts, which hit their peak rates at this time.

Taxes

Hotel prices may or may not include the 19 percent *impuesto de valor agregado* (Value Added Tax), also known as the IVA. Bona fide travelers to Chile are exempt from this tax if they pay in US dollars or with a foreign credit card. Hotels may not volunteer this information and guests need to ask for the exemption and present their passport and tourist card *(see p314)*. Note that not all hotels in Chile participate; budget accommodations are mostly ineligible. Before making a pay-

Explora Patagonia, Parque National Torres del Paine *(see p282)*

◀ Lago Llanquihue, with the snowy peaks of Volcán Osorno in the background

ment, it is best to verify whether the advertised rates are inclusive of taxes.

Chain Hotels

Marriott, **Ritz-Carlton**, **Hyatt**, and **Sheraton** are among the big-name international chains with representation in Santiago and, occasionally, in other areas of Chile. National chains include the **Hoteles Diego de Almagro**, which offers a scattering of utilitarian but comfortable and reliable hotels throughout the country. There is also **A y R Hoteles**, a loosely affiliated group of hotels that range from fairly modest business-oriented accommodations to intimate boutique and luxury five-star hotels.

Living room of the modern Clos Apalta winery at the Lapostolle Residence *(see p277)*

Luxury and Boutique Hotels

Santiago is the site of most of Chile's luxury hotels, which, in this seismically active country, tend to be new constructions with state-of-the-art amenities. The finest are in the eastern boroughs of Vitacura and Las Condes, and they are invariably high-rises with pools, fitness centers, business facilities, and top restaurants. In the rest of the country, luxury hotels are smaller but often include more extensive gardens and access to ocean or lake beaches.

Boutique hotels are becoming abundant throughout the country, and offer some of the best lodging options, especially in the Central Valley, Lake District,

The sleek bar at Explora Rapa Nui is stocked with liquor and Chilean wines *(see p283)*

and Patagonia regions. Some of these, Puerto Natales' Noi Indigo Patagonia *(see p282)* for instance, are among Chile's most eco-friendly accommodations.

Bodegas

The boom in wine tourism has led a number of wineries to install their own luxurious, even super-luxurious, accommodations. The best are found on Colchagua's wine tour, the Ruta del Vino *(see p152)*. These serve as excellent bases to explore the area by road, or by rail on the Tren del Vino.

Budget Accommodations

The range of Chile's budget accommodations includes basic one- and two-star hotels, or cheaper family-run *hospedajes* and *residencias*, which are likely to have a choice of shared or private bath. Some of these are dismal, others surprisingly good,

but they are always inexpensive. Such accommodations usually include a basic breakfast.

Hostales and Hosterías

Relatively small dwellings, *hostales* and *hosterías* are Chile's closest counterpart to bed-and-breakfast options. With rarely more than a dozen rooms, these accommodations vary widely in quality, but the best of them are very good indeed. Those in national parks are usually fine new constructions. They are often, but not always, oriented toward the tastes of Chilean rather than foreign clientele. Some occupy historic homes that have been remodeled, while others are utilitarian and even bland. However, they frequently offer better value for money than comparably priced hotels.

Estancias and Haciendas

Estancias and haciendas are ranches and farms that have chosen to open their often historic facilities to paying guests. These accommodations are mainly found in Patagonia, and a handful are located in temperate central Chile. In some cases, the estates are remodeled to appeal to affluent tastes, and may include the services of gourmet chefs. Most ranches offer activities such as horse riding, and their isolation implies a certain exclusiveness, although not all of them are elite options.

Room with a veranda at Hacienda Tres Lagos in Patagonia

Yurt-style accommodation on a campground in Southern Patagonia

Hostels

For good-value hostels, contact **Hostelling International Chile** and **Backpackers Chile**. Both have private rooms as well as dorms, and they also represent some classy B&Bs.

Self-Catering and Cabañas

Apart-hotels in Chile offer fine accommodation at lower prices than full-service hotels. Apart-hotels have a reception desk, kitchenettes, living rooms, and cleaning staff, but they lack restaurants and other facilities.

Cabañas, suitable for couples and families, range from one to three bedrooms, plus a kitchen. Found all over Chile, they are most common in the Lake District and Patagonia.

Apartment Rentals

German-run **Contact Chile** has nearly 600 rental properties in Santiago, and another 60 or so in Viña del Mar and Valparaíso. In general, rentals are for two or three months, but shorter terms can also be negotiated.

Campgrounds and Refugios

To most Chileans, camping means parking a van or pitching a tent in a campground with electricity, firepits, and bathrooms with hot showers. Such sites, often run by **CONAF**, are common in the Lake District, Patagonia, and some national parks. Many campgrounds charge for a minimum of four or five people. As a result, solo travelers or couples may find them a fairly expensive option.

Refugios in national parks range from basic to elaborate dormitories. They also offer meals and hot showers.

Disabled Travelers

Chilean hotels, especially at the upper end of the spectrum, have at least one room designed with accessibility for disabled travelers in mind. If there are no dedicated facilities, Chilean hoteliers will do everything possible to accommodate the wheelchair-bound with all the necessary assistance.

Tipping

A 1,000-peso note is usually enough for hotel bellmen and porters. In restaurants, a 10 percent tip is customarily left on the table, unless this has already been included in the bill.

Recommended Hotels

The accommodations in this book range from international chains and historic classics to custom-designed boutique hotels and hostels. Quality hotels used to be a feature only of Santiago and beach resorts, but a boom in destinations like San Pedro de Atacama, Easter Island, Pucón, Puerto Varas and Patagonia means there are now great options all over the country.

Entries labeled as DK Choice refer to establishments with exceptional features or qualities. They may occupy a historic building or an unusual location, enjoy beautiful surroundings, offer extraordinary service, have remarkable design features, a superb restaurant, or spa facilities. Whatever the reason, your stay will be memorable.

Chile's Best: Boutique Hotels

Small-scale boutique hotels are a growing phenomenon in the country. Some are recycled buildings in historic locales, such as the hills of Valparaíso or in Santiago's center, while others are purpose-built design hotels in the Lake District and Patagonia. Others are a combination of the two: custom-built accommodations in a style that respects tradition but incorporates contemporary comforts, as in Patagonia and Easter Island.

Colchagua Noi Blend *(see p278)* enlisted members of the ADD (Association of Decorators of Chile) to each design a different room. The results range from shabby chic to French Bohemian.

Elqui Domos *(see p278)* is a spectacular complex of two observatories, glass cabins, and geodesic domes. The best rooms are the domes because guests can remove the roof and sleep under the stars.

Arica
Calama
NORTE GRANDE AND NORTE CHICO
Copiapó

EASTER ISLAND AND ROBINSON CRUSOE ISLAND

SANTIAGO
Rancagua
CENTRAL VALLEY
Concepción
Temuco
LAKE DISTRICT AND CHILOÉ

Coyhaique
NORTHERN PATAGONIA

Punta Arenas
SOUTHERN PATAGONIA AND TIERRA DEL FUEGO

0 km 500
0 miles 500

Hotel Magnolia *(see p276)* blends the old and the new to perfection. The reconstructed stained-glass windows and marble staircases beautifully intertwine with glass walkways and ceilings.

Huilo Huilo Biological Reserve *(see p280)* is home to Magic Mountain Lodge. A waterfall runs down the leafy pyramid past guest's windows.

Easter Island

Explora Rapa Nui *(see p283)* is a luxurious hotel that mimics the traditional architecture of the island.

Hanga Roa

0 km 25
0 miles 25

Awasi Patagonia *(see p281)*, takes its inspiration from old Patagonian shelters and ranch outpost, while drawing on the principles of Scandinavian design.

Places to Stay

Santiago

Santiago Centro

Andes Hostel $
Hostel   **City Map** 2 F2
Monjitas 506
Tel *(02) 2632-9990*
W andeshostel.com
The private rooms at this handsome hostel approach boutique-hotel quality. In a pedestrian-friendly area close to parks, restaurants, and nightlife, the Andes is also ideally located.

Hotel Foresta $
Modern   **City Map** 2 F2
Victoria Subercaseaux 353
Tel *(02) 2639-6261*
W forestahotel.cl
A well-kept but plain establishment that aspires to a Francophile style, this hotel opposite leafy Cerro Santa Lucía offers good service and welcomes many return guests.

Hotel Galerías $$
Modern   **City Map** 2 F3
San Antonio 65
Tel *(02) 2470-7400*
W hotelgalerias.cl
This hotel offers contemporary rooms, as well as public areas that have been filled with a vast collection of museum pieces from all around the country.

Hotel Magnolia $$$
Boutique   **City Map** 2 E3
Huérfanos 539
Tel *(02) 2664-4043*
W hotelmagnolia.cl
Set in a beautiful 1920s building, this glamorous hotel has 42 meticulously designed, comfortable rooms. There is an on site restaurant, rooftop bar, and a library.

DK Choice

Lastarria Boutique Hotel $$$
Boutique   **City Map** 3 B4
Coronel Santiago Bueras 188
Tel *(02) 2840-3700*
W lastarriahotel.com
Barrio Lastarria's first boutique hotel combines a historic exterior with spectacularly contemporary rooms and communal areas. Guests can relax in the appealing, if diminutive, garden pool. There are fine restaurants within easy walking distance.

The Singular Santiago $$$
Luxury   **City Map** 3 A4
Merced 294
Tel *(02) 2306-8820*
W thesingular.com
This purpose-built hotel blends seamlessly into the historic surroundings of Barrio Lastarria. Guests can expect five-star opulence throughout.

West of Santiago Centro

Happy House Hostel $
Hostel   **City Map** 2 D3
Moneda 1829
Tel *(02) 2688-4849*
W happyhousehostel.com
With a pool, decks, and a vast patio, The Happy House might match many boutique hotels. It also has dorms and a few private rooms with shared bath.

Northeast of Santiago Centro

Hotel Orly $
Boutique   **City Map** 4 E2
Avenida Pedro de Valdivia 027
Tel *(02) 2630-3000*
W orlyhotel.com
In a mostly pedestrian-friendly area, the Orly is a French-style mansion with bright bedrooms. Enjoy the home-grown tea.

Meridiano Sur Petit Hotel $
Boutique   **City Map** 4 D2
Santa Beatriz 256
Tel *(02) 2235-3659*
W meridianosur.cl
The accommodations at this former private residence range from small single rooms to expansive apartments.

The modern exterior of chic
W Santiago *(see p277)*

Price Guide

Prices are based on one night's stay in high season for a standard double room, inclusive of service charges and taxes.

$	under $100
$$	$100 to $200
$$$	over $200

Vilafranca Petit Hotel $
Hostel   **City Map** 4 D2
Pérez Valenzuela 1650
Tel *(02) 2235-1413*
W vilafranca.cl
Cozy and with hospitable Catalonian ownership, Vilafranca guesthouse consists of two renovated residences merged into a single building.

Holiday Inn Express $$
Chain   **City Map** 5 A4
Avenida Vitacura 2929
Tel *(02) 2499-6000*
W hilatam.com/cl
Conveniently located for access to business offices, restaurants, and the metro, this is the Santiago branch of a reliable overseas chain.

Hotel Santiago Park Plaza $$
Boutique   **City Map** 4 F2
Ricardo Lyon 207
Tel *(02) 2372-4000*
W parkplaza.cl
The antiques in the lobby of the Park Plaza are contrasted with the contemporary decor of its rooms, which vary considerably in size.

NH Collection Plaza Santiago $$
Chain   **City Map** 5 A4
Avenida Vitacura 2610
Tel *(02) 2433-9000*
W nh-collection.com
This hotel is the ideal choice for business visitors, thanks to its easy access to nearby corporate offices. There are also some quality restaurants within easy walking distance.

DK Choice

The Aubrey $$$
Boutique   **City Map** 3 B3
Constitución 317
Tel *(02) 2940-2800*
W theaubrey.com
Formerly a dilapidated mansion, the restored Aubrey hotel on the lower slopes of Cerro San Cristóbal offers all modern conveniences while retaining its magnificent 1920s details. Barrio Bellavista's lively dining and nightlife scene is nearby.

Grand Hyatt Regency Santiago $$$
Luxury City Map 5 C2
Avenida Kennedy 4601
Tel *(02) 2950-1234*
w santiago.grand.hyatt.com
Towering above the Vitacura neighborhood, the Grand Hyatt Regency offers startling views of the Andean mountains. Its atrium is an architectural marvel.

Hotel Panamericana $$$
Modern City Map 4 E2
Francisco Noguera 146
Tel *(02) 2432-3300*
w panamericanahoteles.cl
Chile's counterpart to the Holiday Inn is a reliable but unremarkable option. In a good Providencia location, it offers easy access to the metro and to restaurants.

Hotel Le Rêve $$$
Boutique City Map 4 E2
Orrego Luco 023
Tel *(02) 2757-6000*
w lerevehotel.cl
Self-consciously Francophile, the boutique Le Rêve occupies a recycled Providencia mansion on a block filled with restaurants and shops. The metro is within easy walking distance

InterContinental Hotel $$$
Luxury City Map 5 A3
Avenida Vitacura 2885
Tel *(02) 2394-2000*
w intercontisantiago.com
Almost completely green, the walls of this vast establishment are covered by drip-irrigated vines and mosses. Expect every possible amenity provided by any hotel of this caliber.

Marriott Santiago $$$
Luxury City Map 5 C2
Avenida Kennedy 5/41
Tel *(02) 2426-2000*
w marriott.com/hotels/travel/scldt-santiago-marriott-hotel
Covered with copper, the Marriott's twin towers rise above Santiago's Vitacura neighborhood and offer splendid Andean views. Frequented by celebrities, including touring rock bands.

The Ritz-Carlton Santiago $$$
Luxury City Map 5 B4
El Alcalde 15
Tel *(02) 2470-8500*
w ritzcarlton.com
The service, amenities, and rooms are comparable to those on offer at the Hyatt and Marriott, but The Ritz-Carlton enjoys a more central location. El Golf metro is just outside, and there are many good restaurants nearby.

Charming detail and opulence at The Aubrey *(see p276)*

Sheraton San Cristóbal Tower $$$
Luxury City Map 4 D2
Josefina Edwards de Ferrari 0100
Tel *(02) 2707-1000*
w sancristobaltowersantiago.com
Sharing its grounds with the Sheraton Santiago, but featuring a number of independent facilities, this is the more affluent version of its sibling hotel.

Sheraton Santiago Hotel $$$
Luxury City Map 4 E2
Avenida Santa María 1742
Tel *(02) 2233-5000*
w sheraton.com/santiago
This high-rise hotel, tucked into the hillside across the Mapocho in Providencia, is a bit isolated from the rest of the city, but it has all the elite amenities its name suggests.

DK Choice

W Santiago $$$
Luxury City Map 5 B4
Isidora Goyenechea 3000
Tel *(02) 2770-0000*
w whotels.com
Sheraton's eccentric cousin, the cutting-edge W has a rooftop pool and bar offering urban and Andean views, in a casual yet efficient atmosphere. It boasts a choice of restaurants, too, including primo sushi. It serves one of the city's best Sunday brunches.

Central Valley

CASABLANCA VALLEY:
La Casona $$$
Boutique Road Map B6
Fundo Rosario, Lagunillas, Casablanca
Tel *(02) 2601-1501*
w matetic.com
The Colonial-style guesthouse of the Matetic winery is set on palm-studded grounds. It offers winery tours and tastings, buffet breakfast, and outdoor activities.

DK Choice

COLCHAGUA VALLEY:
Lapostolle Residence $$$
Bodega Road Map B7
Viña Lapostolle, Apalta, Km 4
Tel *(072) 2953360*
w lapostolle.com
Probably the top vineyard hotel in the whole of Chile, the Lapostolle Residence has four huge hillside suites. Communal areas include a restaurant, a wine bar, a pool, and Clos Apalta – a winery that produces premium offerings from individually selected grapes.

CONCEPCIÓN:
Hotel Alborada $$
Modern Road Map D1
Barros Arana 457
Tel *(041) 2911121*
w hotelalborada.cl
Located in the center of Concepción, this modern, avant-garde, practical hotel is especially suited to short-term visitors.

MAITENCILLO:
Marbella Resort $$
Resort Road Map B6
Carretera Concón-Zapallar, Km 35
Tel *(032) 2795900*
w marbella.cl
North of Viña del Mar, this is a sprawling resort with two golf courses and polo grounds. High on a bluff above the Pacific, it has its own cable car to carry guests to and from the beach.

PICHILEMU:
Pichilemu Surfhostal $
Hostel Road Map B7
Avenida Eugenio Lira 167
Tel *(09) 9270-9555*
w surfhostal.com
This Dutch-run B&B's rooms are small but attractively furnished. Its bar (just across the street) offers simple meals and drinks, plus relaxing saltwater tubs.

For more information on types of hotels *see pages 272–5*

RANCAGUA:
Hotel Mar Andino $$
Modern   Road Map B7
Bulnes 370
Tel *(072) 2645400*
Ⓦ hotelmarandino.cl
This misnamed hotel is nowhere near the ocean. However, it's ideal for a town in which few visitors will spend more than one night.

SANTA CRUZ:
Colchagua Noi Blend $$
Luxury   Road Map B7
Hijuela la Viña s/n
Tel *(02) 2432 6800*
Ⓦ noihotels.com
Located in the middle of a wine region, this beautiful wooden estancia is perfect for a quiet break.

SANTA CRUZ:
Hotel Terraviña $$
Modern   Road Map B7
Camino los Boldos s/n
Tel *(072) 2821284*
Ⓦ terravina.cl
This Chilean-Danish hotel is a calm getaway that is surrounded by vineyards. Several good restaurants are within walking distance.

SANTA CRUZ:
Hotel Santa Cruz Plaza $$$
Historical   Road Map B7
Plaza de Armas 286
Tel *(072) 2209600*
Ⓦ hotelsantacruzplaza.cl
Integrated with the adjacent historical museum, this wine-country resort has a casino and a large souvenir shop.

DK Choice

TALCA:
Lodge Casa Chueca $
Hostería   Road Map B7
Viña Andrea s/n, Sector Alto Lircay
Tel *(09) 9419-0625, (071) 1970096*
Ⓦ trekkingchile.com/casa-chueca
Spread over 17 wooded riverside acres on Talca's eastern outskirts, this hybrid hostel/hotel/apartment complex organizes trips into Talca's Andean backcountry. Evening meals are a communal vegetarian experience; snacks are available through the day.

VALPARAÍSO:
Hostal Luna Sonrisa $
Hostel   Road Map B6
Templeman 833, Cerro Alegre
Tel *(032) 2734117*
Ⓦ lunasonrisa.cl
This hotel is set in a rambling house decorated with modern art. It has small, cheerful rooms and an apartment for families. Breakfast includes home-made fruit preserves.

The pretty facade of historic Zerohotel, Valparaíso

VALPARAÍSO:
Somerscales Hotel $$
Boutique   Road Map B6
San Enrique 446, Cerro Alegre
Tel *(032) 2331006*
Ⓦ hotelsomerscales.cl
Decorated with period furniture, this hotel was once home to the British artist Somerscales. It is the place for a historic experience with contemporary comforts.

DK Choice

VALPARAÍSO:
Hotel Palacio Astoreca $$$
Boutique   Road Map B6
Montealegre 149, Cerro Alegre
Tel *(032) 3277700*
Ⓦ hotelpalacioastoreca.com
The Palacio Astoreca is the result of a colorful Francophile union of two residences that had previously deteriorated after decades of neglect. The communal areas maintain their historic veneer, but the rooms and restaurant all feature contemporary decor.

VALPARAÍSO: Zerohotel $$$
Boutique   Road Map B6
Lautaro Rosas 343, Cerro Alegre
Tel *(032) 2113113*
Ⓦ zerohotel.com
In a building dating from 1880, this hotel boasts high-ceilinged rooms with large baths, plus terraced gardens that offer views of Valparaíso harbor.

VIÑA DEL MAR:
Hotel del Mar $$
Modern   Road Map B6
Avenida Perú & Avenida Los Héroes
Tel *(600) 7006000*
Ⓦ enjoy.cl
Part of the waterfront casino, Hotel del Mar has large rooms with balconies and vast bathrooms. Exceptional buffet breakfast.

ZAPALLAR: Hotel Isla Seca $$
Boutique   Road Map B6
Camino Costero F-30-E No. 31
Tel *(033) 2741224*
Ⓦ hotelislaseca.cl
Despite sitting along the busy coastal highway, it is a quiet hotel, with most rooms facing the ocean. The restaurant serves fine seafood.

Norte Grande and Norte Chico

ANTOFAGASTA:
Hotel del Desierto $$
Luxury   Road Map B3
Avenida Angamos 01455
Tel *(600) 7006000*
Ⓦ enjoy.cl
All the spacious suites at this hotel (part of the Enjoy casino group) have large balconies and panoramic ocean views.

ARICA:
Hotel Boutique Casa Beltrán $
Boutique   Road Map B1
Sotomayor 266
Tel *(058) 2253839*
Ⓦ hotelcasabeltran.cl/en
Set in a historic wooden house, this hotel features modern interior and a solar-heated water supply. Some rooms have balconies. Breakfast and light meals are available.

IQUIQUE:
Hotel Terrado Suites $$
Modern   Road Map B2
Los Rieles 126
Tel *(057) 2363901*
Ⓦ terrado.cl
This high-rise hotel at Playa Cavancha has rooms with balconies and ocean views. It's near some good restaurants.

PAIHUANO: Elqui Domos $$
Boutique   Road Map C3
Camino Publico Pisco Elqui Horcon, Km 3.5, Sector Los Nichos
Tel *(097) 7092879*
Ⓦ elquidomos.cl
Sleep under the stars in this hotel's mini astronomic observatory and enjoy a once in a lifetime experience. Star gazing is also enhanced by the hotel's geodesic design.

SAN PEDRO DE ATACAMA:
Hotel Altiplánico $$$
Luxury   Road Map C3
Domingo Atienza 282
Tel *(055) 2851212*
Ⓦ altiplanico.cl
This hotel re-creates the traditional style of the region with free-standing thatched adobes.

SAN PEDRO DE ATACAMA:
Hotel Alto Atacama $$$
Boutique **Road Map** C3
Camino Pukará s/n, Sector Suchor,
Ayllu Quitor
Tel *(02) 2912-3945*
W altoatacama.com
Stay in thatched adobes set
among cactus and herb gardens.
There is also a swimming pool.

DK Choice

SAN PEDRO DE ATACAMA:
Hotel Awasi $$$
Boutique **Road Map** C3
Tocopilla 4
Tel *(02) 2233-9641*
W awasiatacama.com
A member of the Relais &
Chateaux group, the all-
inclusive Awasi differs from its
competitors in that it occupies
an inconspicuous site in the
center of San Pedro. Tours are
individual – one guide per
room, even for single guests.

Lake District and Chiloé

ANCUD: Hostal Mundo Nuevo $
Hostel **Road Map** D3
Ave. Costanera Salvador Allende 748
Tel *(065) 2628383*
W newworld.cl
The communal areas are stylish
and bright at this hostel/B&B,
suitable for both backpackers
and those with a bit more cash.

CASTRO: Hotel Boutique
Palafito del Mar $$
Boutique **Road Map** D3
Pedro Montt 567
Tel *(065) 2631622*
W palafitodelmar.cl
At Castro's north end, this is a cozy,
informal conversion. Each room
has its own eccentric character.

CASTRO: Palafito 1326
Hotel Boutique $$
Boutique **Road Map** D3
Ernesto Riquelme 1326
Tel *(065) 2530053*
W palafito1326.cl
This was one of the earliest
palafito conversions. The rooms
with views of the sea are more
expensive than those with city
vistas, but anyone can enjoy
the vast rooftop terrace.

DK Choice

CASTRO: Tierra Chiloé $$$
Luxury **Road Map** D3
San José Playa s/n
Tel *(02) 2207-8861*
W tierrachiloe.cl
About midway between Castro
and Dalcahue, this all-inclusive
resort owes its design to the
local naval architecture tradition,
with enormous state rooms and
a gourmet galley, plus ocean
views from an elevated site.

CURACAUTÍN:
Hostal Andenrose $
Hostería **Road Map** E1
Ruta 181, Km 68.5
Tel *(09) 9869-1700*
W andenrose.com
On the northern approach to
Parque Nacional Conguillío, this
is a Bavarian-run B&B with simple
but comfortable rooms. Gourmet
meals are available, and there is
a small riverside campground.

FRUTILLAR:
Hotel Ayacara $
Boutique **Road Map** D2
Avenida Philippi 1215
Tel *(065) 2421550*
W hotelayacara.cl
Located in the Frutillar Bajo
lakefront area, this is a classic
Mitteleuropa-style house. Most
rooms enjoy views of Lago
Llanquihue and Volcán Osorno.

OSORNO: Hotel Lagos
del Sur $$
Modern **Road Map** D2
O'Higgins 564
Tel *(065) 2243244*
W hotelagosdelsur.cl
This central, utilitarian hotel
has an Art Deco facade with a
brick veneer and ample rooms.

PARQUE NACIONAL
VICENTE PÉREZ ROSALES:
Petrohué Lodge $$$
Luxury **Road Map** E2
Ruta 225, Km 64
Tel *(065) 2212025*
W petrohue.com
Boasting outstanding views
from its upper floors, this
hotel includes a museum on
the local settlement. Guided
excursions in the national park
can be arranged.

PUCÓN: Hostería
¡École! $
Hostel **Road Map** E2
General Urrutia 592
Tel *(045) 2441675*
W ecole.cl
Some of this hostel's dorms
and rooms have a private bath,
while others are shared. There
is a vegetarian restaurant and
a grape-arbor patio.

PUCÓN: Aldea Naukana
Posada Boutique $$
Boutique **Road Map** E2
Gerónimo de Alderete 656
Tel *(045) 2443508*
W aldeanaukana.com
With irregular design and
burnished natural woods,
plus pan-Asian decor and
a pan-Asian restaurant, this
is a unique hotel.

PUCÓN: Hotel
Antumalal $$$
Luxury **Road Map** E2
Camino Pucón-Villarrica, Km 2
Tel *(045) 2441011*
W antumalal.com
This Bauhaus-inspired building
offers vast hillside gardens
and a large spa. The service
here is impeccable.

PUCÓN: Villarrica Park
Lake Hotel $$$
Luxury **Road Map** E2
Camino Pucón-Villarrica, Km 13
Tel *(02) 2222 8400*
W hotelvillarricaparklake.com
Located midway between
Villarrica and Pucón, this
lakeside hotel has large
rooms (all with balconies),
but only a small beach.
However, it has an extensive
spa, and it is the area's only
legitimate five-star hotel.

A stylish bathroom at nature-inspired Hotel Alto Atacama, San Pedro de Atacama

For more information on types of hotels *see pages 272–5*

PUERTO MONTT:
Hotel Gran Pacífico $$
Budget   Road Map D2
Urmeneta 719
Tel *(065) 2482100*
W hotelgranpacifico.cl
This is probably the best option
for accommodation that isn't
in nearby Puerto Varas. Rooms
are large, and the tenth-floor
restaurant offers panoramic views.

PUERTO OCTAY:
Hostal Zapato Amarillo $
Hostería   Road Map D2
Ruta U-55, Km 2.5, La Gruta
Tel *(064) 2210787*
W zapatoamarillo.cl
This place offers cabins, private
rooms with shared baths, and a
loft that can accomodate seven.
It also serves excellent breakfasts
and dinners. Excursions and
scooter rental are available.

PUERTO VARAS:
The Guest House $
Boutique   Road Map D2
O'Higgins 608
Tel *(065) 2237577*
W theguesthouse.cl
Enjoying the status of a national-
monument, this German-style
building is within walking distance
of the lakeshore and restaurants.

**RESERVA BIOLÓGICA HUILO
HUILO: Huilo Huilo Biological
Reserve** $$$
Luxury   Road Map D2
*Carretera Internacional CH-203, Km
55 s/n*
Tel *(02) 2887 3535*
W huilohuilo.com
Located in the middle of the
Chilean Patagonian Rainforest,
the Magic Mountain Lodge mirrors
a mountain in its architecture. It
provides a unique opportunity
to experience the jungle. Enjoy
a traditional Chilean meal at the
restaurant before relaxing in a hot
tub carved out of a tree trunk.

TEMUCO: Hotel RP $
Boutique   Road Map D2
Diego Portales 779
Tel *(045) 2977777*
W hotelrp.cl
Downtown Temuco is a bit of a
desert, but with its modern design
and regional decor, including
Mapuche motifs, this hotel is a
small oasis.

TEMUCO:
Hotel Dreams Araucanía $$$
Chain   Road Map D2
Avenida Alemania 945
Tel *600 626 0000*
W mundodreams.com
In a casino complex, with all
the pros and cons that implies,

this is the best-equipped hotel
in town, with decent restaurants.

Northern Patagonia

CALETA TORTEL:
Hostal Costanera $
Hostel   Road Map E5
Antonio Ronchi 141
Tel *(09) 6677 0236*
Of the many B&Bs in Caleta Tortel,
the Costanera is the one with the
longest history and the best facil-
ities, though rooms vary in size and
quality. Be prepared to carry your
bags from the car park above the
town along wooden walkways.

CALETA TORTEL:
Entre Hielos Lodge $$
Boutique   Road Map E5
Sector Centro s/n
Tel *(09) 9579-3779*
W entrehielostortel.cl
The hotel provides suitable
accommodations for a more
demanding clientele. Burnished
native woods cover the rooms and
the communal areas. The restaurant
is open to hotel guests only.

CHILE CHICO:
Hostería de la Patagonia $
Hostería   Road Map E4
Chacra 3, Camino Internacional s/n
Tel *(067) 2411337*
W hosteriadelapatagonia.cl
This B&B consists of a main house
with up-to-date fixtures and a separate campground. They also offer
a unique form of accommodations
– in a vessel that once served as lake
transportation but now functions as
a *cabaña* sleeping up to five people.

**COCHRANE: Hotel
Último Paraíso** $$
Boutique   Road Map E4
Lago Brown 455
Tel *(067) 2522361*
W hotelultimoparaiso.cl
The grounds of the Último Paraíso
are startlingly barren, but the stylish
rooms will appeal to fly-fishermen.
The dining room is for guests only.

DK Choice

**COCHRANE: The Lodge
at Valle Chacabuco** $$$
Luxury   Road Map E4
*Parque Patagonia, Valle
Chacabuco*
W patagoniapark.org
This is a stylish, solar-powered
lodge catering to affluent
guests. The sprawling complex
has a visitor center and a
restaurant (open to the public),
as well as a campground.

**COYHAIQUE: Albergue Las
Salamandras** $
Hostel   Road Map E4
Teniente Vidal, Km 1.5
Tel *(067) 211865*
W salamandras.cl
This beautiful hostel boasts
rustic, wooden spaces and
good value rooms. It also
offers a choice of outdoor
activities such as cycling
and trekking.

COYHAIQUE: Hotel El Reloj $$
Boutique   Road Map E4
Avenida Baquedano 828
Tel *(067) 2231108*
W elrelojhotel.cl
The El Reloj was once the
city's most stylish hotel,
and it still ranks high. The
fixtures, especially the baths,
are modern, but room size
varies. Excellent restaurant
for regional cuisine.

COYHAIQUE:
Nómades Hotel Boutique $$$
Boutique   Road Map E4
Avenida Baquedano 84
Tel *(067) 2237777*
W nomadeshotel.com
The Nómades overlooks the
river and has two roomy
family apartments. The
Patagonian decor includes
native woods, indigenous
artifacts and weavings, and
hide rugs.

FUTALEUFÚ:
Hotel El Barranco $$
Estancia   Road Map E3
O'Higgins 172
Tel *(065) 2721314*
W elbarrancochile.cl
This rustically comfortable
hotel boasts the best facilities
in town. Patagonian seafood
and wild game are the
restaurant's specialties.

The natural wooden interiors of The
Lodge at Valle Chacabuco, Cochrane

FUTALEUFÚ: Uman Lodge   **$$$**
Luxury   **Road Map** E3
Fundo La Confluencia s/n
Tel *(065) 2721700*
W umanlodge.cl
In addition to river valley views
and green-energy measures,
such as semi-subterranean
insulation, this lodge offers spa
facilities and a large wine cellar.

LA JUNTA:
Hotel Espacio y Tiempo   **$$**
Estancia   **Road Map** E3
Carretera Austral 399
Tel *(067) 2314141*
W espacioytiempo.cl
La Junta is only a tiny spot on the
Carretera Austral, but this hotel
offers some of the region's best
roadside accommodations. There
is also an excellent restaurant.

PARQUE PUMALÍN:
Cabañas Caleta Gonzalo   **$**
Cabañas   **Road Map** E3
Carretera Austral s/n
Tel *(065) 2250079*
W parquepumalin.cl
The fairly compact cabins here
have awkwardly low ceilings, and
there are no cooking facilities.
However, the lodge is convenient
to the park's visitor center,
footpaths, and restaurant.

PUERTO BERTRAND:
Lodge BordeBaker   **$$**
Estancia   **Road Map** E4
Carretera Austral, 8 km south of
Puerto Bertrand
Tel *(09) 9234 5315*
W bordebaker.cl
The reception area at this
riverside hotel connects to its
large, free-standing rooms via
a series of boardwalks. There
are river valley views, but no TV.

PUERTO CHACABUCO
Hotel Loberías del Sur   **$$$**
Luxury   **Road Map** D4
José Miguel Carrera 50
Tel *(067) 2351112*
W loberiasdelsur.cl
Probably the best all-rounder in
the entire region, this hotel offers
excursions, including hikes in the
Parque Aiken del Sur. Spacious
rooms and an excellent restaurant.

PUERTO GUADAL:
Parador Austral   **$**
Estancia   **Road Map** E4
Carretera Austral, Km 273/XI
Tel *(067) 2573417*
W paradoraustral.com
On the edge of a great lake
and rivers, and close to glaciers,
this place offers canopy tours,
trekking, and horse-riding. It
also has a restaurant serving
local cuisine.

The inviting superior twin room at Puyuhuapi Lodge & Spa, Puerto Puyuhuapi

PUERTO PUYUHUAPI:
Casa Ludwig   **$**
Hostel   **Road Map** E3
Avenida Übel 202
Tel *(067) 2325220*
W casaludwig.cl
Designated a national historical
monument, this German-
Chilean B&B is one of the
highlights on the Carretera
Austral. The attic rooms, which
have a shared bath, are suitable
for backpackers.

PUERTO PUYUHUAPI:
Cabañas El Pangue   **$$**
Estancia   **Road Map** E3
Carretera Austral, Km 240
Tel *(067) 2526906*
W elpangue.cl
This establishment comprises
a hotel and a number of free-
standing *cabañas*. The decor is
rustic, and the vibe is informal
and comfortable. Package stays
include excursions.

PUERTO PUYUHUAPI:
Puyuhuapi Lodge & Spa   **$$**
Luxury   **Road Map** E3
Bahía Dorita s/n
Tel *(067) 2450305*
W puyuhuapilodge.com
The region's premier hot-spring/
spa resort, this quiet, secluded
lodge is accessible only by
boat. There are short hiking
trails nearby, but the Puyuhuapi
also arranges longer trips
for guests.

VILLA O'HIGGINS:
Hostería El Mosco   **$**
Hostería   **Road Map** E5
Carretera Austral, Km 1240
Tel *(067) 2431821*
W villaohiggins.com/elmosco
The El Mosco combines a
first-floor hostel with an
upstairs B&B; it also includes
a *cabaña* sleeping up to six
people and a rather barren
campground. It is a very
sociable place, with reasonably
stylish decor.

VILLA O'HIGGINS:
Robinson Crusoe Deep
Patagonia Lodge   **$$**
Luxury   **Road Map** E5
Carretera Austral, Km 1240
Tel *(09) 9357-8196; (067) 2431909*
W robinsoncrusoe.com
The first luxury lodge at Villa
O'Higgins, this curiously named
establishment features a large
clubhouse-style reception and
two free-standing wings of
six rooms each. The ideal base
for exploring the Southern
Patagonia Ice Field, the lodge
specializes in excursions

Southern Patagonia and Tierra del Fuego

PARQUE NACIONAL TORRES
DEL PAINE:
Hotel Las Torres   **$$**
Luxury   **Road Map** E6
Sector Las Torres
Tel *(061) 2617450*
W lastorres.com
This hotel, at the eastern starting
point of the W trekking route,
offers comfortable rooms, plus
excursions on horses from its
own stables. Wi-Fi is available
in the communal areas, but it
can be sporadic.

PARQUE NACIONAL TORRES
DEL PAINE:
Awasi Patagonia   **$$$**
Luxury   **Road Map** E6
Parque Nacional Torres del Paine
Tel *(02) 2233-9641*
W awasipatagonia.com
The perfect retreat, Awasi
offers 12 villas in a private
reserve with a strong eco
touch that brings to mind
Scandinavian design. During
the day, personal guides can
be hired to look for pumas
in the national park. At
night, savour the Lodge's
special gastronomic offerings
in the restaurant.

For more information on types of hotels *see pages 272–5*

DK Choice
PARQUE NACIONAL TORRES DEL PAINE: Cascada
EcoCamp $$$
Luxury   **Road Map** E6
Sector Las Torres
Tel *(02) 2923 5950*
w ecocamp.travel
Located in the heart of Parque Nacional Torres Del Paine, near the starting point of the W trekking route, this group of free-standing domes includes basic tents with cots or bunks (with access to shared baths) and dome suites with private baths. Breakfast and other meals are served at a separate restaurant.

PARQUE NACIONAL TORRES DEL PAINE:
Explora Patagonia $$$
Luxury   **Road Map** E6
Sector Lago Pehoé
Tel *(02) 2395-2800*
w explora.com/hotels-and-travesias/patagonia-chile
This was the first of the Explora luxury lodge resorts. Accommodations here pretty much define the concept of "room with a view" – thanks to the vistas of the Paine range, most notably the jagged Cuernos.

PARQUE NACIONAL TORRES DEL PAINE:
Hotel Lago Grey $$$
Luxury   **Road Map** E6
Sector Lago Grey
Tel *(061) 2712100*
w lagogrey.com
On the shore of its namesake lake, the Lago Grey cannot quite match the quality of Explora Patagonia or Hotel Las Torres. However, it does offer easy catamaran access to the glacier at the lake's upper end. Communal areas, such as the bar and restaurant, can get busy.

PARQUE NACIONAL TORRES DEL PAINE:
Patagonia Camp $$$
Luxury   **Road Map** E6
Ruta 9 Norte, Km 74
Tel *(02) 2594-0591*
w patagoniacamp.com
Located just outside the park boundaries, the Patagonia Camp resembles the Cascada EcoCamp (see p282), but its sleeping quarters are housed in yurts rather than domes. It mostly offers all-inclusive deals, but B&B is also available.

PORVENIR:
Hostería Yendegaia $
Hostería   **Road Map** E6
Croacia 702
Tel *(061) 2581919*
w hosteriayendegaia.com
In a classic 1920s house, Porvenir's most distinctive accommodation option recalls the Fuegian past – except for contemporary amenities like flat-screen TVs, a souvenir shop, and a library. There is an in-house laundry service, too.

PUERTO NATALES:
Casa Cecilia $
Hostel   **Road Map** E6
Tomás Rogers 60
Tel *(61) 2412698*
w casaceciliahostal.com
A pioneer in the local hostel movement, this Swiss-Chilean B&B has a bright atrium. It offers a great home-made breakfast.

PUERTO NATALES:
Kau Lodge $
Boutique   **Road Map** E6
Pedro Montt 161
Tel *(061) 2414611*
w kaulodge.com
Some sleeping quarters at this waterfront property are small, with bunk beds, but all rooms offer pleasant ocean views. Breakfast is at the Coffeemaker Café, which is open to the public.

PUERTO NATALES:
Bories House Hotel $$
Estancia   **Road Map** E6
Puerto Bories 13-B
Tel *(061) 2412221*
w borieshouse.com
An Anglo-Chilean enterprise, Bories House has turned a traditional construction into a modern hotel. It has also renovated two other houses into family-friendly lodgings.

The illuminated entrance to Hotel Las Torres (see p281), Parque Nacional Torres del Paine

PUERTO NATALES:
Noi Indigo Patagonia $$
Luxury   **Road Map** E6
Ladrilleros 105
Tel *(061) 2740670*
w noihotels.com/hotel/noi-indigo-patagonia
This hotel features traditional materials on the outside, while the interior is a masterpiece of contemporary design, with metal walkways and a rooftop spa. The pine-paneled, minimalist rooms are small but have modern baths.

PUERTO NATALES:
Hotel Altiplánico del Sur $$$
Chain   **Road Map** E6
Ruta 9 Norte, El Huerto 282
Tel *(061) 2412525*
w altiplanico.cl
A short walk north of town, and built into a mild slope, this innovatively green hotel uses a shield of peat blocks to reduce heat loss through its concrete walls and the roof.

PUERTO NATALES:
Hotel Costaustralis $$$
Modern   **Road Map** E6
Pedro Montt 262
Tel *(061) 2412000*
w hotelcostaustralis.com
This is the city's largest hotel, but it does not have the most innovative design. The rooms are perfectly serviceable, but with practical rather than cutting-edge furnishings.

PUERTO NATALES:
Hotel Remota $$$
Luxury   **Road Map** E6
Ruta 9 Norte, Km 1.5
Tel *(02) 2387-1500*
w remotahotel.com
A short walk from the Altiplánico, Hotel Remota is conspicuous for its high profile – literally – and the dazzling bank of windows that fill it with light even on overcast days.

DK Choice
PUERTO NATALES:
The Singular Patagonia $$$
Luxury   **Road Map** E6
Puerto Bories s/n
Tel *(061) 2722030*
w thesingular.com
This hotel was a crumbling slaughterhouse before it was transformed into a hotel featuring an industrial museum. All rooms have views of Last Hope Sound, and there's a gourmet restaurant and a bar. A range of organized excursions is also on offer.

PUERTO WILLIAMS:
Lakutaia Lodge $$$
Luxury Road Map F7
Seno Lauta s/n
Tel *(061) 2621721*
W lakutaia.cl
Right on the Beagle Channel,
this is the best place to stay
in Puerto Williams. It's a great
base for trekking, fly-fishing,
heli-skiing, and even two-
week yacht trips through the
Fuegian fjords.

PUNTA ARENAS:
Hotel Chalet Chapital $
Hostel Road Map E6
Armando Sanhueza 974
Tel *(061) 2730100*
W hotelchaletchapital.cl
This B&B provides mid-sized
paneled rooms with good
furnishings and modern baths.
The room rates also include a
buffet breakfast. Amenities on
offer range from free Wi-Fi and
cable TV to a laundry service.
Various restaurants and most
city sights are located nearby.

PUNTA ARENAS:
Hotel Rey Don Felipe $$
Modern Road Map E6
Armando Sanhueza 965
Tel *(061) 2295000*
W hotelreydonfelipe.com
The Rey Don Felipe is an
efficient hotel offering
expansive rooms with plenty
of comfortable working space
for its business visitors. It is
also equally appealing to
tourists. Some rooms even
have Jacuzzis.

PUNTA ARENAS:
Hotel Dreams del Estrecho $$$
Chain Road Map E6
O'Higgins 1235
Tel *600 6260000*
W mundodreams.com/hotel/hotel-
dreams-del-estrecho
This gleaming glass-and-steel
tower has contributed greatly
to the gentrification of what
was once a run-down area at
Punta Arenas' waterfront.
The hotel's facilities include
an adjacent casino.

PUNTA ARENAS:
Whalesound $$$
Luxury Road Map E6
Isla Carlos III
Tel *(09) 9887-9814*
W whalesound.com
Whalesound is a tour company
that shuttles visitors to its
dome-tent campground in
the Strait of Magellan, then
out to where humpback
whales go to feed. Meals are
served in a separate dome.

Comfortable seating at Explora Patagonia, Parque Nacional Torres del Paine *(see p282)*

Easter Island and Robinson Crusoe Island

HANGA ROA:
Residencial Kona Tau $
Hostel
Avareipua s/n
Tel *(032) 2100321*
W hostelling.cl
Both dorm accommodation
and private rooms in the main
house are available at this
budget hostel. Visitors can
also feast on abundant free
mangoes from the garden.

HANGA ROA:
Aloha Nui Guest House $$
Hostel
Avenida Atama Tekena s/n
Tel *(032) 2100274*
The owners of this guesthouse –
Ramon Edmunds and Josefina
Mulloy, granddaughter of
the archaeologist William
Mulloy – are among the most
knowledgeable local residents.

HANGA ROA: Hotel Otai $$
Hostería
Te Pito o Te Henua s/n
Tel *(032) 2100560*
W hotelotai.com
With lush gardens sheltering
it from the street, the Otai is a
traditional favorite. Communal
areas have better decor than
the relatively utilitarian guest
rooms, but it's a comfortable
hotel suitable for all.

HANGA ROA: Hotel Taura'a $$
Hostel
Atamu Tekena s/n
Tel *(032) 2100463*
W tauraahotel.cl
Run by a congenial husband-
and-wife team, the Taura'a
pays great attention to detail
in its decor. It also provides
excellent personal service.

HANGA ROA:
Explora Rapa Nui $$$
Luxury
Sector Te Miro Oone
Tel *(02) 2395-2800*
W explora.com/hotels-and-
travesias/easter-island-chile
An all-inclusive luxury resort in an
archaeologically sensitive zone,
offering guided excursions and a
spa, plus its own organic orchard.

DK Choice

**HANGA ROA: Hangaroa
Eco Village & Spa** $$$
Luxury
Avenida Pont s/n
Tel *(032) 2553700*
W hangaroa.cl
On the grounds of a once
deteriorating hotel, outside
investors have created a
scattering of spacious multi-
room suites on luxuriant
subtropical grounds, with spa
facilities, restaurant, and a
business center. The staff are
highly attentive to guests' needs.

SAN JUAN BAUTISTA:
Residencial Mirador de Selkirk $$
Hostel
El Castillo 251
Tel *(09) 8845-7024*
This hillside B&B has an excellent
kitchen, though going full-board
precludes sampling fresh seafood
elsewhere in town. Comfy rooms
and ocean views from the deck.

SAN JUAN BAUTISTA:
Crusoe Island Lodge $$$
Luxury
Sector Pangal
Tel *229461636*
W crusoeislandlodge.com
A short boat ride (or a slightly
longer hike) from San Juan,
this handsome resort offers
B&B-style accommodation,
a spa, and a range of activities.

For more information on types of hotels *see pages 272–5*

WHERE TO EAT AND DRINK

Chile offers an increasingly sophisticated cuisine that uses an assortment of ingredients from the fertile farmlands of its Central Valley and the seas off its endless coastline. Though underrated as a gastronomic destination, the country has a huge diversity of restaurants that range from the roadside *parrilla*, or steakhouse, to eateries serving the freshest possible seafood. Major cities also offer a number of international choices that would draw attention anywhere in Europe or North America. Santiago and other major cities offer outstanding dishes based on beef, lamb, and seafood, but dining can be fairly simple in many smaller towns and in the countryside. Fast food often takes the form of burgers and pizza, but there are also a number of street food stands selling sandwiches and *italianos* (inexpensive hot dogs slathered with mayonnaise, tomatoes and avocado).

Barbecues are very popular in Chile; roadside or campsite *parrillas* are common

Restaurants

The simplest eateries found in markets across Chile are the *comedores* or *cocinerías*, which usually serve fresh seafood that is remarkably good given the affordable price. A *picada* is an informal family restaurant, often starting as a room in the house, that expands as it gains a reputation beyond the neighborhood. A *fuente de soda*, literally a soda fountain, refers to a simple place that does not serve liquor, while a *salon de té*, or a teahouse, is more of a café. A *restaurante* proper is a formal eatery, usually with an elaborate menu. *Parrillas* specialize in grilled beef, but in larger cities they may also serve other meats, seafood, and pastas. Primarily a seafood restaurant, the *marisquería* also serves traditional meat dishes. Reservations are generally required only in upscale restaurants, or on busy weekend evenings and holidays. Guests who are looking for specifics, such as disabled access or a vegetarian menu, should call in advance.

Eating Hours

At most restaurants, and even at some B&Bs, it is hard to get breakfast before 9am. Lunch is served relatively late, around 2pm, and even later on weekends. Chileans often take a third meal of sandwiches and sweets, known as *onces*, between 5 and 7pm; this is accompanied by tea or coffee, and sometimes runs into the dinner hour. Dinner is generally served between 8pm and midnight. However, be aware that smaller restaurants in the countryside usually do not stay open beyond 9 or 10pm.

Payment and Tipping

In addition to the à la carte menu, many restaurants have fixed-price menus at lunchtime that often offer bargains, but this practice is less common at dinnertime.

Prices are inclusive of the 19 percent *Impuesto al Valor Agregado* (IVA) or VAT, but not gratuities. Most restaurants accept MasterCard, Visa, and American Express, although the latter is less common. Payment with traveler's checks is rare. In small, informal eateries, especially outside larger cities, cash is the rule.

There is no fixed standard regarding tipping in Chilean dining establishments; where the service tax is not included in the bill, it is customary for guests to leave a minimum of 10 percent tip, depending on the quality of service.

The dining room at Ancud's upscale Hostal Mundo Nuevo *(see p279)*

The atmospheric and popular Confitería Torres, Santiago *(see p290)*

Disabled Travelers

In Santiago and a few other large Chilean cities, upscale restaurants have ramps or other means of access. However, few traditional buildings have been suitably adapted for guests with limited mobility. In general, Chilean restaurateurs will do their utmost to make the wheelchair-bound feel comfortable and welcome, but toilet access can be a problem. It is advisable to enquire ahead of time about the facilities available.

Children

Chile is a child-friendly country, and children are welcome almost everywhere. Separate menus for children are uncommon, but restaurants do not mind if parents share the often generous portions of food with their children.

Vegetarians

Although Chile's fertile valleys produce abundant ingredients for vegetarian dining, the Chilean diet is based on meat and seafood. Despite this, there are exceptional vegetarian restaurants in Santiago and in tourist destinations such as Pucón; elsewhere visitors may need to insist on salads and pasta with meatless sauces.

Smoking

As of early 2013, Chile's Congress approved legislation to strengthen its anti-tobacco laws. Whereas before then restaurants had the option to allow smoking indoors, or to set up smoking and non-smoking sections, they can no longer do so. Smoking in any enclosed area is now strictly prohibited, and this law also applies to bars and clubs. This has cleared establishments' air indoors making eating out a more pleasant experience all round. Note that smoking is still allowed in outdoor areas including sidewalk seating and patios.

Smoking is also prohibited on public transport, including both local and long distance buses *(see p316)*.

Recommended Restaurants

The restaurants listed on the following pages have been selected to provide a comprehensive cross-section of Chilean dining options; there appears everything from gourmet international cuisine and eateries serving the freshest seafood to good-value pizzerias and sandwich shops.

Chilean seafood, whether prepared in an international style or to local tradition, is among the most diverse in the world. Its popularity here overlaps with what might be called "country cooking", which uses farm-fresh, often seasonal ingredients.

The fine-dining options include some of Chile's top restaurants, mostly in Santiago but also in historic, scenic and sometimes unexpected locations. Grill restaurants with beef but also lamb and seafood are abundant, with menus that can even include game dishes in Patagonia. Grills often have vegetarian options.

Many wineries now have vineyard restaurants that highlight the wines produced on site.

The DK Choice entries highlight exceptional establishments that, on top of outstanding food, offer additional unique features, whether in terms of ambience, location or entertainment.

Sidewalk seating at the vibrant Galindo, Santiago *(see p291)*

The Flavors of Chile

Chilean dishes have always used certain staples sourced from the high Andes: potato; quinoa, the native Andean grain; and the meat of the llama. Chileans are committed carnivores, and eat beef whenever they can, but lamb, primarily from Patagonia, is also popular, as are chicken and pork. Game, such as boar and the ostrich-like rhea, is also gaining popularity. It is the extraordinary marine life of Chile's coastline, however, which is now the star of Chilean cuisine – the cool Humboldt current yields an array of fish and shellfish that is hard to match anywhere else in the world.

Andean quinoa

Baked meat empanadas on display in a traditional Chilean bakery

Creole Cuisine

Comida criolla or Creole cooking is Chilean country cuisine, using staples such as potatoes, sweet corn, onions, garlic, and olives. Stewing is the most common method of cooking them. *Humitas*, similar to Mexican tamales, are steamed corn wraps and can be made with or without meat. Stemming from the Spanish tradition, and common throughout Latin America, the empanada is a pastry turnover, usually filled with ground beef or cheese. The most popular Chilean empanada is *Empanada de pino*. It consists of a seasoned mixture of ground beef, raisins, black olives, onions, and mild aji.

Chilean food in general is quite lightly spiced, if at all. In recent years, however, Mapuche *merkén* (a ground spice mix of dried, smoked red chilies, toasted coriander, and cumin) has grown in popularity, adding some bite to otherwise bland dishes.

Fish and Seafood

Chile's long coastline is the source of some of its greatest

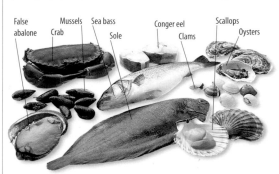

False abalone | Mussels | Crab | Sea bass | Sole | Conger eel | Clams | Scallops | Oysters

A selection from the vast range of superb Chilean seafood

Chilean Dishes and Specialties

The best Chilean dishes are seasonal, linked to the harvests of both land and sea. Chileans tend to eat their largest meal at lunchtime – Santiaguinos throng into the city's restaurants for business lunches, while country dwellers may take two or three hours over a home-cooked meal.

Popular dishes include *pastel de papas* (potato casserole), *caldillo de congrio* (conger eel soup), *chupe de locos* (abalone stew) and *palta reina* (an appetizer of avocado stuffed with tuna, chicken, or ham, heavy on the mayonnaise).

Aji chilies

A favorite condiment, served with bread or spooned over barbecued meat, is *pebre*, a tangy dipping sauce of chopped onion and tomato, fresh coriander, olive oil, garlic, and mildly spicy Aji chili peppers.

Cazuela de Ave is a thin stew of meat (usually beef) with corn on the cob, potato, and rice.

Fresh vegetables at the central fruit and vegetable market in Santiago

Salads and red wine are both essential accompaniments.

Snacks

Chile's favorite snack, the *completo*, is a hot dog smothered in mayonnaise, ketchup, mustard, and sauerkraut. Sandwiches are very popular, usually eaten at *onces* or late afternoon tea. German settlers have given Chile *kuchen*, thick-crusted pastries topped with fruit. *Sopaipilla* (fried sweet or savory flatbread) is a favorite street food.

The Peruvian Connection

Chile and Peru undoubtedly have a contentious political relationship – much of the northern third of Chile was once Peruvian territory, and the two countries even dispute the historical roots of the grape brandy known as *pisco*. But, just as North Americans have embraced Mexican food, so Chileans flock to Peruvian restaurants. In the capital, some of the best kitchens have Peruvian chefs. To discover what Chileans see in their neighbor's cuisine, look out for dishes such as *ají de gallina* (strips of chicken in a creamy walnut sauce with potatoes and olives), *ceviche* (raw fish), and *lomo saltado* (stir-fried steak and vegetables). For those who enjoy spicier food, the Peruvians use a variety of peppers in their dishes; *papa a la huancaína* is a typically spicy potato appetizer.

seafood. Chilean fish includes superb *congrio* (conger eel), *corvina* (sea bass), *lenguado* (sole), and *merluza* (hake), *Reineta* (Brama Australis), among other kinds. However, it is shellfish that sets Chilean seafood cuisine apart from the ordinary. Everyone will recognize such standards as clams, crab, oysters, scallops, shrimp, and squid. The novelties, for first-time visitors in particular, are the many varieties of mussels, including the *choro zapato* (shoe mussel, so named for its size), *erizos* (sea urchins), *locos* (giant abalone), and *picoroco* (giant barnacle). Some of these, of course, are acquired tastes.

Salmon is widely, and controversially, farmed in the lake regions, and trout from there is extremely delicious.

When ordering fish, avoid the *frito* (deep fried) options, often prepared using heavy oils – *a la plancha* (grilled) and *al vapor* (steamed) are healthier options.

Mixed Grill

Chileans enjoy a *parrillada* or barbecue. In addition to cuts of beef, the meal usually includes a variety of sausages such as *morcilla* (blood sausage) and *chunchules* (chitterlings), and sometimes pork or chicken.

Chanco cheese and *longaniza* sausage on a market stall

Pastel de choclo, served in a traditional earthenware bowl, is ground meat topped with corn purée and baked.

Porotos Granados, a thick stew of whole beans and squash, draws its origins from the high Andes. Available only in summer.

Curanto, a typical southern dish of seafood, pork, and vegetables, is simmered for hours in an earth oven.

What to Drink

While Chile's superb wines are renowned globally and are the traditional favorite among people from across the country, it has embraced the Latin American fever for craft beers. *Pisco*, the grape brandy of Norte Chico's deserts, is the basis of *pisco sour*, the national cocktail. Non-alcoholic drinks include a number of standard sugary soft-drinks. Tap water is almost always drinkable, but for those who have any doubts, bottled water is readily available. Chileans drink both black and herbal teas but, except in the capital and major tourist destinations, soluble coffee powder is the default option for caffeine addicts.

Pisco sour, a popular cocktail

Diners at the popular Bar Cinzano in Valparaíso *(see p293)*

Pisco

Distilled from the Muscatel grapes grown in Norte Chico, *pisco* is a clear brandy-like liquor. The final product varies according to its alcoholic content, stated in terms of degrees. Lower quality *pisco* ranges from *selección* (30° or 60 proof) to *especial* (35° or 70 proof), while better versions vary from *reservado* (40° or 80 proof) to *gran pisco* (up to 50° or 100 proof). In general, *reservado* is considered ideal for the emblematic *pisco sour*, Chile's favorite cocktail. This is a potent blend of grape brandy flavored with lime juice, egg white, and Angostura bitters and, at best, a dash of sugar.

Chileans also mix *pisco* with cola drinks to create the *piscola*, Chile's counterpart to the Cuban *libre*. Both lower and higher quality *piscos* may be consumed straight, or mixed as cocktails.

Beer

Chile has marketed its wines brilliantly and they are widely available overseas. It's not all about wine, however; Chileans do also enjoy beer. The most commonly drunk beers are run-of-the-mill lagers produced by companies such as Cristal and Escudo, but increasingly, Chilean breweries are offering microbrews of greater diversity and flavor. For instance,

A worker labeling bottles of beer at the Szot brewery in Santiago

Valdivia's Compañía Cervecera Kunstmann makes excellent ale, honey beers, and bock, and Santiago's Szot has found a niche with its pale ale, amber ale, and stout. The Valparaíso-based Kross has opened Krossbar, a specialised craft beer destination in Santiago's Bellavista, while the traditional Pisco area of Valle del Elqui has its own brewery that uses solar energy.

Non-Alcoholic Drinks

Chilean tap water is drinkable almost everywhere, but short-term visitors with sensitive stomachs may want to stick with bottled water, which comes as either *con gas* (carbonated) or *sin gas* (non-carbonated). Good coffee is not easily available throughout the country. However, coffee-enthusiasts will find espresso and brewed coffee in most major cities and tourist destinations, especially in the better hotels and B&Bs.

Chile boasts a variety of unique herbal teas such as *boldo* and *cachamai*. These are gleaned from the southern forests and, with their unique aroma and woody flavors, are a good substitute to the country's commonly found packaged black tea. In Patagonia, many Chileans drink *mate*, a slightly bitter Argentine brew concocted from a relative of the wild holly and sipped through a bulbous gourd through a metal *bombilla* or straw.

Chilean Wines

Weather conditions in Chile are ideal for cultivating grapes and, by extension, for producing quality wines. In general, whites predominate in the north and give way to reds toward the south, but there are many exceptions to this rule – the Casablanca Valley, northeast of Santiago, produces some of the finest sauvignon blanc and chardonny, but also offers pinot noir and other reds. The country's main wine-growing areas welcome visitors for tours and tastings, but lesser-known vineyards in regions such as the Valle del Elqui are also worth a visit. Climate change has had negative and positive effects on Chilean wine. Producers have started to establish vineyards in areas of the South, widening the spectrum of wine possibilities. Chile's wineries range from large, industrial operations such as Viña Concha y Toro to tiny boutique businesses that produce a few thousand bottles of premium wine per annum.

Sought-after varietals include whites such as Castillo de Molina's sauvignon blanc and Cono Sur's chardonnay. Viña Casa Silva *(see p153)* produces its reds from old vines.

Popular Varietals

Cabernet sauvignon is probably the country's most widely planted grape, but carménère is the most distinctive – the root disease phylloxera nearly killed it in Bordeaux in the 19th century, but French enologists rediscovered it among merlot plantings in Chile in the 1990s. This unintended blending has given Chilean merlot a unique flavor. Other reds cultivated here include syrah and, increasingly, pinot noir. The most common whites, of course, are chardonnay and sauvignon blanc, which are highly regarded.

Casa Silva's Dona Dominga label

The label of Falernia's syrah

Buying and Drinking Wine in Chile

Good drinkable wines are available at most supermarkets for around US$8, but finer vintages can be purchased at a slightly higher price from specialist wine stores. Top vintages, from wineries such as Viña Montes and Viña Lapostolle in the Colchagua Valley *(see pp152–3)*, can be hard to find except at the wineries themselves. In Santiago and other major cities, restaurants usually have extensive wine lists. Wine is generally served by the bottle; the traditional *botellín* or *vino individual* is a single serving bottle. Wine by the glass, however, is usually available at most bars and restaurants.

Clos Apalta, the only wine manufactured by the Franco-Chilean Viña Lapostolle *(see p153)*, is a unique blend of petit verdot, merlot, cabernet sauvignon, and carménère.

Merlot, sauvignon blanc, and syrah served at Tanino in Viña Casas del Bosque

Where to Eat and Drink

Santiago

Santiago Centro

Fuente Alemana $
German   **City Map** 3 B4
Alameda 58
Tel *(02) 2639-3231*   **Closed** *Sun*
The *lomito* (pork loin) is not to be
missed at this popular sandwich
shop. Given the size of the meals
here, some diners might want to
consider sharing.

El Hoyo $
Café   **City Map** 1 B5
San Vicente 375
Tel *(02) 2689-0339*   **Closed** *Sun*
El Hoyo might not look like much,
but the food is delicious and highly
regarded by visitors and locals
alike. Try the *terremoto* (earthquake) of fermented white
wine and pineapple ice cream.

Blue Jar $$
International   **City Map** 2 E3
Profesora Amanda Labarca, 102
Tel *(02) 2696-1890* **Closed** *Sat & Sun*
Blue Jar emphasizes the use of
fresh seasonal ingredients. A
reservations-only dinner takes
place on the first Thursday of
each month, with dishes that are
not on the usual daytime menu.

Confitería Torres $$
International   **City Map** 2 D3
Alameda 1570
Tel *(02) 2688-0751*   **Closed** *Sun*
A popular option at this beautiful
and classy restaurant is the *barros
luco*, a steak-and-cheese sand-
wich favored by President Ramón
Barros Luco.

El Naturista $$
Vegetarian   **City Map** 2 E3
Moneda 846
Tel *(02) 2380-0704*   **Closed** *Sun*
Santiago's venerable vegetarian
restaurant chain dates from 1927,
so the folks here are experts in
the field of veggie cooking. Even
their takes on Chilean staples
such as *pastel de choclo* are meat-
free. Vegan options are fewer.

Richard El Rey Del Mariscal $$
Seafood   **City Map** 2 E1
*Mercado Central, San Pablo 943,
Local 161*
Tel *(02) 2269-6255*
This place offers an alternative
to the classic restaurants of
Santiago's central seafood market.
It has good traditional dishes
such as *chupe de jaiva* (crab) and
locos (false abalone). Friendly
and efficient service.

Salvador Cocina Y Café $$
Chilean   **City Map** 2 E2
Bombero Ossa 1059
Tel *(02) 2673-0619*
Open only during lunch hours,
this restaurant is run by award
winning chef Rolando Ortega.
The menu changes everyday,
however, pig's feet and cow's
tongue feature frequently. It also
has delicious vegetarian options.

DK Choice

Bocanáriz $$$
International   **City Map** 3 A5
Lastarria 276
Tel *(02) 2638-9893*
This is the city's best dedicated
wine bar, with a list of some 400
bottles, and dozens available by
the glass. It also has a food menu
to pair with the wines. Friendly
French ownership, pleasant
contemporary surroundings,
and impeccable service.

Castillo Forestal $$$
French   **City Map** 2 F1
*Avenida Cardenal José María Caro
390 Parque Forestal*
Tel *(02) 2664-1544*
Located in an old castle, this rest-
aurant has an enviable location
and offers scrumptious dishes
that combine French food with
a Chilean twist. The flower
version of their pisco is a must.

Japón $$$
Japanese   **City Map** 3 B5
Barón Pierre de Coubertin 39
Tel *(02) 2222-4517*   **Closed** *Sun*
For authentic sushi, sashimi,
and other Japanese dishes –

The eclectic and vibrant interior of
Boulevard Lavaud

including tempura ice cream –
Japón is probably Santiago's
best choice. The presentation is
creative, and the decor subdued.

Patagonia Sur $$$
International   **City Map** 3 A5
Lastarria 96
Tel *(02) 2664-5341*
If you can't visit Patagonia, you
can at least get a taste of it here,
with South American classics
such as lamb and game dishes,
plus venison, wild boar, and
guanaco on the menu.

West of Santiago Centro

Las Vacas Gordas $$
Grill   **City Map** 1 C2
Cienfuegos 280
Tel *(02) 2697-1066*
Combining quality and value
for money, Las Vacas Gordas
is arguably Santiago's best
parrilla. Don't miss their
version of the tomato-and-
onion Chilean salad. The
restaurant tends to fill up
quickly, so book ahead or
get there early.

DK Choice

Boulevard Lavaud $$$
International   **City Map** 1 B2
Compañía 2789
Tel *(02) 2682-5243*
This is one of Santiago's
most famous restaurants.
In the eclectically decorated
dining room, patrons can
enjoy crêpes, seafood, and
meat dishes, with plenty of
side options. The famous
affiliated barbershop
is still running.

La Diana $$$
International
/Seafood   **City Map** 1 C3
Arturo Prat 435
Tel *(02) 2632-8823*
Built within the walls of a
monastery, the beautiful
and trendy La Diana has its
own culture center. It offers
an array of seafood combi-
nations, a selection of pasta
and interesting desserts.

Price Guide
Prices are based on a three-course meal
per person, with a half-bottle of house
wine, including tax and service.

$	under $15
$$	$15 to $35
$$$	over $35

Ocean Pacific $$$
Seafood **City Map** 1 C3
Avenida Ricardo Cumming 221
Tel *(02) 2770-0300*
Decorated with maritime memorabilia, Ocean Pacific serves good seafood. It is popular with families and can get very busy.

Ostras Azócar $$$
Fish/Seafood **City Map** 1 C3
Bulnes 37
Tel *(02) 2681-6109*
Live oysters are brought into Ostras Azócar from Chiloé, and dinner begins with a sample of them with a glass of Chardonnay. The restaurant has been a presence in Santiago for some 80 years, and dining here is an unforgettable experience.

Zully $$$
International **City Map** 1 C3
Concha y Toro 34
Tel *(02) 2696-1378* **Closed** *Sun*
In a restored mansion with several architectural quirks, including intimate dining rooms and a sunken patio, Zully serves sophisticated international dishes made with Chilean ingredients.

Northeast of Santiago Centro

Kleine Kneipe $
German **City Map** 4 D3
Román Díaz 21
Tel *(02) 2235-1374*
This hole-in-the-wall spot has a menu of burgers and sandwiches and also serves a well-respected wheat beer. It has occasional live music, as well as a 7–10pm happy hour on weekdays.

Baco Vino y Bistro $$
International **City Map** 4 F2
Nueva de Lyon 116
Tel *(02) 2231-4444*
The French-inspired dishes at this popular wine bar, serving wines by the glass, include pepper steak and salmon tartare.

Café Melba $$
Café **City Map** 5 A4
Don Carlos 2898
Tel *(02) 2905-8480*
The Kiwi-run Melba serves breakfast, brunch, and lunch to office workers in and around the neighborhood. There is a diverse sandwich selection, too.

Le Flaubert $$
French **City Map** 4 E2
Orrego Luco 0125
Tel *(02) 2231-9424*
For those in search of French staples such as onion soup,

Vintage posters lining the walls at Bar Liguria

home-made pâté and *crème brûlée*, Le Flaubert, housed in an appropriately Francophile building, is the place to go. It's especially popular with local workers.

Galindo $$
Café **City Map** 3 B4
Dardignac 098
Tel *(02) 2777-0116*
In a neighborhood dominated by gourmet restaurants, Galindo serves Chilean staples such as *pastel de choclo*, *plateada*, and sandwiches – not to mention lots of beer and wine.

El Huerto $$
Vegetarian **City Map** 4 E2
Orrego Luco 54
Tel *(02) 2233-2690*
The delicious vegetarian cuisine served here is so flavorful that carnivores barely notice the absence of meat. International curries and Mexican spices distinguish El Huerto from more conventional vegetarian options.

The attractive facade of Confitería Torres *(see p290)*

Pantaleón II $$
Peruvian **City Map** 3 B3
Antonia López de Bello 98
Tel *(02) 2735-8785*
Try a *ceviche mixto* (mixed seafood) for your appetizer, and the shellfish-heavy *chupe de mariscos* (a traditional stew) as the main course. Don't miss the *pisco sour*. Everything is excellent value for money.

Tiramisú $$
Pizzeria **City Map** 5 B4
Isidora Goyenechea 3141-A
Tel *(02) 2519-4900*
Perhaps the city's most inventive pizzeria, Tiramisú offers a wide choice of creative toppings, plus a variety of beers and a lengthy wine list. Antipasti, *calzoni* and focaccia are also on the menu.

Astrid y Gastón $$$
Peruvian **City Map** 4 F2
Antonio Bellet 201
Tel *(02) 2650-9125* **Closed** *Sun*
Astrid y Gastón differs greatly from other Peruvian restaurants in its ambience, presentation, price, and portion size. Perfect for a romantic night out.

Barandiarán $$$
Peruvian **City Map** 3 B4
Constitución 074
Tel *(02) 2737-0725*
In the Patio Bellavista complex, Barandiarán serves delicious *ceviche*, *parihuela* (seafood soup), and *seco de cordero* (lamb stew). The food-court atmosphere makes for casual dining.

Bar Liguria $$$
Chilean **City Map** 4 D3
Avenida Providencia 1373
Tel *(02) 2235-7914* **Closed** *Sun*
The menu at this informal restaurant celebrates hearty country cooking with meats and stews, plus some seafood dishes. Vintage posters and photos line the walls.

For more information on types of restaurants *see pages 284–5*

DK Choice

Boragó $$$
International **City Map** 5 B2
Avenida Nueva Costanera 3467
Tel *(02) 2953-8893* **Closed** *Sun*
Chef Rodolfo Guzmán seeks out classic Chilean ingredients to create menus that change nightly, with two fixed-price options. Everybody at a given table must order the same menu. Paired wines or juices cost extra.

Divertimento $$$
International **City Map** 4 E1
Avenida El Cerro and Pedro de Valdivia
Tel *(02) 2975-4600*
Divertimento offers everything – from meat, to fish, to pasta dishes, as well as more traditional Chilean cuisine, such as *pastel de choclo* (summer only). It is popular with large groups and families.

Etniko $$$
Asian Fusion **City Map** 3 B3
Constitución 172
Tel *(02) 2732-0119* **Closed** *Sun*
Open until the early hours of the morning, Etniko is a hybrid of an Asian fusion restaurant and a dance club. The sushi is excellent.

Europeo $$$
International **City Map** 5 B2
Alonso de Córdova 2417
Tel *(02) 2208-3603* **Closed** *Sun*
This place serves a largely European menu, featuring dishes such as a venison ragout and a daily risotto. It also offers local fish and even a Nikkei-style *ceviche*.

La Mar $$$
Peruvian/Seafood **City Map** 5 B1
Avenida Nueva Costanera 4076
Tel *(02) 2206-7839*
La Mar specializes in *ceviche* but also Asian dishes, including elaborate seafood and sushi. The Peruvian-style *pisco sours* are spectacular.

OX $$$
Grill **City Map** 5 B1
Avenida Nueva Costanera 3960
Tel *(02) 2799-0260*
This glistening modern restaurant serves the best beef cuts at premium prices, plus a handful of seafood and pasta dishes.

Peumayén $$$
International **City Map** 3 B3
Constitución 136
Closed *Mon*
Priding itself on its "ancestral food," Peumayén has a house specialty of braised oxtail embellished with indigenous Andean ingredients, along with a colorful variety of potatoes.

The beautiful outdoor seating of Peumayén

Pinpilinpausha $$$
Basque **City Map** 5 A3
Isidoria Goyenechea 2900
Tel *(02) 2233-6507*
This place has served Basque-style food for about three-quarters of a century. Besides house specialties such as paella, it also offers risottos, beef and pasta dishes.

Puerto Fuy $$$
International **City Map** 5 B1
Avenida Nueva Costanera 3969
Tel *(02) 2208-8908* **Closed** *Sun*
Renowned for its molecular cooking, as introduced by chef Giancarlo Mazzarelli, Puerto Fuy uses local ingredients to create French-inspired dishes.

Sarita Colonia $$$
Peruvian-Fusion **City Map** 3 A3
Loreto 40
Tel *(02) 2881-3937*
Enjoy delicious fusion Asian-Latin cuisine at this trendy restaurant with kitsch decor. It has one of the best rooftops in town.

Tierra Noble $$$
Grill **City Map** 5 B4
Reyes Lavalle 3310
Tel *(02) 2232-4797*
Primarily a *parrilla* (grill restaurant), Tierra Noble has a wide range of appetizers and side dishes, such as fresh oysters and a traditional Chilean tomato and onion salad. Large wine list, too.

Central Valley

CASABLANCA: Tanino $$$
International **Road Map** B6
Viña Casas del Bosque, Hijuela 2, Ex-Fundo Santa Rosa
Tel *(02) 2377-9431* **Closed** *Mon (except in summer)*
This winery-restaurant pairs a limited seasonal menu with the

winery's own production. Those who prefer to sit outside should be prepared for late-afternoon breezes and fog.

CHILLÁN: Sureño $$
Seafood **Road Map** D1
Constitución 724
Tel *(042) 2210157* **Closed** *Sun*
Sureño is a seafood restaurant that occasionally veers into surf-and-turf territory. Ingredients are purchased from the local fresh produce market. The decor is bright and cheerful.

CHILLÁN: Fuego Divino $$$
Grill **Road Map** D1
Avenida Gamero 980
Tel *(042) 2430900* **Closed** *Sun & Mon*
Fuego Divino cooks its steaks over a central open grill, seasoning side dishes with the Mapuche spice *merkén*. There are some pasta dishes on the menu, and an impressive wine cellar.

CONCEPCIÓN: Las Américas $$
Peruvian **Road Map** D1
San Martín 514
Tel *(041) 2747231*
Offering specialties such as *ceviche*, as well as other dishes, like the seafood stew *parihuela*, this is a solid Peruvian restaurant.

CONCEPCIÓN: Centro Español $$
Spanish **Road Map** D1
Barros Arana 675
Tel *(041) 2224249* **Closed** *Sun*
The facade, interior decor, and menu here predictably evoke the old country. There is a separate bar offering tapas, and there is usually an inexpensive midday menu, too.

CUNACO: Rayuela Wine & Grill $$$
Grill **Road Map** B7
Carretera del Vino, Km 37
Tel *(02) 2379-0020*
Rayuela, as its full name suggests, is the grill restaurant of the Viu Manent winery, preparing beef and fish dishes to be paired with its own vintages. Several shellfish appetizers are available.

CURICÓ: Viña Torres $$$
International **Road Map** B7
Panamericana Sur, Km 195
Tel *(075) 2564100*
This vineyard restaurant makes a great option before or after touring the winery. It has an à la carte menu and a choice of Torres wines. The main dishes lean toward meats, but alternatives include a saffron seafood risotto.

The cheerful exterior of popular
Le Filou de Montpellier, Valparaíso

PAPUDO: Gran Azul $$
Seafood **Road Map** B6
Avenida Irrarázabal 86
Tel *(033) 2791584*
The idyllic coastal location and
fresh fish and seafood at Gran
Azul are what draw patrons here.
However, service can be slow.

PICHILEMU: Casa Roja $$
Italian **Road Map** B7
Avenida Ortúzar 215
Tel *(072) 2841555* **Closed** *Mon*
Thin-crust pizzas and pasta
dishes are on the menu here,
with more sophisticated
ingredients than used in most
comparable Chilean restaurants.

PICHILEMU: Puente Holandés $$
Seafood **Road Map** B7
Eugenio Díaz Lira 167
Tel *(09) 7492-6848*
Enjoy fresh seafood and salads
in designer-style surroundings.
Perfect location, overlooking
the beach.

RANCAGUA:
El Viejo Rancagua $
Local **Road Map** B7
Paseo del Estado 607
Tel *(072) 2222130*
El Viejo Rancagua is primarily
a live-music venue that also
offers fixed-price lunches and
basic Chilean cuisine at night.
It's more a cultural than a
gastronomic experience,
with vintage advertisements
lining the walls.

RANCAGUA: Sapore Italiano $$
Italian **Road Map** B7
Avenida Miguel Ramires 96
Tel *(072) 2768417* **Closed** *Mon*
Surrounded by contemporary
facilities, Sapore Italiano
produces thick-crusted,

cheese-heavy pizzas with a
variety of toppings, as well as
Italian-derived specialties such
as *calzoni* and pasta dishes.

SAN FERNANDO:
Restaurant Casa Silva $$$
International **Road Map** B7
Viña Casa Silva, Hijuela Norte
Tel *(09) 6847-5786* **Closed** *Sun & Mon*
Casa Silva offers meats, fish,
and Chilean country cooking,
but also pasta dishes, tapas,
and sandwiches, as well as a
children's menu.

SANTA CRUZ:
Club Social de Santa Cruz $$
Local **Road Map** B7
Plaza de Armas 178
Tel *(072) 2822529*
Club Social is a traditional, local
restaurant, drawing a Chilean
clientele with its hearty, country-
inspired cuisine. It is Colonial in
style, with a grape arbor covering the patio.

VALPARAÍSO:
Amor Porteño $
Local **Road Map** B6
*Almirante Montt 418, Cerro
Concepción*
Tel *(032) 2216253* **Closed** *Mon*
Come to this charming little
Argentine-style ice-cream
parlor and coffee shop for a
sundae, some churros, or a
mediuluna (a sweet, doughy
croissant). Wash it all down
with a *café con leche*.

VALPARAÍSO: Allegretto $$
Pizzeria **Road Map** B6
Pilcomayo 259, Cerro Concepción
Tel *(032) 2968839*
This casual pizzeria offers a range
of creative toppings, including
curry chicken. In addition to
pasta dishes and risottos, it also
provides a daily lunchtime
special and has an extensive
wine list.

VALPARAÍSO: Bar Cinzano $$
Local **Road Map** B6
Plaza Aníbal Pinto 1182
Tel *(032) 2213043* **Closed** *Sun*
Bar Cinzano's walls are festooned
with maritime memorabilia.
A local crowd comes here for
meats, sandwiches, and seafood
– not to mention the live tango
music featured on Friday
and Saturday nights.

VALPARAÍSO: Café Turri $$
Seafood **Road Map** B6
Templeman 147, Cerro Concepción
Tel *(032) 2252091* **Closed** *Mon*
The modern menu here includes
duck-breast salad, squid-ink
shrimp, and scallop lasagna, but
there are also many Chilean
classics. The terrace is one of
the city's best sites for outdoor
dining, with views of the harbor.

DK Choice

VALPARAÍSO:
Le Filou de Montpellier $$
French **Road Map** B6
Almirante Montt 382, Cerro Alegre
Tel *(032) 2224663* **Closed** *Mon*
Since opening in 1998, this
modest-looking restaurant
has become something of an
institution for excellent but
moderately priced lunches and
Friday and Saturday dinners.
Typical offerings include onion
soup, pâté, and fish or beef.

VALPARAÍSO: Ápice $$$
International **Road Map** B6
*Almirante Montt 462, Cerro
Concepción*
Tel *(032) 2089737* **Closed** *Tue & Wed*
This swish restaurant has
minimalist decor and a creative,
regularly changing menu. Dishes
include octopus with a chorizo
emulsion, oysters with goat's
cheese, and chocolate soufflé
with cinnamon ice cream.

Patrons converse at maritime-themed Bar Cinzano, Valparaíso

For more information on types of restaurants *see pages 284–5*

DK Choice

VALPARAÍSO:
Pasta e Vino $$$
Italian **Road Map** B6
Papudo 427, Cerro Concepción
Tel *(032) 2496187* **Closed** *Mon*
Set inside the Gran Hotel
Gervasoni, Pasta e Vino has
long been a local sensation.
Its main courses include eight
different varieties of gnocchi,
and there's also an imposing
wine list. It has extensive
seating, including outdoors,
but making a reservation is
still essential.

VIÑA DEL MAR: Entre Masas $
Bakery **Road Map** B6
6 Poniente 235
Tel *(032) 2979919*
This tiny bakery specializes in tasty
empanadas. Among its dozens of
varieties are chorizo and goat's
cheese, and spinach and ricotta.
You can eat in or take away.
There is another branch down
the coast in Reñaca.

VIÑA DEL MAR:
Hampton Deli $
Deli **Road Map** B6
Etchevers 174–176
Tel *(032) 2714910* **Closed** *Sun*
What Chileans call a *picada*, the
Hampton Deli is a family business
that produces national classics at
low prices. Patrons include
downtown office workers on
their lunch hours.

VIÑA DEL MAR:
Delicias del Mar $$
Seafood **Road Map** B6
Avenida San Martin 459
Tel *(032) 2901837*
Delicias is a Basque-style
seafood restaurant that is
inexplicably plastered with
countless photos of Marilyn
Monroe, and which has a
mounted trout on the wall that
sings "Take Me to the River"!
Paella is the house specialty,
but there are many other fine
dishes. The use of cell phones
is banned.

VIÑA DEL MAR: Fellini $$
Italian **Road Map** B6
*3 Norte con 6 Poniente, Frente al
Casino Municipal*
Tel *(032) 2975742*
Paying only a passing tribute
to the great film director
(it's more conventional than
surrealistic), the menu at Fellini
offers a diversity of pasta dishes
and other Italian mains, with a
focus on seafood. It is a family-
friendly restaurant, if a little dark.

Paella is a popular choice at Chile's many seafood restaurants

VIÑA DEL MAR:
Jaiba y Cordero $$
Seafood Fusion **Road Map** B6
Siete Norte 76
Tel *(09) 9811-2458*
Primarily a creative seafood
restaurant (though a succulent
Patagonian lamb also features
on the menu), Jaiba y Cordero
has a picturesque dining terrace
with views of the sea.

ZAPALLAR: El Chiringuito $$
Seafood **Road Map** B6
Avenida Zapallar 151
Tel *(033) 2741024*
With fishermen hauling skiffs
on shore within sight of the
restaurant, El Chiringuito
provides arguably the
freshest seafood in the whole
of Chile. There are great views
from the terrace, but take care
that the gulls and pelicans don't
steal your lunch!

Norte Grande and Norte Chico

ANTOFAGASTA:
El Horno de Barro $$
Local **Road Map** B3
Washington 2356
Tel *(055) 2955608* **Closed** *Tue*
The family-run El Horno de
Barro (literally, "the clay oven")
is a *picada* dispensing Chilean
standards such as beef and
pastel de choclo (a dish roughly
equivalent to shepherd's pie).
It hosts folkloric musicians
at dinnertime on Fridays
and Saturdays.

ARICA: Maracuyá $$$
International **Road Map** B1
*Avenida Comandante San Martín
0321*
Tel *(058) 2227600*
Maracuyá's enviable location,
above Playa El Laucho and
beneath the historic Morro,

makes it the best restaurant
in Arica for views. The extensive
seafood menu includes a handful
of Peruvian specialties, and there
is also a selection of pasta dishes
and desserts.

DK Choice

ARICA: Rayú $$$
Peruvian **Road Map** B1
Ingeniero Raúl Pey 2590
Tel *(058) 2216446*
By most accounts, Playa
Chinchorro's Rayú is now
the top dining spot in Arica,
with an elaborate Peruvian
menu and exquisite presentation. *Ceviche* and fish dishes
are the stars, but there are
also Andean dishes such as
seco de cordero (lamb stew
with cilantro).

CALDERA: Nuevo Miramar $$
Seafood **Road Map** B4
Gana 090
Tel *(052) 2515381*
Located right on the water,
Nuevo Miramar serves Chilean
seafood of good to above-
average quality, especially the
shellfish. The decor is kitschy,
but the room is comfortable
and reasonably spacious, with
decent service.

COPIAPÓ: Legado $$
International **Road Map** B4
O'Higgins 12 **Closed** *Sun*
Legado drew international
attention during the famous
rescue of the miners in 2010,
when journalists flocked to the
area. The ambience is subdued,
and the food sophisticated –
much of it being imported game
from elsewhere in the country.

The spectacular Moorish interio of Casino Espanol, Iquique (see p295)

IQUIQUE: Casino Español $$
Spanish   Road Map B2
Plaza Prat 584
Tel *(057) 2760630*
The perfectly decent Spanish food here plays second fiddle to the sumptuous dining room, which is decorated to look like a Moorish palace, with beautiful tiles and hefty suits of armor.

IQUIQUE: El Tercer Ojito $$
Asian Fusion   Road Map B2
Patricio Lynch 1420-A
Tel *(057) 2413847*
In its garden setting, El Tercer Ojito aims to meld Asian dishes with Latin American traditions. In addition to items like Thai rolls, there's sushi, plus Peruvian and even some Italian options. Very low-key ambience.

IQUIQUE: El Viejo Wagón $$
Seafood   Road Map B2
Thompson 85
Tel *(057) 2341428*
With all the artifacts on the walls and the floors, having a meal here is a bit like dining within a regional museum. Fish and seafood are the main focus, but meats also appear on the menu. Unusually for Chile, it's possible to get spicy dishes, thanks to the lingering Peruvian influence.

LA SERENA: Casona del 900 $$
Grill   Road Map B5
Francisco de Aguirre 443
Tel *(051) 2520767*   **Closed** *Sun*
The menu at the cavernous, traditionally decorated Casona del 900 is extensive. Many people share the oversized *parrillada* (mixed grill), but there's also a selection of à la carte cuts and seafood. The wine list is fairly small and conventional.

LA SERENA: La Casona del Guatón $$
Grill   Road Map B5
Brasil 750
Tel *(051) 2211519*
Translating as "The Fat Guy's House," La Casona del Guatón is the locale to feast on meat and potatoes, with a handful of pasta and seafood options, in traditional surroundings. You might even be serenaded by Mexican *charros*.

LA SERENA: Porota's $$
International   Road Map B5
Avenida del Mar 900-B
Tel *(051) 2210937*   **Closed** *Mon*
This incongruous gabled chalet is handsomely furnished, making it a beautiful setting for finely presented dishes such as ravioli, risotto, and Thai chicken. The menu changes seasonally.

OVALLE: Los Braseros $$
Grill   Road Map B5
Vicuña Mackenna 595
Tel *(053) 2624917*
In a handsomely decorated adobe, Los Braseros is a reliable and intimate little *parrilla* where the specialty is beef – and more beef. It also has an impressive wine list.

SAN PEDRO DE ATACAMA: Baltinache $$
Local   Road Map C3
Domingo Atienza, Sitio 2
Tel *(09) 9871-0103*   **Closed** *Wed*
Regional and Andean fusion food is the specialty of this intimate indigenous kitchen, which uses little-known ingredients collected from the surrounding desert, and whose menu changes at every meal. Because the dining room is so small and remarkable, reservations are essential.

SAN PEDRO DE ATACAMA: Café Adobe $$
International   Road Map C3
Caracoles 211
Tel *(055) 2851132*
One of San Pedro's most popular nightspots, Café Adobe serves skillfully presented versions of Chilean specialties. The space itself is an attraction, warmed by an open fire after dark, and there is live Andean music. The decor takes its cues from San Pedro's archaeological museum.

SAN PEDRO DE ATACAMA: Tierra Todo Natural $$
International   Road Map C3
Caracoles 271
Tel *(055) 2851585*
Housed in a space that resembles a thatched Nissen hut, Tierra Todo Natural is a great breakfast spot. It is renowned for its extensive menu of vegetarian specialties, but there is also plenty to satisfy carnivores. An earth oven warms the space at night.

Lake District and Chiloé

CASTRO: La Brüjula del Cuerpo $
Café   Road Map D3
O'Higgins 308
Tel *(065) 2633229*
Situated on the Plaza de Armas, this is a lively café that serves a simple but delicious pub-grub menu of sandwiches, beef, and chicken, as well as a credible selection of ice creams and craft beers. La Brüjula offers arguably the best price-to-quality ratio in town.

CASTRO: Nueva Galicia $$
Seafood   Road Map D3
Pedro Montt 38
Tel *(065) 2532828*
The only shortcoming of this fine restaurant is that it's located on the wrong side of the street for an ocean view. The menu is fairly conventional, but the food itself is excellent. The decor features colorful local weavings.

CASTRO: Octavio $$
Seafood   Road Map D3
Avenida Pedro Montt 261
Tel *(065) 2632855*
Fishing boats are tied up along the bayside windows at stilted Octavio. Seafood is the focus, but there are also meat dishes. The interior is spacious, and there is outdoor seating in fine weather.

CURACAUTÍN: Hotel Andenrose $$
International   Road Map E1
Ruta 181, Km 68.5 + AY19
Tel *(09) 9869-1700*
During high season, this hotel provides exceptional German and Italian meals at moderate prices. Non-guests should phone ahead, but it is worth taking a detour off the highway to see if there is a free table.

Seating at La Casona del Guatón or, "The Fat Guy's House", La Serena

For more information on types of restaurants *see pages 284–5*

DK Choice

OSORNO: Mumbai-Lima $$
International   **Road Map** D2
Manuel Rodríguez 1701
Tel *(064) 2421337*   **Closed** *Sun*
At Mumbai-Lima, South Asian and Peruvian dishes have taken over from the *Bratwurst* and *Leverwurst* staples that are Osorno's historical legacy. Though the exterior suggests a traditional Germanic home, the vast interior – including a handsome mezzanine – and decor are cutting-edge. The kitchen closes an hour before the bar.

OSORNO: La Parrilla de Pepe $$
Grill   **Road Map** D2
Mackenna 1095
Tel *(064) 2249653*
At the end of a row of historic houses built by German pioneers, La Parrilla de Pepe is an architectural landmark and a solid grill restaurant. The interior is more plain and less distinguished, though the paneled walls are attractive, but it has earned – and kept – its place on the local food scene.

PANGUIPULLI:
Gardylafquen $$
Café   **Road Map** E2
Martínez de Rosas 722
Tel *(063) 2310921*
In contemporary surroundings, with a high-beamed ceiling of natural wood, Gardylafquen does a conventional Chilean menu very well, alongside offering assiduous service. At lunchtime, consider sharing one of the pizza-sized stuffed sandwiches.

PUCÓN: ¡École! $$
Vegetarian   **Road Map** E2
General Urrutia 592
Tel *(045) 2441675*
¡École! is a restaurant that draws a mostly tourist and expat clientele seeking out vegetarian specialties in informal surroundings. If you're having breakfast, consider sharing – the portions are large.

PUCÓN: Latitud 39 $$
International   **Road Map** E2
Gerónimo de Alderete 324
Tel *(09) 7430-0016*   **Closed** *Sun*
Run by expat Californians, Latitud 39 is a casual café with a diverse menu that includes hamburgers, sandwiches, burritos, and tacos. There's also a selection of craft beers. Wheelchair patrons may have to settle for sidewalk seating.

Key to Price Guide *see page 290*

PUCÓN: La Maga $$
Grill   **Road Map** E2
Gerónimo de Alderete 276
Tel *(045) 2444277*   **Closed** *Mon; Mar–Dec*
A Uruguayan place, La Maga takes its decor cues from gaucho traditions, though on the menu, they make small concessions to Chilean tastes, too, with such items as the Chilean salad of tomato and onion, and the indigenous *merkén* spice.

PUCÓN: Naukana $$
Asian Fusion   **Road Map** E2
Fresia 236
Tel *(045) 2444677* **Closed** *May & Jun*
Even in non-conformist Pucón, Naukana stands out for its pan-Asian dishes and eclectic South Asian decor. The menu is wide-ranging, with some very spicy options that are unusual in Chile.

PUERTO MONTT:
Club de Yates $$$
Local   **Road Map** D2
Avenida Juan Soler Manfredini 200
Tel *(065) 2282810*
Jutting into the Reloncaví Sound, the modernized yacht club offers a diverse menu that focuses on fish and seafood, plus Chilean countryside specialties and a selection of meat dishes. Understated maritime decor.

PUERTO OCTAY:
El Fogón de Anita $$
Grill   **Road Map** D2
Ruta U-55, Km 49
Tel *(064) 2391240*
A roofed *quincho* restaurant whose name ("The Firepit") stresses its focus on meat (mainly beef, but also game), the friendly and family-run El Fogón also serves afternoon tea and a Sunday lamb barbecue.

Contemporary surroundings at Mumbai-Lima

PUERTO VARAS: Mawen $
Café   **Road Map** D2
Santa Rosa 218-B
Tel *(065) 2236971*
This colorfully decorated coffee shop brews excellent, genuine espresso and serves a menu of sandwiches, salads, and desserts. It also stocks a large selection of teas, both black and herbal.

PUERTO VARAS:
Las Buenas Brasas $$
Grill   **Road Map** D2
San Pedro 543
Tel *(065) 2232154*
"The Good Coals" is a garden restaurant that has meat on the menu plus a rather more elaborate fish and seafood selection. It can get crowded, but the food is well worth a visit.

PUERTO VARAS:
El Cucharón Alemán $$
German   **Road Map** D2
Los Colonos 1175
Tel *(065) 2235309*
"The German Spoon" serves large plates of hearty European food, with a wide selection of beer and wine. It even offers a Chilean version of Klosterbitter liqueur and has occasional live music.

PUERTO VARAS:
Mediterráneo $$
Mediterranean   **Road Map** D2
Santa Rosa 068
Tel *(065) 2237268*   **Closed** *Sun*
In a stylishly renovated lakefront house, Mediterráneo uses local ingredients to create southern European favorites, including pasta dishes, risottos, and tempting desserts. There are spectacular views of the lake and the volcano.

PUERTO VARAS: La Olla $$
Seafood   **Road Map** D2
Ruta 225, Km 0.9
Tel *(065) 2234605*
This is an immensely popular fish and seafood restaurant whose offerings are well above average, though the enormous dining room is a spartan, no-frills affair. Note that parking can be very difficult.

PUERTO VARAS: Ibis $$$
International   **Road Map** D2
Vicente Pérez Rosales 1117
Tel *(065) 2235533*
Ibis has earned a reputation throughout Chile for its gourmet seafood, which is served with a range of sauces, and its small selection of pasta dishes and meats. It occupies an attractive contemporary space with high wooden ceilings.

TEMUCO: El Corralero $$
Grill **Road Map** D2
Vicuña Mackenna 811
Tel *(045) 2401355*
Arguably downtown Temuco's
most notable restaurant, this
is a fine grill, with a handful of
fish dishes to complement the
meats. The decor is exuberant,
and the service excellent.

TEMUCO: El Criollito $$
Local **Road Map** D2
San Martin 250
Tel *(045) 2911370*
One of numerous *puestos*
in the Mercado Municipal, El
Criollito is popular with Chilean
families in search of cheap but
wholesome, filling meals. Lots
of good seafood is offered, but
there are also huge sandwiches
and slabs of meat.

TEMUCO:
Madonna Pizza & Pasta $$
Pizzeria **Road Map** D2
Avenida Alemania 0660
Tel *(045) 2329393*
Thick-crust and cheese-heavy
pizza is the rule here. The pastas,
with seafood sauces, are also
appealing. Seafood appetizers
and some meat dishes are
available, too. The wine list is
more impressive than the food.

VALDIVIA: La Calesa $$
Peruvian **Road Map** D2
O'Higgins 160
Tel *(063) 2225467* **Closed** *Mon*
La Calesa's Peruvian kitchen
serves spicier dishes than most
Chileans prefer. The building's
exterior is unremarkable but
cheerfully decorated. Dishes
such as *lomo saltado* (stir-fry
beef) are comparably colorful.

VILLARRICA: The Travellers $
International **Road Map** E2
Valentín Letelier 753
Tel *(045) 2413617*
It started as a hangout for tourists
and expats, but over the years
The Travellers has become more
of a Chilean party scene, with a
pub-grub menu featuring diverse
snack plates and curries. Closing
time is 4am.

VILLARRICA: Fuego Patagón $$
Grill **Road Map** E2
Pedro Montt 40
Tel *(045) 2412207*
Despite its rustic affectations,
this urbane lakeside restaurant
is an unmissable choice for grilled
meats – including roast goat
and even game dishes such as
wild boar. The presentation is
good, and there is a reliable
wine list.

The modernized yacht club, Club de Yates *(see p296)*

VILLARRICA:
El Rey del Marisco $$
Seafood **Road Map** E2
Valentín Letelier 1030
Tel *(045) 2412093*
A longtime favorite in town,
"The King of Seafood" may be
a destination restaurant for
Chilean celebrities, but it's also
family-oriented. In a lakeshore
location, it is a reliable choice
for shellfish dishes in particular.

Northern Patagonia

COYHAIQUE:
Café de Mayo $
Café **Road Map** E4
21 de Mayo 543
Tel *(067) 2210720* **Closed** *Sun*
A welcome newcomer on
Coyhaique's food scene, this
casual café prepares espresso,
quiches, sandwiches, and *kuchen*
in a rustically stylish interior. It
also has excellent garden seating
for fine weather.

COYHAIQUE: La Casona $$
Local **Road Map** E4
Obispo Vielmo 77
Tel *(067) 2238894*
In a spacious converted residence
with high ceilings, this is a
conventional but very reliable
seafood restaurant that also has
a dedicated grill for meats. It
has no accessibility ramp, but
staff will gladly help wheelchair
users in and out.

COYHAIQUE: Lito's $$
Local **Road Map** E4
Lautaro 147
Tel *(067) 2254528* **Closed** *Sun*
From the outside, Lito's looks
like a dive bar, but the beef,
fish, and seafood menu is a near-
revelation. This is about as good
as local food gets. In addition,
the restaurant offers arguably

the best value for money in
Coyhaique, and there is a
congenial atmosphere, too.

DK Choice

COYHAIQUE:
Mamma Gaucha $$
Pizzeria **Road Map** E4
Paseo Horn 47
Tel *(067) 2210721*
This engaging establishment
operates mostly as a pizzeria:
their thin-crust offerings, with
minimal cheese and a variety of
creative toppings, are baked in
a clay oven. It also has a good
selection of craft beers, while
the photographs and artwork
displayed pay tribute to the
region's gaucho heritage.

COYHAIQUE: Tamango $$
Peruvian **Road Map** E4
Arturo Prat 176
Tel *(067) 2242588* **Closed** *Sun*
Coyhaique's first Peruvian
restaurant, Tamango has been
spicing up the local food scene
ever since it opened. The usual
favorites *ají de gallina* (chicken in
a cream sauce) and *lomo saltado*
(stir-fry beef) are good, but also
worth trying is the *parihuela*
(seafood stew)

Pebre, a traditional Chilean salsa made with
coriander, onion, garlic and aji peppers

For more information on types of restaurants *see pages 284–5*

COYHAIQUE: El Ovejero $$$
Local   Road Map E4
Baquedano 828
Tel *(067) 2231108*   **Closed** *Sun*
Boasting what may be
Coyhaique's best views, the
restaurant of the Hotel El Reloj
focuses on Patagonian lamb. Wild
hare and salmon are also on the
menu. Reservations are advisable,
especially for non-hotel guests.

FUTALEUFÚ:
Martín Pescador $$
International   Road Map E3
Balmaceda 603
Tel *(065) 2721279*
In a rustic, sophisticated building
that even has its own private
library, Martín Pescador serves
mainly salmon but occasionally
also dishes such as king crab
quiche, gnocchi with almond
pesto, and beef or vegetable
stir-fries. The afternoon hours
are unpredictable.

Southern Patagonia and Tierra del Fuego

Monumento Natural
CUEVA DEL MILODÓN:
Caverna del Milodón $$
Grill   Road Map E6
Ruta Y-290, Km 8
Tel *(09) 9940-8276*
Located across the highway from
the Cueva del Milodón, this
modern restaurant specializes in
mixed *parrillada*, but it also serves
sandwiches and seafood. It is a
convenient lunch stop for visitors
heading to the park.

PARQUE NACIONAL TORRES
DEL PAINE:
Coirón $$$
International   Road Map E6
Sector Las Torres
Tel *(061) 2617450*
Despite its proximity to the
famous granite needles, Coirón,
in the Hotel Las Torres, can't offer
the same views as Hotel Lago
Grey or Hostería Pehoé. The same
can be said for the quality of the
food on offer.

PARQUE NACIONAL TORRES
DEL PAINE:
Hostería Pehoé $$$
International   Road Map E6
Sector Lago Pehoé
Tel *(061) 2617727*
Like Hotel Lago Grey, Hostería
Pehoé has a restaurant with
views over the Paine range, but
its picture windows are smaller.
It offers fixed-price buffets for
guests and non-guests.

The charming, rural setting of Martin Pescador, Futaleufú

PARQUE NACIONAL TORRES
DEL PAINE:
Hotel Lago Grey $$$
International   Road Map E6
Sector Lago Grey
Tel *(061) 2712100*
At Hotel Lago Grey, where diners
can view floating icebergs from the
eponymous glacier, there are fixed-
price buffet lunches and dinners
for guests and non-guests. The food
may not be as great as the views.

PORVENIR:
Club Social Croata $$
Seafood   Road Map E6
Señoret 542
Tel *(061) 2580053*   **Closed** *Sun*
Croatians played a major role in
settling Tierra del Fuego, and
while the food here is strictly
Chilean, the venue provides a
glimpse into that past. Formal
dining room, with sea views.

PUERTO NATALES: El Living $
Café   Road Map E6
Arturo Prat 156
Tel *(061) 2411140*
Cozy, with sofas and easy chairs,
El Living is a vegetarian venue.
The menu stresses sandwiches,
soups, snacks, and sweets, all
washed down with coffee, tea,
and juices. The owners also
operate a book exchange.

PUERTO NATALES: Angélica's $$
Seafood   Road Map E6
Manuel Bulnes 501
Tel *(061) 2410007*
One of the region's best fish and
seafood restaurants, Angélica's
also serves meat and pasta.
Try the king crab cannelloni,
grilled hake, or roast lamb.
An adjacent deli sells coffee,
sandwiches, pizza, and *kuchen*.

PUERTO NATALES:
El Asador Patagónico $$
Grill   Road Map E6
Arturo Prat 158
Tel *(061) 2413553*
This is a fairly conventional grill
restaurant, but it has largely

preserved the decor of the
classic apothecary it once was.
Good for regaining energy
after a hard week's hike in
Torres del Paine.

PUERTO NATALES:
Cormorán de las Rocas $$
Local   Road Map E6
Sánchez 72
Tel *(061) 2413723*
The menu here is diverse,
and portions of dishes like
entraña (skirt steak) can easily
feed two hungry diners. There's
an adjacent bar with pub grub
like shrimp empanadas, as well
as a wine shop and specialty
chocolates on the ground floor.
The restaurant offers panoramas
of Last Hope Sound and the
distant Paine.

PUERTO NATALES:
Mesita Grande $$
Pizzeria   Road Map E6
Arturo Prat 196
Tel *(061) 2411571*
A Natales institution, the "Little
Big Table" is both a culinary
and a social experience – diners
sit on either side of two long
wooden tables to order any of
25 thin-crust pizzas and chat to
neighbors. Salads, pasta, and
ice cream are also available.

DK Choice

PUERTO NATALES:
Afrigonia $$$
African Fusion   Road Map E6
Eberhard 343
Tel *(061) 2412877*
The menu at Afrigonia
offers a unique combination
of Zambian and Chilean
flavors, with decor to match.
The chef adds spice to
Patagonian ingredients
such as shrimp and scallops
to produce a curried seafood
masala. Try the *cordero
MacLean à la menta* (roast
lamb chops with mint).

PUNTA ARENAS: Lomit's $

Café   **Road Map** E6

José Menéndez 722

Tel *(061) 2243399*

Usually packed, Lomit's has diner decor and is a local landmark for sandwiches and beer. It offers excellent quality, especially by fast-food standards.

DK Choice

PUNTA ARENAS: Damiana Elena $$

International   **Road Map** E6

Magallanes 341

Tel *(061) 2222818*   **Closed** *Sun*

In a magnificent Magellanic house with small and intimate dining rooms, this is almost consensually considered the city's best restaurant. The menu changes nightly, but the wine list is quite conventional. Reservations are usually essential, and Spanish is useful. (Waiters explain the menu, but not all of them speak English.)

PUNTA ARENAS: Los Ganaderos $$

Grill   **Road Map** F6

O'Higgins 1166

Tel *(061) 2225103*

Los Ganaderos merged with the same owners' Puerto Viejo seafood restaurant, and those maritime dishes are still on the menu here. Both meat and seafood are well above average.

PUNTA ARENAS: La Leyenda del Remezón $$

Local   **Road Map** E6

21 de Mayo 1469

Tel *(061) 2241029*   **Closed** *Sun*

A low-key but quality Patagonian restaurant, La Leyenda has a full menu of lamb, king crab, and game dishes, including guanaco and rhea. The interior decor reflects Patagonia's golden period in the wool industry.

DK Choice

PUNTA ARENAS: La Luna $$

Seafood   **Road Map** E6

O'Higgins 1017

Tel *(061) 2228555*

With its eccentric decor, La Luna is a visual delight for locals and tourists alike, even before they sip a *pisco sour* or sink their teeth into a king crab casserole. This is an obligatory stop for foreign visitors, who pin their home towns onto various maps.

Walls decorated by patrons at La Luna, Punta Arenas

PUNTA ARENAS: El Mercado $$

Seafood   **Road Map** E6

Mejicana 617

Tel *(061) 2242746*

Once an unmissable bargain, El Mercado has since lost ground in the increasingly sophisticated local food scene. Most popular with locals, it still offers good-value dishes, such as king crab, in utilitarian surroundings.

PUNTA ARENAS: Santino Bar e Cucina $$

Italian   **Road Map** E6

Avenida Colón 657

Tel *(061) 2710882*

The bar here is prioritized over the kitchen, and it doesn't close until the early hours of the morning. Pizzas, pastas, and Chilean dishes, including seafood, will satisfy your hunger, but they are an afterthought.

PUNTA ARENAS: Sotito's Bar $$

Seafood   **Road Map** E6

O'Higgins 1138

Tel *(061) 2243565*

Despite the name, this is a restaurant first and a bar second. Do not miss the king crab cannelloni or, in season, the calafate mousse. Well established and professional, Sotito's has gleaming but minimal decoration.

Easter Island and Robinson Crusoe Island

HANGA ROA: Au Bout du Monde $$

Seafood

Policarpo Toro s/n

Tel *(032) 2552060*   **Closed** *Tue*

This Franco-Belgian-Polynesian place serves flavorful fish dishes, Polynesian curries, and some vegetarian choices, plus excellent desserts. On some nights, it has live local music and folkloric dance shows.

HANGA ROA: Tataku Vave $$

Seafood

Caleta Hanga Piko s/n

Tel *(032) 2551544*   **Closed** *Sun*

A little off the tourist track (though they will pick you up if necessary), Tataku Vave draws a crowd for its fish and seafood dishes served with subtropical sauces. The daily lunch special is a bargain, but the cost of the à la carte menu can add up.

HANGA ROA: Te Moana $$

International

Av Policarpo Toro s/n

Tel *(032) 2551578*   **Closed** *Sun*

A great spot for a sunset cocktail or beer (try the Tahitian lager, Hinano), this classy restaurant/bar is in a prime spot directly overlooking the sea. The fish and seafood dishes are also well worth a try.

HANGA ROA: La Taverne du Pecheur $$$

International

Caleta Hanga Roa s/n

Tel *(032) 2100619*   **Closed** *Sun*

A meal at La Taverne du Pecheur could be your best meal on Easter Island. The French owner chef cooks brilliantly, and the coveside location is a destination not to be missed.

The humble exterior of La Taverne du Pecheur, Hanga Roa

For more information on types of restaurants *see pages 284–5*

SHOPPING IN CHILE AND EASTER ISLAND

Chile is not among the world's shopping meccas, but there are several items that are worth taking home. The open economy has meant a massive influx of foreign goods, but typical Chilean products remain popular with shoppers. Visitors will find alpaca and sheep woolens from the Andean north and Patagonia, *huaso* riding gear from the Central Valley, and Mapuche basketry, silver jewelry, and weavings from the Lake District.

The country's lapiz lazuli jewelry is greatly prized by experienced buyers. Wine is a favorite purchase, as is the noteworthy drink, *pisco*. Among the most eye-catching artifacts in Chile are the wooden or stone replicas of the massive *moai* statues of Easter Island. Handcrafted by skilled Rapa Nui artisans, these can be found across the country.

A row of souvenir shops reached by the Ascensor Artillería, Valparaíso

Opening Hours

Shops and shopping malls usually open after 10am and stay open until 9 or 10pm. Many stores are open on Saturday mornings but close around 1pm, except in tourist destinations, such as Santiago's Barrio Bellavista, where shops and malls, particularly those in Patio Bellavista *(see p92)*, also open on the weekend. In smaller cities and towns, shops tend to close for lunch and a siesta that lasts from around 1 to 5pm.

Payment, Taxes, and Bargaining

Payment in cash, preferably Chilean pesos, is the default option, especially in rural areas, street stalls, and artisans' markets. However, most large shops in major cities accept credit cards. Visa and MasterCard are most widely accepted, although American Express is not uncommon. No surcharge is added to credit card purchases, but credit card agencies at home may deduct an amount on overseas purchases *(see p320)*. Most tourism-oriented businesses, with the exception of hotels, don't accept US dollars, and euros are a relative novelty in Chile. A Value Added Tax (VAT or IVA) of 19 percent is customarily included in the price of most goods and services.

In Chile, bargaining is not the usual custom as in other South American countries. Haggling may be expected in crafts markets, but is considered inappropriate if the vendor has a fixed address.

Crafts and Souvenirs

Popular handicrafts such as ceramics, ornaments, basketry, woodcarvings, and alpaca woolens are available in crafts markets and stalls across Chile. Los Andes in Central Valley is known for its decorative ceramics. **Cerámica Cala**, one of the many ceramic workshops here, is open for tours and offers a range of handcrafted pottery items.

Museum Shops

A couple of Chile's museums have shops that are worth visiting. Santiago's Museo Chileno de Arte Precolombino *(see pp64–5)* sells books, videos, and replicas of its own pieces, particularly of Andean pottery and textiles.

Operated by the **Fundación Neruda**, Pablo Neruda's three houses, located in Santiago, Valparaíso, and Isla Negra, have

Browsing through craft stalls along a cobbled street in Pucón

ceramics, crafts, and books by and about the poet.

Almacruz in Santa Cruz's Museo de Colchagua (see p150) has an abundant selection of regional souvenirs and wines from the area.

Located on the outskirts of the northern city of Arica, the Museo Arqueológico San Miguel de Azapa (see p165) – home to the world-famous Chinchorro mummies – offers alpaca woolens and bags produced in the region, as well as reproductions of historic ceramics.

Artisans' Markets

The quality of Chile's local arts and crafts has greatly improved since the end of the 20th century, partly due to the development of non-profit associations such as the Artesanías de Chile (see p101), who work with artisans to manufacture fine products and provide a network for the sale of wares.

The Centro de Exposición de Arte Indígena (see p101) is Santiago's most accessible crafts market, while Pueblo Los Dominicos (see p95) is the capital's biggest artisans' market. It is open daily and gets especially lively on Sundays. Located in the heart of Mapuche territory, Temuco's Mercado Municipal (see p194) offers finely crafted ornaments, basketry, and woodcarvings made by ethnic groups across Chile, as well as by indigenous peoples from the Andean countries of Peru and Ecuador.

Held in Puerto Montt, in the Lake District, the **Feria Artesanal de Angelmó** is one of the country's largest crafts fairs, featuring rows of well-stocked stalls displaying locally made textiles, pottery, woolens, and jewelry.

On the Chiloé archipelago (see pp218–25), artisans' markets in Ancud and Castro, as well as in the smaller settlements of Dalcahue, Achao, and Chonchi, are well worth a visit. On Easter Island, Hanga Roa's Mercado Artesanal (see p262) offers custom-made *moai* and *rongorongo* tablets.

Cabernet sauvignon and carménère wines from the Colchagua Valley

Food and Wine

During the summer months, visitors to Chile will find highly prized temperate fruits such as blueberries, raspberries, cherries, grapes, and olives.

Puerto Varas, in southern Chile, is the place to buy chocolates. Based in town, **Vicki Johnson** creates a range of delicious homemade chocolates and other mouth-watering treats such as smoked salmon, flavored sugar and honey, liqueurs, jams, and marmalades. Organic honey and fruit preserves can be purchased from the Parque Pumalín (see p230) project's retail outlet Puma Verde, which also sells books and local crafts.

Chile produces prodigious amounts of wine, and though the 2010 earthquake destroyed part of what was in storage, the industry has recovered quickly. The best wine can be found at specialist wine shops or at the wineries themselves. Two of the best specialty shops in Santiago are La Vinoteca and El Mundo del Vino (see p101), both located in Las Condes.

The majority of Chile's best vineyards are found in the fertile Central Valley. These include the excellent Viña Cousiño-Macul and Viña Concha y Toro (see p144), both open for tours and tastings. In the Casablanca Valley (see pp142–3), located northwest of the capital, the best choice is Viña Veramonte.

Many Colchagua Valley wineries (see pp152–3), such as Viña Montes and Viña Casa Silva, sell their premium vintages. The information center of Colchagua's Ruta del Vino, in Santa Cruz, also provides a wide selection of wines from the region's various vineyards.

A popular beverage across South America, *pisco* is one of Chile's favorite drinks. Good *pisco* is readily available throughout the country, and it is advisable to buy at least the 40° (80 proof) *reservado* (with 40 percent alcohol) in order to make the well-known cocktail, *pisco sour*. Major brands such as Planta Capel (see p186) and **Centro Turistico Capel** are sold almost everywhere, but small producers such as **Fundo Los Nichos** are also worth seeking out, though this may require a visit to remote distilleries, in this case, to the Valle del Elqui (see pp186–7).

The exterior of Temuco's Mercado Municipal

Books and Music

Most large bookstores in urban centers stock titles in Spanish and English. The popular Feria Chilena del Libro (see p101) and Librería Antartica have branches across the capital. For second-hand books, there is a cluster of shops along Calle San Diego, just south of the Universidad de Chile Metro station.

In Santiago Centro, **La Tienda Nacional** is known for its collection of Chilean music, books, and cinema. It also offers a range of vintage toys and souvenirs that present Chilean culture in a stylish way.

Music stores across Chile offer popular international music, Chilean classical recordings, and folkloric rhythms. Providencia's **Billboard** carries a wide selection of CDs. Hotel Santa Cruz Plaza (see p278) in the Colchagua Valley has a small store that specializes in books and music on Chilean themes.

Antiques

In the 19th century, Chile's elite and middle class could afford furniture and other items imported from Europe. Many of these, along with a range of local pre-Hispanic artifacts, have made their way to antique shops in Santiago and Valparaíso. In Santiago, Antiguedades Bucarest and Antiguedades Balmaceda (see p101) are warehouses

where several vendors display their goods. The capital also has a fine Sunday antique market on Plaza Perú, in Las Condes. Valparaíso's Plaza O'Higgins market is open on weekends and holidays. Other than archaeological items, visitors are allowed to carry most antiques out of the country.

Department Stores

Chain department stores across Chile sell everything from clothing to electronics and furniture. The biggest name is **Falabella**, but **Almacenes París** and **Ripley** stores can also be found in most major cities.

Shopping Malls

Most malls and shopping centers are massive constructions in suburban Santiago. Mall Costanera Centre and Alto Las Condes (see p101) are among the largest malls in the capital.

Cities such as Antofagasta, Iquique, Puerto Montt, and Temuco also have modern shopping malls. A large variety of products are available at the duty-free Zona Franca de Iquique and at Punta Arenas' **ZonAustral**. Most malls include a food court, multiplex cinemas, and play areas for children. Temuco's mall on Avenida Alemania also has a casino.

Exterior of Falabella, one of the most popular department store

Lapis Lazuli

A semiprecious gemstone, the intensely blue lapis lazuli has been valued since ancient times. The early Egyptians utilized it in decorative art and as a cosmetic – Cleopatra is said to have used powdered lapis as eyeshadow. The Romans considered it an aphrodisiac, and in pre-Columbian Chile, the stone formed part of ornaments and objects of functional and ritualistic use. Today, the only sizable deposits of lapis are found in Afghanistan and in the high Andes of Chile's Norte Grande and Norte Chico. Specialty stores, mostly in Santiago, offer intricate lapis lazuli jewelry, figurines, and decorative boxes.

From Workshop to Shop

Once lapis lazuli is mined and brought to workshops, it is cut with a diamond disk and carved with abrasive emery for shape. Subsequently, sandpaper is used to remove any roughness and the gem is polished for shine. The stone is then combined with precious metals, especially gold and silver, to create prized ornaments and artifacts. These are sold at specialty stores such as the Lapis Lazuli House (see p101).

An uncut, unpolished block of lapis lazuli

Polished gems of varying sizes

Heavy necklaces, earrings, and bracelet

Sterling silver brooches fashioned to resemble an elephant and a woman

Dangle designs in lapis lazuli

Flower pendant

Earrings in shades of blue

Gold and silver is inlaid with lapis lazuli to make valuable and attractive accessories. The price of each piece depends on the amount of the metal used, the uniqueness of the design, and the size and number of gems inlaid. Popular items include necklaces, bracelets, earrings, cuff links, and brooches.

Ornamental and utilitarian articles made of lapis lazuli include finely handcrafted vases, small figurines, paper weights, ashtrays, cutlery, and key rings. Lapis lazuli is often combined with crystal and metal, as well as with other gems to create unique items.

Carved candlesticks

A silver amphora

Turquoise and lapis lazuli mask

A cutlery set decorated with lapis lazuli

Blue-and-white patterned chess set

A house-shaped table clock

Replica of a classic car in metal and stone

ENTERTAINMENT IN CHILE

The range of entertainment in Chile is a reflection of its rich culture and the spirit of its people. Spectator sports form an integral part of life here. Soccer, in particular, fills stadiums all over the country despite the difficulty of the national team reaching the World Cup in a continent dominated by soccer powerhouses Argentina and Brazil. Equestrian sports are also popular, as racetracks across the country draw enthusiastic fans. Chile comes alive during the night and there are numerous bars and nightclubs that cater to its genial crowds. The vivid world of music and dance runs the gamut from folkloric music to contemporary rock and reggae, classical music and dance, with many artists of international fame. Chile also has an active theater scene, most notably in Santiago, and Chilean films have begun to generate worldwide interest.

Practical Information

Local newspapers such as *El Mercurio's Wikén* and the online *Revolver Magazine* (in English) are good sources of information in Santiago. Hotel receptions and tourist offices also offer guidance and events calendars. **Punto Ticket** is an online ticket broker that also sells through Ripley department stores in Santiago, La Serena, Antofagasta, and Concepción. Another alternative is **Ticketek**, which has outlets at Falabella department stores.

Spectator Sports

Chilean soccer lacks the high international profile of neighboring Argentina – though it won the Copa Americas for the second successive year after defeating Argentina in 2016. It also hosted the 1962 World Cup at its Estadio Nacional. Real First Division *clásicos* (classics) between **Universidad de Chile** and **Colo Colo** take place in this venue, but there are many other stadiums in the city. A number of regional teams such as the team of Universidad Católica, also play in the First Division. Tickets are arranged through individual soccer clubs. Racetrack enthusiasts in Santiago watch horses compete at Club Hípico *(see p85)* and Hipódromo Chile *(see p105)*. The **Valparaíso Sporting Club** also hosts prestigious races, notably the Chilean Derby Stakes. Tennis is popular thanks to many high-profile players *(see p34)*.

Bars and Nightclubs

Chilean cities, in particular Santiago and the coastal resort of Viña del Mar, are notable for a nightlife that starts early in the afternoon but gets into full swing only after midnight. Discos and dance clubs stay open until dawn, especially in the capital city's Barrio Bellavista, which also has an active gay scene. Lake District resorts, such as Pucón and Puerto Varas, also attract partygoers.

Musicians at Mil Guitarras para Víctor Jara, Santiago

Folk Music

Thanks to politically conscious musicians such as Violeta Parra and Víctor Jara *(see p29)*, Chilean folkloric music has gained many fans throughout Latin America and beyond. Performing in *peñas*, small informal clubs, these artistes modernized folk tradition that originated among the poor and dispossessed. Groups such as Quilapayún and Inti-Illimani absorbed Andean highland traditions from Peru and Bolivia, including characteristic instruments such as the *charango* and *zampoña* in their music. The political content of their work is obvious in albums such as *Cantata Popular Santa María de Iquique*, which features songs about the army's slaughter of nitrate miners and their families in the Atacama desert city.

Throughout Chile, there are clubs that focus on conventional folkloric entertainment such as the *cueca*, a music and dance form that mimics the courtship of the rooster and hen.

Match between Universidad de Chile and Colo Colo, Torneo Clausura 2015

Spirited performance of Chile's national dance, the *cueca*

Particularly popular during the mid-September patriotic holidays *(see pp36–7)*, the *cueca* is the traditional face of Chilean folkloric music, and may have African as well as Spanish influences.

Despite its Argentine origins, tango has earned a niche in many urban areas, and is particularly popular in Santiago, Valparaíso, and Coquimbo.

Classical Music

Having produced musical prodigies such as the pianist Claudio Arrau and the opera tenor Tito Beltrán, Chile has a small but significant classical music and dance community, centered mainly on the capital. Opera and classical music concerts take place at Santiago's Teatro Municipal and Teatro Universidad de Chile *(see p105)*. Many touring companies from Europe and North America play at these venues.

Contemporary Music

Chile's pop and rock scene has a lower international profile than its folk tradition, but new artists such as Pedropiedra, Gepe, Javiera Mena o Francisca Valenzuela and Grammy nominated artists Anita Tijoux and Mon Laferte have gained some attention in Latin America. The best place for live music is Santiago *(see pp102–103)*.

International headliners, and big Chilean names in contemporary music, perform annually at **Lollapalooza** – a weekend of pop, alternative rock, heavy metal, punk rock and hip-hop held in Santiago's Parque Bernardo O'Higgins *(see p85)*.

Theater and Film

Chile has an active theater community, with many major venues and dozens of small theater companies. Among the contemporary playwrights of note are Ariel Dorfman, who writes in both English and Spanish, and Marco Antonio de la Parra. Roberto Parra's *La Negra Ester*, about a prostitute in San Antonio, is the nation's most frequently produced contemporary play. Major venues include the **Teatro Nacional Chileno** and Universidad de Chile's **Sala Agustín Sire**, but these, and more intimate locales such as the Teatro La Comedia *(see p105)*, are for Spanish speakers.

Grammy nominated, Anita Tijoux

Film directors have made an impact beyond national borders in recent years, but most cinema halls show foreign films, primarily Hollywood fare. Most of these films are subtitled, but animated movies are invariably dubbed. Chain multiplexes include **Cine Hoyts** and **Cinemark**, but there are also repertory houses such as the **Cine Arte Biógrafo** and the **Cine Arte Normandie**.

OUTDOOR ACTIVITIES AND SPECIALIZED HOLIDAYS

With a splendid geographical diversity, ranging from the tropics to sub-Antarctica and from the Pacific shoreline to the highest Andean summits, Chile has outdoor activities to cater to every interest. The numerous national parks offer hiking, climbing, nature-watching, and horseback riding, and, in winter, the southern hemisphere's top skiing. Water sports are also popular, such as rafting and kayaking on some of the world's wildest rivers, trout fishing in the gentler streams, and year-round surfing along the coastline. For the less sporty, the Atacama desert boasts some of the continent's best-preserved archaeological sites, and its clear skies offer glimpses of constellations and planets that are invisible elsewhere on Earth. Finally, there are a number of hot springs and spas, and tours of world-class vineyards which offer great wines and gourmet cuisines.

Hikers in the Parque Nacional Torres del Paine, Southern Patagonia

Hiking

Fine wild hiking can be had along the length of the Andes and the coastal mountain range, while Parque Nacional Torres del Paine in Southern Patagonia is regarded by many to be the international gold standard for this pursuit. In most areas, good hiking trails are no more than half an hour away, and the Sendero de Chile will, upon its completion in 2040, be a pedestrian, bicycle, and horseback trail that runs the length of the country.

Apart from Parque Nacional Torres del Paine, the most popular bases for hiking are the towns of Pucón and Puerto Varas in the Lake District. There is also plenty of good hiking an hour from downtown Santiago, in the Cajón del Maipo. Also south of Santiago, the mountains east of the city of Talca offer lesser-known, but excellent trekking opportunities. The backcountry of Reserva Nacional Cerro Castillo, south of the Northern Patagonian city of Coyhaique, is gaining popularity among distance trekkers, but still gets just a fraction of those going to Parque Nacional Torres del Paine. Talca-based **Trekking Chile** not only provides accommodations and information on its immediate surroundings, but also covers destinations throughout the country. Santiago's **Cascada Expediciones** operates an eco-camp as the base for its multi-night treks in and around Parque Nacional Torres del Paine. Based outside the city of Cochrane in Northern Patagonia, the US-operated **Patagonia Adventure Expeditions** specializes in the Aisén Glacier Trail, to which it has exclusive rights.

Climbing

Chile offers climbing for both novice and experienced climbers. Casual visitors might undertake recreational climbing along with several other outdoor activities. However, safety measures should be strictly followed. The ascent of Volcán Villarrica, just outside of Pucón in the Lake District, can be undertaken in a day trip, but seismic and volcanic activity frequently shuts down access. Recreational climbing is also possible on Volcán Osorno outside Puerto Varas, but can require an overnight stay. Usually with these excursions, the view is the prime purpose of the climb. Among the tour operators who can help recreational climbers are **Sol y Nieve Expediciones**, based in Pucón, and **Alsur Expeditions**, based in Puerto Varas.

Climbing the snowbound Volcán Villarrica

For technical climbers, there are more difficult routes up peaks such as Osorno and Villarrica, but there are also other climbs that are challenging in terms of sheer altitude, such as the 22,609-ft- (6,893-m-) high Volcán Ojos del Salado in the desert north. Among climbs rated for their technical difficulties are the steep granite faces of Torres del Paine in Southern Patagonia. **Antares Patagonia Adventure** in Puerto Natales and **Azimut 360** in Santiago can arrange more challenging climbs and provide logistic support.

Bird-Watching

Chile's diverse ecosystems are home to a variety of birdlife and, for first-time visitors, almost everything is a novelty. Guides are provided by professional enterprises such as **Birds Chile**, based in Puerto Varas, which covers all of Patagonia, from the Lake District to Tierra del Fuego. **Birdwatching in Chile** is an online resource that enables enthusiasts to meet up with a "birding pal" who is well versed in the local habitat. In Punta Arenas, **Natura Patagonia** operates in the Strait of Magellan, Tierra del Fuego, and the Patagonian steppe.

Horseback Riding

The riding tradition is strong throughout Chile, and two comfortable lodges, both founded by Germans but with substantial Chilean input, specialize in providing backcountry trips. In the high desert, east of Ovalle city, Hacienda Los Andes *(see p188)* is a Colonial-style lodge that offers guided horseback-riding trips across the Andes. East of Puerto Varas, **Campo Aventura** provides rides into rugged terrain surrounded by dense Valdivian rain forest. The Mapuche operator **Kila Leufú** organizes day trips and longer rides near Pucón in the Lake District.

A cyclist on the Carretera Austral, stretching across Patagonia

Cycling and Mountain-Biking

Chile is suitable for both local and long-distance cycling and mountain-biking. Most cities and resorts, from the Atacama to the Lake District and beyond, offer rental bikes at reasonable rates. The best destinations are San Pedro de Atacama, Pucón, and Puerto Varas, but given the progress of the Sendero de Chile, the path that is due to cover the length of the country, cycling is possible almost everywhere.

Long distance cyclists often use the famous Pan American Highway or Ruta 5 to travel from Alaska to Tierra del Fuego, but in the Lake District, there are many loop rides that avoid the busy highway. The Carretera Austral is another iconic route for travelers through Patagonia. For those who prefer logistic support, California-based **Backroads** organizes cycling trips through this part of Chile and certain areas of Argentina.

Driving Holidays

As most seasoned visitors to Chile know, the Carretera Austral is best enjoyed on a driving tour. Spectacularly scenic, this highway is a discontinuous route that starts in Puerto Montt and, with numerous ferry connections, ends just beyond Villa O'Higgins. The segment from Chaitén north to Parque Pumalín was restored following damage caused by the eruption of Volcán Chaitén. The easiest way to explore Carretera Austral is to rent a car in Coyhaique and travel either north or south. The road is mostly gravel, but paved segments are increasing, especially north of Coyhaique; 4WDs are advisable.

Also ideal for automobile touring is the Lake District, from Temuco south to Puerto Montt and Chiloé, especially on trunk roads away from the four-lane Pan-American Highway. The bulk of these roads are paved, but there is the occasional gravel route.

While driving in the Atacama desert allows visitors access to remote areas, it can mean great distances and, when moving off the main roads, slow speeds. Operating out of Santiago, **Pachamama by Bus** offers van services north to San Pedro de Atacama and south to Puerto Varas and Puerto Montt. These hop-on, hop-off services operate with a minimum of just one passenger, stop at notable sights en route, and allow travelers to re-board at their convenience, with no time limit.

Horseback riding over the slopes near Playa El Faro, La Serena

Skiing and Snowboarding

Chile is one of the few places where skiers and snowboarders can hit the slopes between July and September. The traditional choice for most is Ski Portillo *(see p138)*, near the Argentine border, but there is splendid skiing near Santiago, at resorts such as El Colorado and Valle Nevado *(see p144)*. Farther south, Nevados de Chillán *(see p156)* is the best choice, but there are good opportunities at Volcán Villarrica *(see p202)*, Volcán Osorno *(see p214)*, and Parque Nacional Puyehue's Centro de Ski Antillanca *(see p209)*. Santiago's **Skitotal** arranges day trips to resorts near the capital. The US-run **PowderQuest Ski Tours** offers tours to the top areas in both Chile and Argentina.

White-Water Rafting

The steep-gradient transverse rivers of Chile offer runnable white-water barely an hour from downtown Santiago and well into Patagonia. The most popular destinations for river running are Río Trancura near Pucón, Río Petrohué near Puerto Varas, and the rivers of Cajón del Maipo. However, the gold standard is northern Patagonia's Río Futaleufú, one of the world's top-ten white-water experiences.

Day trips are organized by operators such as Santiago's **Cascada Expediciones**, which is also ideal for hikes, Pucón's **Politur**, and Puerto Varas' **KoKayak**. Some agents, such

White-water rafting on Río Futaleufú

as **Expediciones Chile**, **Bío Bío Expeditions**, and **Earth River Expeditions**, have comfortable camps along the Futaleufú for week-long programs, but they also do day trips.

Fishing

Chile attracts trout fishermen from around the world to its placid lakes and clear rivers, from south of Temuco to Aisén and Tierra del Fuego. **Southern Chile Expeditions** operates fly-fishing lodges such as Yan Kee Way near Puerto Varas and El Patagón in the more remote Aisén region. It is also possible to make arrangements with local operators and guides in towns including Coyhaique in Northern Patagonia and Pucón in the Lake District.

Surfing

With a coastline that runs for thousands of miles and hundreds of long sandy beaches, some of which are hidden in

coves among dramatic headlands, Chile has almost limitless surfing potential, except in Patagonia. The most popular stretches for surfers are found along the coast of central Chile, in places such as Viña del Mar and its suburbs, the vicinity of Pichilemu, and also in and around the northern Chilean cities of Iquique and Arica. While surfing is a year-round activity, the most challenging waves occur in winter, when large swells hit the Pacific coast. The cold Humboldt current makes a wet suit essential for avoiding hypothermia, and some beaches have dangerous rip currents.

A number of local lodges specialize in surfing, including the **Pichilemu Surf Hostal** and **Posada Punta de Lobos**, which offer classes and rental gear. In most areas where surfing is possible, windsurfing is also an alternative.

Sea Kayaking

Predictably, given the region's extensive coastline, Chile is a delight for sea kayakers. However, areas facing the open Pacific may be less appealing than the coves and inland sea around the Chiloé archipelago. On the mainland, Northern Patagonia boasts some truly remote coves, access to which may require major logistic support. Santiago's **Altué Sea Kayaking**, based in the Chiloé town of Dalcahue in summer, is the major operator, but another option in the region is Alsur Expeditions, which also offers climbing expeditions.

Diving

In the cool eastern Pacific Ocean, diving is not the pastime it is in tropical waters such as the Caribbean. However, Juan Fernandez and Easter Island are popular spots with two diving companies, **Mike Rapu Diving Center** and **Orca Diving Center**. Other areas include Los Molles, Las Tacas and Punta de Choros. There is also a PADI diving school in Santiago.

Underwater exploration off Playa Anakena, Easter Island

A cruise ship moored off Punta Arenas in Southern Patagonia

Cruises

Many large cruise ships round Cape Horn on journeys between Santiago and the Argentine capital, Buenos Aires. Smaller, locally run cruise ships permit frequent, and more interesting, land excursions into remote areas on itineraries of 3 to 5 days. Among the better companies is **Cruceros Australis**, which shuttles back and forth between Punta Arenas and Ushuaia, in Argentine Tierra del Fuego. **Cruceros Marítimos Skorpios** covers some spectacular territory from Puerto Montt and Puerto Chacabuco to Laguna San Rafael, and from Puerto Natales to the fjords of the Campo de Hielo Sur, but the level of service does not compare with that of Cruceros Australis.

Whale-Watching

In Chile, whale-watching is still developing and sometimes the logistics can be difficult. Nevertheless, there are blue whales in the Golfo de Corcovado, off Chiloé, in Punta de Choros, North of La Serena, and, more notably, accessible humpback feeding grounds in the Strait of Magellan. On Isla Carlos III, near the feeding grounds, **Whalesound** operates an island eco-camp, with accommodation in dome tents.

Paragliding

Behind Iquique, the coastal range rises almost vertically, and the offshore westerlies are ideal to carry paragliders off the escarpment. Here, the local government has dedicated a take-off site to encourage paragliding. Local operators take visitors on tandem flights that offer bird's-eye views of the city and its astounding dunes, before landing on sandy beaches. Experienced paragliders can occasionally ride the breezes as far as Tocopilla, 162 miles (260 km) to the south. The **Escuela de Parapente Altazor** helps paragliders get started and also provides accommodation for its clientele.

Golf

Golf is not the phenomenon it is in neighboring Argentina, and Chilean courses are invariably private and clubby – it usually takes a member's invitation to get in. However, some hotels arrange passes for their guests and the coastal **Marbella Resort**, at Maitencillo north of Viña del Mar, has its own course open to guests.

Astronomy

The skies of the southern hemisphere so differ from those of the north that several major international observatories have placed state-of-the-art astronomical facilities in Chile, such as the advanced Cerro Paranal Observatory (see p181) and ALMA Observatory in Llano de Chajnantor. The easiest to visit are **Cerro Tololo Inter-American Observatory**, near La Serena, and **La Silla Observatory**, near Santiago. Smaller municipal observatories include the Cerro Mamalluca Observatory (see p186). Near San Pedro de Atacama, Frenchman Alain Maury's private **San Pedro de Atacama Celestial Explorations** is very informative.

Cerro Mamalluca Observatory in the arid Valle de Elqui, Vicuña

The Clos Apalta winery as seen from Casa Lapostolle

Archaeology

The nearly perfect aridity of the Atacama desert, preserving ruins and artifacts over millennia, has made northern Chile a mecca for archaeological research. The most priceless and conspicous relics of the region are the enormous hillside geo-glyphs, linked geographically and historically to the Andean highlands. In addition, pre-Columbian fortresses and villages still survive throughout the desert, and Arica's Chinchorro mummies *(see p165)* are a land-mark discovery. Evidence of historical archaeology, which is concerned with ancient societies that used writing, can be seen in ghost towns of the Atacama, such as Santa Laura and Humberstone *(see p172)*.

Far Horizons Archaeological and Cultural Trips, based in California, offers excursions to the Atacama, but its specialty is in trips to Easter Island; its guides are globally known scholars on the island's enigmatic past.

The country's most notable archaeological site is Monte Verde, near Puerto Montt in the Lake District. Dating from 13,000 BC, this site offers evi-dence of the earliest human settlement in the Americas. Around 12 miles (18 km) south of downtown Santiago, in the basin of the Río Maipo, is the location of the Cerro Chena site, where ruins of an Incan fortress have been excavated.

Spas and Hot Springs

As part of the Pacific Ring of Fire, Chile's numerous active volcanoes also mean abundant geysers and hot springs, espe-cially, but not solely, southward of Santiago. Many of the sites are open for day trips, notably Termas Geométricas near

Pucón, but others are full-scale hotels with spa facilities. The best known are the all-inclusive Termas de Puyehue *(see p209)* and Northern Patagonia's Puyuhuapi Lodge & Spa *(see p232)*. Both offer day passes as well.

Wine and Food

Chile has numerous wine routes, significantly through the Colchagua and Casablanca valleys, that offer not just wine but also fine cuisine and, in some cases, accommodation. The Ruta del Vino *(see p152)* offers the most complete services, and individual mem-bers such as **Viña Casa Silva** and the Casablanca valley's **Viña Matetic** combine wine and gourmet food with elite lodging. **Santiago Adventures** arranges trips to these wineries and to the scenic but lesser-known Aconcagua valley.

Tour Operators

Many international operators offer tours focusing on different kinds of outdoor activities and specialist interests. **LAN Vacations** is the tour branch of Chile's flagship airline, while US-based **Wildland Adventures** is highly regarded for its Patagonian trips. In the UK, **Journey Latin America** specializes in the region, while **Birdwatching Chile** offers just what you would expect.

The hot-spring resort Termas de Puyehue, near the Parque Nacional Puyehue

DIRECTORY

Hiking

Cascada Expediciones
Las Condes, Santiago.
Tel (02) 2923-5262.
W cascada.travel

Patagonia Adventure Expeditions
Puerto Bertrand.
Tel (067) 2411330.
W patagonia
adventureexpeditions.
com

Trekking Chile
Talca. **Tel** (071) 1970096.
W trekkingchile.com

Climbing

Alsur Expeditions
Puerto Varas. **Tel** (065)
2232300. W alsur
expeditions.com

Antares Patagonia Adventure
Puerto Natales.
Tel (061) 2414611.
W antarespata
gonia.travel

Azimut 360
Eliodoro Yáñez 1437,
Providencia, Santiago.
Tel (02) 2235-1519.
W azimut360.com

Sol y Nieve Expediciones
Lincoyan 361, Pucón.
Tel (045) 2444761.
W solynlevepucon.com

Bird-Watching

Birds Chile
Puerto Varas.
Tel (09) 9269-2606.
W birdschile.com

Birdwatching in Chile
W birdingpal.org/
Chile.htm

Natura Patagonia
W naturapatagonia.cl

Horseback Riding

Campo Aventura
Cochamó.
Tel (09) 9289-4318.
W campo-aventura.
com

Kila Leufú
Tel (09) 9876-4576.
W kilaleufu.cl

Cycling and Mountain-Biking

Backroads
Tel (800) 462-2848 (USA).
W backroads.com

Driving Holidays

Pachamama by Bus
Moneda 2350, Santiago.
Tel (02) 2688-8018.
W pachamama
bybus.com

Skiing and Snowboarding

PowderQuest Ski Tours
Tel (888) 5657158 (USA).
W powderquest.com

Skitotal
Las Condes.
Tel (02) 2246-0156.
W skitotal.cl

White-Water Rafting

Bío Bío Expeditions
Tel (800) 2467238 (USA).
W bbxrafting.com

Cascada Expediciones
Las Condes, Santiago.
Tel (02) 2923-5950.
W cascada.travel

Earth River Expeditions
Tel (800) 643-2784 (USA).
W earthriver.com

Expediciones Chile
Tel 208 629-5032 (USA).
W exchile.com

KoKayak
Puerto Varas.
Tel (065) 2233004.
W kokayak.cl

Politur
Pucón. **Tel** (045) 2441373.
W politur.com

Fishing

Southern Chile Expeditions
Tel (866) 881-9215 (USA).
W southernchilexp.com

Surfing

Pichilemu Surf Hostal
Tel (09) 7492-6848.
W pichilemusurf
hostal.com

Posada Punta de Lobos
Tel (09) 8154-1106.
W posadapunta
delobos.cl

Sea Kayaking

Altué Sea Kayaking
Dalcahue.
Tel (09) 9419-6809.
W seakayakchile.com

Diving

Mike Rapu Diving Center
Hanga Roa. **Tel** (032)
2551055. W mikerapu.cl

Orca Diving Center
Hanga Roa.
Tel (032) 2550375.
W seemorca.co.cl

Cruises

Cruceros Australis
Santiago. **Tel** (02) 2840-
0100. W australis.com

Cruceros Marítimos Skorpios
Santiago. **Tel** (02) 2477-
1900. W skorpios.cl

Whale-Watching

Whalesound
Punta Arenas.
Tel (09) 9887-9814.
W whalesound.com

Paragliding

Escuela de Parapente Altazor
Iquique.
Tel (057) 2380110.
W altazor.cl

Golf

Marbella Resort
Km 35, Camino
Concón Zapallar.
Tel (032) 2795900.
W marbella.cl

Astronomy

Cerro Tololo Inter-American Observatory
La Serena.
Tel (051) 2205200.
W ctio.noao.edu

San Pedro de Atacama Celestial Explorations
San Pedro de Atacama.
Tel (055) 2566278.
W spaceobs.com

La Silla Observatory
Ave. Alonso de Córdova
3107, Vitacura, Santiago.
Tel (02) 2464-4100.
W eso.org

Archaeology

Far Horizons Archaeological and Cultural Trips
Tel (415) 482-8400 (USA).
W farhorizons.com

Wine and Food

Santiago Adventures
Tegualda, 1352,
Providencia, Santiago. **Tel**
(02) 2244-2750; (802) 904-
6798 (USA). W santiago
adventures.com

Viña Casa Silva
Hijuela Norte s/n,
San Fernando.
Tel (072) 2716519.
W casasilva.cl

Viña Matetic
Fundo Rosario,
Lagunillas, Casablanca.
Tel (02) 2611-1501.
W matetic.cl

Tour Operators

Birdwatching Chile
W birdwatching
chile.com

Journey Latin America
401 King Street,
London W6 9NJ.
Tel (020) 3131-7959 (UK).
W journeylatin
america.co.uk

LAN Vacations
Tel (888) 335-9055.
W grayline.com/
lanvacations

Wildland Adventures
3516 NE 155th Street,
Seattle, WA 98155.
Tel (800) 345-4453 (USA).
W wildland.com

SURVIVAL GUIDE

PRACTICAL INFORMATION

Chile's modern infrastructure is one of the best among Latin American countries, and compares well with that of most developed nations. Santiago, for instance, boasts hi-tech highways and an immaculate metro system. Telephone services, for both land-lines and cell phones, are excellent, and Internet connections are abundant. All the important tourist destinations are well equipped to receive international visitors, however facilities may be limited in remote rural areas. Chileans in general are polite and helpful, and the police are professional – to be consulted and trusted rather than feared or bribed. National tourist offices, usually with English-speaking personnel, are found in every regional capital and many other cities and towns, sometimes complemented by municipal offices. Off the main roads, however, it can be hard to find an English speaker, except in popular tourist destinations.

Skiing, a popular winter activity at the Andean resorts in Chile

When to Go

Since Chile extends from the subtropical deserts of Atacama to the sub-Antarctic icefields of Patagonia, the country offers recreation for every season. Spring and autumn *(see pp38–41)* are usually pleasant, with prices and crowds reaching their peak in January–February.

Visas and Passports

Citizens of most countries, inclu-ding Australia, Canada, the USA, and members of the EU, do not need visas to enter Chile. How-ever, citizens of countries that require Chileans to obtain visas must pay "reciprocity fees" equi-valent to the cost of those visas – Mexicans pay US$23 and Australians US$117. These fees, valid for the life of the passport, are collected only at Santiago's international airport. Passports should be valid for at least six months. On arrival, visitors receive a tourist card, valid for 90 days, which can be extended for another 90 days for US$100.

Travel Safety Advice

Visitors can get up-to-date travel safety information from the Foreign and Commonwealth Office in the UK, the State Department in the US and the Department of Foreign Affairs and Trade in Australia.

Customs Information

Visitors may bring 17 oz (500 g) of tobacco, 6 pints (3 liters) of spirits (for adults over 18), and small amounts of perfume into Chile. However, import of fresh fruit or other agricultural prod-ucts is strictly prohibited. The northernmost desert cities of Iquique and Arica, along with the southernmost region of Magallanes, have duty-free zones; travelers from these regions may experience internal customs checks.

Embassies

Consulates of most nations, including **Canada**, the **USA**, and the **UK**, are located in Santiago. Queries can be addressed to these centers, although much of this information is available on their official websites.

Tourist Information

Sernatur, the national tourism service, has offices at interna-tional airports, in Santiago and every regional capital, and in most tourist cities. Most towns have municipal tourist offices. Hostels and hotels also provide good information.
  CONAF is the governing body for all national parks, reserves, and other sanctuaries in Chile, and offers information about them.

Tourist information center in Castro's Plaza de Armas, Chiloé

◀ Hikers above Río Paine, in Parque Nacional Torres del Paine, Southern Patagonia

Travelers on a tour boat to the Glaciar Gray in Southern Patagonia

What to Wear

Chile is mostly a temperate mid-latitude country, and seasonally appropriate clothing – light summer clothes, with a raincoat for the wetter areas, and warm clothes for winter – should be suitable for most purposes. Nights at high altitudes in the Atacama and the Andes can turn very cold, so winter clothing becomes necessary in all seasons.

Opening Hours and Admission Charges

Museums can charge a minimal fee for entry, but many public museums are free of charge. Private facilities, however, can be expensive. Museum hours vary daily and seasonally, but many are closed on Mondays.

National parks are open year round, but a few limit access to daylight hours. Some of the parks are free, while most charge up to US$8 for foreigners and US$4 for residents. Torres del Paine is the most expensive, and charges US$32 for foreigners, and US$9 for nationals.

Language

Spanish is Chile's official language, but the local variant, which omits final and even some internal consonants, can cause problems for those who have learned the language elsewhere. Many Chileans in the tourism industry speak English, but in areas off the main highways, a working knowledge of Spanish is useful.

The indigenous groups, mainly Mapuche but also Aymara and some smaller groups, have their own languages, but almost all of them speak Spanish as well.

Street Names and Addresses

As in most Latin American countries, street names and addresses differ from those in English-speaking nations. The main difference is that the street name goes before the number. Most Chilean street names are not abbreviated, and while Calle is usually omitted from street addresses, Avenida and others are not.

The Chilean custom of double surname, in which an individual's father's name comes first and the mother's name second, is also applicable to road names. In Santiago, for example, Avenida Vicuña Mackenna is not the same as Mackenna (another street), and this can be problematic when asking for directions.

Religion and Social Etiquette

Historically, Chile is a Roman Catholic country and the Church is still influential here. However, its inability to attract priests has created a vacuum in which evangelical Protestantism is growing. The indigenous peoples, especially the Mapuche and Aymara, have their own religious traditions, but many are Catholic or evangelicals. Although Chilean society is not particularly conservative about dressing, visitors are advised to dress modestly when visiting religious venues.

Chileans value courtesy and are polite in their public behavior. When addressing a stranger, the formal titles *señor* (sir or mister), *señora* (madam), or *señorita* (miss) are used. The correct greetings are *buenos días* (good morning), *buenas tardes* (good afternoon), or *buenas noches* (good evening). Nudist beaches, though not rare, are restricted to a few areas along the central coast.

Women Travelers

Despite electing a female president in 2006 and again in 2014, Chile is not entirely free of sexism. The likeliest hassle is the verbal *piropo* (unsolicited comments), which can range from the relatively innocuous to the truly vulgar – even for those who do not understand the language, the tone is usually clear. The best tactic is to ignore the offender or seek refuge in a public place such as a hotel or a café. It is best to avoid walking alone at night; if it becomes necessary, or if stranded, it is advisable to call for a radio taxi.

Traveling with Children

Chile is a child-friendly nation. Parents traveling with small children are not required to pay their bus fares unless the children occupy a separate seat. Nor do they pay for their children's stay in hotels. However, families of four or more persons should look at *cabana* accommodations, which can be cheaper than hotels on a per person basis.

Locals and visitors thronging the Plaza José Francisco Vergara, Viña del Mar

Senior Citizens

In Chile, senior citizens can anticipate a great deal of respect and, when they need it, assistance. Reduced admission charges enjoyed by Chilean seniors do not apply to foreign visitors, but there are discounts to be had on the metro.

Gay and Lesbian Travelers

Historically, Chile is a socially conservative country and public homosexuality is frowned upon. Since the end of the Pinochet dictatorship, however, many Chilean people are now open about their sexuality, and Santiago celebrates a gay pride parade in late September. There is an active gay nightlife scene in the capital's Barrio Bellavista, and in beach resorts such as Viña del Mar.

Disabled Travelers

Chile can be challenging for wheelchair-bound travelers, as narrow sidewalks, rough surfaces, and the lack of ramps can make most cities difficult to negotiate. However, many newer hotels have constructed rooms with wheelchairs in mind and others have retrofitted them. In the countryside, especially in the backcountry, wheelchair access is limited.

Student Information

Many North American and European students spend a semester abroad in Chile

The LGBTQ pride walk held at Santiago in 2016

through their home universities, with the main destinations being Santiago, Valparaíso, and Concepción. A student visa, obtained through a Chilean consulate in the home country, is required for such trips. Many visitors also take advantage of their stay to study Spanish. Santiago has a great number of quality language schools, although Valparaíso and resort-towns such as Pucón also offer courses. Courses are usually on a weekly or monthly basis, and may include homestays with Chilean families. No special visa is required for this.

Tipping

In formal restaurants – that is, those with table service and a printed menu – a 10 percent tip is usual and often "suggested" on the check.

When paying by credit card, guests can choose to either pay the tip in cash or fill in the appropriate amount in the tip box on the card statement. Taxi drivers do not expect tips unless they have provided some extra service, such as hauling luggage. A small tip is proper for a gas station attendant who cleans the windshield and for students who help at various supermarkets.

Smoking

Many Chileans are heavy smokers, but they almost always observe the prohibition on smoking on public transport, the workplace, and other restricted areas. The government has placed some of the grisliest possible health warnings on tobacco packaging. The nationwide tobacco law prohibits smoking in all restaurants and bars, though smokers are allowed to light up in outdoor dining areas. Compliance is close to perfect.

Universidad de Chile, one of many centers in Santiago offering Spanish classes to overseas students

Public Toilets

Sanitation standards are higher in Chile than in tropical Latin American countries and, in general, public toilets are safe to use. At bus stations and service stations, for instance, there is almost always a caretaker who keeps the facilities clean. However, travelers sometimes need to pay a small charge for their use and to purchase toilet paper. Many service stations also offer shower facilities, which are used primarily by truckers, but are also open to the public at large.

Measurements

The metric system is official and universal in Chile except for a few vernacular measures and oddities such as tire pressure, which is measured in pounds per sq inch, and airport elevation, which is measured in feet. To convert degrees Celsius to degrees Farenheit, multiply by 1.0 and add 32.

Imperial to Metric
1 inch = 2.5 centimeters
1 foot = 30 centimeters
1 mile = 1.6 kilometers
1 ounce = 28 grams
1 pound = 454 grams
1 US pint = 0.473 liter
1 US quart = 0.947 liter
1 US gallon = 3.78 liters
Metric to Imperial
1 centimeter = 0.4 inch
1 meter = 3 feet 3 inches
1 kilometer = 0.6 mile
1 gram = 0.04 ounce
1 kilogram = 2.2 pounds
1 liter = 2.1 US pints
1°C = 33.8°F

Electricity

Chile's electric system operates on 220 volts, 50 cycles, similar to the European and UK systems, but travelers from North America may need converters. However, appliances such as laptop computers and cell phones operate on both 220- and 100-volt systems. Most plugs take two rounded prongs, and adapters are necessary. A surge protector is a wise investment.

The eco-lodge Casona Distante in Valle del Elqui, Norte Chico

Time

Chile used to be four hours behind Greenwich Mean Time (GMT) and one hour ahead of New York's Eastern Standard Time (EST). In 2015, however, the clock was set ahead another hour throughout the year. This means that in the northernmost tropical latitudes, near the Peruvian border, sunrise does not come until after 8am for much of the summer. Easter Island is two hours behind the mainland.

Responsible Tourism

Although some of Chile's forest trees have received official protection for many decades, public awareness of broad environmental issues has developed only recently. Chile lacks major energy resources except for hydroelectricity, which makes its scenic areas vulnerable to massive dam projects. Due to Chile's fossil fuel shortage, many operators have made efforts to reduce their energy consumption, and newer hotels have state-of-the-art facilities that help reduce their carbon footprint (see p329).

Developments in locally based ethnotourism have been slower, but the Kunza communities of San Pedro de Atacama are gaining control over access to Geisers de Tatio, and the Aymara residents of the Parque Nacional Lauca operate hotels and serve as guides. The indigenous residents of Easter Island are increasing their control over their home. In the south, Mapuche-run tourism businesses include farmstays.

In Patagonia and the desert north, distances are great and, in some areas, public transport is limited. Here, many mountain lodges operate their own excursions, which can be a more efficient option to private car rentals.

Some of Chile's marine resources have suffered overexploitation. In particular, the farming of salmon in the Lake District and Patagonia has drawn criticism for overuse of chemicals that contaminate the waterways and oceans.

DIRECTORY

Travel Safety Advice

Australia
Department of Foreign Affairs and Trade
Ⓦ dfat.gov.au/
Ⓦ smarttraveller.gov.au/

UK
Foreign and Commonwealth Office
Ⓦ gov.uk/foreign-travel-advice

US
US Department of State
Ⓦ travel.state.gov/

Embassies

Canada
Nueva Tajamar 481, Santiago.
Ⓦ canadainternational.gc.ca

UK
Avenida El Bosque Norte 0125, 3rd floor, Las Condes, Santiago.
Ⓦ britemb.cl

USA
Avenida Andrés Bello 2800, Las Condes, Santiago.
Ⓦ chile.usembassy.gov

Tourist Information

CONAF
Paseo Bulnes, 265, piso 1, Santiago.
Tel (02) 2663-0125. Ⓦ conaf.cl

Sernatur
Avenida Providencia 1550, Providencia, Santiago. **Tel** (02) 2731-8310. Ⓦ sernatur.cl

Personal Security and Health

By international standards, Chile is a safe country for visitors who take routine precautions. Incidents of crime directed at tourists are few, but in any event, it is best to avoid displaying conspicuous valuables. Chilean medical care is among the continent's best, especially in Santiago, and there are few serious health hazards – Chile has no poisonous snakes or malaria, and no vaccinations are needed for entering Chile. Altitude sickness can be an issue, and, in the far south, polar ozone depletion makes sunburn a serious matter requiring protective measures.

A green-and-white police car at the coastal resort of Viña del Mar

Police

Latin American police have a reputation for corruption, and often for much worse, but the **Carabineros de Chile** – identified by their sharp khaki-and-green uniforms and pentagonal badges – are the exception to the rule. Generally considered firm but fair, the *carabineros* are rarely implicated in any sort of misdeed, and travelers should never attempt to bribe them. Their behavior toward foreign visitors borders on the deferential and tourists need feel no hesitation in approaching the *carabineros* for directions or other forms of assistance. That said, few street patrolmen speak English, especially outside the larger cities, and they may need to call in someone from the precinct office in case of an emergency.

Carabinero in khaki uniform

areas, avoid poorly lighted areas where people are few.

Armed assaults on anyone, and particularly on foreign visitors, are unusual. As a general precaution, however, it is best to avoid traveling with or displaying expensive personal items that might attract unwanted attention. Valuables can be secured in the electronic safes provided at most mid-range and upscale hotels; any cash that needs to be carried on a journey is best kept in a money belt or leg pouch. Those who are traveling by car need to park in secure lots at night, and avoid leaving visible valuables in their vehicles.

General Precautions

Crimes directed at tourists are few, and most of those are crimes of opportunity such as pickpocketing and purse snatchings. Visitors must therefore be aware of their surroundings and, in urban

Lost and Stolen Property

While the odds of recovering lost or stolen property are low unless it is reported immediately, the *carabineros* will generally do their best to provide assistance. They should be asked to take a *denuncia* (a report necessary for insurance claims) that includes a *narración de los hechos* (account of the incident) and a *declaración jurada de pre-existencia de especies sustraídas* (declaration of losses). Visitors must report lost passports to their embassy or consulate (*see p317*), which will issue a replacement. Lost credit cards shold be reported to the issuing bank (*see p320*).

Health Precautions

Chile is a country with high public health standards. Tap water is drinkable almost everywhere and, other than common illnesses such as colds and flu, there is little to fear. Even the 2009 swine flu breakout has had little impact. There have been cases of Chagas' disease, dengue, and hantavirus, but instances of tourists developing these infections are few. Chile requires no vaccinations for entry, though visitors from the tropics may be asked for a yellow fever certificate.

Altitude Sickness

Chile's northern and central Andes encompass some of the highest altitudes in the western hemisphere, with areas such as the altiplano in Parque Nacional Lauca reaching elevations of over 14,440 ft (4,400 m). Even

High-altitude tablelands of Parque Nacional Lauca

Private ambulance operated by the SAMU organization

the young and healthy are affected in such oxygen-poor environments, and more than one tourist has suffered fatally from acute mountain sickness. When traveling to altitudes above 8,000 ft (2,440 m), it is best to spend a night at an intermediate altitude for acclimatization. Symptoms of altitude sickness include headaches, nausea, fatigue, dizziness, and dehydration, and it is best to turn back at the first manifestation of these signs.

Natural Disasters

Chile is one of the world's most seismically active countries, with frequent earthquakes and many active volcanoes. Hotels across the nation have evacuation plans that guests need to be familiar with. Chilean cities and towns such as Pucón and Curacautín maintain volcano warning systems, and most coastal towns have signs indicating evacuation routes in case of tsunamis. Fires can be a hazard in the woodlands of the Central Valley, especially in summer and autumn. There is a nationwide phone number for the **Fire Department**, and another number, monitored by **CONAF**, for forest fires.

Emergencies

In Santiago, in the capitals of every administrative province, and in many smaller cities, public hospitals and clinics are prepared to deal with almost any emergency. There is also a national phone line for **Ambulance** services. Most doctors speak at least some English, but the waiting time can be substantial except for critical cases. Even the smallest villages have emergency clinics that, while they may not have doctors, can deal with intensive care until it is possible to arrange a transfer to a more complete facility.

Medical Treatment

In Santiago, the medical care available meets the highest international standards, especially at private hospitals such as **Clinica Las Condes** and **Clinica Alemana de Santiago**. Regional hospitals are also good, but in sparsely populated areas, they can be few and far between. **Hospital Mutual de Seguridad** has branches in several cities.

Public hospitals provide competent basic care, but can be overburdened with patients from the state health system. Health insurance, including a policy for emergency evacuation, is highly advisable as Chilean hospital care is not cheap. Most hospitals accept credit card payments, and provide bills for reimbursement.

Pharmacies

Compared to Europe and the US, Chile has fairly liberal pharmacy laws. A number of medications that would be obtained by prescription elsewhere are available over the counter here, and pharmacists may dispense some of these based on the symptoms described to them. However, medicines are not cheap.

Pharmacies do not have fixed hours. Big pharmacy chains such as Cruz Verde, Ahumada, and Salcobrand keep open for long hours in the cities, but in smaller towns, there may only be a modest public pharmacy for emergencies.

DIRECTORY

Police

Carabineros de Chile
Tel 133.

Natural Disasters

CONAF
Tel 130.

Fire Department
Tel 132.

Emergencies

Ambulance
Tel 131.

Medical Treatment

Clinica Alemana de Santiago
Avenida Vitacura 5951, Santiago.
Tel (02) 2210-1111.

Clinica Las Condes
Estoril 450, Santiago.
Tel (02) 2210-4000.

Hospital Mutual de Seguridad
w mutual.cl

An outlet of the Cruz Verde pharmacy chain

Banking and Currency

Chile's unit of currency is the peso, but US dollars are accepted only in hotels. Traveler's checks get a lower rate of exchange than dollars and can be time-consuming to change. Exchange rates are higher in Santiago than elsewhere in Chile. Credit cards are widely accepted, except at very small businesses. In rural Chile, small denomination pesos become necessary. In border areas, merchants may accept Argentine pesos, but the rate of exchange can be unfavorable. There are no restrictions on the import or export of Chilean or foreign currency, but amounts greater than US$10,000 must be declared to Chilean customs.

An armored car with an ATM for public use

Banks

There are numerous banks in Chilean cities and even in many small towns, where the state-run **BancoEstado** usually has a branch. Opening hours are generally 9am to 2pm, from Monday to Friday only. Bank processes can be slow and bureaucratic, and it is best to visit in the mornings. *Casas de cambio* (foreign exchange bureaus) are more efficient and stay open until 6pm, but may close for lunch. Some also open on Saturday mornings. *Casas de cambio* are abundant in Santiago, but far fewer in other parts of Chile. They will change euros and most other currencies, but the exchange rates will be lower than for US dollars.

ATMs

Chile has perhaps the greatest availability of ATMs, known locally as *cajeros automáticos*, in any Latin American country. They are found at banks, super-markets, service stations, and many other places. There are also exchange counters at Santiago's international airport,

but better rates are available from ATMs in the lobby. Mobile ATMs are found at summer resorts that may not have their own banks. Visitors with ATM cards from their home country can withdraw up to the peso equivalent of US$300 per day, but cannot withdraw any foreign currencies.

ATMs usually dispense large bills of $10,000, with a couple of $5,000 notes, so obtaining small change can be trouble-some. Most Chilean banks, apart from BancoEstado and CorpBanca, charge US$3–4 per transaction. Visitors using foreign ATM cards need to check what charges are imposed – some banks collect substantial fees for foreign transactions even at their own overseas ATMs. Others, such as Wells Fargo, are even more expensive. The most inexpensive cards come from credit unions.

Credit Cards and Traveler's Checks

Credit cards are widely used in Chile, in hotels, restaurants, and shops, although the less expensive accommodations and eateries often take only cash. Credit card companies usually deduct a commission on overseas purchases, and it is advisable to check what this is to avoid any surprises. The most widely used cards are **MasterCard**, **Visa**, and **American Express**;

other cards are almost unheard of. If a credit card is lost or stolen, the home company or a Chilean affiliate should be contacted, with the card number.

Currency cards are among the easiest ways of carrying money. Companies such as Caxton, FairFX and Travelex offer easy to use pre-loadable cards. Customers can manage the balance on their cards online whilst traveling.

Electronic Transfer

Western Union arranges electronic transfers to Chile through *casas de cambio*, and through the domestic courier service **Chilexpress**, which has nearly 200 locations throughout the country.

In addition to the usual exchange commission, Western Union collects a substantial charge per transaction. **Thomas Cook** also arranges wire transfers. Money Gram can be used in the Correos (postal) offices.

Taxes

All price tags include the 19 percent *impuesto de valor agregado* (IVA or VAT), but at most mid-range and upscale hotels, tourists are exempt from this tax if they pay in US dollars or with a foreign credit card. However, not all hotels participate in this government rebate program, and even if they do it is not automatic: in some cases, guests must request the hotel complete a *factura de exportación*, for which they must show their tourist card (*see p314*). In some cases, restaurant and excursions charges are exempt from IVA for guests who pay through their hotel bills. To avoid confusion, it is best to ask whether hotel rates are *con IVA* (with taxes) or *sin IVA* (without).

Currency

The Chilean peso, the nation's official currency, has a symbol ($) similar to that of the US dollar (US$). There should be no confusion between the two, however, as a single Chilean peso is worth very little. This unit was further divided into 100 centavos, but, since 1984, inflation has rendered the centavo obsolete and these coins are no longer in circulation. For Chile's bicentennial year of 2010, the government planned to introduce $20 and $200 coins, but there was not enough

enthusiasm for the project, so it never came to fruition.

It is best to carry some small banknotes and coins for minor purchases, particularly for services such as city buses and taxis. This becomes necessary in rural areas, where many businesses do not have large amounts of cash on hand. The custom at most shops is to round up prices to the nearest $10. A thousand pesos is known as one *luca*, a slang term that helps make large amounts of cash more comprehensible.

Coins

Peso coins occur in denominations of $500, $100, $50, $10 and $5. While $1 and $5 coins still exist, they are uncommon and almost worthless.

10 pesos

50 pesos

100 pesos

500 pesos

1,000 pesos

Banknotes (Bills)

Issued in denominations of $1,000, $2,000, $5,000, $10,000, and $20,000, banknotes usually bear portraits of national heroes. In commemoration of the bicentennial of the Republic, new notes were released between 2009 and 2012, with a different look and dimensions.

2,000 pesos

5,000 pesos

10,000 pesos

20,000 pesos

Communications and Media

In Chile, media and communications services are well developed and modern. The telephone is the most versatile means of communication. While public telephones, operated by coins and cards, are still common, cell phones have become increasingly popular. Internet services are readily available throughout the country, even in remote areas. The mail delivery network is reasonably efficient, but private courier services are a quicker alternative. Chile has innumerable television networks and radio stations. Santiago and other major cities have multiple dailies; however, English-language newspapers and magazines are conspicuous by their absence.

Callers at one of Santiago's public phone booths

Telephones

There is no single national telecommunications agency in Chile. Instead there are several competing companies known as *portadores* or carriers. Of these service providers, **Movistar** and **Entel** are the largest. Each individual agency has its own public and private telephones, phone cards, and a specific three-digit access code. To make a call from a phone owned by a particular company, you can use the phone card of any other carrier service by dialing its access code. However, no access code needs to be dialed if the card belongs to the same company as the phone. Instructions, in Spanish, are written on each phone card. While an increasing number of public phones accept only fixed-value or rechargeable phone cards, many also accept pesos. The basic rate for a local call is 100 pesos for 5 minutes. Phone cards can be purchased from news kiosks, pharmacies, and most stores, and can be used for local cell phones as well.

It is easy to make national and international calls from *centros de llamados*, or call centers, found throughout the country. In most cases, users can enter the booth and dial directly, but in some centers, an on-site operator is available to connect the call.

While many hotels have telephones, the cost of making calls through their switchboards can be high. It is possible to make *cobro revertido* (collect or reverse charge) and *tarjeta de crédito* (credit card) calls from public and private telephones, but these can be substantially more expensive than using the *centros de llamados*. It is especially expensive to make overseas collect and credit card calls from the conspicuous bright blue telephones found across the country.

Cell Phones

Cell phones are the most popular means of communication in Chile and have, in fact, exceeded the number of landlines. Cell phone coverage, however, can be weak in thinly populated areas such as the Atacama desert and Patagonia, and in areas of rugged terrain. While most international cellular services also work in Chile, overseas visitors should first check whether their service providers offer coverage in this country. A majority of network operators offer roaming facilities, but this often entails higher outgoing and incoming rates, as well as paying a substantial premium. While quad-band phones (supporting four frequency bands) from abroad continue to work in Chile, tri-band phones (supporting three frequency bands) may have limited coverage. Visitors are advised to keep their network operator's helpline number handy for emergencies and carry the insurance papers of their

Dialing Codes

- In Chile, telephone numbers have one- or two-digit area codes and seven- or eight-digit local numbers.
- To call Chile from abroad, dial the international access code, followed by Chile's country code (56), the area code, and the local number.
- Cell phone numbers have the prefix 07, 08, and, most frequently, 09, followed by eight digits. Calls between cell phones, as well as between local landlines within the same area code, do not require dialing a prefix.
- To make a regional call, dial the area code (where necessary), followed by the local number.
- To make an international call, dial the carrier code (where necessary), followed by 0, then the country code, area code, and number.
- For directory inquiries, dial 103.

phone in case of loss or theft. Local SIM cards are easily available and many travelers prefer to either hire or buy a cell phone.

Internet, Email, and Fax Facilities

Cybercafés can be found across Chile, and most establishments also offer *banda ancha* (broadband) and wireless Internet access. The north of the country has reliable internet connection, however lack of fibre optic causes disruption as one moves towards south of the country. Although unreliable, Santiago's international airport has free Wi-Fi. Most hotels and hostels include Wi-Fi in their rates. High-end international chain hotels may charge extra for Internet access, but their Chilean counterparts generally do not. A number of *centros de llamados* offer Internet access at reasonable rates, usually by the hour.

Newspapers and Magazines

There are almost 7 national and 100 regional newspapers in Chile. While *El Mercurio* (*see p126*) is the country's major daily newspaper, it offers limited coverage of international news. *La Tercera*,

Entrance to a *centro de llamados* in Valparaíso

a tabloid daily, provides some competition, but the publishing phenomenon of the new millennium is *The Clinic*, a satirical weekly. *Estrategia* is the voice of Chile's business and financial community. Santiago lacks an English-language newspaper. A wide selection of non-Chilean magazines and papers is available at Santiago's airport.

Television and Radio

Chile has several television stations, most notably Televisión Nacional, owned by the government, and Canal 13, owned by one of the richest men in the country, Andronic Luksic. Cable television is found in most Chilean households and at restaurants, bars, and cafés. Most hotels also have cable TV installed in the rooms. However, an English-speaking station is rare.

Radio is quite popular in Chile. However, reception outside of towns and cities can be weak. There are over 20 FM stations broadcasting a variety of popular music and classical tunes.

Postal and Courier Services

Correos de Chile, the country's privatized postal service, has offices in every city and town. Although slow, it is reasonably reliable. Foreign visitors can

receive mail at any of their post offices via the *lista de correos* or by general delivery to their address. There are ample courier services in Chile. Along with the international **DHL** and **Federal Express**, the more affordable local **Chilexpress** has hundreds of offices and affiliates throughout the country. Courier services are a faster, although more expensive, alternative to Chile's postal system.

DIRECTORY

Telephones

Entel
w entel.cl

Movistar
w movistar.cl

Postal and Courier Services

Chilexpress
Avenida Providencia 1709, Santiago.
Tel (02) 2355-2500.
w chilexpress.cl

Correos de Chile
w correos.cl

DHL
Avenida Nueva Providencia 2070, Santiago.
Tel (02) 2666-2050.
w dhl.cl

Federal Express
Avenida Providencia 2519, Providencia, Santiago.
Tel (02) 2361-6000 (general information).
w fedex.com/cl

Magazines for sale at a kiosk in Valparaíso

TRAVEL INFORMATION

While most travelers arrive in Chile by air, overland crossings from neighboring Argentina – and to a lesser degree from Bolivia and Peru – are also fairly common. The airport at Santiago is served by major international airlines from across the world. Cruise ships connect ports such as Valparaíso with Buenos Aires in Argentina. Within the country, there are reliable air services from the Peruvian border in the north to the tip of Patagonia and to Easter Island, but it is usually necessary to change planes in Santiago. On land, passenger trains are few and slow but most main roads are paved and often excellent. High-quality bus services are frequent and car rentals are often useful. Traveling by ferry is most convenient in southern Chile.

Arriving by Air

Most overseas visitors arrive at **Aeropuerto Internacional Arturo Merino Benítez**, located 10 miles (17 km) northwest of Santiago. The airport is a state-of-the art facility, with flights that connect to other Chilean cities as well as to international destinations. Airports elsewhere in Chile only receive flights from neighboring countries, except Easter Island's Aeropuerto Mataveri, which is also accessible by flights from Tahiti and Australia.

The main international carrier is **LATAM Airlines**, which links Chile with Europe, North America, and the Pacific Islands. **Air France KLM**, **Air Europa**, and **Iberia** are popular European carriers, while important North American airlines include **Avianca**, **American Airlines**, **United Airlines**, **Delta Airlines**, and **Air Canada**. Continental Airlines partners with Panama's airline **Copa**, while **Qantas** flies from Australia and New Zealand.

Air Fares and Passes

In general, air fares to Chile are expensive, but prices vary seasonally and depend on how early tickets are booked. Fares are highest from mid-December to February and lowest during the winter months. Special packages and promotional fares may be available on airline and travel websites such as **Travelocity**, **Expedia**, and **Orbitz**. Apex tickets, booked well in advance, are cheaper than unrestricted tickets, but incur penalties for changes.

LATAM Airlines is part of the alliance of airlines called **One World** that offers a Visit South America pass. This can be used for a trip to Chile alone or to other countries in the continent as well.

Passengers arriving in Chile should have an onward ticket, but this regulation is rarely enforced. Combined airline and hotel packages are ideal for shorter trips.

Shuttle Services

Santiago-based operators such as **Transfer Delfos** and **Transvip** provide on-demand shuttle services from the capital's international airport. These vans accommodate between 4 and 5 passengers who travel to the same area in Santiago. Trips to the eastern boroughs of Providencia and Las Condes cost slightly more than those to downtown Santiago. A number of other cities also have airport shuttles, but most travelers rely on taxi services.

Shuttle van at Santiago's international airport

Aeropuerto Internacional Arturo Merino Benítez, near the capital Santiago

A cruise ship allowing passengers to explore a fjord in inflatable boats

Arriving by Land

Chile has numerous Andean crossings from Argentina, some of which are connected by comfortable buses. Of these crossings, the Los Libertadores pass, between Santiago and Mendoza, Argentina, has most of the traffic, but winter snow can close it for days at a time. Another busy route connects Osorno in the Lake District to the Argentine city of San Carlos de Bariloche via the Paso Cardenal Samoré, whose lower altitude keeps it open year round. Other overland crossings include the Paso de Jama from Chile's San Pedro de Atacama to Jujuy and Salta in Argentina; and the road from Punta Arenas to Río Gallegos in Argentina. During summer, the roads from Puerto Natales and Torres del Paine to El Calafate in Argentina experience heavy traffic.

The main routes to Bolivia are paved highways from the cities of Arica and Iquique to La Paz and Oruro, respectively, while the route from San Pedro de Atacama across the Bolivian salt flat Salar de Uyuni is a favorite with adventurous backpackers. Arica has convenient coastal highway crossings to and from the Peruvian city of Tacna.

Rented cars can be taken from Chile into Argentina and vice versa, but this requires additional paperwork and insurance coverage. It is even more difficult to rent a car from Bolivia or Peru into Chile, and vice versa.

Arriving by Sea

While there is no regular, scheduled maritime service to Chile, cruise ships sail down the Pacific coast from Peru, around Cape Horn to Argentina, Brazil, and back. Possible Chilean ports of call en route include Iquique, Arica, Antofagasta, Valparaíso, Puerto Montt, Coquimbo, Puerto Chacabuco, Puerto Natales, and Punta Arenas. It is possible to leave a cruise at any of these ports and continue overland.

Organized Tours

Many companies in North America, Europe, and the UK offer organized tours to Chile. The UK-based Journey Latin America (see p311), and the US-based **Pan American Travel Services** provide many custom-made packages across Chile. In addition, several reputed Chilean operators arrange a variety of deals. Organized tours generally comprise flight transfers, local transportation, accommodations, and guides.

Activity-oriented packages are the most common, with adventure tour agencies organizing everything from skiing, snowboarding, mountain-biking, hiking, surfing, white-water rafting, and wildlife-watching. Operators also arrange vineyard accommodations in Chile's fertile Central Valley, informative trips to Easter Island's archaeological resources, and stargazing excursions in San Pedro de Atacama.

DIRECTORY

Arriving by Air

Aeropuerto Internacional Arturo Merino Benítez
Casilla 79, Santiago.
Tel (02) 2690-1752.
W nuevopudahuel.cl

Air Canada
Tel (02) 2460-2206 (Canada & US).
W aircanada.com

Air Europa
Tel (02) 2938-1525.
W aireuropa.com

Air France KLM
Tel (02) 2580 9696.
W airfrance.com

American Airlines
Tel (02) 2679-0000.
W aa.com

Avianca
Tel 800 536 022.
W avianca.com

Copa
Tel (02) 2835-8200.
W copaair.com

Delta Airlines
Tel 800 202 020.
W delta.com

Iberia
Tel (34) 901 111 500 (Spain). W iberia.com

LATAM Airlines
Tel 1866 4359 526 (US).
W latam.com

Qantas
W qantas.com.au

United Airlines
Tel 2728-9300.
W united.com

Air Fares and Passes

Expedia
W expedia.com

One World
W oneworld.com

Orbitz
W orbitz.com

Travelocity
W travelocity.com

Shuttle Services

Transfer Delfos
Aeropuerto Internacional Arturo Merino Benítez, Santiago.
Tel (02) 2913-8800.
W transferdelfos.cl

Transvip
Aeropuerto Internacional Arturo Merino Benítez, Santiago. **Tel** (02) 2677-3000. W transvip.cl

Organized Tours

Pan American Travel Services
Tel 1800 364 4359 (US).
W panam-tours.com

Domestic Flights

Chile's boundaries, stretching from the tropics to the sub-Antarctic, but nowhere wider than 186 miles (300 km), make air travel the preferred mode of transportation. Flying between the northern and southern parts of the country usually requires changing planes in Santiago. The more isolated destinations in southern Chile can be reached on smaller planes run by regional airlines. Bargain fares can be found on most airline websites, which, in some instances, are updated on a weekly basis. In-flight services vary depending on the airline, with the national carrier providing amenities that live up to the highest international standards.

Passengers waiting for their flights at the airport in Arica

Domestic Airlines

There are two primary domestic airlines in Chile. Other airlines occasionally join the local market, but none of them has survived longer than a few years. At the forefront is LATAM Airlines (see p325), dominating at least 85 percent of the domestic market. LATAM offers the widest selection of flights and is also the only scheduled airline to Easter Island. **Sky Airline** has also managed to carve a niche for itself over the years, but has fewer flights and services.

Based in Santiago, **Lassa** and **Aerolíneas ATA** connect the city to Robinson Crusoe Island. Carriers such as **Aerocord**, **Aerotaxis del Sur**, and **Cielomaraustral** operate air taxis from Puerto Montt to Chaitén. Air taxi companies, including **Transportes Aéreos San Rafael**, offer services from Coyhaique in Northern Patagonia to lesser-known destinations such as the island settlement of Melinka, Parque Nacional Laguna San Rafael, Villa O'Higgins, and Cochrane. Small planes from

Puerto Montt depart for the Chiloé archipelago farther south. Based in Punta Arenas, **Aerovías DAP** offers flights to Porvenir, in Tierra del Fuego, and to Puerto Navarino and Chile's Antarctic base at Isla Rey Jorge, where they connect with smaller cruise ships sailing around the Antarctic peninsula.

Domestic Airports

The main airport is Santiago's busy Aeropuerto Internacional Arturo Merino Benítez (see p325). Other major mainland airports are located in **Arica**, **Iquique**, **La Serena**, **Calama**, and **Antofagasta** in Norte Grande and Norte Chico; **Temuco** and **Puerto Montt** in the Lake District; and **Punta Arenas** and **Coyhaique** in Patagonia.

Reservations

At both LATAM Airlines and Sky Airline it is easy to make reservations online. Electronic tickets are valid, but travelers need to carry a printout of the reservation or a copy of the confirming email. Websites of these two major airlines also offer bargain fares, but some of these deals may only be available for purchase in Chile. Most of the smaller airline companies also take bookings via phone or email, but reservations made in person or through a travel agent are the most reliable.

A LATAM Airlines plane on the runway of Easter Island's Aeropuerto Mataveri

Flight Duration Chart

1:15 = Duration in hours: minutes

Santiago					
2:45	Arica				
2:30	0:45	Iquique			
2:00	4:35	0:55	Antofagasta		
1:40	4:35	4:40	4:25	Puerto Montt	
4:00	8:05	6:10	2:20	2:10	Punta Arenas

Getting Around

Air travel across the length of the country entails flight transfers in certain cities. The chart reflects minimum flight times. Flying may take longer depending on available flight connections.

Family disembarking at Puerto Montt's airport

Checking In

The process of checking in at Chile's modern airports is similar to that at European or North American airports. Travelers need to carry their paper ticket or flight number and their passport in hand. It is advisable to arrive at least 60 minutes prior to departure at Santiago's large Aeropuerto Internacional Arturo Merino Benítez. This may not be required in the extremely efficient airports in other cities and at the informal aerodromes that are served by the smaller airlines.

Concessionary Fares

Children up to the age of two travel free, but are not entitled to a separate baggage allowance or their own seat. Those between two and eleven years pay around two-thirds of the fare and are entitled to the full baggage allowance.

Advance purchase can lower fares substantially. There are no direct discounts for students or senior citizens, but the Santiago-based **Student Flight Center** can arrange cheaper tickets for students and young adults.

Baggage Restrictions

On domestic flights, LATAM Airlines passengers can check in up to 50 lbs (23 kg) per person, plus one handbag and a personal item such as a laptop. Business class passengers on LATAM can check in up to three bags of 51 lbs (23 kg) each, plus one carry bag of up to 35 lbs (16 kg). Sky Airline passengers can check up to 45 lbs (20 kg) per person, plus one handbag weighing up to 11 lbs (5 kg). There is no business class seating on Sky Airline.

Smaller airlines, especially air taxis, have lower baggage weight limits. Airlines may charge extra for recreational equipment such as bicycles, surfboards, and skis in addition to penalties for exceeding the weight limit.

DIRECTORY

Domestic Airlines

Aerocord
Aerodromo La Paloma,
Puerto Montt.
Tel (065) 2246300.
W **aerocord.cl**

Aerolíneas ATA
Aeropuerto Arturo
Merino Benítez,
Santiago.
Tel (02) 2611-3670.
W **aerolineasata.cl**

Aerotaxis del Sur
Aeródromo Teniente
Vidal, Coyhaique.
Tel (09) 9256-2293.
W **aerotaxisdelsur.cl**

Aerovías DAP
O'Higgins 891,
Punta Arenas.
Tel (061) 2616100.
W **aeroviasdap.cl**

Cielomaustral
Quillota 254,
Puerto Montt.
Tel (065) 2263654.
W **cielomaustral.cl**

Lassa
Avenida Larraín 7941,
La Reina, Santiago.
Tel (02) 2273-1458.

Sky Airline
Santa Elena 1763,
Santiago. **Tel** 600 600
2828. W **skyairline.cl**

**Transportes Aéreos
San Rafael**
18 de Septiembre 469,
Coyhaique.
Tel (067) 2573083.

Domestic Airports

Antofagasta
Tel (055) 2254998.

Arica
Tel (058) 2212773.

Calama
Tel (02) 2222-8400.

Coyhaique
Tel (067) 2272126.

Iquique
Tel (057) 2473473.

Puerto Montt
Tel (065) 2294161.

Punta Arenas
Tel (061) 2238181.

La Serena
Tel (051) 2270353.

Temuco
Tel (045) 2201901.

Concessionary Fares

Student Flight Center
Antonio Bellet, 77,
Oficina101, Providencia.
Tel (02) 2577-1200.
W **studentfc.cl**

Traveling Around Chile

While flying is an important mode of transportation in Chile, overland travel is also worth consideration, especially in the country's heartland. Overnight buses are comfortable and cost a fraction of flight prices. The best of them are air-conditioned and have onboard meal service and entertainment. Long-distance trains, which are few, are a slower option. An abundance of city buses known as *micros*, taxis, and *colectivos* or shared taxis make getting around cities and towns cheap and efficient. In the Lake District and archipelagic south, ferries are an indispensable part of the transportation system.

A brightly painted and spacious overnight bus

Buses

Long-distance coaches have several categories of service. The most basic have reclining seats and are adequate for 3- or 4-hour trips. With seats that recline almost horizontally and greater leg room, *semi-cama*, (semi-bed) and *salón cama* (full-bed) buses are ideal for overnight travel. Longer trips can be a little tiring, but include meals, snacks, and drinks on board; the buses may also stop en route for meals. Shorter trips, particularly in some rural areas, may require taking buses that are smaller and cramped. Private buses also take visitors to specific destinations.

For instance, **Expediciones Manzur** provides transport to various attractions in the Cajón del Maipo.

Most cities and towns have central bus terminals, but individual companies may also have their own separate departure points. In general, these terminals are safe, although they can be dreary and congested. Fortunately, it is only necessary to arrive 20 minutes before departure time.

Trains

The Empresa de Ferrocarriles del Estado or EFE *(see p97)* is the state-run railroad system, whose long-distance services, although inexpensive, are slower and less efficient than those offered by privately run bus systems. However, southbound commuter trains from Santiago to Rancagua and San Fernando offer good service. Operated by the EFE, TerraSur trains make the 5-hour trip, five times daily, between Santiago and Chillán in the Central Valley, with a bus link to Concepción. One of Chile's greatest rail experiences is traveling by the meter-gauge train on the short Buscarril line connecting Talca with the beach resort of Constitución.

Ferries and Catamarans

Traveling by catamarans or ferries is a crucial means of getting around in the Lake District and Patagonia, where roads and highways are interrupted by large waterbodies. In Northern Patagonia, the most useful services are **Navimag**'s overnight ferries that depart from Puerto Montt to Puerto Chacabuco, and the 3-day ferry to Puerto Natales, the gateway to Parque Nacional Torres del Paine *(see pp246–9)*. From Puerto Chacabuco, catamaran services sail to Parque Nacional Laguna San Rafael *(see p237)* on day trips. Also starting from Puerto Montt, and sometimes from Quellón on Chiloé's Isla Grande, **Naviera Austral** serves the port of Chaitén. There is also a bus–ferry shuttle from Puerto Montt and Hornopirén to Caleta Gonzalo, the northern access point to Parque Pumalín *(see p230)*, continuing to Chaitén on the Ruta Bimodal. Shuttle ferries connect the mainland town of Pargua in the Lake District with Isla Grande and the hamlets of La Arena and Puelche, located southeast of Puerto Montt.

In Southern Patagonia, **Transbordadora Austral Broom** provides a ferry service from Punta Arenas to Porvenir, on the Chilean side of Tierra del Fuego. It also has ferries that shuttle buses, cars, and passengers across the Strait of Magellan at Primera Angostura, located northeast of Punta Arenas.

Those who wish to travel to Argentina *(see pp256–7)* can also

One of Empresa de Ferrocarriles del Estado's long-distance trains

take ferries to certain border points. At Puerto Yungay, on the southernmost part of the Carretera Austral, a free public ferry shuttles vehicles on the Mitchell fjord to Villa O'Higgins, where a seasonal catamaran carries hikers to a border post with overland connections to El Chaltén in Argentina. A ferry from Puerto Fuy crosses Lago Pirihueico to Puerto Pirihueico, the link to the Argentine city of San Martín de los Andes. **Cruce Andino** is a bus-catamaran-bus shuttle that crosses the Andes from Puerto Montt and Puerto Varas to the city of Bariloche in Argentina.

Driving

Stretching from the Peruvian border to Puerto Montt and Chiloé, Chile's improving highway network is ideal for driving. There is a four-lane highway from La Serena in the Norte Chico to Puerto Montt in Patagonia and many excellent, but sometimes narrow, secondary roads. The main highways are all toll roads and, in Santiago, they require either an electronic permit or a daily fee permit. These are available with most rental cars or can be bought up to 48 hours after entering the network. Daily passes can be bought online at **Servipag**. Chile's Gringo Trail has been a favorite with visitors, particularly backpackers, for many decades. It includes the country's popularly traveled areas from San Pedro de Atacama to Santiago, parts of the Lake District, and Torres del Paine in Patagonia. Today, this area can be explored by driving over scenic roads and highways. Much of the southerly Carretera Austral, Chile's most exciting drive through the forested Andes, is still narrow, with loose gravel and blind curves in its wildest segments. It does not require a 4WD, as long as drivers are careful. There are no SOS phones and cell phone coverage is spotty at best, but people will stop to help in case of accidents. Drivers on this highway must, by law, carry warning triangles that indicate

Driving on the Carretera Austral in Northern Patagonia

an accident or car breakdown, a fire extinguisher, and a first-aid kit.

Driving is on the right, and all passengers are required to wear seat belts. There are firm laws about driving under the influence of alcohol or drugs.

Renting Cars

International rental companies such as **Avis** and **Hertz** have affiliates in major cities. In addition, there are numerous local companies, including **Verschae, Free Rent a Car** and **Seelmann**, that rent cars at cheaper rates. Unlimited mileage rates are the rule but prices are usually higher in Chile than in the US or Europe. A client must be at least 21 years old and have a driver's license, passport, and credit card. In theory, an international driving permit is required, but this is almost never enforced. The rental agency must provide the car's ownership documents, which need to be presented at police request. In general, deductibles are high on rental car insurance policies – as much as 20 percent of the vehicle's value. Cross-border rentals require a power of attorney and additional insurance.

Green Travel

Public awareness about green travel is not widespread in Chile, but it is a practical concern for many in a country with high oil prices and levels of pollution. While increasing prosperity has led many Chileans to buy cars, traveling by metro in Santiago, Valparaíso, and Viña del Mar is faster, cheaper, and eco-friendly. The Transantiago bus network in the capital also covers tremendous ground. Chile's rail

network is not too efficient, but long-distance buses are frequent, comfortable, and quick. An overnight sleeper bus is often cheaper and more environmentally friendly than a flight, and also reduces hotel costs. Nevertheless, great distances make flights essential, particularly on longer trips and over water.

Tour agents (see p311) are conscious of the environment. Patagonia's tour operators, for instance, are outspoken defenders of the region's natural resources.

New hotels also have state-of-the-art insulation that lessens their carbon footprint. Some, especially in desert areas, have low-consumption toilets and showers that reduce water usage.

General Index

Acknowledgments

Dorling Kindersley would like to thank the many people whose help and assistance contributed to the preparation of this book.

Contributors
Wayne Bernhardson has been visiting Chile for more than three decades. He has written extensively for newspapers, magazines, and guidebooks including Moon Handbooks, Lonely Planet, and National Geographic Traveler. Wayne has also co-authored the DK Eyewitness Guide to Argentina.

Declan McGarvey is a travel writer and journalist based in Buenos Aires, where he has lived since 1999. He is the co-author of the *Eyewitness Guide to Argentina* and of the *Eyewitness Top 10 Guide to Buenos Aires*, and has also contributed to DK's *Where to Go When* series.

Kristina Schreck moved to Chile in 1998 following several years as editor of *Adventure Journal* magazine. She has since worked in every aspect of the travel industry, as a trekking guide in Patagonia, travel writer and author of the first edition of Frommer's *Chile & Easter Island*, and as the head of media relations for the Chilean tourism board.

Cartography
The maps on pages 59, 79, 87, and 106–112 are derived from © www.openstreetmap.org and contributors, licensed under CC-BY-SA; see www.creativecommons.org for further details.

Fact Checker Rodrigo Cabezas
Editorial Consultant Nick Rider
Proofreaders Kathryn Glendenning, Janice Pariat
Indexers Hilary Bird, Vanessa Bird
Design and Editorial
Publisher Douglas Amrine
List Manager Vivien Antwi
Project Art Editor Shahid Mahmood
Project Editor Michelle Crane
Senior Cartographic Editor Casper Morris
Jacket Design Tessa Bindloss, Stephen Bere
Senior DTP Designer Jason Little
Senior Picture Researcher Ellen Root
Production Controller Rebecca Short

Revisions Team Namrata Adhwaryu, Vicki Allen, Marta Bescos, Subhadeep Biswas, Louise Cleghorn, Thomas Connelly, Rebecca Flynn, Fay Franklin, Anna Kaminski, Sumita Khatwani, Carly Madden, Hayley Maher, Shafik Meghji, Lucy Richards, Akanksha Siwach, Sands Publishing Solutions, Ankita Sharma, Neil Simpson, Joanna Stenlake, Anna Streiffert, Hollie Teague, Priyanka Thakur, Ana Patricia Luna Tomás, Ed Wright

Additional Photography Geoff Brightling, Tony Briscoe, Demetrio Carrasco, Frank Greenaway, Nigel Hicks, Dave King, Greg Roden, Rough Guides / Tim Draper, Jerry Young, Ian O'Leary Studios

Design Assistance Janice Utton

Special Assistance Dorling Kindersley would like to thank the following for their assistance: Lawrence Lamonica at Lapis Lazuli House, Aya Nishimura from Hers Agency, and Preeti Pant.

Photography Permission
Dorling Kindersley would like to thank the following for their assistance and kind permission to photograph at their establishments:
Bar La Playa, Basilica y Museo de la Merced, Biblioteca de Santiago, Biblioteca Nacional, Bolsa de Comercio, Cancellería, Casa Museo Isla Negra, Casino Español in Iquique, Catedral Metropolitana, Centro Cultural Estación Mapocho, Centro Cultural Palacio La Moneda, Cerro Central, Iglesia de San Francisco in Chiu Chiu, Iglesia de Santo Domingo, Hotel Indigo and Spa, Isabel Aninat Galleria, Lagos in Patagonia, Mamiña Hot Springs, Mercado Central, Museo Chileno de Arte Precolombino, Museo de Colchagua in Santa Cruz, Museo de la Moda, Museo de Santiago in Casa Colorada, Museo Ferroviaria Pablo Neruda, Museo Ferroviario, Museo Muncipal Juan Pablo II, Museo Nacional de Bellas Artes, Museo Nacional de Historia Natural, Marítimo Nacional, Museo Regional Braun Menendez, Palacio Cousiño, Palacio de los Tribunales de Justicia, Puyuhupai Lodge & Spa, Teatro Municipal, Termas de Socos, Hotel Zero, Zona Franca Zofri.

Picture Credits
Key: a-above; b-below/bottom; c-center; f-far; l-left; r-right; t-top.

Works of art have been reproduced with the kind permission of the following copyright holders:
Absent Feet Airmail Painting No. 153 2002-03 tincture, photo-silkscreen, sateen, and stitching on 4 sections of duck fabric 82 x 220 1/2 in/ 210 x 560 cm, courtesy of the artist and Alexander and Bonin, New York © Eugenio Dittborn 32bl; *New Nature I* and *New Nature II* © Pedro Tyler 57crb; *Fotografo II*, 2008, Ed 6 Originales Alto 165cms, Base 55 x 33cms, Height 65 x 21 x 11/16 x 13 in © Aurora Cañero 99cb; *Historia de Concepción*, Gregorio de la Fuente © Pablo de la Fuente 156br.

The publisher would like to thank the following individuals, companies, and picture libraries for their kind permission to reproduce their photographs:

© **Unesco**: CODELCO 149bc, 149cra. **123RF.com**: Ekaterina Pokrovsky 252-253. **4Corners**: H P Huber 258. **Eduardo Abasolo**: 198cla, 199tl. **Alamy Images**: Alaska Stock LLC / John Hyde 25br; Arco Images /Stengert, N. 154bc; The Art Archive/ Gianni Dagli Orti 46clb; Roussel Bernard 20t, 130–31cl; Blickwinkel/ Brehm 23br; Cephas Picture Library/ Matt Wilson153cla; Chile /Chris Howarth 94bl; Chile DesConocido 161bl, 185tl, 218br; Danita Delimont 297tr; Dennis Cox 152tr; Creative Trails 173tr; Jan Csernoch 169bl; Celso Diniz 314cl; Eagle Visions Photography/ Craig Lovell 26crb; Reiner Elsen 86, 293br; Peter Flaco 291bc; David R. Frazier Photolibrary, Inc. 320cl; GM Photo Images 161b; Fabian Gonzales Editorial 25cr, 289c; FAN travelstock 183t; Chris Gomersall 22crb; Blaine Harrington III 27cra; Hemis.fr 103b,/ Hughes Hervé 191b, 293tl; Nigel Hicks 301br; Marla Holden 263cr; Chris Howarth / Chile 12tc; Ildi.Travel.Chile 302bl; Imagebroker 22cla/Christian Handl 214clb/Nico Stengert 32tr; Infocusphotos.com/ Malie Rich-Griffith 161b; Interfoto 26br, 49br; John Warburton-Lee Photography 35tl; Mooney-Kelly 298br; Russell Kord 22tr, 324b; Karol Kozlowski Premium RM Collection 290bc; Frans Lemmens 255c; Keith Levit 275crb; Yadid Levy 39tl, 39c; LOOK Die Bildagentur der Fotografen GmbH/ Michael Boyny 35cra,/ Hauke Dressler 17br; Chris Mattison 224bl; Yannis Emmanuel Mavromatakis 247cla; Megapress 96br; Randy Mehoves 289bl; Florian Neukirchen 197b; Newzulu 304cra, 316tr; Nifro Travel Images 203tc; North Wind Picture Archives 46bl, 139br; M. Timothy O'Keefe 8-9; Astrid Padberg 264cr; Photoshot Holdings Ltd 198bc; Picture Contact/ Jochem Wijnands 26bl, 74tl; Sergio Pitamitz 25clb, 241b; Leonid Plotkin 116tr, 119b; Radharc Images 299br; StockShot/ Dan Milner 35br; Top-Pics TBK 246cla; MARCELO DE LA TORRE 305tl; travelbild.com 14tc; V1 41tr; Simon Vine 127cl; David Wall 285br; John G. Walter 123tl; Wide Eye Pictures 37clb; WoodyStock/ Begsteiger 41b; World History Archive 47br; Fernando Zabala 215tl. **Alto Atacama**: 279br; Hector Hugo Gutierrez Alvarado: 48bc. **Alexander and Bonin**: Bill Orcutt 32bl. **Altos De Lircay**: 155bl. **Atacama Photo**: Gerhard Huedepohl 4-5tc, 24cl, 24br, 24bl, 248cl, 259b, 261t, 269cl, 269br. **The Aubrey**: 277tr. **Carolina Alicia Dagach Avila**: 104tl. **AWASI - San Pedro De ATACAMA**: 275tr. **AWL Images**: Paul Harris 118; Karol Kozlowski 285tl. **Bio Bio Expeditions**: 5cra, 231tl, 308tc. **The Bridgeman Art Library**: Naval Combat beween the Peruvian

Ship 'Huascar' against the Chilean 'Blanco Encalada' and the 'Cochrane' in 1879, Monleon y Torres, Rafael (1847-1900) / Private Collection / Index 49fclb. **La Casona:** 295br. **Centro De Ski Araucarias:** 198clb. **Joao Colella:** 223br. **Colibri Music:** 29crb. **Niall Corbet:** 147t. **Corbis:** Lucien Aigner 29tl; Bettmann 30bc, 48br, 51ctc, 51crb; Julio Donoso 224cla; Ric Ergenbright 266clb; Martin Harvey 34tr; Blaine Harrington III 22cl; Jon Hicks 81tl; Dave G. Houser 242b; Masterfile / Graham French 78./ R. Ian Lloyd 212-213. NewSport/ Chris Trotman 34bc; Gregg Newton 52tl; Jonathan Selkowitz 35bl; Hubert Stadler 23cr, 210b; Sygma/Sophie Bassouls 30tr,/Carlos Carrion 51br,/Diego Goldberg 52bc,/Thierry Orban 34cr; Xinhua Press/ Zhang Yuwei 34bl. **Danita Delimont Stock Photography:** Bill Bachmann 40tr; Ric Ergenbright 27bl; Wendy Kaveney/ Jaynes Gallery 36bc, 288cl; John Warburton-Lee 221b.
Dawsonlapelicula.cl: 255tc. **Juan Eduardo Donoso:** 319tr.
Marcela Donoso: 219cla, 219crb, 219cb. **Dreamstime.com:** Steve Allen 226; Andreviegas 240; Maciej Bledowski 4cb; Byvalet 234-235; Francisco Javier Espuny 5cr; Alexandre Fagundes De Fagundes 270-271; Marcelo Vildósola Garrigó 37cra, 195tl; Alejandro Gherardi 306cl; Ildipapp 296bc; Michal Knitl 114-115; Jesse Kraft 70-71; Larissapereira 29clb; Marconi Couto De Jesus 176-177; Ghm Meuffels 13tl, 15tr; Dmitry Pichugin 4crb; Kelly Price 15br; Kseniya Ragozina 244b. **Ejecutiva Comercial Hoteles Huilo Huilo:** La Montana Magica Hotel 205br. **Elqui Domos:** 275cra. **Endémica Expediciones:** 308bl. **Paz Errazuriz:** 65cr. **Explora:** 273tc, 283tr. **Caroline Fink:** 147bl. **Fotoscopio Latin America Stock Photo Agency:** 37bc. **Pablo De La Fuente:** 156br. **Fundación Artesanias De Chile:** 10tc, 19c, 32cb, 32clb, 32fclb, 98cl, 158tr, 158ctr, 158bc, 158br, 159tr, 159tc, 159cr, 159clb, 159bl, 159bc. **Fundación Sewell:** 148cla, 149crb. **German Del Sol - Arquitecto:** 204tl. **Getty Images:** AFP /Staff/ Pablo Porciuncula 53bc,/Martin Bernetti 35cl, 3/crb, 53cr, 53crb, 144tl,/ Maurico Lima 34cla,/Pedro Ugarte 53tl; AFP/ STF 51bl,/ STR/ Stringer 199bc; AFP/ Stringer 36tr,/ Raul Bravo 288bc, 327cl/ David Lillo 36-7c; Aurora/ Bernardo Gimenez 231cr; FoodPix/ Sheridan Stancliff 36bl; Gems/ Redferns 29tr; Krzysztof Dydynski 102bc; The Image Bank/ Frans Lemmens 306br ,/Eastcott Momatiuk 117br; John Warburton-Lee 231bc; Kean Collection/ Staff/ Archive Photos 47ca; Lonely Planet Images/ Bethune Carmichael 116cl; Agencia Makro / CON 3/tl; Jason Merritt 305cb; National Geographic/ Stephen Alvarez 267crb,/Joel Sartore 22bl; Popperfoto 34cb, David Redfern 21ca; STF / Gabriel Rossi 92br; HECTOR RETAMAL 103tr; VICTOR ROJAS 137tl; Travel Ink/ Gallo Images 137br, 179tc, 326cla; Carlos Vera 304bl. **Andrew Gould:** 130br. **The Granger Collection, New York:** 151cla. **Hacienda Los Andes:** 307br. **Isabel Aninat Galeria De Arte:** 57crb. **iStockphoto. com:** billyfoto 54-55; Piet Veltman 139c. **François Jolly:** 328br. **La Sonora Palacios:** 29cl. **Lapis Lazuli House:** 303cla, 303ca, 303cr, 303fcr, 303cra, 303fclb, 303cl, 303c, 303cb, 303cra, 303fcrb, 303fbl, 303bl, 303br, 303fbr. **Lapostolle:** 153clb; Clos Apalta Winery 151bl, 273cl, 310tl. **Latin Photo:** Felipe Gonzalez V. 28bl, 39br; Nicolas Nadjar 158cl; Ely Negri 29cr. **Marco Lillo:** 32cr, 103b. **Lindsay Simmonds Design:** 215br. **Lonely Planet Images:** John Elk III 225tl; Oliver Strewe Randy Mehovestl. **Los Huasos Quincheros:** 29bc. **Magical Andes Photography:** James Brunker 23cl. **Mary Evans Picture Library:** Aisa Media 44. **MASTERFILE:** Graham French 88tr. **Restaurante Martin Pescador:** 299tr. **Declan Mcgarvey:** 158clb. **Montgras Properties:** 152cl. **Mumbai-Lima:** 297br.

Museo Historica Nacional De Chile: 50tl. **MUSEO NACIONAL DE BELLAS ARTES, Chile:** Colección Museo Nacional de Bellas Artes de Santiago de Chile 32br. **Noi Hotels:** 275cla. **Santiago Rios Pacheco:** 154tl. **Gregory Panayotou:** 266cla. **Peter Langer/Associated Media Group:** 28crb, 130clb, 131crb, 148tr. **Peumayén:** 292tc. **Photographers Direct:** Alimdi.net/ Thomas Muller 202br. **Photolibrary:** 140–41; age fotostock/ Wojtek Buss 268clb; Armytage/ Anne Green 205cb; Wojtek Buss 20bl; Rob Crandall 21br; Denkou Images 255bb; Fresh Food Images/ Steven Morris Photography 22cr; Garden Picture Library/ J S Sira 23cb; Oliver Gerhard 249tl; Christian Handl 56cla; Paul Harris 27crb; Imagebroker.net/ Oliver Gerhard 210tc,/Sepp Puchinger 28tr,/ Nico Stengert 169crb, 169tl; John Warburton-Lee Photography 146tl,/Paul Harris 151br, 230br,192tr, 214br/ Nick Laing 272cl/ John Warburton-Lee 246clb, 254tl,/Diego Martin 11br; Jon Arnold Travel/ Michele Falzone 11tl; Christophe Lehenaff 181br; Lonely Planet Images/ Grant Dixon 199cr,/ Richard I'Anson 130cl,/ Paul Kennedy 150bl,/Oliver Strewe 97tl; Mary Evans Picture Library 46br, 47cb, 49tr, 65tl, 269bl; Aris Mihich 202cl; Laurence Mouton 42cla; Peter Arnold Images/ James L Amos 267cra,/Fred Bruemmer 268b, 269tr,/Alexandra Edwards 45br,/Kevin Schafer 249c,/Gunter Ziesler 23fbr; Photononstop/ Bruno Barbier 214cla,/Marc Vérin 322cl; Pixtal Images 11b, 265b, 266tr; The Print Collector 50cb; Robert Harding Travel/ Ken Gillham 220cla,/ Geoff Renner 96cl,/Marco Simoni 198tr, 249br/Michael Snell 57bl,/Tony Waltham 25t; Robin Smith 251tc; Tips Italia/ Wojtek Buss 263tc,/Paolo Olaco 1c; Wave 203crb; White /Medio Images 38br; Bob Wickham 10cra. **Photoshot:** C2070 Rolf Haid 134bc; UPPA 91tc; World Pictures 192bl. **The Picture Desk: The Art Archive:** Museo Nacional de Historia Lima / Dagli Orti 49clb; The Kobal Collection: Cine Experimental de La Universdad de Chile 31br. **David Pin:** 56clb. **DON PORTER:** 131tl. **Private Collection:** 45clb, 50br. **Qantas Airways Limited: Javiera Quenaya:** 4hr, 36cl. **RANCHO-DE-CABALLOS:** 203bl. **Random House Mondadori:** 30cl. **ALVARO RIVAS.** 197tr. **Robert Harding Picture Library:** Barbara Boensch 294br; Blaine Harrington 18; Peter Langer 58; Robert Seitz 312-313. **South American Pictures:** Robert Francis 40bl; Sue Mann 38cl; Tony Morrison 26cl; Karen Ward 27tc; Rebecca Whitfield 26tr. **SuperStock:** Hemis.fr 219tr. **Vasile Tomoiaga:** 27cl. **Topfoto.co.uk:** Chilepic/ Rose Deakin 28cl. **Travel-Images.com:** Craig Lovell 202tr, 323bl. **Turtransfer:** 324c. **Valle Chacabuco:** 280br. **Vina Casas Del Bosque:** 142cl, 289br. **Viu Manent:** 152br, 153crb. **W Santiago:** 276bc. **WIKIPEDIA, The Free Encyclopedia:** 48t. **www.macondo.cl:** Clara Salina 31c.

Front Endpaper: Left: 4Corners: H P Huber cl; **AWL Images:** Paul Harris tl; **Dorling Kindersley:** Rough Guides / Tim Draper tc, bc.
Right: Alamy Images: Reiner Elsen c; **Corbis:** Masterfile / Graham French tr; **Dreamstime.com:** Steve Allen bc,/ Andreviegas br. **Robert Harding Picture Library:** Peter Langer tc.

Cover images: Front: Alamy Images: Inge Johnsson. **Back: Dreamstime.com:** Gábor Kovács. **Spine: Alamy Images:** Inge Johnsson.

All other images © Dorling Kindersley
For further information see: www.dkimages.com

Phrase Book

Chileans themselves sometimes apologize for speaking bad Spanish, and anyone who has learned the language elsewhere may find it a challenge. Still, it is fairer to say that, given the country's geographical isolation, Spanish simply developed differently here. Additionally, because of Mapuche influence, there are many non-standard words, and pronunciation can also be difficult.

Chileans often omit the terminal "s," making it difficult for outsiders to distinguish singular from plural, and sometimes even the internal "s." On the tongue of a Chilean, for instance, las escuelas (the schools) may sound more like "la ecuela." Similarly, Anglicisms such as "show" sound more like "cho" in local speech.

In everyday informal speech, Chileans may also use non-standard verb forms. For instance, second-person familiar verbs often end in an accented "í," as in "¿Querí?" (Do you want?) rather than the conventional "¿Quieres?".

Some Special Chilean words

carrete	kahrehteh	party
chupe	choopeh	a seafood stew
completo	kohmplehtoh	Chilean hot dog
copa	kohpah	glass (of wine)
galería	gahlehree-ah	shopping mall
oficina	ohfeeseenah	office; in the Atacama nitrate-mining towns
parcela	pahrsaylah	country home or small farm
parrilla	pahreeyah	grill restaurant
paseo	pahsayoh	pedestrian mall

In an Emergency

Help!	¡Socorro!	sokorro
Stop!	¡Pare!	pareh
Call a doctor!	¡Llamen un médico!	yamen oon mehdeeko
Call an ambulance	¡Llamen a una ambulancia	yamen a oona amboolans-ya
Police!	¡Policía!	poleesee-a
I've been robbed	Me robaron	meh robaron
Where is the nearest hospital?	¿Dónde queda el hospital más cercano?	dondeh keda el ospeetal mas sairkano
Could you help me?	¿Me puede ayudar?	meh pwedeh a-yoodar

Communication Essentials

Yes	Sí	see
No	No	no
Please	Por favor	por fabor
Pardon me	Perdone	pairdoneh
Excuse me	Disculpe	deeskoolpeh
I'm sorry	Lo siento	lo s-yento
Thanks	Gracias	gras-yas
Hello!	¡Hola!	o-la
Good morning	Buenos días	bwenos dee-as
Good afternoon	Buenas tardes	bwenas tardes
Good evening	Buenas noches	bwenas noches
Night	Noche	nocheh

Morning	Mañana	man-yana
Tomorrow	Mañana	man-yana
Yesterday	Ayer	a-yair
Here	Acá	aka
What?	¿Cómo?	komo
When?	¿Cuándo?	kwando
Where?	¿Dónde?	dondeh
Why?	¿Por qué?	por keh
How are you?	¿Cómo está?	komo estah
Very well, thank you	Muy bien, gracias	mwee byen gras-yas
Pleased to meet you	Encantado/a/ mucho gusto	enkantad o/a/ moocho goosto

Useful Phrases

That's great!	¡Qué bien!	keh b-yen
Do you speak English?	¿Habla usted Ingles?	abla oo-sted eenglehs
I don't understand	No entiendo	no ent-yendo
Could you speak more slowly?	¿Puede hablar más despacio?	pwedeh ablar mas despas-yo
I agree/okay	De acuerdo/bueno	deh akwairdo/ bweno
Let's go!	¡Vámonos!	bamonos
How do I get to/ which way to...?	¿Cómo se llega a...?/¿Por dónde se va a...?	komo se llega a/por dondeh seh ba a

Useful Words

large	grande	grandeh
small	pequeño	peken-yo
hot	caliente	kal-yenteh
cold	frío	free-o
good	bueno	bweno
bad	malo	malo
sufficient	suficiente	soofees-yenteh
open	abierto	ab-yairto
closed	cerrado	serrah-do
entrance	entrada	entrada
exit	salida	saleeda
full	lleno	yeno
right	derecha	dairehcha
left	izquierda	eesk-yairda
straight on	derecho	dehrehcho
above	arriba	arreeba
quickly	rápido	rahpidoh
early	temprano	temprahno
late	tarde	tardeh
now	ahora	a-ora
soon	pronto	pronto
less	menos	menos
much	mucho	moocho
in front of	delante	delanteh
opposite	enfrente	enfrenteh
behind	detrás	detrahs
second floor	segundo piso	segoondo peeso
ground floor	primer piso	preemair peeso
bar	bar	bar
discoteque	boliche	bohleecheh
lift/elevator	ascensor	asensor
bathroom	baño	ban-yo
toilet paper	papel higiénico	papel eeh-yeneeko
bribe	coima	koyma
girl/woman	mina	meena
women	mujeres	moohaires
men	hombres	ombres
child (boy/girl)	niño/niña	neen-yo, neen-yah
camera	cámara	kamara
batteries	pilas	peelas
passport	pasaporte	pasaporteh
visa	visa	beesa
tourist card	tarjeta turística	tarheta tooreesteeka

driver's license	licencia de conducir	leesensyah de condooseer
thief	ladrón	lahdrohn
cop	carabinero	ka-ra-bin-air-oh
money	dinero	deenehroh
lazy	flojo	flohoh
mess	lío	lee-oh
shanty town	callampa	kayahmpah
to eat	comer	koh-mehr
to steal	robar	rohbahr
to back away	arrugar	ahroogahr
to put up with	soportar	sohportahr
No way	¡De ningun manera!	Day neengoonah manehra

Health

I don't feel well	No me siento bien	No meh s-yento been
I have a stomach ache/ headache.	Me duele el estómago/ la cabeza	meh dweleh el estohmago/ la kabesa
He/she is ill	Está enfermo/a	esta enfairmo/a
I need to rest	Necesito decansar	neseseeto deskansar

Post Offices and Banks

I'm looking for a...	Busco una...	boosko oona
bureau de change	casa de cambio	kasa deh kamb-yo
What is the dollar rate?	¿A cuánto está el dólar?	a kwantoh esta el dohlar
I want to send a	Quiero enviar una	k-yairo en-vyar-oona
letter	carta	karta
postcard	postal	postal
stamp	estampilla	estampee-ya
withdraw money	sacar dinero	sakar deenairo

Shopping

I would like...	Me gustaría...	meh goostaree-a
I want...	Quiero...	k-yairo
Do you have any?	¿Tiene...?	t-yeneh
How much is it?	¿Cuánto cuesta?	kwanto kwesta
What time do you open/close?	¿A qué hora abre/ cierra?	a ke ora abreh/ s-yairra
May I pay with a credit card?	¿Puedo pagar con tarjeta de crédito?	pwedo pagar kon tarheta deh kredeeto
expensive	caro	karo

Sightseeing

beach	playa	pla ya
castle, fortress	castillo	kastee-yo
guide	guía	gee-a
hamlet	aldea	ahdayah
motorway	autopista	owtopeesta
neighborhood	barrio	bahreeoh
road	carretera	karretaira
street	calle	ka-yeh
tourist bureau	oficina de turismo	ofeeseena deh tooreesmo
town hall	municipalidad	mooneeseepaleedad

Getting Around

When does it leave?	¿A qué hora sale?	a keh ora saleh
When does the next train/bus leave for...?	¿A qué hora sale el próximo tren/ autobús a...?	a keh ora saleh el prokseemo tren/ owtoboos a
Could you call a taxi for me?	¿Me puede llamar un taxi?	meh pwedeh yamar oon taksee
departure gate	puerta de embarque	pwairta deh embarkeh
boarding pass	tarjeta de embarque	tarheta deh e embarkeh
customs	aduana	adwana
fare	tarifa	tareefa
insurance	seguro	segooro
car hire	alquiler de autos	alkeelair deh owtos
bicycle	bicicleta	beeseekleta
gas station	estación de servicio	estas-yon deh serveeseeoh
garage	garage	garaheh
I have a flat tire	Se me pinchó un neumático	seh meh peencho un nayoomahtikoh

Staying in a Hotel

I have a reservation	Tengo una reserva	Tengo oona rresairba
Is there a room available?	¿Hay habitación disponible?	I ahbitahseeohn deesponeeble
single/double room	habitación single/ doble	abeetas-yohn senglay/dobleh
twin room	habitación con camas gemelas	abeetas-yon kon kamas hemelas
shower	ducha	doocha
bathtub	tina	teenah
I want to be woken up at...	Necesito que me despierten a las...	neseseeto keh meh desp-yairten a las
hot water	agua caliente	agwa lak-yenteh
cold water	agua fría	agwa free-yah
soap	jabón	habohn
towel	toalla	to-a-ya
key	llave	yabeh

Eating Out

I am a vegetarian	Soy vegetariano	soy behetar-yano
fixed price	precio fijo	pres-yo feeho
glass	vaso	baso
cup	taza	tahsah
cutlery	cubiertos	koob-yairtos
Can I see the menu, please?	¿Puedo ver la carta, por favor?	pwedoh vair la carta, por fabor
The check, please	la cuenta, por favor	la kwenta por fabor
I would like a glass of water	Me gustaría un vaso de agua	meh goostaree-a oon baso deh agwa
breakfast	desayuno	desa-yoono
lunch	almuerzo	almwairso
dinner	cena	saynah

Menu Decoder

parrillada	pahreeyada	mixed grill
lomo	lohmoh	beefsteak
lomo a la pimienta	lohomo ah la peemee-entah	pepper steak
lomo vetado	lohmoh vettudah	ribeye
lomo liso	lohmoh leesoh	sirloin
barros luco	bahros lookoh	beef sandwich with melted cheese
cazuela de vacuno	kahswaylah de vahkoonoh	beef and vegetable stew
cazuela de ave	kahswaylah de ahvay	chicken and vegetable stew
centolla	sentoyah	king crab
pebre	pehbray	Chilean salsa
chorizo	chohreezoh	pork sausage
choripán	choreepan	pork sausage in a bun
churrasco	choorrasko	thin boneless steak on bread
cola de mono	kohlah de mono	aperitif of coffee, milk, and liqueur
curanto	kooranhntoh	stew of shellfish, meat, and potatoes
lúcuma	lookoohmah	eggfruit
mollejas	moyehas	sweetbreads
pastel de choclo	pahstel deh chohcloh	sweet corn pie
plateada	plahte-ahda	stewed beef and vegetables
terremoto	tairehmohtoh	cocktail of white wine, Fernet, and pineapple ice cream
humita	oomeeta	mashed sweet corn mixed with onion and milk
arroz	arrohs	rice
atún	atoon	tuna
azúcar	asookar	sugar
bacalao	bakala-o	cod
camarones	kamarones	shrimp
carne	karneh	beef
cebolla	sebo-ya	onion
chirimoya	cheereemoyah	custard apple
huevo	webo	egg
jugo	hoogo	fruit juice
langosta	langosta	lobster
leche	lecheh	milk
mantequilla	mantekee-ya	butter
marisco	mareesko	shellfish

pan	*pan*	bread
papas	*papas*	potatoes
pescado	*peskado*	fish
pimienta dulce	*peemee-entah*	sweet pepper
	doolsay	
pollo	*po-yo*	chicken
postre	*postreh*	dessert
roseta	*rroseta*	bread roll
sal	*sal*	salt
salsa	*salsa*	sauce
sopa	*sopa*	soup
té	*teh*	tea
vinagre	*beenagreh*	vinegar
zapallito	*sapa-yeeto*	squash

Time

minute	**minuto**	*meenootoh*
hour	**hora**	*ora*
half an hour	**media hora**	*med-ya ora*
quarter of	**un cuarto**	*oon kwarto*
an hour		
Monday	**lunes**	*loones*
Tuesday	**martes**	*martes*
Wednesday	**miércoles**	*m-yairkoles*
Thursday	**jueves**	*hwebes*
Friday	**viernes**	*b-yairnes*
Saturday	**sábado**	*sabado*
Sunday	**domingo**	*domeengo*
January	**enero**	*enairo*
February	**febrero**	*febrairo*
March	**marzo**	*marso*
April	**abril**	*abreel*
May	**mayo**	*ma-yo*
June	**junio**	*hoon-yo*
July	**julio**	*hool-yo*
August	**agosto**	*agosto*
September	**septiembre**	*sept-yembreh*
October	**octubre**	*oktoobreh*
November	**noviembre**	*nob-yembreh*
December	**diciembre**	*dees-yembreh*

Numbers

0	**cero**	*sairo*
1	**uno**	*oono*
2	**dos**	*dos*
3	**tres**	*tres*
4	**cuatro**	*kwatro*
5	**cinco**	*seenko*
6	**seis**	*says*
7	**siete**	*s-yeteh*
8	**ocho**	*ocho*
9	**nueve**	*nwebeh*
10	**diez**	*d-yes*
11	**once**	*onseh*
12	**doce**	*doseh*
13	**trece**	*treseh*
14	**catorce**	*katorseh*
15	**quince**	*keenseh*
16	**dieciséis**	*d-yeseesays*
17	**diecisiete**	*d-yesees-yeteh*
18	**dieciocho**	*d-yes-yocho*
19	**diecinueve**	*d-yeseenwebeh*
20	**veinte**	*baynteh*
30	**treinta**	*traynta*
40	**cuarenta**	*kwarenta*
50	**cincuenta**	*seenkwenta*
60	**sesenta**	*sesenta*
70	**setenta**	*setenta*
80	**ochenta**	*ochenta*
90	**noventa**	*nobenta*
100	**cien**	*s-yen*
500	**quinientos**	*keen-yentos*
1000	**mil**	*meel*
first	**primero/a**	*preemairo/a*
second	**segundo/a**	*segoondo/a*
third	**tercero/a**	*tairsairo/a*
fourth	**cuarto/a**	*kwarto/a*
fifth	**quinto/a**	*keento/a*
sixth	**sexto/a**	*seksto/a*
seventh	**séptimo/a**	*septeemo/a*
eighth	**octavo/a**	*oktabo/a*
ninth	**noveno/a**	*nobeno/a*
tenth	**décimo/a**	*deseemo/a*

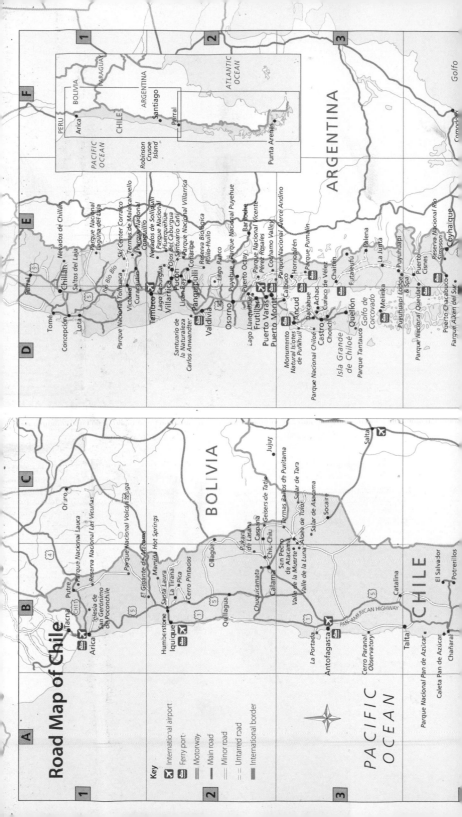

Road Map of Chile

Key
- ✈ International airport
- ⛴ Ferry port
- ▬▬ Motorway
- ▬▬ Main road
- ── Minor road
- == Untarred road
- ▬▬ International border